CHRIST VICTORIOUS

Selected Writings of Hugh Martin

Rev. Hugh Martin D.D.

CHRIST VICTORIOUS

Selected Writings of Hugh Martin

Edited by
Matthew J. & Catherine E. Hyde

*But grow in grace, and in the knowledge of our Lord and
Saviour Jesus Christ. To him be glory both now and
for ever. Amen.*—2 Peter 3:18

THE BANNER OF TRUTH TRUST

THE BANNER OF TRUTH TRUST

Head Office
3 Murrayfield Road
Edinburgh
EH12 6EL
UK

North America Office
PO Box 621
Carlisle
PA 17013
USA

banneroftruth.org

First published 2019
© The Banner of Truth Trust 2019

*

ISBN
Print: 978 1 84871 252 2
Epub: 978 1 84871 254 6
Kindle: 978 1 84871 253 9

*

Typeset in 10.5/13.5 pt Adobe Garamond Pro
at The Banner of Truth Trust, Edinburgh

Printed in the USA by
Versa Press Inc.,
East Peoria, IL.

CONTENTS

INTRODUCTION

E VERY pastor must be a theologian. This book contains the writings of a pastor-theologian par excellence. Hugh Martin (1821–1885) was never a seminary professor, but he had deep and clear doctrinal insights which shaped his pulpit ministry, and his pastoral work.

≈

Born and brought up in Aberdeen, Martin studied mathematics at Marischal College, graduating a Master of Arts in April, 1839, aged barely 18 years. He remained involved in the study of mathematics for the rest of his life.[1]

At the formation of the Free Church in 1843, Martin was a student training for the ministry in the Church of Scotland. He left the Established Church at the Disruption and was ordained and inducted to the charge of Panbride (midway between Dundee and Arbroath) in 1844. Martin was one of the galaxy of brilliant ministers who served in the Free Church of Scotland during its early years. He was a close friend of John ('Rabbi') Duncan (1796–1870), George Smeaton (1814–1889), John Kennedy (1819–1884), William Nixon (1803–1900) and Alexander Auld (1821–1904), among other gracious, like-minded ministers.

Martin ministered at Panbride for fourteen years, then in 1858 he was translated to the charge of Free Greyfriars, Edinburgh. In 1863 he was forced to resign from the pastorate due to ill health, at the early age of forty-two years. In his retirement in Lasswade, and later Montrose, he continued to preach whenever possible and gave the rest of his time to writing. He died in Dundee in June, 1885.

[1] The best biographical accounts of Martin published to date are: D. Taylor, 'Biographical Introduction,' in Hugh Martin *Christ for Us* (Edinburgh: Banner of Truth Trust, 1998), pp. i-xvi.; D. Somerset, 'Life of Hugh Martin,' *The Bulwark: Magazine of the Scottish Reformation Society* (Oct.–Dec., 2008), pp. 14-25.

As someone robustly committed to the Westminster standards and the attainments of the Scottish Reformation, Martin wrote strongly against the errors of Higher Criticism, strenuously opposed the union of the Free Church and the United Presbyterian Church, because of the latter's dubious doctrinal standards, and resisted the introduction of hymns and musical accompaniment in public worship.

❧

Today Martin is best known, and highly respected, for his writings. According to *Principal John MacLeod* (1872–1948), Martin was 'a masterly exponent and a singular ornament of the Reformed faith.'[1] Several of his books are currently in print. His first book, *The Abiding Presence* (originally titled *Christ's Presence in the Gospel History*) was published in 1860. This was followed by his commentary on Jonah, *The Prophet Jonah* (1866), *The Atonement* (1870) (for which the University of Edinburgh conferred on him a Doctorate of Divinity in 1872), *The Shadow of Calvary* (1875), and *The Westminster Doctrine of the Inspiration of Scripture* (1877).

Besides these, Martin wrote a number of pamphlets, and published several sermons. He was an established essayist, regularly contributing essays and reviews to two Free Church publications, *The British and Foreign Evangelical Review* and *The Watchword*. These he invariably signed with his pen-name μ, the Greek letter *mu*, corresponding to the first letter of his surname. Lurking scatteredly in already long defunct magazines, these writings were referred to by Principal Macleod as 'fugitive' pieces, and at the same time he called them 'Martin's best work.'[2] Yet with the passage of time, these valuable writings are becoming only harder to obtain and access.

The Banner of Truth has republished several items from Martin's pen. First to be reprinted were some of his 'fugitive' pieces from the *Family Treasury of Sunday Reading* for 1869 under the title *Simon Peter* (1967), and then later publishing a volume of his previously uncollected and unpublished sermons, *Christ For Us* (1998). However, there is more material which has not been included in these two volumes. The preface

---

[1] John Macleod, *Scottish Theology in Relation to Church History Since the Reformation* (1943; repr. Edinburgh: Banner of Truth Trust, 2015), p. 338.

[2] *Ibid.* p. 326.

to *Christ For Us* details a number of Martin's other pamphlet sermons and essays in various rare and inaccessible periodicals. An extensive list of such material is provided by John C. A. Ferguson in his doctoral thesis on Hugh Martin's federal theology.[1]

In this volume we can give no more than a selection. Ten items have been chosen from Martin's sermons and essays, and to these we have added all the personal correspondence which we know to be extant. On occasions footnotes which provide context, or which help to clarify some of Martin's remarks have beeen added to the text. To distinguish these later editorial additions from Martin's original composition such footnotes are contained in square brackets.

∾

The material collected for this volume consists of sermons, essays, and letters. Each of these types of writing showcases in its own way Martin's gift not only for diving deep in his exposition of a text, but for doing so with accuracy and great precision. Additionally, his exposition never goes without an application. His sermons and letters teem with practical applications of the truth—and so, perhaps surprisingly, do his essays written for theological journals. Martin's aim was never simply to stimulate the mind, but to nourish the soul. His personal desire, and his evident desire for others, was for growth in grace and in the knowledge of the Lord Jesus Christ.

Three emphases in Martin's thought stand out in this volume. They are all Christological, reflecting what is perhaps Martin's main contribution—his grasp and articulation of the atoning work of a divine Christ.

1. The *first* is that his view of Christ is Trinitarian. The divine Saviour who accomplished redemption was sent by the Father and equipped by the Spirit to do this work. Specifically, for example, in his humiliation, the incarnate Son of God relied entirely on the Spirit to access the resources he needed from his Father in order to carry out his saving work. On this point, like his close friend and colleague, George Smeaton, Martin shares the view of the Puritan giant, Dr John Owen (1616–1683).

[1] John C. A. Ferguson, *The Atonement in Its Relations: The Doctrine of Salvation in the Federal Theology of Hugh Martin* (1822–1885). Doctoral Thesis submitted to the University of Aberdeen, 2012.

2. The *second* is Martin's view of the relationship between Word and Spirit. For Martin, the Word and the Spirit are not to be thought of as independent of each other—the one modulates our understanding of the other. We have to think in terms of the Christ-sent Spirit and the Spirit-anointed Christ. This is true not just for the inscripturated Word but also for the personal Word. The believer certainly goes no further than the inscripturated Word allows, but the believer must go every bit as far as the inscripturated Word allows, getting to know Christ and leaning more heavily on Christ and receiving more and more comfort from Christ—all as empowered by the Spirit.

3. *Thirdly*, Martin insisted on the activeness and the victoriousness of Christ's death. His work, *The Atonement*, provides an expanded development of this point, but Martin never missed an opportunity to utterly reject the idea that Christ died passively, as a mere victim. It is Christ *crucified* who personifies Life in his sermon on Galatians 2:20, and as crucified he is 'Life living in death: Life living death down: Life, by being crucified, crucifying death dead!'

These three themes appear repeatedly in Martin's sermons and essays, and they are also prominent in the two sets of his letters included here. This is all the more remarkable given that these were personal letters written to friends and family members. Meaty theological reflections sit side by side here with the standard pleasantries and expressions of affection. Writing to his daughters, Martin does not hesitate to thrash out some very weighty points about Christ's mediatorial work. Writing to his friend, Martin's detailed and penetrating theology is clearly the underpinning of his kind and warm pastoring.

Although Martin's correspondent was apparently a believer of long standing and a minister, he was nevertheless sometimes hesitant about taking advantage of the comforts which belong to believers. Martin repeatedly and gently encourages him to trust God's promise and dive deeper and deeper into the oceans of God's grace. Yet he does so without claiming to enjoy exultant heights of assurance himself. In fact he speaks frankly about his own struggles and the weariness of the way. It is striking however that he does not try to comfort his friend primarily by sharing similarities or differences in their experience. Instead, he helps his friend by pointing out some relevant part of Scripture and how faith can make use of it, and then by moving the conversation on to share some meditation or reflection he had had on some other part of Scripture. These thoughts are miniature sermons—expositions with application to the heart—and are just as remarkable as his fully fledged essays and sermons for homing in on an under-appreciated facet of a text with the effect of deriving a great deal of edification and comfort.

Hugh Martin's evident desire—in the pieces reproduced here—was for an increasing knowledge of Christ, his person and his work. It is true that mere knowledge can never save of itself; to possess a saving knowledge of the truth is to have knowledge in conjunction with the grace of faith. But grace will seek a greater knowledge of Christ. Grace is defective or weak where it does not thirst after greater views of Christ. We hope that souls desiring to know more of Christ will find their faith strengthened in reading the contents of this book.

The publishers would like to thank the librarians at The National Library of Scotland, and New College Library, The University of Edinburgh, for copies of some of Martin's rare pamphlets reproduced here, and to the London Mathematical Society for permission to reproduce the frontispiece portrait of Hugh Martin from their collections.

SERMONS

VOICES AT BETHLEHEM[1]

Let us now go even unto Bethlehem.—Luke 2:15

He that hath ears to hear, let him hear.—Matthew 11:15

THERE are voices to be heard in Bethlehem, as well as a great sight to be seen. And the voices explain what we see. No doubt, if we had been present, we would have heard the voices of Mary and Joseph, as they softly communed together beside the rude cradle of the heaven-born babe. And we would have heard the rapturous and joyful voices of the shepherds, as they told of the vision of the angels and the angels' songs. And we would have heard the reverential voices of the wise men, who had seen the royal child's star in the east, and were come to worship him. But there were far other voices than these resounding in the stable at Bethlehem—voices that we, at this distance, and after so long a time, may hear as well as they who were present then; and which they had no better means of hearing then, than we have now. Yes, there were voices sounding there that have never become silent since; and he that hath an ear to hear let him hear them.

The Spirit was speaking. And the little child was speaking. And the Father was speaking. And the whole Church, in the Spirit, was speaking—at Bethlehem.

---

[1] [From *The Christian Treasury* (1858), pp. 505-7.]

I. The Spirit's voice

The Spirit was speaking expressly, and saying: 'But thou, Bethlehem Ephratah, though thou be little among the thousands of Judah, yet out of thee shall he come forth unto me that is to be ruler in Israel: whose goings forth have been from of old, from everlasting' (Mic. 5:2).

Ah! this little babe may be born in a low condition, but he is born under the glorious welcome of the Holy Spirit's voice—a voice louder than all the thunders of heaven, or the songs of all the angels. No palace receives him as the Royal One of Israel. If he is a Prince, he is indeed in disguise. Even the inn of an insignificant village—'little Bethlehem'—has no room for him. Behold the babe in swaddling bands, and lying in a manger. But though all things on earth conspire to his humiliation, the Spirit bears witness—and the Spirit is truth—that he is the ruler in Israel, and that his goings forth have been of old from everlasting.

Happy they who hear the Spirit's voice, who listen to the Spirit's truth and testimony. He can show them glory when all around looks mean. He can show them peace, when all around is war. He can tell of life, and light, and joy, where, without his voice, there would be nothing but terror, and darkness, and the shadow of death. The God of glory has come down to dwell with men. The kings and nobles of the earth know nothing of his coming. But a little child, taught by the Spirit, can see in the manger of Bethlehem the creator of the heavens and the earth, the teacher of eternal truth; the sin-bearing Lamb of God, and sacrifice-bringing priest for sinners; the King of Israel. 'O send forth thy light and thy truth; let them lead me; let them bring me unto thy holy hill, and to thy tabernacles.' Let them bring me to the manger of Bethlehem, to the cross of Calvary, to the right hand of the throne of the majesty in the heavens within the veil. Thither will I go, as unto the altar of God, unto God my exceeding joy.

II. The Child's voice

But another sweet voice breaks upon our ear. It is the voice of the child himself.

But what? The child's voice! The new-born infant speaks! Yes. He is the Word of God. In the beginning was the Word. And the Word was made flesh. Surely it is the very office of the Word to speak. And shall his coming into the world make him silent? Surely not.

But this child in swaddling hands, lying here in the manger—he does not speak to me. His lips do not even move. No sound issues from them. And how can you say then that you hear a voice from the new-born speechless babe?

But I also will ask you one question. As you gaze into the manger of Bethlehem, and listen in vain, as you say, to hear the voice of Jesus—so do I now look up to the right hand of the throne of God, where Jesus now is, and I also may complain as well as you that I listen in vain, that I hear no voice from Jesus. As little sound of words do I hear coming down from the throne of God, as you now hear coming forth from the new-born king. But is Jesus therefore silent unto me? Has he nothing to say to me? And does he take no means of saying it? Am I doomed not to hear the voice of Jesus? Do I really not hear him? Then I am not of his sheep. For his sheep hear his voice. And other sheep he has that are not yet of his fold, them also he will bring, and they shall hear his voice.

His voice is heard in the word—in that word of the Lord which liveth and abideth for ever. By his word he speaks, now that he is set down on his throne of glory. By his word also he speaks, even when lying a helpless babe in Bethlehem. Yes—'When he cometh into the world he saith, sacrifice and offering thou wouldest not, but a body hast thou prepared me: in burnt offerings and sacrifices for sin thou hast no pleasure. Then said I, Lo, I come (in the volume of the book it is written of me) to do thy will, O God' (Heb. 10:5-7; Psa. 40:6-8).

In his very coming into the world, he speaks of himself as a sacrifice for sin. He willingly accepts, he gladly welcomes, the body prepared for him—the body in which he is to bear our sins upon the tree. It is his Father's will that he should lay down his life, and he delights to do his will. 'Lo, I come, I delight to do thy will, O my God.'

What wondrous love to his father! What wondrous love to us! And how do we receive, or reply to, his love! Shall he welcome so joyfully that body in which he was to be wounded, and wearied, and grieved, and bruised, and crucified, and buried? And shall not we welcome him in that body in which he suffers all this for us? Is our flesh so dear to him that he rejoices to receive the body prepared for him? and when he thus presents to us the fullness of his Godhead, joyfully sojourning among us in our flesh, even though the penalty of doing so be the burden of our sin, and the sting of our death, and the battle with our foes, and the curse of our God, shall we not give him joyful welcome, even when the issue of our doing so is, deliverance from the curse and from death, and from Satan and from sin? Surely this body is prepared for us as much as for him. He bore our sins in his own body on the tree. He was wounded for our transgressions, he was bruised for our iniquities. And shall we leave it to him alone to welcome this body in which our redemption is to be accomplished? Nay, we join with him in rejoicing at his birth. Bethlehem is the very birth-place of our hope and salvation. 'Lo, we come,' to see and to embrace, and to give praise for the body prepared for bearing our sins, and carrying our sorrows. And being reconciled in the body of his flesh through death, 'lo, we come,' with him and like him, 'to do thy will, O God. Put thy law into our hearts as it was in his.'

III. The Father's voice

There is the Father's voice also: 'When he bringeth in the first begotten into the world, he saith: And let all the angels of God worship him' (Heb. 1:6).

Blessed voice!—which the Word of God alone enables to hear. And what a boundless scene of glory it opens to our view! The babe may be very lowly in his manger-cradle. The kings of the earth may scorn the knowledge of his birth. The mighty nations may carry on their wars as if the Prince of Peace and Life were not yet come. His own nation may give him no kind reception. The young child's life even may be sought. And when his hour is come, he may, by wicked hands, be slain. But the countless glorious host of heaven's holy ones are commanded by the Father to worship him. Angels and principalities and powers are made subject to him. The little child is made the head of all principality and power.

We know how the angels visited the world in his service, and for his sake. And it is only for his sake that they could ever visit it. It is in his name that they come forth to minister to them that shall be heirs of salvation. They would otherwise abhor this world. They could not move in the wake and train of Jehovah's curse. But they can follow in the train of a curse-bearing Redeemer—the man who is Jehovah's fellow. By his visit to the world, heaven is opened, and the angels of God may ascend and descend upon the Son of Man. They can never be ashamed, nor afraid, to follow where he leads; though it be in a world that is defiled with sin, and dark with the shadow of death. Nor can they ever refuse to worship the Eternal Godhead, though its throne be the manger of Bethlehem, and its dwelling-place be fixed in the infant there. 'Let all the angels of God worship him.'

And shall not we also welcome him and worship him? Yea, we will join with the whole Church of God and welcome him.

IV. The Church's voice

The Spirit welcomes him as the ruler of Israel, the eternal King. The Child himself welcomes the body prepared for him. The Father welcomes him, and calls all his angels to worship him. Oh! there are glorious ones present at the birth of our Prince and Brother in Bethlehem. All the elect and redeemed ones of God also are present in the Spirit, and speaking by the Word; and they say: 'Unto us a child is born, unto us a son is given, and the government shall be upon his shoulder, and his name shall be called Wonderful, Counsellor, the mighty God, the everlasting Father, and the Prince of Peace' (Isa. 9:6).

Such is the noble song of joy with which the redeemed of the Lord—all believing souls—welcome their Father's unspeakable gift in Bethlehem, celebrating his most glorious rank and name, and singing his most worthy praise. There is no cold-heartedness here. There is no half-slumbering negligence, listlessly and dreamily looking on as at a distance. There is no delay, no doubting, no questioning of whether the gift is bestowed on them, whether the child is born for them. They draw near in earnest to see this great sight. They look steadfastly upon the child in swaddling bands, lying in the manger. They see the Eternal Son of God in their own flesh. And it is enough. At once they embrace, as designed for them, as hereby given to them, what God, they see, has sent to be welcomed and received. 'Unto us a child is born, unto us a son is given.' Marvels of mercy they know that they need; marvels of pardon; unsearchable wonders and riches of grace. But behold the marvel of all marvels, given already: the most wonderful of wonders, the Everlasting God committed to us in this little child, that we may welcome him and love him. Behold the Wonderful! Counsels they will need; counsels and light in their unspeakable ignorance and darkness. But behold the Counsellor! Strength to do battle with sin and death, with hell and Satan. But behold the mighty God! Eternal life they need; but this is the everlasting Father. Peace with the God whom they have a thousand times offended; but here is the Prince of Peace. There is nothing wanting on his part. And as to all that is wanting on their part, 'the zeal of the Lord of hosts will perform it.' Thus is he all their salvation and all their desire, and they cannot find a reason for refusing him although they would.

And neither, I am sure, can we. If we do not receive him, it can only be because we will not have him. But will we stand in Bethlehem and say, 'We will not have this child, we have no room for him in our hearts'? When we had altogether lost our God—and lost the knowledge and the favour, and the image of God, lo, God is restored to us in the most wonderful and sweet and acceptable form—in the form of Bethlehem's little child. And he has come to be our Light, that we may know the Lord; and our Lamb for a burnt-offering, that we may have peace with God; and our King, gentle and meek and loving, yet very strong to change our hearts and to destroy our foes, that we may love the Lord and serve him without fear, in holiness and righteousness before him all the days of our life. And do we not receive him? Yea, by the grace of God, we will receive him. For, he is freely given; he is infinitely worthy to be received; and to as many as receive him he gives power to become the sons of God. And being thus, by our Father's sovereign grace, the sons of God—through the birth of our Elder Brother, his Eternal Son, in Bethlehem, and by our believing reception of him as our Father's free and unspeakable gift—let us freely receive also the Spirit of his Son into our hearts, crying, 'Abba, Father.' Now, therefore, we are no more strangers and foreigners—outcasts, enemies, and slaves. We are sons. Let us live as the sons of God, blameless and harmless, the dutiful brethren of God's holy child Jesus. Amen.

'CHRIST LIVETH IN ME'[1]

Christ liveth in me.—Galatians 2:20

HERE is a very marvellous thing, calling for thoughtful examination, and surely worthy of it. 'Christ liveth in me,' says Paul.

Is this a highly figurative statement, or has it actual reality to rest upon? Is it really true that the believer can have solid grounds for saying, 'Christ liveth in me!' Glorious things are spoken of the people of God, but few things could be said of them more glorious than that Christ—God manifest in the flesh—liveth in them. Is this marvellous assertion the high-wrought utterance of religious mysticism, or is it the simple expression of a spiritual fact?

We may observe that the text is far from being a solitary or unparalleled statement in the Word of God. The truth contained in it is even declared to lie at the foundation of all personal and living Christianity: 'Examine yourselves, whether ye be in the faith. Know ye not your own selves, how that *Jesus Christ is in you*, except ye be reprobates?' To convey this astonishing privilege of having Christ living in us, is the great end for which the gospel ministry is established and exercised: 'My little children, of whom I travail in birth again till *Christ be formed in you*, I desire to be present with you now, and to change my voice; for I stand in doubt of you.' The realizing of this great marvel among the Gentiles is 'the mystery which hath been hid from ages and from generations, but now is made manifest unto

---

[1] [From *The Family Treasury of Sunday Reading* (1859), p. 153ff.]

God's saints, to whom he would make known what is the riches of the glory of this mystery among the Gentiles, which is *Christ in you*, the hope of glory.' It is the great object, for the attainment of which Jesus knocks, by his gospel and his Spirit, at the hearts of sinners: 'Behold, I stand at the door, and knock: if any man hear my voice, and open the door, *I will come in to him*.' It is the realization of the great covenant promise: 'For ye are the temple of the living God: as God hath said, *I will dwell in them and walk in them*; and I will be their God, and they shall be my people.' It is the object for which believers are commanded to abide in Christ: 'Abide in me, and I IN YOU.' It is the scope of Paul's prayer for the Ephesians: 'For this cause I bow my knees to the God and Father of our Lord Jesus Christ, of whom the whole family in heaven and earth is named, that he would grant you, according to the riches of his glory, to be strengthened with all might by the Spirit in the inner man; that *Christ may dwell in your hearts* by faith.' Nay, it is the grand and ultimate aim of Christ's own intercession; the utmost and terminal desire of his heart, as expressed unto the Father on their behalf; the resting-place of his heart concerning them, where he sees of the travail of his soul and is satisfied: for even thus does his intercessory prayer for them terminate, 'That the love wherewith thou hast loved me may be in them, and *I in them*.'

But in none of these statements, confirmatory and parallel to the text as they evidently are, is the great truth set forth so simply and emphatically as in the text itself—'Christ liveth in me.' We propose to consider the *causes and consequences* of Christ living in the believer. The rich meaning and import of this truth may thus in a measure open up to us; while its intense and glorious literality will become manifest.

I. First, how is Christ living within the believer actually realized? To what causes can it be assigned?

1. The great leading cause is the Holy Spirit. This great effect is to be attributed to him—to the operation and indwelling of the Holy Spirit.

Regeneration, which is the Spirit's work, is the implantation in a soul, formerly dead in trespasses and sins, of a new life, a vital[1] principle

---

[1] [vital = indispensable to the continuance of life; absolutely necessary, essential.]

of holiness. The will is renewed; and from being ungodly and enmity to God, it is turned to choose God, satisfying itself with him as its Supreme Good, subjecting itself to him as its Sovereign Lord. This is a new life—spiritual, God-ward, altogether new—a new creature. With this new principle of life, this new creation in the soul, the Spirit of God, who is the author of it, maintains a vital and uninterrupted connection, thereby dwelling in the believer henceforth as in a living temple. It is in virtue of this in-dwelling, this in-living of the Spirit, that Christ liveth in us. For, in all this, the Spirit acts as the Spirit of Christ. For 'if any man have not the Spirit of Christ, he is none of his.' And 'hereby we know that he abideth in us, by his Spirit which he hath given us.'

Christ, as God the Son, is of one substance, power, and eternity with God the Holy Spirit. Christ also, as the Son of man, had the Spirit bestowed on him without measure. His human nature was formed, in body and soul, and sanctified from the first, by the special operation of the Spirit. He was anointed with the immeasurable plenitude of the Spirit. By the light of the Spirit, the man Christ Jesus thought all his thoughts; by the grace of the Spirit, willed all his purposes; by the strength of the Spirit, wrought all his works; till finally he, 'through the eternal Spirit, offered himself without spot to God,' thereafter rising from the dead by the Spirit of holiness, and ascending to pour out that Spirit of truth and consolations which he had promised so graciously to his disciples. In his Godhead, our Lord is one with the Spirit; and as man, by the Spirit he was what he was.

When Christ, therefore, sends his Spirit, not to speak of himself, but to take of what is Christ's and show it unto us; to create us again in Christ and like Christ; to dwell in us as in a living temple, as ourselves living spirits to which he has given a new and Christ-like life—can we fail to see that there is something here which in no respect falls short even of the great marvel of our text, 'Christ living in us'? Christ, the eternal Son, lives in us, when the Spirit lives in us; for the Spirit and the Son with the Father are inseparable in their joint possession of the all-fullness of the Godhead. And Christ, as God-man, the Son of man, the very Christ that tabernacled with men upon the earth, lives in us, when the Spirit living in us confines himself to revealing Christ as the

God-man, whose glory his disciples saw in human flesh, as the glory of the only-begotten of the Father, full of grace and truth.

It is as the agent and ambassador of the God-man that the Spirit is given in the Church; it is the God-man whom the Spirit reveals and glorifies in the Church; it is within the limits of what he himself revealed and wrought in the God-man that he restricts himself in working in the Church or body of the faithful. He lives in them as he lived in him. He works to reveal in them progressively the truth which he implanted and developed in unclouded spiritual splendour in the mind of the man Christ Jesus; to establish in them progressively the grace with which he replenished the heart of the man Christ Jesus—to conform them, in a word, to the 'firstborn of many brethren.' And how then can his in-dwelling, in-working, in-living in them be other than most adequately expressed by the doctrine that 'Christ liveth in them'?

Christ, by his Spirit, lives in them. By his Spirit he quickens them to new and spiritual life; and by his Spirit he takes possession of them as his living temple. As a living temple, he always regards them and acts in them. Their faculties as living men—alive from the dead—he animates and controls. Whatever in their thoughts, affections, purposes, actions, is opposed to his own, he sets himself to suppress; and the faculties themselves he undertakes to sanctify—to form, and mould, and guide into harmony with his own. Nay; their whole character, their very natures, as living men—spiritually living—he works by his Spirit to assimilate unto his own. So far as this work advances, the very thoughts that he thinks they think; the affections he entertains they entertain; the purposes of his mind are theirs also; his work is their work; his nature theirs. And up to the limit to which this blessed result has in its onward progress been achieved, how can a better, a briefer, a more perfect expression be found for it, than to say that, to this extent, 'Christ liveth in them'? It is, then, literally, profoundly true that Christ lives in his people. He lives in them by his Spirit which he has given them.

2. Another cause, holding, indeed, a different place, but indispensable, is the gospel. The Spirit is the efficient cause, the gospel is the formal cause of Christ living in his people.

We know nothing of Christ save as revealed and set forth in the Word—'the word of the truth of the gospel.' God is manifest in the man Christ Jesus—the invisible, inaccessible Godhead is brought near and manifested in Christ—but it is in the gospel that the manifestation is given. Take away the gospel, and you take away Christ. He has bound himself inseparably to his gospel in all his dispensations to the sons of men. He hath has seated himself in the chariot of his gospel, and all his goings forth have been, and to the end of time will be, as seated there. He has clothed himself with his own gospel, and in these robes alone does he appear in his Church below. He that is blind to the gospel is blind to Christ. He that believes not the gospel believes not on Christ; he that rejects the gospel, it is Christ whom he is rejecting. When we receive Christ, it is by the heart, it is into the heart, that we receive him; but we can in this life receive him only as he is offered to us in the gospel. When another gospel, therefore, was preached in the Church at Galatia, Paul felt that *the Christ in them* was endangered: 'My little children, of whom I travail in birth again till Christ be formed in you.' When to the Church at Colosse he spoke of 'Christ in them the hope of glory'—knowing that only by means of the gospel could Christ be in them—he added, '*whom we preach,* teaching every man, and warning every man.' If his word dwells in you, Christ dwells in you. 'Let that, therefore, abide in you which ye have heard from the beginning. If that which ye have heard from the beginning shall remain in you, ye also shall continue in the Son and in the Father.' And if ye continue in the Son, he continues in you, according to the sacred oracle: 'Abide in me, and I in you.'

3. Another cause, holding still a different place, but equally indispensable, is faith. The Spirit is the efficient cause on Christ's part; the gospel is the formal cause on Christ's part; faith is the instrumental cause on our part.

The place and operation of faith in this matter are attested emphatically by the apostle in his prayer for the Ephesians—'That Christ may dwell in your hearts by faith.' The new life which the Spirit in regeneration gives, acts all its operations by faith. It acts primarily in all things by faith. All its forthgoings and energies are in the acting of faith. And it is this that reconciles Paul's apparent contradiction—that he himself lives, and yet that it is Christ that liveth in him; bringing it about that while he himself liveth, and Christ liveth in him, these are not two lives, but one. It is by faith that they are really one.

'I live; yet not I, but Christ liveth in me.' Does Paul, then, retract the assertion, 'I live,' by saying, 'yet not I, but Christ liveth in me'? Does he deny that he lives, by declaring that Christ lives in him? Nay, he asserts it; he re-asserts it; for he goes on to say, 'And the life that I live in the flesh.' And how does he make these two lives to be really one? Why, 'The life that I live in the flesh I live by the faith of the Son of God, even him who loved me and gave himself for me.' By the faith of him I live on him; I live his life; he lives in me by faith. By faith I receive, I retain the living Christ—living in me; Christ my life. By faith I live the life which Christ lives in me.

Mark also very specially that it is by faith in a dying Christ that Christ lives in his people. It might have been supposed that it must be by faith in a living Christ that Christ should live in us; but it is not so. It is by faith in a dying Christ. 'I live by the faith of the Son of God,' says Paul. Be it so. But under what view of Christ—in what aspect of Christ's relation to you and his work for you—do you exercise your faith in him? 'Who loved me, and gave himself for me,' is Paul's answer. It is as loving him and dying for him that Paul exercises faith in Christ, in order that Christ may live in him. Nay, this singular verse, with its rich and unfathomable wonders, both begins and closes with this truth—that it is by faith's communion with a substituted, crucified, dying Saviour, that that Saviour lives in his people: 'I am *crucified* with Christ: nevertheless I live; yet not I, but Christ liveth in me: and the life that I live in the flesh I live by the faith of the Son of God, who loved me, and *gave himself for me.*'

It is this great truth that the Lord himself sets forth in his startling discourse concerning eating his flesh and drinking his blood. For it is faith's participation of his sacrifice of himself in death, in the wounding of his flesh and the shedding of his blood, that he is there describing: 'The bread that I shall give is my flesh, which I shall give for the life of the world. Verily, verily, I say unto you, Except ye eat the flesh of the Son of man, and drink his blood, ye have no life in you. Whoso eateth my flesh, and drinketh my blood, hath eternal life, and I will raise him up at the last day. For my flesh is meat indeed, and my blood is drink indeed.' And then he comes nearer to the doctrine before us: 'He that eateth my flesh, and drinketh my blood, dwelleth in me, and I in him.' And at last he exactly states it: 'As the living Father hath sent me, and I live by the Father; so he that eateth me, even he shall live by me.'

The apostle Paul, also, in writing to the Corinthians, puts this truth in a very beautiful light—the truth, I mean, that it is by faith in a dying Saviour that that Saviour lives in us—when he says, 'Always bearing about in the body the dying of the Lord Jesus, that the life also of Jesus may be made manifest in your mortal body.' If I would have Christ living in me, I must be crucified with Christ; if I would have Christ living in me, it must be by the exercise of faith in Christ dying for me.

Nor is this mysterious. For if I would have life reigning in me, I have a prior death that reigns in me to dispose of. I have a judicial death, a death in the anger of God—a wrathful but righteous sentence of death—barring me from all life and blessing; strengthening, also, and riveting in me, the dominion of spiritual death—my death in trespasses and sins. I must, therefore, find a life that shall suppress my death, and that shall not itself die in doing so—that shall not expire in the effort, but shall conquer and live on—the true and only life everlasting. Such a life is Christ's death. Marvel not at this. Christ's death is vital—Christ's death is life—Christ's death is life eternal, swallowing up death in victory—suppressing my death, and living for me and in me—eternal life still. The life that I need is a life that can live in the midst of death, seeing that I am dead—dead under the law of God, and dead in trespasses and sins. Show me Eternal Life made under the law of God, and giving itself in death for my trespasses and sins. Show me a life in the midst of death, if you would show me a life that can live in me.

A singular demand! but one that is exactly met in Christ—the Living One—the Life, giving himself a sacrifice in death for me, and living still—living in the inviolable depths of his divine person; never more living than when actively and livingly giving himself in death for me,—laying down his human life, that, in the unabated life and living energy of his divine person, and in the legal triumph of his mediatorial office, he might—after the power of an endless life which his death never for a moment interrupted—resume that human life once more. Give me that death of Christ in which, even when dying, he lived and conquered—that death of Christ in which through death he destroyed him that had the power of death—that death of Christ which, far from extinguishing the life which he brought from heaven to me, only broke open for me that 'fountain of life' (Psa. 36:9) in his Godhead which had otherwise been for ever sealed and inaccessible, till there poured forth from it 'a river of the water of life,' sweeping away and swallowing up death in victory. Give me that death of the Prince of Life. It is a vital death: it is a real life: it is the very life for me; for it is the life which can live in death—the only life that can live in me. I am crucified with Christ: nevertheless I live. If I would have Christ living in me, it must be by the faith of Christ dying for me. The life which I live in the flesh I must live by the faith of the Son of God, who loved me, and *gave himself for me.*

Apart from Christ, what am I, and what is my position or place? I am shut up within the gates of death. And apart from me, what is Christ? He is 'the Life'—Life eternal and inviolable—no death in his lot at all. What, then, is Christ's death, if in redeeming love he dies for me—if he gives himself a substitute, a sacrifice in death for me—if he comes into my place and stead, and dies for me? What have I here but Eternal Life bursting open the gates of death, and coming in to adjoin and identify himself with me? And as he bursts them open, and comes in, do they close again, and imprison both him and me? Is the fountain of life, is Godhead in the man Christ Jesus, the prey and prisoner of death? God forbid. He is not death's prisoner: he is death's plagues and death's destruction. He has come to me, not in the suppression, but in the unabated energy and in the glorious triumph of his character and power as the Life Eternal; his triumph being this—that in dying he has burst the gates of death; Christ crucified, the only life that could ever find its way into me, and that has done so by dying for me. Yes; give me life in the midst of death, if you would give me a life that will suffice for me. The cross alone meets my demand. For this is the marvel of the cross, and of the decease accomplished there. It is Life in the midst of death. Not Life extinguished in death—and by death. But Life living in death: Life living death down: Life, by being crucified, crucifying death dead. I am crucified with *this* Life. No wonder, therefore, if—'nevertheless I live.'

Therefore, always as I would have Christ live in me more and more, let me have communion more and more with Christ dying for me. For thus only the death that is always rising up over me, to claim me, through the sin that is always dwelling in me—for sin rises up in me, and death by sin—suppressed and set aside, even by my faith ever bringing in the death of Christ for me. For if by sin being ever in me, death enters by sin, by faith there ever enters also death for sin—Christ's perfect death, always conquering death, and always giving life to me. Only by bearing about in the body the death of Jesus, can the life also of Jesus be made manifest in my mortal body. Only as Christ crucified does Christ live in his people. Only as always crucified with Christ do I continue to live. I *am* crucified with Christ, nevertheless I live. I not only get my life, I live it, by the faith of the Son of God, who loved me, and gave himself for me. Not only as Christ crucified does he come into my soul, it is as Christ crucified that he dwells and lives there. Faith in Christ dying for me is the means whereby Christ lives in me.

Such, then, are the means and causes by which Christ lives in his people—the Spirit, the gospel, faith—the Spirit working faith in us by the gospel. Christ as revealed in the gospel, and therein apprehended by faith, comes into his people's hearts by his Spirit, and there he dwells and lives.

II. Consider some of the consequences of Christ living in his people.

1. *First,* their holiness is hereby secured. For what is their holiness but their likeness to Christ? And how true must that likeness be, if verily Christ himself lives in them! So far as Christ lives in you, so far you will inevitably and exactly be like Christ.

For, whether living in his own person or in you, there is but one Christ, unchanged—the same yesterday, today, and for ever. He will not contradict himself; he will not misrepresent himself. He will not live in you any otherwise than he lived in the days of his flesh upon the earth. It is just the very Christ whom we read of in the gospel, and just as he lived when tabernacling with men upon the earth, who lives in you; and what he was then in his own person, exactly that will he be in you, to the full extent to which by faith you suffer him to live and dwell in you. In you, as in himself, he will still be the same meek and lowly one; the same kind and condescending one; the same dutiful, diligent, obedient son; the same uncomplaining, unflinching sufferer. In you, as in himself, he will still go about doing good; or you will, when he lives in you. In you, as in himself, he will long after lost souls, and love the souls of the saved; or you will, when Christ lives in you. In you, as in himself, he will say—he will say in you, or you will say in him—the ever same, unchanged, obedient one, 'It is my meat and drink to do the will of him that sent me: wist ye not that I must be about my Father's business?'—the same submissive one: 'Father, if it be possible, let this cup pass from me: nevertheless, not as I will, but as thou wilt! The cup which my Father hath given me to drink, shall I not drink it?'—the same forgiving one: 'Father, forgive them, for they know not what they do!'—the same relying one even in death: 'Father, into thy hands I commit my spirit.' All this will he be in you, as all this he was in himself: all this will he be in you to the full extent to which he lives in you. He will reproduce himself in you. He will re-present himself in you. Even as he was, so will you also be, in the world. His thoughts will be yours; for the same mind that was in Christ will assuredly be in you, when Christ himself is in you. His will will be yours; for he will work in you to will and to do of his good pleasure. His work will be yours, 'for he that abideth in me, and I in him, the same bringeth forth much fruit.' Surely Christ living in you is the truest and profoundest security for your being like him, for your being made holy even as he is holy.

And mark how holiness on this principle—holiness thus secured—cannot fail to be based upon humility and pervaded therewith, as all true holiness must be. You live—you live a holy life; but you have no credit, you have no ground of glorying, thereby. For it is really not you that lives; it is Christ that lives in you. The thoughts of purity and light and wisdom that you think, are not your own; they are the mind of Christ—they are Christ living in you, thinking his own truth in you, wielding by his Spirit your faculty of thought, and bringing its perceptions of heavenly knowledge into harmony with his own. The purposes of meek obedience and uncomplaining patience which you cherish are not your own; they are the will of Christ—they are Christ living in you, willing his own purpose in you, wielding your will by his Spirit, and bringing its desire and choice into unison with his. Your good works are not your own; they are Christ living in you, working in you to will and to do of his own good pleasure. You resign all ground of glorying: you renounce all claim to honour. Nay, far more: you renounce, indeed, your very self. It is not I, it is Christ. Christ is all in all. 'By the grace of God I am what I am: and his grace which was bestowed upon me was not in vain, for I laboured more abundantly than they all; yet not I, but the grace of God which was with me.' 'I live; yet not I, but Christ liveth in me.' Oh! who that knows himself in all his sinfulness and emptiness, would not renounce himself, that he might be filled with Christ, that he might have Christ reproduced in him, Christ living in him—Christ, the chiefest among ten thousand, the altogether lovely, fairer than the sons of men!

2. As a *second* consequence, take the mutual love that subsists among the members of Christ. 'Hereby know we that we have passed from death to life, because we love the brethren.' Hereby know we that we ourselves live, that Christ lives in us, because we love them in whom Christ lives. Our love to him inevitably goes forth as love to them. Nay, our love to them is just our love to him—recognising, receiving, resting on him, as living in them also. For if Christ lives in them, then his word is literally and profoundly true—'He that receiveth you receiveth me.' 'Inasmuch as ye did it unto the least of my disciples, ye did it unto *me*.' When a Christian brother ministers to me in Christian love, it is not he, but Christ living in him that ministers to me. When I, in turn, minister in love to my brother, it is to Christ living in him that I minister. Thus in his people Christ himself ministers to me here: Christ will own me as having ministered to himself

in them hereafter. Not a cup of cold water, given in the name of a disciple, should fail of being met with gratitude to Christ for it now; nor shall fail of obtaining from Christ for it its reward at last.

Hence, also, the secret of that pure and exalted feeling of honour and esteem with which the blessed grace of love to the brethren is characterized. For when I truly love a believer, it is with an emotional ascription of honour to him as one of the excellent of the earth. I recognise him as a child of God—as an heir of God. I recognise him as a king and a priest by the divine appointment and in the estimation of our Father who is in heaven. But honourable and exalted as this, his recognised rank and renown, must be, my estimate of him rises higher still when I recognise the truth that Christ lives in him, when I recognise Christ himself living in him. Then I not only honour him in Christ, but I honour Christ in him. Nor does the element of his earthly rank or estate enter into this consideration at all. *That* dwindles into insignificance, and comes not at all into account. Nay, his nation, kindred, people, tongue, becomes a matter of pure indifference. Christ living in him obliterates all distinctions of social or national estate, throws down all barriers of social or national separation. 'There is neither Greek nor Jew, circumcision nor uncircumcision, barbarian, Scythian, bond nor free; but Christ is all, if Christ is in all, if Christ is all in all.' 'Inasmuch as ye did it unto the *least* of my disciples ye did it unto me.' Well, therefore, may this mutual love be assigned as the grand evidence of discipleship: 'Hereby shall all men know that ye are my disciples, if ye have love one to another.'

3. As a *third* consequence, observe the explanation, the origin, of persecution.

It originates in the world's hatred to Christ, and is directed against him. It must be so, seeing that Christ lives in his people. 'Saul, Saul, wasting the Church, why persecutest thou *me?*' And it is no extenuation of the world's guilt in hating the saints, that they do not believe that Christ lives in them—that they do not know or recognise Christ in *them.* Their rejection of those that are *his* stands exactly on the same footing with their rejection of *him:* 'Henceforth the world knoweth us not, because it knew him not.' Depravity blinded the world to the glory of Christ when he came in his own person, and blinds them to the measure of his glory in which he comes in the persons of his people. The bitter Ishmaelitish laugh and jest with which you, the worldling, scorn the Isaac of God, the promised seed; the hard words or hard deeds with which you, born after the flesh, persecute him that is born after the Spirit, will bear no excuse from your assertion that you did not know, you did not think, you did not see, that Christ was living in him—that it was really the promised Seed of the woman, Messiah himself, you were persecuting. For it is only your hatred and bitter prejudice that blind you. If you feared God and loved Christ, you would see him in his people: 'They that fear thee shall rejoice when they see me trusting in thy word;' 'they shall glorify Christ in me.'

Ah! consider, in your dislike of those that are Christ's; in your suspicion of them; your hard thoughts and hard speeches concerning them; your discomfort in their presence when their godliness, their Christliness, comes out; your scornful joy over their infirmities and failures—consider what a proof you have in all this of your deadly enmity to that Christ who lives in them. You cannot but know that as yet Christ lives in them only partially. If Christ is in them, the body is dead because of sin, though the Spirit is life because of righteousness. A body of sin and death is in them, as well as a living Christ. And that body of sin and death is a drawback on the completeness of the life and likeness of Christ in his people. They profess to give no more than a partial, though still a real, representation of Christ. They profess no more, though they long that it were far more, yea, long that it were unbroken and complete. But were it so—were their infirmities removed, their remaining corruption finally suppressed and extinguished; were there absolutely nothing seen or extant in them any more save Christ—'Christ living in them' in the unabated fullness and energy of his holy grace and life—ah! you know that their society would be unspeakably more painful to you still; their Christliness would rebuke you more powerfully than now; your withdrawal from them, if withdrawal were possible, would be more complete: or if you could not escape their presence and their intercourse—if you found yourself in relations to them which you could not set aside—if you found them a people with whom, in their perfect righteousness, and holiness, and likeness to Christ, yon could not but have to do—ah! would not your dislike to them, your rejection of them, your resentment against them and their piety, break out in manifold strength and bitterness? And what is this but just a proof that the more clearly Christ is revealed to you, the nearer Christ is brought to you, so much the more do you dislike him; and that were Christ, therefore, to come to you, not only in his own personal perfection in his people, but in himself, in his own perfect person, you would fully and finally reject him, and say, 'Depart from us, for we desire not thee, nor the knowledge of thy ways'? Ah! forget not that it is this, indeed, you do say, when now you reject his people. You reject, you persecute, him in them; for 'Christ liveth in them.'

But let believers know what they are to expect at the world's hands, and why. 'Christ living in you' will not fare any better at the world's hands than Christ sojourning in the world in the days of his flesh. The world is the same now as then. Christ in you is the same Christ as then. If they have kept his sayings, they will keep yours also; if they have persecuted him, they will persecute you. The servant is not greater than his Lord; it is enough if the servant be as his Lord. And it must be so, if his Lord lives in him. Christ in his own person was the object of the world's malice. Christ living in you will be so still.

4. But, *fourthly,* as another consequence of Christ living in you, take the words of Paul to the Colossians: 'Christ in you the hope of glory.'

Christ living in you by his Spirit is the seal, the hope, the earnest of the glory to be revealed. Not the glory itself as yet; the seal only, not the substance; the hope only, not the realization; the earnest merely, not the fullness or completion. And the reason is, that Christ lives in you as yet, not as he lives in his glory: when he does so, that will be your glory realized. When Christ as glorified shall live in you, ye also will be glorified thereby. But not yet does Christ live in you as he lives in his glory. Christ lives in you as he lived in his humiliation, in his work and travail, in his sorrows and sufferings; his glory veiled in the tabernacle of his flesh and beneath the thick covering of his deep abasement. The Christ who now lives in you is not the Christ as sitting in the fullness of his blessed reward; but the Christ as labouring in the yoke and toil of his humble service; the Christ as going about Judea and Galilee doing good and suffering evil—overcoming evil with good—enduring the contradiction of sinners against himself; living, indeed, a glorious life in the favour of his Father even then, but with his glory hidden. This is the Christ who now lives in you. Your life, therefore, also, is hid with Christ in God. To suffer with Christ is your portion now, even to fill up what is behind of the sufferings of Christ. Christ, when glory comes, will live in you in glory as he lives in glory himself. Christ, ere glory comes, will live in you in the world even as he himself in the world did live. 'Ought not Christ to have suffered these things, and to enter into his glory?' Ought not ye to suffer with him, that ye may be also glorified together?

It is, then, only 'the hope of glory.' But it is that hope most sure and blessed—most animating for duty, most comforting for patience. For living in you, and working in you, Christ will perfect that which concerneth you. He will gradually suppress, and finally extinguish, all that is not 'Christ in you;' and he will then shine forth in you in the unabated splendour of his perfect image. You know not what you shall be; but you know that when he shall appear, you shall be like him, for you shall see him as he is. There will then be nothing in you but Christ. Already you have said, and do habitually say, 'None but Christ for me;' and blessed be God that is already realized in full perfection: Christ for me; Christ, 'who loved me, and gave himself *for me;'* Christ, who 'appeareth in the presence of God *for me.'* But then there shall also be realized fully that other cry, which as yet is but the object of desire and hope, and towards which there is only as yet a progress—'None but Christ in me;' and you will be satisfied when you awake in the attainment of it. Meantime, bear patiently the sufferings; for I reckon that the sufferings of this present time are not worthy to be compared with the glory that is to be revealed in us. The seal, and earnest, and hope of that glory is Christ living in us already. Engage an in-living Christ more and more, by faith, by vigilance, by prayer, by diligence and dutifulness—engage the Christ who lives in you to mortify and crucify the sin that dwells in you. So will you realize and manifest his inward presence with you. And you will say, with growing faith and wonder, and with deepening apprehension of the rich grace and marvels of the saying, 'I am crucified with Christ: nevertheless, I live; yet not I, but Christ liveth in me: and the life which I live in the flesh, I live by the faith of the Son of God, who loved me, and gave himself for me.' Amen.

'YEA AND AMEN'[1]

Preface to the Second Edition

A N impression of the following sermon being printed for private distribution among the members of Free Greyfriars, it has been thought right to publish a second edition. In doing this, I am tempted to retain here a portion of what I had said in a prefatory note to my friends of the Greyfriars, the topic being one of general interest and great importance.

'I take the opportunity of affectionately counselling you to see to it, that yourselves and families be intelligently rooted and grounded in the great fundamental truths of our most holy faith. At all times, it is good to call to mind the words of the Lord Jesus, how he not only said, 'Read,' but *Search* the Scriptures.' It is specially so in times like these. Much of the current Christian literature of the day, even where it is not positively unsound, seems more and more bent on cultivating what is shallow and superficial; presenting us at best with men's own thoughts dipped in a weak solution of religious truth, and abdicating the infinitely grander function of setting forth the glorious treasures of the intellect of God. I warn you against this great evil. Be not deceived. Take no hair-thin lacquered silver filigree, for the solid gold of Havilah, which is good. Buy ye the truth, and sell it not. Be really rooted and grounded in it. And to this end, make full proof of the help which our Catechisms and Confession of Faith afford. You know how these venerable documents are being, in some quarters, despised. Some say

---

[1] [Originally published as a pamphlet: *'Yea and Amen.' A Sermon on the Steadfastness of God's Promises,* 2nd ed. (Edinburgh: John MacLaren, 1866).]

they contain *too much* truth; others say, *too little* And they both follow up these contradictory complaints with a statement of their preference for the Bible! Very misleading representations! Our symbols are indeed full of truth. They are not the mine. Holy Scriptures—the Inspired Word of God—alone is. But they are very full of pure gold from that mine—mined and made ready for our use; and that the coin of this treasury is genuine, really from the true mine, is plainly written down before our eyes. Speak of the gold that perisheth, and who complains that his inherited exchequer is too full? The children of this world are wiser. As to our Catechisms and Confession containing too *little* truth; more particularly, as to any risk of your Christian intelligence being cramped, and your Christian worth weakened, by too much attention to these subordinate standards of your Church; you would think me sarcastic, would you not, were I expressing any apprehensions in that direction? We must all be very conscious that our error lies on quite the other side. Study these standards in the light of Holy Scripture—the only authoritative divine rule of faith and duty. Study Holy Scripture with the great help which these documents afford. And you will not be like the best and holiest of Scotland's pious patriarchs if you do not own, that, with the Holy Ghost sent down on you from on high, you are, even unto hoar hairs, being more and more fed on the finest of the wheat.'

I would add that our Standards are too often spoken of as if they were exclusively *doctrinal,* and afforded no guidance in setting forth the *practical,* side of Christian life and character. I venture to say, however, that the old moderates would have made their 'good moral discourses' considerably better had they been more familiar with the Standards of their Church. Look, for instance, at the Larger Catechism under the question, 'What are the sins forbidden in the ninth commandment?' Where have the moralists presented us with anything more searching and complete? The subject is so fully discussed, and the alphabetically noted references to Scripture are so numerous, that the whole alphabet is exhausted twice over, with the exception of the letter a, which is only once called into play; and the preceding question, 'What are the duties required?' had already once exhausted the alphabet without excluding a single letter. Under this vast amount of Scripture reference, no fewer than 126 passages of the Word of God are brought under review! I say *passages* : for many of them are not mere verses, but paragraphs. I call this Biblical. I call it Biblical exposition of the very highest order. We do not need *less* less, but *more* preaching in accordance with our Standards. No doubt the Bible contains history, poetry, proverbs, and prophecy. And by all means, if possible, let the preacher be at once as doctrinal as Paul, as practical as James, as narrative as Luke, as apothegmatical as Solomon, and as poetical as Isaiah. And let it be understood that literary slovenliness in the pulpit is to be condemned. Still, with full scope for all literary refinement, and all Biblical variety, it must be borne in mind, that the Scriptures principally teach what man is to believe concerning God, and what duty God requires of man. The Scriptures *principally* teach doctrine and duty. So must the pulpit. So do our Standards. And whether is the preacher more like to be faithful and efficient who essays his duty under the wonderful and wise guidance which our Standards afford, or he who roams through the Bible unguided and at random? Or, which of them does the greater honour to Holy Scripture? The heavens are the workmanship of God; the Newtonian theory is the product of enlightened reason studying them. I should not think that I honoured God by lecturing on the starry heavens as if Newton had never lived. No! nor by lecturing on the Bible as if the Westminster Assembly had never sat.

H. M.

Edinburgh

February, 1866

All the promises of God in him are Yea, and in him Amen,
unto the glory of God by us.—2 Corinthians 1:20

THE theme brought before us by these words is—the sureness, the certainty, the stability of the promises.

It is not of any particular promise, nor of any particular set or section or portion of the promises, that this certainty or unchangeableness is affirmed; but of the promises as a whole—of all the promises of God—the promises in their whole fullness, range, and amplitude. 'All the promises of God in him are Yea.'

And how amazing is the amplitude and all-embracing sweep of these promises! How numerous these promises in themselves! How marvellously great, and full, and rich, and varied the matter of them! God himself, even our Father—'I will be a God unto you,' 'I will be a father unto you, saith the Lord Almighty.' Christ, the good shepherd, who giveth his life for the sheep—'I will set up one shepherd over them, and he shall feed them; he shall feed them, and he shall be their shepherd.' The Spirit—'Behold, I will pour out my Spirit unto you.' Regeneration and renewal of our depraved natures dead in sin; 'A new heart will I give you, and a right spirit will I put within you.' Entire and free remission of iniquities;—'Your sins and your iniquities will I remember no more.' And time would fail me to tell of the promises and pledged words of God concerning justification, adoption, sanctification, and the assurance of his love; the peace of conscience, the joy in the Holy Ghost, the increase of grace, the perseverance to the end; the death in peace and victory, the resurrection in honour, power, and glory, the acquittal and acknowledgment at the great white throne, the presentation in faultlessness and in exceeding joy unto the Father, and the life everlasting, Amen. All these things are again and again, in every variety of form, and down to the most minute detail, declared and guaranteed to the Church in promises. 'Look now towards heaven,' one might almost say, adopting, concerning the promises, the memorable words of Jehovah communing with Abraham his friend concerning the promised seed,—'Look now towards heaven and tell the stars, if thou be able to number them, so shall the promises be.' 'All the promises.' Yet in this vast multiplicity there is unity. Insomuch that the Spirit of inspiration, gathering them all up into one, hath said, 'This is the promise that he hath promised us, even eternal life.' The promises, thus summed up and collected in one, are also called the covenant—'This is the covenant that I will make with them, saith the Lord,'—and then follows an enumeration of promises, specifying particularly the two grand branches, regeneration and remission of sins. It is this covenant-bond that makes all the promises one. 'If ye are Christ's, then are ye Abraham's seed, and heirs according to the promise.' And it is worthy of remark that this unity of the promises—this unity in multiplicity—stands closely connected with the attribute of their sureness, their stability, their certainty. For Paul, arguing this very certainty, seems very specially and designedly to use the word in the singular number—'For the *promise* to Abraham and his seed was not through the law, but through the righteousness of faith. Therefore it is of faith, that it might be by grace, to the end the promise might be sure to all the seed.'

There is unity, then, in multiplicity. Look again towards heaven, and tell the stars, if thou be able to number them. Yet though the vast multiplicity of heaven's bright hosts baffles reckoning, you see that heaven's blue vault is *one*. It is even so with the promises. And it is of all the promises in their wholeness and unity that perfect stability or unchangeableness is asserted in our text. 'All the promises of God in him are Yea, and in him Amen, to the glory of God by us.'

The text invites us to consider the steadfastness of the promises. *First,* as on the side of God; *secondly,* as on the side of man; *first,* on the side of God and his faithfulness; *second,* on the side of man and his faith; *first,* on the side of God and his fullness and faithfulness; and *second,* on the side of man and his emptiness and empty-handed faith.

Standing, then, as it were, *first,* on the side of God, we have three successive truths set before us:—

I. On the side of God, all the premises are sure.—'All the promises of God are Yea.'

II. On the side of God the promises have this sureness in Christ, he as the God-man being on God's side, 'All the promises of God in him are Yea.'

III. On the side of God the promises are sure in Christ to the glory of God; 'All the promises of God in him are Yea, *to the glory of God.'*

Turning now, *secondly,* to man's side, we have three exactly corresponding truths or facts to consider:—

I. On the side of man, and his empty-handed, simple, and implicit faith, all the promises are sure, 'All the promises are, Amen;' so it is.

II. On the side of man, the promises have this sureness in Christ, he, as the God-man, being on man's side, 'All the promises of God in him are, Amen.'

III. On the side of man, the promises are to God's glory, through man's possession of them, 'to the glory of God by us'—each of us who believe.

Firstly then, the steadfastness of the promises on God's side. In this view, then, we are to consider the sureness of the promises on the side of God.

I. And, in the first place, God's promises are sure. The promises of God are, 'Yea,' firm, absolute, unchangeable.

The import of this may, by God's blessing, be made to appear, by the three following remarks; and, following the example of the apostle, we shall use expressions somewhat brief and memorable.

1. *First,* then, the promises of God are not 'Perhaps,' they are 'Yea.' You become alive to your lost condition as a sinner. You realize the conviction that you are spiritually dead; dead in law and dead in sin; on the one hand, guilty under the righteous wrath of God as a rebel; and on the other hand, depraved, helpless, under the love, and grasp, and power of sin as a slave. You carry this ruined and wretched estate to God for his consideration, for his commiseration, for his merciful and gracious aid. You carry it to his throne, to his word, to his covenant, to his promises. And how does he meet you? What does he say to you?

He does not meet you with a 'perhaps,' but with a 'yea.' He does not give you a weak, wavering, half-audible 'perhaps;' he gives you a strong, clear, outspoken 'yea.' He does not say: he will try what he can do for you; he will consider your case; when he hath convenient season he will call for you; and possibly in the meantime something may turn up in your favour, and you may call upon him again and see. Ah! he deals not so with the poor afflicted one. The prospect he holds out to you is not a possibility, not a probability, not a probability even however strong; not a 'perhaps,' however closely verging on a 'yea.' At once, without scruple, whole and entire, without limit and without reserve, sounding clear and strong, he gives you his 'yea' itself; not probability, but certainty. 'Though your sins be as scarlet, they shall be white as snow.' 'Him that cometh unto me I will in no wise cast out.'

2. *Secondly*, all the promises of God are not 'If,' they are 'Yea.' That is to say, they are not conditional, but unconditional. Their truth and firmness are not suspended on some consideration or event beyond themselves, so that were that event or consideration failing, the promises also must fail; or, so that they hold good only *if* it holds good. No. But apart from every event save those which they themselves express and secure; apart from every consideration save those which they themselves involve and explain, they are in themselves, and by themselves, unconditionally and absolutely sure. God does not say, 'This is the covenant that I will make with them—if.' He says, 'This is the covenant I will make with them.' He does not say, 'I will be your God—if.' He says, 'I will be your God.' He does not say, 'A new heart will I give them, and their sins will I remember no more—provided.' But absolutely, without condition, with no 'if,' with an undiminished, unmingled, 'yea,' he says, 'A new heart I will give you, and I will be merciful to your unrighteousness, and your sins and your iniquities will I remember no more.'

Yes, the God of the everlasting covenant, the covenant of promise, reserves no condition in his own hand, and he requires no condition in mine. On his own part, he keeps no condition in reserve. He does not say to me, for instance, I will be a God unto you if I see it would be for my glory. And on my part, he calls no condition into play. He does not say to me, for instance, I will be a God unto you if you are faithful and deserve it. Abjuring all condition which might bring suspense on his side, and forbidding all condition which might breed suspense on mine, his word to me is absolute, simple, unconditional, yea, 'I will be a God unto you.'

Of course there are conditional promises in the gospel. There are promises which for their fulfilment do depend on the prior accomplishment of some event with which they stand connected—the prior realization of some gift on God's part, or some grace on ours. There are promises, limited and bounded by an 'if.' The believer is familiar, for instance, with this one, 'If we confess our sins, God is faithful and just to forgive us our sins, and to cleanse us from all unrighteousness;' where the sweet experience of pardon and cleansing is made to depend on our having first made confession of our guilt and impurity. But then, this merely indicates the order in which God fulfils his promises; it does not make them, as a whole, conditional and uncertain. It tells us that the promise of pardon and cleansing is fulfilled in due order after the promise of repenting and relenting grace. The very confession on which pardon is made to depend—the grace to make such confession—is itself promised. It lies wrapped up in the promise of a new heart, which is a holy, contrite, true, confessing heart. And taking this promise first, and then the promise of pardon and cleansing as surely and orderly following upon it, the whole is not conditional, but sure; not 'if,' 'but 'yea.'

For again, it is well to remember that the text does not assert the absolute sureness of any one promise by itself—but of all the promises in their fullness and their oneness. 'All the promises of God are Yea.' They may be arranged in such order, and connected by such ties, that the second can be fulfilled only 'if' the first has been already accomplished, and that the third can be accomplished only when the second has been realized, and the fourth in like manner might be suspended conditionally on the third, each link following its predecessor. But the whole chain—all the promises, first, second, third, and all—all in one—the multiplicity in unity—is not conditional, not dependent, not 'if,' but 'yea.'

Look again toward heaven and its stars. The rising of Orion may be conditional on the prior rising of the Pleiades. Such maybe the constitution of the heavens, and the relation of star to star in its mighty vault, that one particular star can be visible above the horizon only *if* some other star hath risen first. And in like manner such may be the constitution of the covenant, and such the relation of promise to promise, that one particular promise, say, for instance, that of conscious sweet forgiveness, can be fulfilled to me only if another promise, that of a new and contrite heart to confess my sin, has been already fulfilled. Thus, indeed, you introduce an 'if,' a necessary and prior condition. But what of that? Does that make the covenant conditional and uncertain? Does that make all the promises—the promises whole and in their unity—to hang upon an 'if'? Does it interfere with their sure stability—their 'yea'? By no means. Look again towards heaven. The rising of Orion may be conditional. But the permanence of the whole vault is sure. Orion will rise only 'if' certain constellations rise first. But concerning the steadfastness of heaven's vault there is no 'if,' no doubt, no condition,—'for ever singing as they shine, the hand that made us is divine.'

Precisely so, one promise may be fulfilled to you only if certain others have been already realized. But the covenant—all the promises in their unity—the promise according to which being Christ's you are Abraham's seed, and heirs according to the promise,—the one vault of promise in heaven's kingdom of grace and glory, is not 'if,' but 'yea,' not conditional, but absolute and sure for ever.

3. All the promises of God are not 'Yea and Nay;' they are 'Yea.' They are not 'Yea' now and then, and 'Nay' in the intervals. Always, unalterably, without fluctuation, without variableness or shadow of turning, they are 'Yea,' the same yesterday, today, and for ever.

Ah! this is a blessed truth. Always, in all ages, in all circumstances, for all souls alike, these promises are invariable—continually 'yea.' For Abraham—were these promises solid, and steadfast and true? For me, for my use, they have unchangeably, identically, all that sureness and steadfastness still. For all who have found boldness to come within the veil by faith, and have found grace in the sight of the Lord, and peace and joy in believing, have these promises been sufficient and secure? They have all their sufficiency, all their security, identical and invariable, for the chief of sinners, farthest gone in guilt and alienation, trembling to think of drawing near, scarcely venturing to move towards a return, scarcely venturing to hope for grace. They have their identically invariable sureness for me. For yon white-robed throng with palms of victory before the throne, were all the promises sure? For me, also, they are sure; for always they are 'yea,' they are never 'yea and nay.'

Nay, more: Was there a time when the sun shone brightly and I saw and believed; a time when, with wholly broken, bleeding heart, and simple, child-like trust, I tried the promises, and found them sure? Well may I say:—Bless the Lord, O my soul; these promises are not Yea and Nay; always they are Yea. They are not 'yea'—good and firm— today, because I am enjoying them, strong in the faith; and then 'nay' tomorrow, because I am changed, and dark in mind, and fluttering between hope and fear, and groping in darkness to recover my faith, and regain my foundation. They are not 'yea' today, because my sky being clear, and my eye healthful and open, and the mists all gone, and the purity great, and the telescopic help of ordinances powerful, I see the shining vault of the covenant, and believe its promises, and am sure; and then 'nay' tomorrow, when the clouds may gather and screen the bright vision from my view. No. They are not thus, 'yea and nay.' Always, in all my changing moods, in my bounding hope and deep despondency; in my bright clear sunshine, and in my dark and cloudy day, the promises, still alike, always are sure. Could my bright day return if it were not so? 'Thy mercy, O Lord, is in the heavens; and thy faithfulness reacheth to the clouds.' Even though the clouds return after the rain; still thy mercy is in the heavens. Yonder shine all the promises ever safe and sure as before. And though the clouds should long prevail, and the day be dark and weary, thy faithfulness reacheth to the clouds, and shall prevail to sweep them all aside; and again, many times, at least at evening time, it shall be light. 'Why art thou cast down, O my soul, and why art thou disquieted within me? Hope in God, for I shall yet praise him, who is the health of my countenance and my God.'

Such then is the stability of all the promises. (1) They are not, 'Perhaps,' they are 'Yea;' not uncertain, but sure. (2) They are not 'If;' they are 'Yea;' not conditional, but absolute. (3) They are not 'Yea and Nay;' they are 'Yea,' not fluctuating, but invariable. All the promises of God—in all their fullness, and in their thorough unity-more sure, absolute, invariable. All the promises of God are 'Yea.'

The nature and truth of this stability may become still clearer, if the four following remarks be considered.

1. The promises are sure—in God's own mind. As originally in the mind of God, the promises indicate his eternal goodwill to sinners. And in this respect they are steadfast. They reveal a stable, sincere, unchangeable disposition of mercy, kindness and compassion. The God of compassion, and the compassion of God, are not fickle. They are the same yesterday, today, and for ever. In this respect he is of one mind. And he knoweth the end from the beginning. I know, saith he, the thoughts that I think concerning you. God is love. As I live, saith the Lord, I have no pleasure in the death of the sinner, but rather that he should turn and live. Viewed thus, in their origin, their spring, and eternal first cause and fountain, the promises are seen to have in them nothing untrue, insincere, insecure, fickle or changeable. They are absolutely free from every such evil attribute. They are Yea.

2. The promises are sure—in *God's recorded mind*. He hath recorded his mind in Holy Scripture. And there, as much as in his own mind from eternity, his promises are Yea. For he hath recorded all his mind concerning them, without scruple, without reserve. This revelation of his mind in Holy Scripture is not partial, unsatisfactory, reserved, and insufficient. The mighty God, even the Lord, hath spoken—and spoken out, and spoken out on this point all his mind. There is nothing equivocal in what he has said; and there is nothing suppressed of what he has thought. He hath had no mental reservation with us. Full and distinct as his promises were in his own mind, to the same fullness and distinctness hath he recorded them. O the glory of the firmness and fullness and simplicity with which God speaks out in his promises; a clear, complete, full, outspoken 'Yea.' Yes; this is the covenant that I will make with them. He speaks as with firm voice. He is giving forth a clear understanding.

3. The promises are sure—*as proposed to your mind*. Against all your objections they continue unchangeably 'Yea.' No effort of yours can make them otherwise. You cannot make them 'Nay.' You cannot negative them. They give back, in the face of every question and every query—of every objection, scruple, doubt, or difficulty—they give back their secure and triumphant 'Yea!' You say, 'I would embrace them but for this guilt, and this shame and cannot draw near.' But the promises ring back the loud, clear answer:—I will sprinkle clean water upon you, and ye shall be clean: 'And if the blood of bulls and of goats, and the ashes of an heifer, sprinkling the unclean, sancti-fied to the purifying of the flesh, how much more shall the blood of Christ, who, through the eternal Spirit, offered himself without spot, to God, purge your conscience from dead works to serve the living God.' You complain that you are dead in sin, and held in the fetters of depravity, and therefore you cannot have an interest in the promises. But again they triumph in their answer, in their unshaken 'Yea:'—'A new heart will I give you, and a right spirit will I put within you; I will take away the hard and stony heart out of your flesh, and give you an heart of flesh. I will put my Spirit in you, and ye shall live.' You may reply that even then you could not walk in the holy ways of the Lord, so weak, and wicked, and wayward do you feel yourself to be. But the masterly and ever-ready word of the promise answers—still abiding by its Yea—'I will put my Spirit upon you, and I will cause you to walk in my statutes, and ye shall keep my commandments and do them.' Drawing on their all-sufficiency, their all-fullness—'all the promises of God'—they answer and annihilate all your opposition, and remain master of the field, having always and unchangeably their 'yea.' In no ignoble sense these promises of God, in their conflict with your unbelief, always have the last word. They tear off every mask that could hide the unreasonable and offensive character of unbelief. They follow unbelief into all its hiding-places, and dislodge it from them all; and they demonstrate, in a flood of light, that your unbelief is the only reason of your ruin; if, within the sound of these promises you should, alas! be ruined still. In a word, their fullness and sureness shut us up into the faith.

4. Being sure, originally, in God's mind; and sure in God's recorded mind; and sure as proposed to your mind;—the promises abide sure whether received or rejected by your mind. Whether welcomed by you or refused, all the promises of God are 'Yea.'

Of course, if welcomed, their sureness is admitted; it is when rejected that a doubt seems to rise. The believer owns that they are 'yea.' It is the unbeliever with whom alone any question can be held. Hitherto, then, you have not believed; and you come and ask: 'Are the promises sure?' We refer you to the proofs that have been already given. But you say: 'All that I have heard, hitherto, of their steadfastness, is merely general; are they sure to me—to me in particular?' And I answer that what has been already said goes to show, that for you, as material and ground of faith to you, all the promises of God are sure; all the promises of God, in all their fullness and in all their steadfastness, are, to you, for a sure foundation of faith, identically what they are to me; identically to you and me alike, what they were to Abraham. And what answer can you give? Will you have the folly to ask the question: 'Will they be surely fulfilled to me whether I believe them or not?' By nature you are a lost soul, dead in sin. Holy faith can never be of yourself; it must be wrought in you of the Lord. 'By grace are ye saved, through faith, and that not of yourselves, it is the gift of God.' The gift of faith is itself one of the promises. And can you fail, then, to see that your question is a contradiction? When you ask, Will they be fulfilled whether I have faith in them, whether I embrace them, or no? you just ask, Will they be fulfilled, whether they are fulfilled or not? Surely we may be released from defending their faithfulness any farther.

Do you resign absurdity and betake yourself to impiety? Do you say, 'Then if I believe not, the promise will not be fulfilled, its truth and sureness will be compromised, and the faithfulness of God will fail'? And who are you that have power over the faithfulness of God, to bend and break it at your pleasure? What if you do not believe? 'Shall your unbelief make the faithfulness of God without effect? God forbid. Yea, let God be true, and every man a liar. As it is written, That thou mightest be justified in thy sayings, and mightest overcome when thou art judged.'

The case, in fact, is this—These promises in their fullness meet all thy case. Art thou guilty? They provide pardon free and full, now, and for ever. Art thou dead?—life. Art thou an outcast?—adoption, gratuitous, without money. Art thou blind?—a new eye and the light of the Lord. What is thine evil?—The promises can free thee from it. What is thy want?—They can supply it. Hence, all thine honest scruples, difficulties, and objections, they answer and remove: all thy dishonest scruples, they answer and expose, tearing off every mask. They prove that thou wilt not come; that nothing but thine own will prevents. They prove thee unwilling, untrue, insincere, false; yes, they prove thee insincere; thou doest not prove them insincere or insecure. Thy doubt of their truth springs from thine own falseness. Thy distrust of their sincerity is only thine own insincerity. They reach thee, and show thy falseness. Thou canst not reach them to alter their truth. They have thee always within their range; they besiege thee, and hem thee in; they dominate thee. But thou canst not master their range. All thy turbulent and unbelieving passions cannot affect the promises, cannot stain their purity and truth. All thy objections and refusals have their limit, 'hitherto shall they come;' but not nigh the promises, to shake or stain them; yea, though they toss themselves, yet can they not pass over.

Yon flag of the promise floateth high above thee, stainless as the undriven snow. Thou canst not reach to tarnish or dishonour it. Ah! why shouldest thou desire? It is Jehovah's flag of truce to thee, his rebel, and his enemy, to thee his long lost child. It is the white flag of a free and full forgiveness, of a free and full reconciliation, of promise all-sufficient, all-secure. Let every one that heareth do it honour. 'And the Spirit and the bride say, Come, and let him that heareth say, Come, and let him that is athirst come, and whosoever will, let him come.' You cannot falsify nor stain that flag. Let him that heareth do it honour. 'And he brought me to his banqueting house, and his banner over me was love.'

II. Secondly, and still viewing the promises on God's side; they are all. Yea, in Christ. They have their sureness in him. 'All the promises of God in him, are Yea.'

Now, there are four respects in which the promises have their stability in Christ. (1) He shares them with the Father, in all their original fullness and sureness, in virtue of his Godhead. (2) He declares them undiminished and unaltered in the office of his ministry. (3) He seals and confirms them by the sacrifice of his death. And, (4) He has fully received, and securely possesses them, as his reward in glory.

1. First, then, they are Yea in Christ, as he, being God, shares them in all their fullness, and all their sureness, with the Father. In none, save a Divine Redeemer, could they assuredly be Yea. No mind, save one co-extensive with the Father's, can hold all the promises at once, in all their full proportions, in all their glorious rich details, in all their manifold and wonderful relations. But the Son dwelleth in the bosom of the Father. The Son's mind reflects the Father's mind. He is the brightness of the Father's glory, and the express image of his person. Such as the promises are originally in the Father's mind, such are they, undiminished, underanged, altogether unaltered, in the Son.

2. Second; clothing himself in our nature, the Son cometh forth to declare the Father. And still in our flesh he abideth the image of the invisible God. Unaltered still are all the promises in the Son. It pleased the Father that in him should all fullness dwell, all the treasures of wisdom and knowledge. Would you see the Father, and read the Father's mind, in all its truth and faithfulness? Behold God manifest in the flesh. 'He that hath seen me,' saith Jesus, 'hath seen the Father.' And all the Father's will Jesus declares without deterioration, without diminution, without reserve. 'I call you friends, for all that I have heard of my Father, I have made known unto you.'

3. The Son seals and confirms the promises by the sacrifice of his death. He bears my sin on his own body on the tree. He expiates, in my room, the guilt that alone could make God's good-will and promise to me impossible or doubtful. He brings in, in my room, and on my behalf, a perfect obedience to the law, which makes God's goodwill and promise to me righteous and secure. My title to the promises is

thus in Christ; in Christ crucified and accepted; in Christ finishing the work which the Father gave him to do; in Christ wholly fulfilling every condition, and thus placing the promises on a footing, a platform, a rock of security, which neither you nor I, nor sin, nor earth, nor hell can ever shake.

4. And now, the Son himself, my surety and legal representative, having fulfilled every condition, and fulfilled all righteousness, and done so for me, doth—for me also, still for me—ascend on high and receive in his own person, all the promises. 'This Jesus hath God raised up; and being, by the right hand of God exalted, he hath received the promise of the Holy Ghost.' Yes! Thy mercy is in the heavens, and thy faithfulness reacheth to the clouds. I may be down here beneath the clouds, in a sphere which clouds have it in their power to darken; but yonder, beyond the region of the clouds, where doubt and darkness cannot come-in the heavens, as Stephen saw them opened, and the Son of man standing at the right hand of God-there are all the promises, sure, fulfilled, enjoyed, 'Yea' in Christ. The king shall joy in thy strength, O Lord! in thy salvation how greatly shall he rejoice. Thou hast given him his heart's desire, and hast not withholden the request of his lips. He asked life of thee—with strong crying and tears in the days of his flesh he cried unto thee who wast able to save him from death, and was heard in that he feared—he asked life of thee and thou gavest it him, even length of days, for ever and for ever. His glory is great in thy salvation; honour and majesty hast thou laid upon him. For thou hast made him most blessed for ever; thou hast made him exceeding glad with thy countenance. For the king trusteth in the Lord, and, through the mercy of the Most High, he shall not be moved. Thus it is with the king. Literally in him—in his own experience and joy—in him, the promises are Yea.

III. The sureness of the promises in Christ glorifies God. 'All the promises of God in him are Yea—to the glory of God.'

Now, the sureness of the promises we have seen is singularly bound up with their fullness; their all-sufficiency to supply every want; their all-sufficiency to master every hindrance. Hence their sureness specially glorifies God in two respects; *first*, as regards his all-sufficient fullness of sovereign grace; and, *secondly,* his all-successful supremacy of sovereign will. Regarding the first:

1. All the premises are Yea in Christ, to the glory of God's all-sufficient sovereign grace. In the depths of his own fullness and love, he found all that was required for the recovery of ruined rebellious man. In himself, in his all-sufficiency, he found Righteousness—not only his own infinite eternal righteousness, but a righteousness also for myriads of unrighteous guilty criminals; and, in himself, in his all-sufficiency, he found Life—not only life in himself, but life for myriads dead in sin, infinitely further from life than if they had never had a being. This Righteousness and this Life he found in himself, and he provided and sent them forth in his Son. In him the Righteousness proved all-sufficient, even when weighed down by the unrighteousness of the guilty, as he bare their guilt on the tree. Still his Righteousness abode and overcame. In him also, the Son, the Life proved all-sufficient, even weighed down by the death of the dead, when 'the Life' died their death, and yet outlived it, and liveth for evermore. And this all-sufficiency of righteousness and life is provided in infinite free grace, to the praise of the glory of sovereign grace;—that he may show unto the ages to come, the exceeding riches of his grace.

2. The faithfulness of the promises glorifies God's supreme and sovereign will. He ruleth king by the sureness of his promises. He executeth the good pleasure of his loving will. He overcometh every objection, every enemy, every obstacle. Not even my backslidings can make void his sovereign will. For the promises are not, Yea *in me*, but in Christ. If I break his commandments he may chastise me, but, he adds, 'My lovingkindness will I not take from him, nor alter the word that hath gone out of my mouth.' Ah! it is difficult for me to feel this and hold this with a pure and purifying faith. But in proportion to its difficulty, it is powerful in its truth to exalt and glorify God, and powerful by the Spirit to abase and purify me. 'Fear not, little flock, it is your Father's good pleasure to give you the kingdom.' His sure promise glorifies his high supremacy, and it does so, as being Yea in Christ. 'For I am persuaded that neither life nor death, nor angels nor

principalities nor powers, nor things present nor things to come, nor height nor depth, nor any other creature, shall be able to separate us from the love of God, which is in Christ Jesus our Lord.'

Thus are all the promises Yea in Christ to the glory of God.

We turn now briefly *to view the stability of the promises as on* the *side of man and man's faith.* And here the principle is, that as God on his side is full and faithful, man on his side is empty, and his faith, when true, is empty-handed. His faith neither adds to, nor diminishes, the promises; it owns the certainty that is in them, and embraces them as they are. His reception of them, and his response when truly in faith, is a simple 'Amen;'—So let it be; So it is: a simple Amen, leaving them in all the strength and sureness of their own 'Yea.' Thus faith takes God at his word. Valuable consequences are involved.

1. My Amen comes after God's Yea. My faith follows God's promise. It never can appear save in the wake of the promise. You say you cannot believe—you have tried to look to the Lamb of God, to the cross of Christ, to the perfect sacrifice and propitiation, but without success, without any sense of pardon and of peace. What if you have been silencing God's promise; deaf to it, instead of believing? What if you have been putting out of view God's Yea, God's word—God's sure promise? If you put aside God's Yea—God's promise—your effort at faith will end in an effort of fancy; your thoughts of the power of Christ's blood will be mere acts of intellect. Your believing Amen— your faith—can follow only on God's word—on God's Yea. Look again to that bleeding victim on the cross, and as you look, listen: let the Lord now speak—speak to you, 'Look unto me and be ye saved.' Behold, indeed, the Lamb of God; but hear the promise while you are beholding him—'Behold the lamb of God that beareth away the sin of the world.' 'Though your sins be as scarlet, they shall be white as snow; though red like crimson, they shall be as wool;' Yea, they shall be as wool. Does your Amen not come? Hath God spoken and you not believed? Be ashamed and confounded. Believe, be forgiven, be cleansed, be peaceful. Do you press it back another step and say you cannot believe of yourself; you need the grace of the Spirit. Behold again the Lamb of God, and hear God's word, 'He hath redeemed us

from the curse of the law, being made a curse for us, that we might receive the promise of the Spirit. Behold, I will pour out my Spirit upon you.' And can you not believe and receive the Spirit in truth, as God in truth doth promise? If God be true, cannot you believe? If God give his Yea, will you withhold your Amen? You could not believe till he hath spoken; when he hath spoken can you doubt? 'Faith cometh by hearing, and hearing by the word of God.' 'Be it unto me, thy servant, according to thy word.'

2. My Amen ought to come immediately after God's Yea. Faith ought not to tarry a moment after God's promise. This follows at once from the views already presented. Were the promise of God a mere 'Perhaps,' I might naturally, and with some show of reason, wait till it became a trustworthy and decided 'Yea,' before consenting to put my trust in it. Were the promise of God an 'If,'—conditional— I would have to fulfil the condition first, or at least wait till it were fulfilled. And were the promise of God 'Yea and Nay'—Yes and No alternately—I would be quite sure that my time of deepest conscious guilt and misery, my time of sorest need, was precisely the very time of the 'Nay.' And in all these cases immediate believing would be impossible. But God's promise is at once and wholly, by itself alone, sure and sufficient—an immediate, firm, self-supporting, unchanging, Yea. It needs no work of mine to complete or to confirm it; no proposal of mine; no suggestion of mine. I am, in fact, peremptorily called upon to cease from all suggestion of my own, all proposal, all work, all scruple, all hesitation; and the promise being Yea, my faith must give an immediate Amen. 'Behold! now is the accepted time. Behold! now is the day of salvation.'

3. My Amen needs nothing more than God's Yea. For his promise meets all my, case, and is sure. It is, therefore, all my salvation and all my desire.

4. My Amen ought to embrace nothing less than God's Yea. Faith ought to embrace all God's promises. For it is 'all the promises,' in their unity, that are Yea. Would I escape the curse, and refuse the moral image of him who redeems me from the curse? Would I have remission of sins, and reject renewal of heart and holiness of life? Then

I am rejecting God's Yea; for his premises are one. 'This is his promise which he hath promised us, Eternal Life;' life in the forgiveness of sins; life in the favour of God; life in nearness and holy fellowship with God; life in the service, the society, the holiness, the happiness, the heaven, the home of God. This is the promise which is Yea; one promise in all, many promises in one. Can I view it on every side, and give my joyful Amen?

5. If I can, then my faith, being true, has infallible sureness in it; for my Amen cannot but carry in it the same certainty as God's Yea. The living faith of the renewed heart—the true Amen—what is it but the echo of God's Yea? It is the Holy Spirit in the heart answering and echoing back to himself in the word. Your believing Amen is simply the Yea of God's faithfulness translated into the language of faith, and, echoed back to its native heaven. And as the original voice has sureness, clearness, unmingled steadfastness in it, so also has the echo. Said the disciples, 'We believe and are sure.' No doubt, in every actual case of believing, the voice of remaining unbelief may mingle its tremulous discordant tones with the clear and firm-ringing tones of faith, and the soul's utterance, as a whole, may seem to waver; but all the wavering is from unbelief alone. Even as the clang of a hammer, or the rumble of a vehicle may mingle with and mar the pure echo of a trumpet, which, itself, gives no uncertain sound; while yet the echo has in itself nothing but the very key and tone and firmness of the sound original;—So it is with faith. The believer may be able to say nothing more,—in this life he can say nothing higher— than, 'Lord I believe, help thou my unbelief.' Still, let the noble grace of living faith be accredited with all its glorious sureness; 'a true heart and the full assurance of faith.' Fear not, Oh believer, to assert the full thorough sureness, the Divine certainty that lives in thy living faith. It derives all that sureness solely from the sureness of the promise. It is the reflex and echo of the steadfastness of the promise. For if the promise is sure, and you believe it, can you not say, 'we believe and are sure'? Verily, your Amen, being a humble and mere Amen, is, for that very reason, imbued with all the certainty of God's firm and unchangeable Yea.

On the side of man, and man's faith, the promises have their sureness in Christ. All the promises of God *in him* are Amen.

To see this, revert for a moment to the consideration of their sureness in Christ as on God's side. There are three progressive steps: *First*; Christ, as God, shares the promises with the Father, in eternal covenant design, in the counsel of peace which is between them both: *Secondly*; as God-man, he secures and seals the promises on the cross, purchasing them all by the blood of the everlasting covenant: *Thirdly*; as man, in his human consciousness and experience, he securely possesses and enjoys them now at the Father's right hand. 'Thou hast ascended on high; thou hast received gifts in the man' (Psa. 68:18, *Margin*). Thus on God's side they are Yea in Christ: in him as God from everlasting; in him as God-man on the cross; in him as man, 'and because he is the Son of man,' on the throne.

And now it is at this point that the God-man, standing now on your side, claims your faith—your Amen. In him, therefore, let them be Amen to you; and the three progressive steps or stages of certainty in these promises re-appear on your side in reverse order. Give Christ your Amen, your faith, your simple consent and confidence, and then: *First*, himself, as man, enjoying them, he shares them all with you, even as from eternity, being God, he shared them with the Father. *Secondly*, as God-man, he carries you by his cross into the conviction of their irrefragable certainty, as righteously and for ever sealed there. And *thirdly*, by the way of that same cross he carries you at length to his Father and your Father, that you may enjoy them all, and the love which they imply, and in which they all originate, according to his own majestic intercessory appeal—'Father, I will that those whom thou hast given me be with me where I am, that they may behold my glory which thou hast given me, for thou lovedst me before the foundation of the world.'

Here let us pause and contemplate Christ's noble office—Christ's glorious position.

Eternal God, and ever dwelling in the Father's bosom, he comes forth clothed in my flesh. In one hand he brings to me 'all the promises,' the one covenant of promise running up into eternal life; all the promises in their fullness, and freeness, and sureness; God's unchangeable Yea. Moved of his Spirit, who striveth with me and persuadeth me, I receive his testimony, and set to my seal that God is true. I do not work, I believe; I make no suggestion or proposal, I simply believe. I give my signature to his covenant. To his Father's 'yea' I give my simple 'amen.' In one hand now he holds God's Yea, in the other my Amen. From the Father to me he brings and reports the Father's Yea; from me to the Father he carries back and reports my Amen. Glorious daysman! His hand is upon us both. His hand, with God's gracious, glorious 'Yea,' is on me; his hand, with my trembling, 'Amen,' is on God. Let my hand be on this man of my right hand, in continual acknowledgment of my guilt and obligation. Let thy hand, O God, be on this same man of thy right hand, in continual acknowledgment of thy grace and satisfaction. 'So shall we not go back from thee.' Oh, glorious and eternal stability!

And this must be to the glory of God by us. God thus glorifieth himself in each particular soul that gives his Amen. God gaineth his glory, no doubt; but it can be no abstract, no ideal glory. It must be glory in individual souls, in yours and mine, in your salvation, my brother, and in mine. No doubt God can want both me and you. Though we be not gathered, his glory shall not fail. All whom the Father hath given to Jesus shall come to him. But then also, you and me he will in nowise cast out. Yea, you and I have an opportunity of being to his glory. He seeks in you, and in me, an occasion for his glory. By you and by men 'by us'—he seeks to glorify unto the ages to come the exceeding riches of his sovereign grace, and the exceeding strength of his sovereign will. Brother, shall we not give him this opportunity? Shall we not give him this gratification? His glory comes this day to our door. His glory standeth at the door and knocketh. Shall we send the glory of the Lord a-begging? 'All the promises,' full, immediate, irrevocable remission of sin; new life to throb in penitence, and love, and holiness, within our hearts; peace, strength, light, liberty, joy, hope boundless, endless;— all free, all sure, all Yea. Do you not say, Amen? And the glory of the Lord seeking to overshadow, and shine forth in you for ever. Oh come in, then blessed of the Lord; wherefore standest thou without? And as thou comest there is a glory of God shines forth that could never shine forth but 'by thee'—'To the glory of God by us.'

And then, always for God's Yea, in the Word, have in readiness your Amen, in the Spirit.

Take one or two cases in concluding application.

1. You have many duties to discharge, many lusts to mortify, many trials to bear, many foes to vanquish. Have you God's Yea for them all? You have. For hark! 'My grace is sufficient for you; my strength is made perfect in weakness.' Amen, 'I can do all things through Christ which strengtheneth me.'

2. Thus moving onward in your pilgrimage, thus serving your generation, you come to the closing scene at last. Have you still God's Yea to hear you through the dark waters? You have. For you hear a voice from heaven saying, 'Blessed are the dead that die in the Lord from henceforth: Yea, saith the Spirit, that they may rest from their labours, and their works do follow them.' Amen. It is enough. You have 'a desire to depart, and to be with Christ, which is far better.'

3. And when you are gone, can you cherish hopes for this weary, sin-racked, wretched world? Your soul is sick of its wide-wasting woes, misunderstandings, oppression, violence, cunning, ambition, wars, and blood. Is there no unsullied day of purity and peace to dawn and bless the world when you have left it? Have you God's Yea for this? You have. 'Yea, all kings shall fall down before him, all nations shall serve him: men shall be blessed in him, and all nations shall call him blessed.' Again, it is enough. Amen. 'Blessed be his glorious name for ever, and let the whole earth be filled with his glory. Amen, and Amen.'

4. Still, there is one more longing, though only one. The earthly house of this tabernacle is dissolved. It mingles with the still loved dust of your beloved dead, that are not lost, but gone before. For their dust, and yours, is there hope? Is there 'Yea and Amen' concerning this also? Ah! yes. God's faithfulness here also is Yea; here also your faith, even now, may be Amen By faith you may see the light: by faith you may already hear the voice. Yonder! where the light breaketh; lo! once more the Child's star in the east; nay, himself, the root and the

offspring of David, the bright and morning star. And yonder! whence the sound cometh. 'Tis the voice of your beloved, 'tis the rushing chariot of your Lord. And hark! Once more God's grand mighty Yea in Christ; 'Behold, I come quickly.' 'Amen: Even so come, Lord Jesus.' Amen.

'OTHER SHEEP I HAVE'[1]

Prefatory Note

MY reason for publishing this sermon is simply that I have often been asked to do so, and latterly so urgently that I have consented.

It was originally prepared and preached at a time when I was, for some weeks on end, engaged in evangelistic work; and I take this opportunity of saying that I believe the permanent success, under God, of such work, depends on the clearness and fullness with which Calvinistic doctrine is preached. I should consider myself not only most unfaithful, but very foolish, could I conceal or tone down the special doctrines of grace, in order to present the gospel in a more cheering aspect to the sinner. What could be more hopeful to a lost sinner than the blessed utterance of our Lord in the verse on which the following discourse is founded? It is such a glorious outburst of that 'grace and truth' which 'came by Jesus Christ,' that I suppose no ambassador of his could ever satisfy himself with any exposition of it he could give. But all the light and hope with which it is replenished, depend upon the doctrine of the sovereign grace of the Father, providing the certainly efficacious, and therefore particular redemption accomplished by the Son, which, in its turn, secures the certainty of the Divine Spirit's regenerating, life-giving work. If these truths are trenched upon, I, for one, could not preach on this text,—in short, I could not understand it.

---

[1] [Originally published as a pamphlet, *'Other Sheep I Have: Them I Must Also Bring'* (Edinburgh: Duncan Grant & Co., 1875).]

May a blessing accompany my poor attempt to expound and apply one of the most gracious and remarkable utterances of him into whose lips grace is poured.

H. M.

And other sheep I have, which are not of this fold: them also
I must bring.—John 10:16

THE immediate reference is to the Gentiles. Some sheep Jesus already had; a few disciples that knew his voice and followed him; a little flock; a Jewish fold; lost sheep of the house of Israel—lost sheep brought home. But the nations of the world, on all sides, and in all ages, rose to his view as lost sheep still; sheep without a Shepherd, stumbling on the dark mountains, ready to perish. And looking around a wide world and waste of heathenism, of darkened, destroyed souls; and looking adown the course of time till the end come; realising in divine joy the countless multitude, out of every kindred and people and nation and tongue, to be redeemed by his blood, and renewed by his Spirit, and presented faultless before the presence of his Father; he breaks out in the mingled gratulation[1] and prediction of the text:—'Other sheep I have, which are not of this fold: them also I must bring, and they shall hear my voice, and there shall be one fold and one shepherd.'

Glorious are the results already gathered in, in terms of this blessed declaration. Who are these that are arrayed in white robes around the throne of God, and whence came they? These are they that have heard the chief shepherd's voice, and been brought out of great tribulation, having washed their robes and made them white in the blood of the lamb. They are the fruits of the promise or prediction of the text. So also are all those upon the earth now who, with consciences purged from dead works, adore and serve and glorify the living God.

But the pledge or prediction before us is not yet exhausted. At every moment along the lapse of ages, and now even at this present time, is Jesus in the Church, renewing and repeating, as still true and valid, still in force, still ever dear to him and to all the faithful, this most

---

[1] [gratulation = a feeling of happiness, joy, satisfaction, pleasure.]

precious utterance, 'Other sheep I have;' still other sheep I have; and 'them also I must bring.' Going forth conquering and to conquer; on no haphazard work; claiming triumphantly, and securing savingly all his own; his banner bears this motto—indicating his work, explaining his movements, animating his under-shepherds, rejoicing all his loving flock,—'Other sheep I have; them also I must bring.'

A deep saying! In little words, for children. Laden with thought, also, more than enough for them that are of full understanding.

We are here invited to consider, *first*, Christ's present relation to these other sheep; and, *secondly*, his coming work upon them.

Firstly, Christ's present Relation to these Sheep.

Jesus expresses his present relation to these other sheep by the assertion that he 'hath' them,—qualified by the admission that, as yet, 'they are not of his fold.'

But is not this a contradiction? He hath them: yet they are not of his fold. It is admitted that 'they are not of his fold,' and yet it is asserted that he 'hath' them. These other sheep are not of this fold, and there is but one fold. It is into this fold they must be brought; for when they shall hear his voice, and be brought, there shall be only 'one fold,' even as there is only 'one shepherd.' They are not of this fold. They are not in any sense in Christ's fold. They are not in any fold of his, for he has but one fold,—this fold alone, and they are not of it. They are lost sheep. They have gone, and are still going astray. They have turned everyone to his own way, and they have not returned to the shepherd and bishop of souls.

Yet Jesus says, 'I have them.' Not,—I expect to have them; not,—I will one day have them; not,—I will have them when I shall have brought them: but even now, and as they are; not yet brought, not of this fold; wayward, wandering, strangers, aliens, lost; still, even as they are, already, at this present time, 'I have them,'—these other sheep.

How is this? On what *grounds* can Jesus say this? And in what sense can Jesus say this?

I. On what grounds can Jesus say, 'I have them'? On grounds the best, the most valid: and chiefly two.

1. *First*, on the ground of his Father's promise. In designating his Only-begotten Son, in eternal counsel, to the office of Mediator, the Father did not leave in loose, unsettled, haphazard uncertainty how many, or whom the Son should have from among mankind as his flock, his heritage, his reward. The Father did not leave this most momentous matter to circumstances, to contingencies, to the signs of the times, the spirit of the age, or the wills of men. *No*; he gave him a people, he promised him a sure reward. 'And now, saith Jehovah, that formed me from the womb to be his servant, to bring Jacob again to him' ('them also I must bring'), 'Though Israel be not gathered, yet shall I be glorious in the eyes of Jehovah, and my God shall be my strength. And he said, It is a light thing that thou shouldest be my servant to raise up the tribes of Jacob, and to restore the preserved of Israel' ('other sheep thou hast that are not of this fold'): 'I will also give thee for a light to the Gentiles, that thou mayest be my salvation to the end of the earth' (Isa. 49:5, 6). And again, 'Behold, thou shalt call a nation that thou knowest not, and nations that knew not thee shall run unto thee' (Isa. 55:5). And yet again, in the eighty-ninth Psalm, in vision to his Holy One, how often does the Father pledge and assure unto him a seed, a generation, a continual succession of sheep,—of sheep who, even if they wander, shall nevertheless be brought back and retained within the fold; children who, if they trespass, shall be chastised, but not disowned; not cast away world without end. 'His seed also will I make to endure for ever, and his throne as the days of heaven. If his children forsake my law, and walk not in my judgments; if they break my statutes, and keep not my commandments; then will I visit their transgressions with the rod, and their iniquity with stripes. Nevertheless my loving kindness will I not utterly take from *him*, nor suffer my faithfulness to fail. His seed shall endure for ever' (Psa. 89:29-36). And, finally, we may observe that in prosecution of the theme which Jesus in the text dwells upon, he not only attributes his 'having' of these sheep to his Father's gift and promise, but is content to rest on that, as it were, singly and alone, his own certainty of 'having' them, of having them even forever. 'My sheep hear my voice, and I know them;

and they follow me: and I give unto them eternal life, and they shall never perish, neither shall any pluck them out of my hand. My Father, *which gave them me*, is greater than all; and none is able to pluck them out of my Father's hand' (verses 27-29).

2. But there is a *second* ground on which Jesus can say of these other sheep, 'I have them.' He hath purchased them. Yes: he hath redeemed them; redeemed them with a great price; not with silver and gold, but with his own, precious blood, as of a lamb without blemish and without spot. Therefore they are his: he 'hath them;' they are his sheep; his, own sheep. 'The good shepherd, whose own the sheep are.' 'Whose else are they, or can they be? They are not Satan's. He never had a right to them. Always he was a usurper. The bond which he malignantly pleaded, bound them not to him, but to the justice of God. And that bond being now satisfied,—torn and nailed to the cross,—their usurper is non-suited and ashamed, while they are free. They are not Satan's. And they are not the world's. They are redeemed out of the world. They are not even their own: they are bought with a price. They are Christ's wholly: bought up by him: bought up for him: their bodies and their spirits are his. They are his sheep: he is their Shepherd. He is the Shepherd, and the Buyer, and the Bishop of their souls.

In the fifty-third chapter of Isaiah, the sheep are abundantly assured, or made over, to him as his, that he may 'have' them: and the transfer, the conveyance, the thoroughly legal collation or bestowment, proceeds upon a recognition of his sufferings as the redemption-price whereby they have become his. 'All we like sheep have gone astray; we have turned everyone to his own way.' 'Tis the voice of the elect Church of God, not of mankind in general. Alas! mankind in general have not come to make that confession, and therefore dare not claim the consolation that follows; but the contrite confessing Church of God can, as she adds,— 'And the Lord hath laid on him the iniquity of us all.' 'When thou shall make his soul an offering for sin he shall see his seed.' 'He shall see of the travail of his soul, and shall be satisfied' (verses 6, 10, 11).

And finally, to adduce no further proof on this point, let it be observed that Jesus both introduces and follows up this text,—this declaration, that these other sheep he 'hath—by most pointed and powerful asseveration of his priestly action in his redeeming death; as if both before and behind, on the right hand and on the left, he would compass about, and support his claim to them, by pointing to the price he hath paid for them. For, in the verse preceding the text, he declares, 'As the Father knoweth me, so know I the Father, and I lay down my life for the sheep.' I lay down my life *for* them; for them; with a view to 'having' them: as surely as Abraham laid down the four hundred shekels for the cave of Macpelah, that was before Mamre,—*for* it, and nothing else and nothing less; with a view to 'having' it, 'having' it as his own for ever. Even so I lay down my life for the sheep. And I know my Father, my righteous Father, into whose hands I lay down my life for the sheep—for the other sheep that are not of this fold: and therefore I 'have' them. These 'other sheep I have.' And, in like manner, Jesus follows up this text and the claim which it contains, by another allusion to the ground on which he rests the claim, and in joyful confiding assurance that his Father owns and honours it. 'Therefore doth my Father love me, because I lay down my life for the sheep.'

These, then, are the grounds on which Jesus claims a present possession, of his other sheep,—those that are not yet of this fold: First, his Father's promise; Second, his own purchase.

The second question still remains:

II. In what sense does Jesus say, 'I have them'?

We have seen on what *grounds* Jesus claims to have these other sheep,—to have them already, though they are not yet of his fold. But this scarcely goes all the length of reconciling the apparent contradiction. Good and valid as the claim must be which rests on his Father's promise and his own purchase,—on these grounds combinedly; the promise, on the faith of which he purchased them; the purchase which has sealed the promise;—still this seems merely to justify Jesus in holding assuredly, that these sheep shall come to him and be his; that most certainly in due time he shall have them; while meantime it is admitted, as is obvious, that they are not of his fold. In what sense, then, even on these grounds, can Jesus assert a true present possession? In what sense can he say, these 'other sheep I have'?

To this the reply is most interesting and instructive. It is indeed a very simple, a very obvious, reply: and remembering that Jesus here speaks not as God, but as God-man, Mediator, the Father's servant, it is this:—I have them *by faith*.

Will you discover any other sense, any other way, in which Jesus, the man Christ Jesus, can have them,—have them even now,—has had them all along, when he spoke among the Jews that day, when he sits at his Father's right hand at the present time,—than by faith? Multitudes of them are not yet born. Many of them are, but are going astray like lost sheep. The last thought in the minds of many of them at this moment would be that of reposing, as they shall yet repose, as gathered lambs in the good shepherd's bosom. They are not of this fold, and how then can Jesus say he has them, save by faith?

Do you object against this way, or kind, of 'having,' that it is a fancy?—that it is a mere illusion?—that it is unreal?—that it is an evasion of the difficulty?—that this is not true 'having,' but merely expecting to 'have'?

I grant that it is not true 'having,' if Jesus have not his Father's promise to lean upon, or if that promise be unreliable—if he have not his own purchase to plead, or if it be imperfect. But do you call his Father's promise unreal; his own redemption, the travail of his soul, unreal? He thinks not so. 'I know the Father, and I lay down my life.' I know what the promise of the Father, and the laying down of my life, make sure to me,—what they make my own. And by *faith*, I have the substance of the promise, the matter of the purchase; by faith, the substance to me of things hoped for, the evidence of things not seen. By the eye of faith I already see all the wandering sheep brought home. By the hand of faith I 'have' and hold these other sheep,—not yet of my fold though they be.

O the blessed marvel and mystery of faith! O noble, skilful grace of faith,—by which we may 'have' the blessings we desire, though they be not yet actually come! And is it not at once directive and consoling, to see our Lord acting out and exemplifying, both on earth and in glory, that very faith which he calls for in us,—which often, faithless that we are, we find so trying?

See, brother, he says; thou hast gone astray like a lost sheep: thou hast an immortal soul to be saved, a lost soul to care for. I also have lost souls to care for; many souls; countless sheep; not yet of this fold. And knowing the value of a soul, as thou knowest not, and seeing into eternity as thou seest not, I feel a deeper, keener interest in these souls than ever, at the uttermost, thou hast felt in thine own. But, brother, I doubt not, I falter not. I have them. By faith I have them all. Brother, be as I am, not faithless but believing.

Ah, good shepherd! but thou hast grounds for thy faith, I never can aspire unto, thy Father's everlasting covenant promise; thy own redemptive act of sacrifice on Calvary! If I dared, I could almost find it in my heart to envy thee grounds of faith like these.

What! I hear the Good Shepherd answer. Have I been so long with thee, and yet hast thou not known me? Hast thou not known, hast thou not heard that freely I lay open to thee these self-same grounds of faith, to share them with thee in all their fullness, in all their sureness? My very grounds of faith I give to thee, when I give myself to thee. And my Father giveth them, when he giveth me for a covenant. Thou enviest me, my grounds of faith! Then I take thee at thy word. I hold thee on thine honour. Only there need be no envy, for there is room for none. My Father's promise, my own purchase; these, these alone, have I. These, these wholly, I give to thee: my great redemption to thee; my Father's promise to thee. Whereof the Holy Ghost also is a witness, saying, 'This is the covenant that I will make with them after those days, saith the Lord, I will put my laws into their hearts and in their minds will I write them, and their sins and iniquities will I remember no more.' Hark! my Father's voice. Look! my flowing blood. Hear the promise in the word. See the purchase of the cross. Hear, and thy soul shall live. Look unto me, and be thou saved. Be not faithless, but believing. On my Father's promise, through my perfect purchase, by faith thou hast forgiveness, righteousness, peace, sonship, and the hope of glory; a new heart also, a sweet, contrite, thankful, new heart, within thee. Say not thou hast them not. By faith thou hast them all. 'The word is nigh thee, even in thy mouth, and in thine heart—the word of faith,' by which thou hast them all. And let thy broken, wondering, believing, peaceful, joyful heart tell whether this be not true 'having,' whilst thou singest in thy glad relief,—'Return unto thy rest, O my soul, for the Lord hath dealt bountifully with thee.'

And as for all thy future supplies, as for all thy needed, coming blessings; be thou content to 'have' them, to have them all now and already—by *faith*; and in due time thou shalt have them all in *fact*. Be thou only true to the promise and the purchase, as Christ is true. Be thou only true to the Covenant and the Cross, as Christ is true. And fear not to maintain that all spiritual blessings in heavenly places thou 'hast' already; 'hast' them all by faith; 'hast' them as Christ is content to have his 'other sheep'—as he was long content to have *thee*! Is it not enough for the disciple that he be as his Master, and the servant as his Lord?

Consider, now, Christ's future work upon these other sheep. 'Them also I must bring.'

Here besides the great specialty in this marvellous utterance, 'I *must*'—a crowd of questions presses on our notice. Why must Jesus bring them? Whither—to what or to whom—must he bring them? How must he bring them? By what way or door must he bring them?

III. Why must Jesus bring them?

First, because they are his Father's promise and gift. Therefore must he take order that all whom the Father giveth 'him shall come to him' (John 6:37). How profoundly Jesus feels the force of this reason, he himself shows in his intercessory prayer for them to the Father (John 17:6-8). *Secondly*, because they are his own purchase: therefore must he bring them. To this end he died for them. 'For Christ also hath once suffered for sins, the just for the unjust, that he might bring us to God' (1 Pet. 3:18). *Thirdly*, because, though given to him by the Father's love, and purchased with his own blood, yet, left to themselves, they '*will* not come unto him that they may have life' (John 5:40), and, '*cannot* come except the Father,' through the Son, by the Spirit, 'draw them.' (John 6:44) Therefore doth Jesus say, 'I must bring them.' And what heart would not break to hear him say it? O Jesus! 'grace is poured into thy lips.'

IV. To what, or to whom, must Jesus bring them?

Jesus himself supplies; the answer when he adds, 'And there shall be one *fold* and one shepherd.' He must bring them to the fold, and he must bring them to the shepherd.

1. He must bring them to the fold. And this implies two things: he must bring them under the means of grace; and he must bring them under power of grace. If they are wandering beyond the pale of the visible Church,—out of which, as our Confession of Faith says, there is no ordinary possibility of salvation—he must bring them into the bonds of that outstanding society upon the earth, within which the word and ordinances of salvation are enjoyed. In that sense, he must bring them into the fold. From the company of scoffers, in a Christian land, who scorn the Scriptures, break the Sabbath, live as they list, and despise the Lord; yea, from the company of the blinded heathen in foreign lands, worshipping idols and all abominations; from such society he must bring them, bring them out into the Church visible,—the fold wherein the chief shepherd feeds his flock. He must bring them under the means of grace. But that is not enough. The kingdom of God is not in mere means, but by the Spirit; not in word, but in power. He must bring them under the power of grace. From the company of formal Worshippers, he must bring them into the true fold invisible, the society of those who worship God in spirit and in truth. He must bring them under the renewing—the sweet but strong renewing—power of grace; into the company of the household of faith even of those that are born again.

2. But he must bring them to the *shepherd* to himself, as well as to the fold. It is indeed by bringing them to himself that he truly brings them to the true fold. And he brings them to himself now in faith, by grace: 'All whom the Father giveth me, shall come to me' (John 6:37). And he brings them to himself, hereafter, in glory: 'The king's daughter is all glorious within, her clothing is of wrought gold. She shall be brought unto the king in raiment of needlework: the virgins her companions that follow her (the other sheep that thou hast) shall be brought unto thee. With gladness and rejoicing shall they be brought: they shall enter into the king's palace' (Psa. 45:13-15).

3. In a word, 'he must bring them unto God.' And he does bring them unto God, by bringing them to his fold and to himself. He brings them to God in the first true repentance and return of the lost sheep: 'I will arise and go unto my father.' And he brings them unto God on the second return of the shepherd: 'Behold I and the children whom thou hast given me.'

V. How—by what means or agency, or by what agency and means combined—must he bring them?

The answer is, by his 'voice.' 'They shall hear my voice.' Now his voice is in his Word, and by his Spirit. Or rather, his voice is his 'Word and Spirit.' Not his word alone: alone, his Word to a sinner dead in sin, were a dead letter—intelligible, but dead. And not his Spirit alone: alone, his Spirit were a living and life-giving but inarticulate power—living, yet unintelligible. But let the intelligible but lifeless Word be quickened and wielded by the Spirit: let the otherwise inarticulate and unintelligible Spirit express his mind by the articulate intelligible Word. Let the Word live by the Spirit: let the Spirit speak by the Word. Then may Jesus say, 'The words that I speak unto you, they are spirit and they are life;' not in word only, but in power.

'They shall hear my voice.' 'The hour is coming, and now is, when the dead shall hear the voice of the Son of God, and they that hear shall live' (John 5:25).

So does Jesus bring.—'O, send out thy light and thy truth; thy Spirit and thy Word: let them lead me: let them bring me' (Psa. 43:3).

VI. By what way, what path, what door must Jesus bring them? Jesus himself gives the answer.

'I am the way, the truth, and the life: no man cometh unto the Father, but by me' (John 14:6). He is himself, at once, the shepherd of the sheep, and the door by which he brings them in. 'I am the door: by me, if any man enter in, he shall be saved' (verse 9). And 'he that entereth not by the door in to the sheepfold, but climbeth up some other way, the same is a thief and a robber' (verse 2). Law and justice are evaded by such an one. But by the good shepherd, law was magnified, and justice satisfied, when he gave his life for the sheep. Hence the good shepherd is to be actually identified by this very mark. 'But he that entereth in by the door, the same is the shepherd of the sheep' (verse 2). All his work is then competently and legally transacted, accepted, and acknowledged. 'To him the porter openeth' (verse 3). And this, and nothing less than this; nothing less than his entering in by the door, which is himself, in the rending of the veil, which is his flesh; nothing less than this gives him a word to speak, and a voice to wield with power and sweetness to the sheep; even as nothing less than this gives him a finished work to which the Father gives acceptance, and all authorities of law and justice do obeisance. 'To *him* (that entereth in by the door) the porter openeth, and the sheep hear his voice' (verse 3).

Yes: Jesus himself enters by the same door by which we must enter. He enters in *by himself.* He himself, our risen righteousness, enters in *by himself* as our crucified righteousness. The forerunner enters by the door by which his followers enter even by his own broken humanity. 'By a greater and more perfect tabernacle'—that is, the temple of his body—'and by his own blood, he entered in' (Heb. 9:11, 12). And thus have the sheep 'boldness to enter into the holiest' by the self-same way, even 'by the blood of Jesus, through the veil, which is his flesh' (Heb. 10:19, 20). As the shepherd-king of Israel, Christ, by the skilfulness of his hands, brings in the sheep by himself as the slain lamb; by the open door of his own wounds; by that death in which he laid down his life for the sheep; by that death, which is the gate of righteousness, the very gate of heaven; by that death, through which he himself entered into heaven itself, having obtained eternal redemption for us. 'I am the door.'

But now, passing from all these questions, let us concentrate our regards on what. I have called the great specialty of this wondrous word. Let the marvellous language which the LORD God Messiah, Jehovah-Jesus, here condescends to use, be solemnly weighed:—'Them also I must bring.' *I must bring them. I must.*

Two things are couched in this great word. There is Responsibility, and there is Resoluteness.

1. There is responsibility.

Towards the Father there is responsibility. It is the language of one under authority,—of one acting on his allegiance, acting by commandment. Thus it has ever been with Jesus, the God-man, mediator. In the days of his flesh, made under the law, God's righteous servant, even when but twelve years old, he owns his responsibility:— 'Wist ye not that I must be about my Father's business?' (Luke 2:49). When doing his glorious works of miracle and mercy, it was as one realising his solemn responsibility:—'I must work the works of him that sent me' (John 9:4). And when he had one poor lost sheep to 'bring,' one 'not of this fold,' one with whom the Jews would have no dealings, that poor woman at the well—O! with what artlessness does Holy Scripture tell, that, to speak with her, to bring her, 'He must needs go through Samaria' (John 4:4). Acting under law to his Father,—'this commandment received I of my Father,'—he never was ashamed to use the words which indicate paramount obligation; strict, unreserved, severe responsibility; the responsibility of one learning obedience, though he were a son; the responsibility of God's righteous servant. Equal in the undivided Godhead with the Father, and therein the Father's 'fellow;' yet as 'the man that is Jehovah's fellow,' the shepherd to be smitten to save the little ones; he could say, 'My Father is greater than I; and I *must* be about my Father's business.'

Nor was this responsibility confined to the days of his flesh. It subsists even now at the Father's right hand within the veil. 'This man continueth ever;' and as God-man, mediator, a shepherd, and bringer of sheep, still can he say, 'My Father is greater than I.' Nay, more; it was in reference to his going away to occupy his exalted throne that he loyally and joyfully made that avowal. 'If ye loved me, ye would rejoice because I said, I go unto the Father; for my Father is greater than I' (John 14:28).

Within the veil, therefore; in the highest heights of the heavenly glory; far above all principality and power and every name that is named; every knee bowing at his own name, at the name of Jesus every tongue confessing that he is Lord; Jesus—still the Father's righteous servant, his servant exactly and solely because he wears our nature, his servant exactly and chiefly for our sakes—owns loyal responsibility to the Father. And by all the urgency of that responsibility, he exclaims— 'Father I delight to do thy will; these sheep I *must* bring.'

2. There is resoluteness in this word, as well as responsibility.

Towards the Father, responsibility: resoluteness towards all else beside:—responsibility, as in reference to the authority of Godhead, to which authority he bows, the Son also himself in subjection, that God may be all in all: resoluteness, in reference to all opposition that may from any quarter arise, for the Son also hath a name above every name, that at the name of Jesus every knee should bow, and all power in heaven and earth is given unto him. In the exercise of that power, with calm and glorious dignity, quietly facing all opposition, he says, 'These sheep I *must* bring.'

Behold, their sins are as scarlet, red like crimson. Canst thou bring vile sinners, lost sheep, like these? Though their sins be as scarlet, they shall be white as snow; though red like crimson, they shall be as wool. I can bring even such sinners as these,—and I will. Such were some of you, and such are some of those whom I will bring. Yea, 'them also I must bring.' Behold, they hate thee; they have hated thee without a cause; their hearts are hard and stony, harder than the flinty rock: no groan for sin, no tear of sorrow, no sigh of penitence can come from adamantine rocks like these. A new heart I can give them. They shall be willing in the day of my power. These also I must bring. Behold their tempters are cunning; their lusts strong as the grave; their circumstances baffle hope; their enemies from hell are legion. Canst thou still bring them, O thou mighty to save? I have spoiled principalities and powers, and the hosts of darkness flee before me. I make old circumstances bend at my pleasure, and I make new circumstances. I make, and I unmake. I kill, and I make alive. The strong man armed may keep his house, but I am stronger than he. He may seem to 'have' these other sheep. But it is I who really 'have' them; and 'them also I must bring.' If need be, I will give Egypt for their ransom, Ethiopia and Seba for them. Fear not, O Israel! I will bring thy seed from the east and from the west. I will say to the north, Give up; and to the south, Keep not back; bring my sons from far, and my daughters from the ends of the earth. For still other sheep I have, and them also, every one of them, *I must bring*.

Christian parent, mourning over thy prodigal child! Hear this! Hear Jesus! 'Other sheep I have,' besides those already brought; 'them also I must bring.' Jesus owns his responsibility for bringing wandering sheep home. Jesus asseverates his resoluteness. Roll it continually on him, in never-ceasing fellowship of prayer.

Anxious soul! trembling under guilt; tortured by the power of sin; casting an eye of wistful longing towards the fold, envying the peaceful folded sheep, wondering whether such as thou art may venture near, and seek the mercy to pardon thy heavy guilt, the grace to cure thy hard and corrupt heart! Still there is room! Still other sheep Jesus hath, and them also he must bring. Thee, longing, wistful, he is calling. Thee, willing, coming, he is bringing. If he is *not* bringing thee, it is certain thou art not coming, thou art not willing. And if thou art neither coming, nor willing to come (John 5:40), how canst thou dare to blame him for not bringing thee? The blame is all thine own. It is impossible thou canst be willing, and yet Jesus bringing thee not. Thy willingness is the fruit, the first fruit, of his bringing (Psa. 110:3). Therefore take to thyself the great guilt of being unwilling to come, and give to him, the great glory of being able to bring thee. Not coming, not willing, art thou not therein very vile,—very vile in thine own eyes? Able to bring thee, responsible and resolute to bring lost sheep like thee, is he not therein very precious in thine esteem? And if, in thine own sight, thou art very vile and this great 'bringer' very precious, surely it looks as if he were indeed bringing thee. But oh! make sure. Deal directly with the good shepherd himself. Lord, there is no other name but thine given under heaven whereby we *must* be saved. I *must* come to thee. Whether able or not, whether willing or not, I *must* come to thee. Commandment is laid upon me, and I must come. And there are those whom—blessed be thy condescension and thy love!—thou *must* bring. Wilt thou not bring *me*? If ever I am saved, my salvation is in thy wondrous word, 'Other sheep I have; them also I must bring.' Not one of them, any more than I, ever will be either able or willing to come, except and until thou bring. Herein, therefore, thou art all my salvation and all my desire. Turn thou me, and I shall be turned. Bring thou me, and I shall be brought.

Graceless soul! despising thy day of grace: neglecting the throne of grace: refusing the gift of grace: resisting the Spirit of grace: deaf to the good shepherd's voice! Thou wilt not come unto him that thou mayest have life? Thou wilt not be of this fold? Thou wilt not have this shepherd-king to rule over thee? Then, what is that to him? Other sheep he hath: he will bring them. He can afford to let thee be lost, if thou must have it so. Canst thou afford? He hath other sheep, though thou be not gathered. Hast thou other souls, when the one thou hast is lost? Ah! take heed, today, if ye will hear his voice!

VII. A concluding exhortation

And now let me exhort two classes of persons; those who desire that Jesus would bring them, and those whom he hath already brought.

1. *Would you be brought into the sheepfold*—brought unto the Father within the veil? It is Jesus who must bring you—Jesus acting on his responsibility, Jesus acting in his resoluteness. Therefore make a deliberate study of the power and office of Christ, in the light both of his responsibility and his resoluteness.

Within the veil; in the light of the most holy place; at the Father's right hand; Jesus stands, the representative of lost men, the God-man, man with God, the advocate with the Father, God's righteous servant, the shepherd, responsible: responsible alike for bringing lost sheep to God, and for the government of all the universe. Thus he is within the veil. And without the veil, here, by his Spirit, Jesus stands at our right hand, the representative of God to lost men, the God-man, God with us, our rightful Lord, the shepherd, resolute: resolute to bring lost sheep to God, though opposed by all the universe.

Mark the glorious twofold position and relations. Mark, I say, and study this contrast of positions; this combination, also, of powers to save. And, behold, with what thankfulness and confidence you may welcome this redeemer.

Within the veil he is continually in his glorified body: 'I go to prepare a place for you;' and 'Him the heavens must receive till the restitution of all things.' Without the veil he comes also continually in his Word and Spirit,—his most intelligible Word, his quickening and enlightening Spirit: 'Lo, I am with you alway, even unto the end of the world.' Within the veil, at the Father's right hand; without the veil, at your right hand. Within the veil, the representative of lost men to God: without the veil, the representative of God to lost men. Within the veil, an advocate with the Father, pleading for lost sheep: without the veil, an advocate, or pleader, from the Father, pleading with lost sheep for him. Within the veil, God's righteous servant: without the veil, your rightful Lord. Within the veil, adoringly responsible, as in the utmost loyalty of a creature's responsibility—responsible for bring-ing lost souls to God as much as for the government of all the universe: without the veil, most resolute, as in all the omnipotence of a Creator's *fiat*,—resolute to bring lost sheep to God, though opposed by all the universe. Within the veil, and without, alike and always, the shepherd, the good shepherd that giveth his life for the sheep and *must* bring them.

Responsible within the veil to the Father for lost sheep, and saying, in recognition of his official duty, 'I must bring them,' becomes forth without the veil, in the might of his providential arrangements, and in the clear calls of his blessed Word, and in the energy of his striving Spirit, resolute to fulfil his responsibility, and he pleads with lost sheep. He thus pleads with you. Brother! wilt thou go with me, within the veil, to the home of grace and glory, to the Father's throne and love?

Ah, good shepherd, my guilt! my guilt! I cannot go before the Holy One. I have done evil in his sight, and he is clear in judging. 'Tis at my peril if I appear before him. 'Tis as much as my soul is worth. For he is a consuming fire, and on my own responsibility I cannot go.

Be it so, brother. Be it at my peril then. Be it on my responsibility. As much as *thy* soul is worth! As much, rather, as my soul was worth when I gave my soul a ransom for sin. Therefore be it on my respon-sibility, for I am responsible before the Holy One for poor lost sheep, such as thou art. Come, under my cover, my name, my righteousness, my responsibility. He cannot cast thee out. 'Therefore doth my Father love me, because I laid down my life for the sheep'—lost sheep like thee; because 'I died, the just for the unjust, that I might bring them unto God.' Be it all, then, on my responsibility, and prove him herewith and see.

But, ah, good shepherd, even still; my weakness! my weakness! I cannot come. I am without strength. My feeble heart misgives me. My resolution fails me, and the bruised reed gives way.

Be it so. Not *thy* resolution settles, rules, carries this glorious case this day, but *mine*. Not that thou art resolute to come; but that I am resolute to bring. Rest nothing on thine own resoluteness: rest everything on mine. Take hold on my resoluteness; let go thine own. O trust me, trust me! It cannot fare otherwise than well with thee to let go thine own strength and take hold on mine, 'I am the good Shepherd;' and when lost sheep cannot come, I can, and will, and *must* bring. And even now, while I speak unto thee, let thy broken-hearted surprise, and shamefaced thankfulness, and assuaging terrors, and dawning hopes tell that thou art coming,—and not because thou art good at coming, but because I am good at bringing!

Yea, Lord, my heart is fixed; my heart is fixed! Entreat me not to leave thee, nor to return from following after thee. If thou must bring, I must come. I must, I can, I will, I do come,—the shepherd-king bringing me. 'The king hath brought me to his banqueting-house, and his banner over me was love.'

2. *Is that really the case with you?* Have you been brought into the fold? Have you been within the veil? Have you seen the light of your Father's reconciled countenance, and heard his words of love and reconciliation? Have you shed there the tears of holy shame and sorrow for your offences, looking on him whom you have pierced; the tears, also, of full relief and of astonishment in the new and strange enjoyment of an instant, perfect, unchangeable, everlasting forgiveness? Have you found sweet and holy courage, too, to lift up your eyes from the footstool, and look around the holy place, the sweet and holy fold, the dwelling-place of 'an innumerable company of angels and of the Church of the first-born which are written in heaven,' and heard them all in song because of your arrival, and because this their brother 'was dead and is alive again, was lost and is found'? And realising

this infinite and wondrous grace, have you turned your eyes again to 'God the judge of all, and to Jesus the mediator of the new covenant, and to the blood of sprinkling that speaketh better things than that of Abel,' and yielded up your whole soul to the all-searching light of that mingled majesty and mercy that dwell and shine between the cherubims? Then, has it not been brought home to your inmost heart, and riveted there as with a nail in a sure place by the master of assemblies, that you also 'must work the works of him who sends you'? For you share your Lord's responsibility and righteousness; and, you are now welcome to wield your Lord's resoluteness and strength. Abide in him. Both within the veil and without the veil, abide in him, in respect both of his responsibility and his resoluteness. No demands of justice, no frowning aspects of law, no reclaimings of conscience, may bar the access to a willing coming sinner, that looks to that shepherd-priest who, in the terms of Jehovah's oath, makes himself responsible for the satisfaction and abolition of them all. And no messengers of Satan, no thorns in the flesh, no besetting sins, no temptations, trials, toils, may warrantably affright or vanquish him who looks to that shepherd king, whose resoluteness, invincible, is, through the one indwelling Spirit, enough for himself and for every 'member of his body, of his flesh and of his bones.' Abide in him—the responsible—the resolute. Accept your responsibility, when Jesus shares it with you,—yours with him, his with you. Quarrel not with your responsibility, however weighty. It is an exceeding weight of glory when seen on Jesus,—and on you in him. Surely, also, it sits gracefully, when seen on Jesus,—and on you in him. Is it not a graceful, a glorious thing that, along with him, you too can say, 'I *must* work the works of him that sends me'? Is it not your highest conceivable honour to be responsible to Jehovah,—the living and the true God and an everlasting king? Is it not a grand and blessed destiny of yours, that you must compear[1] before the majesty of heaven, and say, 'Thou hast *commanded* me to keep thy precepts diligently'? Nor need you fear that the prayer which this deep responsibility prompts—'O that my ways were directed to keep them!'—shall fail of an answer. Your faithful shepherd-priest upon his throne,

[1] [Scots: to appear in court.]

king in Zion, will give you of his own spirit of resoluteness, his own Holy Spirit of might, and zeal, and power, to qualify you to meet your responsibility.

Yes, O believer! Thou who hast been within the veil, 'and now livest in a weary, troubled, and sinful world,' thine own sinfulness troubling and wearying thee more than the world can! Thou must work the works of him that sends thee. Responsibility is laid upon thee. But resoluteness is given unto thee. Abide in Christ. Concerning both thy worship and thy work,—thy duty both within the veil and without,—abide in Christ. So shalt thou 'go in and out, and find pasture' (John 10:9). For it is not within the veil only that thou shalt find pasture,—plenty, wine and milk, mercy and peace, grace and love. But without the veil also thou shalt find pasture,—plenty, plenty of work,—thy meat and drink to do it,—success in thy work, comfort in thy toil, liberty of spirit, and a great reward. Therefore again I say, abide in Christ. For if thou wouldst purpose well, as a faithful servant, enter thou into the responsibility of thy Lord. If thou wouldst perform well, as a good servant, enter thou into the resoluteness of thy Lord. Then, in the evening, in the recompense of the reward: 'Well done, good and faithful servant; enter thou into the joy of thy Lord.' Amen.

PRINCIPLES OF HARVEST IN THE SPIRITUAL WORLD[1]

They joy before thee according to the joy in harvest.

—Isaiah 9:3

THERE can be no doubt that this prophecy refers to the first advent of Christ. The verses preceding the text are quoted by Matthew as therein receiving their fulfilment: 'And leaving Nazareth, he came and dwelt in Capernaum, which is upon the sea-coast in the borders of Zabulon and Nephthalim; that it might be fulfilled which was spoken by Esaias the prophet, saying, The land of Zabulon, and the land of Nephthalim, by the way of the sea, beyond Jordan, Galilee of the Gentiles; the people which sat in darkness saw great light; and to them which sat in the region and shadow of death light is sprung up' (Matt. 4:13-16). The verses following the text, also, contain the well-known and heart-stirring doxology, in which the Church is represented as welcoming the birth of her Warrior-Redeemer: 'Unto us a child is born, unto us a son is given; and the government shall be upon his shoulder; and his name shall be called Wonderful, Counsellor, The mighty God, The everlasting Father, The Prince of Peace. Of the increase of his government and peace there shall be no end upon the throne of David.' The increase of the Church at this epoch was wonderful. Messiah assumed the throne of his father David; was inaugurated King of Zion—'Thy king cometh unto thee, O Zion;'—and, on his ascension, the kingdom of David threw off

---

[1] [From *The Free Presbyterian Magazine* (1930), vol. 35, p. 205ff.]

its beggarly elements—its carnal envelope—and stood forth trusting to its spiritual powers alone, received immense accessions from the middle wall of partition being broken down and the Gentiles being admitted among the Israel of God, and Jesus very largely 'saw of the travail of his soul' and of 'the joy set before him.'

The language of the prophet, in fact, was verified: 'thou hast multiplied the nation, and increased unto him the joy.'[1] And in these circumstances it is that the joy of the Church is announced and described: 'They joy when they divide the spoil.' First of all, Messiah himself is joyful: 'Thou hast increased unto *him* the joy;' or, as in the language of the 21st Psalm, 'The king shall joy in thy strength, O Lord; and in thy salvation how greatly shall he rejoice.' Then the Church, loyal to her husband, rejoices in his joy, being admitted by him, in his love, to share the gladness of his heart: 'Thou hast increased unto *him* the joy'—and now—'they joy before thee.'

For, all warrantable joy in this world of death and sorrow is Christ's joy. All the true joy of the Church is the joy of Christ, her living Head. It is so in this life: 'These things have I spoken unto you, that my joy may remain in you, and that your joy may be full' (John 15:11). It is so in the life to come: 'Well done, good and faithful servant, enter thou into the joy of *thy* Lord.'

Now, there are three views given in Scripture of the joy of the Church—whether it be the joy of Christ personally, or in his members; and they are all fitted to show that such joy has its root in sorrow, in suffering, in self-denial, and conflict. *First*, there is the joy that succeeds travail. Such us Christ's joy: 'He shall see of the travail of his soul, and shall be satisfied.' Such also is the joy of his members: 'Verily, verily, I say unto you, that ye shall weep and lament, but the world shall rejoice; and ye shall be sorrowful, but your sorrow shall be turned into joy. A woman when she is in travail, hath sorrow because her hour is come; but as soon as she is delivered of the child, she remembereth no more the anguish for joy that a man is born into the world. And ye now, therefore, have sorrow; but I will see you again and your heart shall rejoice, and your joy no man taketh from you.' Then, *secondly*, there is

[1] [Marginal translation.]

the joy of the harvest; which, as we shall see, presupposes sacrifice and self-denial. And, thirdly, there is the joy of victory, which, of course, is preceded by conflict. The text sets Christian joy in the light of the second of these analogies. It is the joy of harvest. We propose to consider Christian joy under that particular aspect; the joy of harvest.

Now, to see what is peculiar in the joy of harvest, it will be necessary to analyse the idea of harvest. It is a complex idea. Especially when introduced, on the principle of analogy, into the unseen affairs of the moral and spiritual world, it requires a careful examination before it yields up all the special truths for which it becomes a ready vehicle—a comprehensive expression. At the outset, however, let me show—of course from the Scripture, our only source of knowledge— that the idea of harvest, I might almost say the principle of harvest, is eminently applicable to the kingdom of Christ; and hence the joy of harvest may well be expected to be found there. There is a real harvest in the Church, and, therefore, there is the joy of harvest. Nay, the principle and power of harvest, whatever these may be, are universally present and continually in action in the Church. To illustrate Christian joy by the joy of harvest is not a mere illustration. Nor is it merely a passing expression of the pen inspiration—an occasional, happy phrase or turn. Deep inlaid in the whole scheme of redemption, the complex and comprehensive idea of harvest is to be met with; so much so that it applies—First, to the person and work of the Redeemer; Secondly, to the person of the redeemed; and, Thirdly, to the good work of the redeemed.

First, as to the person and work of the Redeemer, let the passage in the 12th chapter of John be considered. Towards the close of the Lord's ministry, there were 'certain Greeks that came up to worship at the feast; the same came, therefore, to Philip, which was of Bethsaida of Galilee, and desired him, saying, Sir, we would see Jesus.' The disciples convey the expression of this request to their Master, Jesus sees in these Greeks the first-fruits of all the Gentile nations, one day to be brought unto him. He looks forward and sees in anticipation 'all nations blessed in him, and all nations calling him blessed.' He sees the whole world one great and golden harvest-field, waving in autumnal plenty and beauty. And knowing that all this rich ingathering is from his own redemption-work in death, through which alone he could thus be glorified in this world, and comparing his own person and work to the seed-corn from which, through death and burial, new and plenteous life springs again, he exclaims, 'The hour is come that the Son of man should be glorified. Verily, verily, I say unto you, except a corn of wheat fall into the ground and die, it abideth alone; but if it die, it bringeth forth much fruit.' The harvest principle has its first and greatest verification in the Redeemer himself, and in the work of the cross.

Not only so but, *secondly,* Jesus goes on immediately to apply it to his people also. For certainly this is his design in adding: 'He that loveth his life shall lose it, and he that hateth it in this world shall keep it unto life eternal' (John 12:25). He that 'loveth his life' as 'to keep it'—like the husbandman in spring preferring to retain the seed—such an one shall not really keep his life; but rather lose it; as the husbandman by keeping the seed would be only providing famine. But he that 'hateth his life' in this world—he who can deal with his life like the husbandman who seems to hate the seed, and throws it from him, and parts with it, and buries it out of his sight—he shall not lose his life; it shall be he only that shall really keep his life; yea, 'keep it unto life eternal.' He shall have a harvest of life. So that the harvest principle applies to the persons of the redeemed. Yea, it applies to their whole person, soul and body alike. The soul is especially mentioned in a passage in Matthew exactly parallel to what we have now quoted from John: 'For whosoever shall save his life shall lose it: and whosoever shall lose his life for my sake shall find it. For what is a man profited, if he gain the whole world, and lose his own soul?' (Matt. 16:25, 26). The salvation of his soul is on the principle of harvest. It applies also to the body: 'It is sown a natural body, it is raised a spiritual body.' The resurrection is a harvest. The soul has been quickened, raised, and ripened in glory. To the entire person this idea of harvest applies.

Thirdly, to complete the full range and sweep of its application, as really embracing all that is to be found in the kingdom of Christ, it applies to the works of the redeemed, as well as to their person, and to the person and work of their Redeemer. All their good works are so much sowing; and all their reward is so much reaping. 'Let us not be weary in well-doing; for in due time we shall reap, if we faint not' (Gal. 6:9). 'They that sow in tears shall reap in joy. He that goeth forth and weepeth, bearing precious seed, shall doubtless come again with rejoicing, bringing his sheaves with him' (Psa. 126:5, 6). Again, it is just the harvest. The idea of harvest, whatever that may imply, is all-pervasive in the kingdom of faith.

What, then, is implied in *harvest*? Let us analyse it, and we shall find that it contains the ideas of:—

    I. Surrender.
    II. Surrender unto death.
    III. Life in, and by means of, death.
    IV. Abundance of life.
    V. Beauty of life.
    VI. Variety of life.

I. Harvest implies and presupposes surrender.

You surrender the good seed. You give up, as it would seem, all personal interest in it. Apparently and comparatively, you hate it. You cast it away. Like a thing which you have quitted and abandoned and are done with—which you are to make no use of, and turn to no good account—you throw it from you, and bury it in the ground, and there you leave it. You most thoroughly and completely give it up. You make a most entire surrender. This, first of all, is involved in the idea or principle of harvest, and, therefore, in the joy of harvest.

There is this, also in the case of his members. They part with themselves. 'They give their own selves to the Lord.' They surrender all personal interest in themselves—all right and desire to call themselves their own. The wicked do not so; they do precisely the reverse. They say, 'Our lips are our own,' and they ask, 'Who is Lord over us?' But conversion revolutionises this. It brings with it the feeling—the resolution—'We are not our own,'—no, neither in soul nor in body; we will glorify God in our bodies and our spirits, which are his; we will live not unto ourselves, but unto him that died for us, and that rose again. We surrender ourselves. We present ourselves to God a living sacrifice.

But this applies also to the good works of the redeemed, as well as to their persons, and to the person and work of their Redeemer. All their good works are offerings, sacrifices, surrendering. And the surrendering must be complete, unreserved, ungrudging; 'a matter of bounty and not of covetousness.' Here the principle and analogy of harvest comes in very expressly: 'He that soweth bountifully, shall reap also bountifully'—'And God is able to make all grace abound towards you, that ye, always having all sufficiency, may be able to abound unto every good work'—'And let us not be weary in well-doing, for in due time ye shall reap if ye faint not.' In all these cases, then, to which, as we have seen, the idea of harvest applies, there is first of all a surrender; and that surrender is voluntary, unreserved, and in faith.

II. Harvest implies surrender unto death.

In the idea of harvest there is implied not only the idea of surrender, but of surrender unto death. Without this, no harvest is attainable. 'Thou fool, that which thou sowest is not quickened except it die.' 'Except a corn of wheat fall into the ground and die, it abideth alone.' To this extent is the surrender required; and to this extent is the surrender yielded, where it is complete and true. It is even unto death.

This is verified, first, and very eminently, in Christ himself. It was, indeed, concerning his own death that he uttered the pregnant maxim—'Except a corn of wheat fall into the ground and die, it abideth alone.' When he gave himself for us, it was a giving of the most complete kind; it was giving himself unto death. Without this, in fact, the surrender would not have been complete nor thorough—nor, indeed, real. Himself he is the Life—the Fountain, and the fullness of life; and it is inconceivable that he could, as such, surrender himself, except in death. It would be a contradiction. He would not have been surrendering, but, on the contrary, retaining himself, unless he had died. He who was rich as the Fountain of Life, could, in that respect, become poor, only by dying. He did so. 'I lay down my life.' 'The Good Shepherd giveth his life for the sheep.' That it might not 'abide alone,' the Seed-corn fell into the ground and died. He surrendered himself unto death.

This is verified, also, in his people, wherever there is that surrender that shall issue in a harvest of life, it is surrender unto death. The old life in sin—which is a life unto self—given up to be destroyed. It is submitted and subjected to the power of the Cross, which is a power fatal and deadly to self, and to sin, and to Satan. The old man is crucified with Christ to the end that the body of sin may be destroyed. Christ's members share Christ's death. They are dead indeed unto sin. For it is impossible to surrender myself truly or safely or acceptably unto God, except with and in Christ. To surrender myself to God apart from Christ is that 'fearful thing' which Paul speaks of with trembling—'falling into the hands of the living God.' But, by faith, I adjoin, I conjoin, myself with Christ. I surrender myself as he surrenders himself; I surrender myself where he surrenders himself—at the cross. I surrender myself in and with his surrender of himself. But his surrender of himself is in death; so, therefore, is mine. 'Ye are dead, and your life is hid with Christ in God.' 'Reckon ye yourselves dead indeed unto sin.' 'Know ye not that as many of you as were baptised unto Christ were baptised unto his death?' Conversion is the surrender of ourselves unto death.

This is verified, yet again, in the believer's good works, as well as in his person, and in his Lord's. If you believingly present the sacrifices of good works unto God, you give up all passing, temporal, earthly interest in them. You submit to have no more lot or part in them than Abraham in Isaac when he was about to resign all personal interest in him, and all personal intercourse with him, till they should meet on the other side of time and the grave. This is involved in all sincere good works. You do not, for instance—if observant of your Lord's injunction—invite to your feast those that can 'bid you again,' for then a recompense is given you in this life. That is not sowing. That is lending, hoping to be paid again. 'But when thou makest a feast, call the poor, the maimed, the lame, the blind, for they cannot recompense thee; for thou shalt be recompensed in the resurrection of the just.' This is sowing, not lending. This is sowing, not bartering. This is heavenly agriculture, not earthly commerce:—for the recompense is on the other side of death; heavenly agriculture, waiting for the great harvest-home. Yes, death intervenes where harvest comes into play. Sowing is surrendering unto death—looking for recompense on the other side of death. 'Except a corn of wheat fall into the ground and die, it abideth alone.' If you surrendered it not to death, you may receive it again as what you gave in loan, or gave in hire. But you do not reap, for you did not sow. You did not give up all interest in it on this side of death. And death is necessary—pre-requisite—to harvest. It is so, we have seen, in Christ personal, in Christ's people, and in their good works.

III. Harvest implies a life that is reached and reproduced through death.

But now, thirdly, tracing out yet farther the fullness of this idea—the idea of harvest—we find in it not only the principle of surrendering, and surrendering unto death; we find also the grand principle of *life in death,—life reached and reproduced through death*. This is the very core of what is implied in harvest. 'That which thou sowest is not quickened except it die, but if it die,' it is quickened, 'it bringeth forth much fruit.' The seed-corn cast into the ground undergoes a process of disorganisation and decomposition. The outer body, or shell of it, really dies; it becomes assimilated to the soil and lost in it; 'dust to dust, and ashes to ashes.' But an inner and central germ of vital power is thus set free, which bursting the rapidly disorganising integuments, and setting them aside, sprouts into principles of harvest in the spiritual world. A new life, urging, pressing, securing its resurrection, and claiming our notice, as 'first the blade, then the ear, then the full corn in the ear.' Here is vitality in the original grain more powerful than death; nay, not only so, but turning death into its service—making death the occasion, the means, and minister of its own development.

Most completely is the analogy in this respect met in the person and work of Christ, and in the very nature of things, it never could have been met in the moral government of God and the spiritual world except in a redemption and a Redeemer—yes, a Divine Redeemer. In a sinless universe, the phenomenon of harvest in the natural world could have had no analogue, no parallel, in the moral. And in that case, would the physical world, with its splendid scheme of organism, developing and reproductive, have been constituted as it is? Who will venture to say that it would? One is apt, at least, to think that it would have cast a splendour and a wealth of purpose and idea round the physical, overbearing and depreciatory of the spiritual. It would have given the humbler aspects of nature a power of expressing the simpler things of moral and spiritual relation for the grandest aspects of nature to illustrate or express. It would have given materialism a claim for admiration with which comparatively tame spirituality could not have competed. And to the soul that rebelled against worshipping Development, it would have given to nature's undeniably grandest mystery the aspect of a splendid hand-post.[1] pointing to nothing!—of an elaborate system of telegraphy that never sent a message! I have said that only in redemption and a Redeemer can the analogy of harvest be truly met; and I add emphatically, a *Divine* Redeemer—God manifest in the flesh—dying, a substitute for sinners. For, observe what it is that the analogy demands. It demands an inner life that shall prove more than a match for death; nay, that shall serve itself at death's hands—that shall turn death into its help and minister, and make death the very means of liberating it into full and free development, and crowning it with glorious triumph. No creature can do this—no creature has such an inner and invincible vitality. For that vitality is invincible which passes unhurt, I say not through danger and disease, but through very death itself; which outlives death, and breaks forth into its grandest triumph in the valley and shadow of death. That surely is life invincible. The 'child born,' the 'Son given,' must in very truth be 'Wonderful' if he can realise this. He must be 'The mighty God, The everlasting Father.'

A Divine Person, he is life itself—the very fullness, the fountain of life. *A Divine Person in human nature* , he is not only the Life; he is capable of death. As a Divine Person, he answers to that element of the analogy in which the seed-corn is seen to have a secret life capable of prevailing over death itself. As a Divine Person in human nature in the room of sinners, he meets the analogy also in respect of the seed-corn falling into the ground and dying. That death which would have

---

[1] [hand-post = sign-post.]

engulfed in everlasting ruin the sinner suffering in his own person, Christ, in his Divine Person, taking the sinner's nature, and place, and condemnation, can suffer, can conquer, and set aside. And the Fountain of Life, which death hitherto had sealed against us, bursts forth for us by death itself, triumphing not only in death, and over death, but, most marvellously, by death; and the life that could not come to us direct from the celestial throne, has come through an earthly grave. Heaven could not be—what the grave has become—the birth-place of life for sinful men. 'For except a corn of wheat fall into the ground and die, it abideth alone;' and 'that which thou sowest is not quickened except it die.'

This principle of 'life in death'—'life by death'—reappears in Christ's members. You are baptised into his death. You are engrafted into Christ, expressly and especially, as a dying Christ. You take hold on his death by faith, and make it your own. This is the very value of the cross to you. It becomes full of meaning, and full of worth, exactly when you see and believe this; namely, that when conscience and the law are denouncing death to you, the cross is that very death—death complete, death harmless to you. You embrace death, when you embrace the cross. It is not any less the very death the law was denouncing, because it is Christ's death. On the contrary, it is for that reason exactly the death which the law was denouncing, nay, has exacted and received. But it is the death of him who is the Fountain of Life. Receiving it; being baptised into it; being also, by your baptism or engrafting into it, buried with Christ; you are so buried with him, that like as he was raised from the dead by the glory of the Father, so you also now walk in newness of life. Being planted with him in the likeness of his death, you are also in the likeness of his resurrection. In union with him, you partake of his death; let it be said, you receive death—the death which the law exacts and inflicts for sin. But receiving death in virtue of union with him who is the way, and the truth and the Life, you receive life also, yea, everlasting life. Everlasting life has thus reached you through death; first, Christ's death for you, and then your death in him. You see Christ dying on the cross; offering himself to God a sacrifice in death. As between you and Christ and God, you see no reason for this, no justification of this, no possible fruit of this, unless it be that the cursed death of the cross shall be held as suffered for your sin and unto your salvation. To furnish reason, therefore, and justification, and fruit, of this wondrous death of Calvary—the highest, grandest, loyal duty man or angel can discharge—you conjoin yourself, by faith, with Christ in his death. You offer yourself up to God in and with him on the Cross. You render up the old life to be extinguished. You thus judge, that if One died for you, then you also died, that you, now living, may not live unto yourself, but unto him that died for you, and that rose again. Thus you are crucified with Christ; nevertheless you live. You are part, in fact, of Christ's harvest. It is the life of Christ reproduced in you. Christ doth not now 'abide alone.' He has you with him. 'Except a corn of wheat fall into the ground and die, it abideth alone; but, if it die, it bringeth forth much fruit.'

The Christian life is 'life in death;' and the death is helpful to the life, on the harvest principle:—'If ye through the Spirit do mortify the deeds of the body, ye shall live.' This also is the quickening power of sanctified affliction. It is just so much death, liberating and emancipating so much more life; procuring and conveying great scope for the unhampered development of life. It is 'bearing about in the body the dying of the Lord Jesus, that the life also of Jesus may be made manifest in our mortal body. For which cause we faint not; but though our outward man perish, the inward man is renewed day by day.' Our outward man is the shell of the seed-corn; and it must be disorganised, that the secret germ of life may burst into its plenitude, and power, and triumph.

IV. Harvest as an abundance of life

In the idea of harvest, there is not only the thought of 'life through death,' but of *abundance of life*. 'Except a corn of wheat fall into the ground and die, it abideth alone: but if it die, it bringeth forth much fruit.' The life produced by the dying of the seed-corn is not merely sufficient to compensate for the death which has taken place, but exceedingly abundant above that. The result is not another seed-corn, as a substitute, replacing that which has been surrendered, but a manifold return—'in some thirty, in some sixty, in some an hundred-fold.' Thus harvest is enriching. The surrender that is required to procure harvest is the source of riches. Political economists, in fact, tell us that agriculture is the only real source of wealth. The literary, scientific, and professional men of a community may ornament and dignify a nation; the talented and energetic men of commerce may re-distribute and circulate, to the advantage of the greatest number, the materials of necessity, convenience and luxury; but it is the cultivators of the soil who alone, positively and immediately, increase the coun-try's wealth. The aggregate increase of the world's wealth in any year is the total of its harvests. A fine thought this nature itself teaching that, under this world's constitution, surrender unto death is the con-dition of plenteousness and abundance of life. Need I say that this is illustrated very gloriously in the person and work of Christ? His death is the root and source of life multiplied by numbers without number. Himself the first-fruits and first-begotten from the dead, he is by his death, the cause of life to a people whom no man can number. In him is the transcendent exemplification. It was concerning himself he said, 'Except a corn of wheat fall into the ground and die, it abi-deth alone; but if it die, it bringeth forth much fruit.' And when he said this, the harvest-field his eye really rested on was the countless myriads of his people in Gentile days and Gentile climes, as it is written also in the 72nd Psalm: 'There shall be an handful of corn in the earth upon the top of the mountains; the fruit thereof shall shake like Lebanon; and they of the city shall flourish like grass of the earth. Men shall be blessed in him: all nations shall call him blessed.'

The same thing is exemplified in the Christian as in Christ; the life which the believer has through death is an abundant life—plenteous, overflowing, eternal life. 'I am come,' says Jesus, 'that ye might have life, and that ye might have it more abundantly.' They that receive abundance of grace and of the gift of righteousness shall 'reign in life.' They shall have a royalty, a kingliness of life. 'He that hateth his life' surrendering it, as we have seen, on the principle and on the faith of harvest—shall not only keep it, but 'shall keep it unto life eternal.' That which he receives is abundant and plenteous compared with that which he surrendered. He surrendered a life unto self; he receives a life unto God. He lives henceforth not unto himself, but unto God. And greater as God is than self, so much greater is the amount of real life he receives than he surrendered. For before the surrender the seed-corn was 'alone;' now it has brought forth 'much fruit.'

This is exemplified also in the Christian's good works. His good works are each of them a seed-corn cast into the ground; and it doth not re-appear 'alone.' Let it simply be surrendered unselfishly and unreservedly; let all personal interest of your own in it be abjured—for the principle holds good only in that case—the work is really good only when it is disinterested. But thus meeting the analogy of the seed-corn put away, abandoned, given up, it will in due time reappear in harvest in manifold and plenteous return. Yea, our Lord hath declared that no man can act thus for his sake in any case, without receiving 'an hundredfold more in this life, with persecutions'—there is one form of the dying of the seed—'with persecutions, and in the world to come life eternal.' There is a vitality in every good work, every work of faith, which absolutely nothing can extinguish. No opposition can crush or quench it. The world's utmost hostility, when it comes nearest to killing a Christian's good work, is only hastening its fertile harvest, only disimprisoning the life that is in it, and making it reproduce itself more rapidly; and when reproduced, it is far more abundant. Handfuls of corn; bosomfuls of sheaves!

V. In analysing the idea of harvest we find, still farther, the element of beauty.

There is not only 'life through death,' and that life abundant; it is also beautiful. There is not only more life than was surrendered, but it is much more lovely also; insomuch that no imagination could have anticipated the result.

The pen of inspiration speaks of this very finely. 'That which thou sowest, thou sowest not that body that shall be, but bare grain; it may chance of wheat, or some other grain.' The bare naked grain; the seed corn; there is no beauty in it. A rough husk, with no pretension whatever to fine form, or tracery, or colouring, or delicacy; there is no violation of good taste in casting it out among the clods of the valley. But mark the exquisite delicacy of the fresh and tender little blade. Mark the stately, graceful from of the full-grown stalk in earing time. Mark the queenly dignity with which it bows its more than mitred head with crowning autumn's rich tiara of the full-grown corn in the ear. This you have now, replacing what Paul so finely calls the 'bare grain.' And he accounts for this change. 'Thou sowest bare grain; but God giveth it a body as it hath pleased him.' Yes, 'as it hath pleased him.' He consults his own 'pleasure,' his own good taste—to speak with deepest reverence, for good taste, like all that is good, is of God—he consults his own good taste, and his own good pleasure, his own sovereign sense of what is fit, becoming, beautiful; and so it comes to pass that every seed acquires a body that 'pleases' even God.

I might apply this again to Christ—to the Christian—to Christian good works. To Christ, dying and living through death as the root of David, the root of all the Israel of God; to him God giveth a body as it pleaseth him—the Church, which is his body, the fullness of him that filleth all in all. That Church, that body, is called Zion; and Zion is called 'the perfection of beauty.' Glorious things are spoken of thee, O city of God, O body of Christ. Thou art Beulah; thou art Hephzibah; thou art a crown of glory; thou art a royal diadem; thou art adorned as a bride for her husband; thou art beautiful, O my love, as Tirzah; comely as Jerusalem—and Jerusalem is beautiful for situation; the joy of the whole earth. Beauty appears also in the individual Christian. The Lord beautifies his people with salvation. The life that springs up from the surrender of the old life is beautiful. It is the image of God. The fruit of the Spirit is love, joy, peace, longsuffering, gentleness, goodness, faith, meekness, temperance. All these are beautiful. They are the beauteous life that in regeneration is developed from communion with Christ crucified. There is beauty also in the good works of the believer. Each of them is as a seed-corn from which manifold return accrues; and the harvest, here, too, is beautiful as well as abundant; so beautiful, as shining in the beauty of holiness, which is the beauty of the Lord, that believers will not know their own good works again, but will be ready to deny them, saying, 'Lord, when saw we thee an hungered and fed thee?'

VI. Harvest as diversification

Lastly; in Harvest, in Harvest life, there is not only the idea of beauty, but of variety too—diversification—and that abundantly. Paul goes on to speak of this also, in a passage already quoted. He not only speaks of the great difference in respect of beauty between the bare, naked grain you sow and the lovely plant that springs from it— 'God giveth it a body as it hath pleased him;' but he brings into view the principle of diversification, which God illustrates and honours in this department of his works perhaps more than in any other— 'God giveth it a body as it hath pleased him, and *to every seed his own body.*' God has variety of forms at his disposal—boundless variety in the compass of his grand creative idea—at the disposal of his great creative fiat. And he hath given 'to every seed his own body.' 'All flesh is not the same flesh,' continues the Apostle; and then follows a detailed protest against the idea of tame repetition and insipid uniformity, every region of the universe being summoned to be witness against it. 'There is one kind of flesh of men; another flesh of beasts; another of fishes; and another of birds. There are also celestial bodies, and bodies terrestrial; but the glory of the celestial is one, and the glory of the terrestrial is another. There is one glory of the sun, and another glory of the moon, and another glory of the stars; for one star differeth from another star in glory. So also is the resurrection of the dead.' So also is it in harvest; of which resurrection is but a single, special case. In harvest, the whole autumnal plain of nature is not one field of wheat, or of any one grain. No, nor in that harvest in which the Church of God rejoices as in harvest joy.

See, rather, a garden tastefully laid out! See where botanic skill, and finest taste, and the resources of many climes have contributed to produce some lovely specimen of nature's wealth of flora. There is the glory of the blushing rose; and another glory of the chastely lily; and another glory of the lowly daisy; and another glory of the humble violet: and one flower differeth from another flower in glory. There is one glory of the monarch oak; and another glory of the spreading cedar; and another glory of the stately palm; and another glory of the weeping cypress; and one tree differeth from another tree in glory. So in the harvest of Christ's death; of the Christian's death in reunion with Christ; and of the Christian's good work. There is variety—diversification—in them all. I shall not speak of the variety of beauty in Christ—the Rose of Sharon; the Lily of the valley; the good Olive Tree; the Vine out of Egypt, its goodly branches like the cedars of Lebanon, as it fills the land. Nor shall I speak of the 'diversities of gifts, of ministrations, of operations,' among believers; all wrought by that self-same Spirit who divideth to everyone severally as he will.

I specify only the good works of believers. And I would put the case somewhat as Paul's language puts it. 'Be not weary in well doing; for in due time ye shall reap, if ye faint not;' for 'he that soweth bountifully shall reap also bountifully;' and he that soweth variously shall reap also variously not bare grain again, but something unutterably more beautiful; with wonderful variety also, on which indeed beauty so much depends. For, 'to every seed' you sow God giveth 'its own body.' Now all seed is not the same seed. For there is one kind of seed of prayers; and another seed of silent tears, and anxious cares, and thoughtful devising for the good of others; and another seed of liberality; and another seed of alms-giving; and another seed of kind, gratuitous tuition of the young; and countless others, of which we cannot now speak particularly. Yea, there are good works, which, because of God being their more immediate object, we might—culling some more of Paul's vocabulary on the mysteries of harvest—all 'celestial;' such as worship of God, and meek submission and obedience to him. And there are good works, which, because of man being the object of them, may be called 'terrestrial'—such as scrupulously just transactions; and carefully kindest courtesies; and generous forgivenesses; and charitable constructions; and all mutual helpfulness, and sympathies, and love. 'But the glory of the celestial is one, and the glory of the terrestrial is another.' To each of all these kinds of good works—and to every individual instance of them all—considered as a seed which you sow in faith, 'God giveth a body as it hath pleased him, and to every seed his own body.' When you reap, therefore, after God hath given the increase, you will be gathering the produce of a variedly lovely garden which the Lord hath blessed:—'I, the Lord have watered it; lest any should hurt it, I have kept it day and night.' With what joy unspeakable and full of glory will the reaping be! Rejoice in the Lord, ye righteous; and shout for joy all ye that are upright in heart. Light is sown for the righteous, and gladness for all them that are upright in heart. In due time ye shall reap them. Think of sheaves of light—bosomfuls of gladness; gladness and light most rich, beautiful, variegated. And blessed rule!—'they that sow in tears shall reap in joy; he that goeth forth and weepeth, bearing precious seed, shall doubtless come again with rejoicing, bringing his sheaves with him.' Verily, 'they joy before *thee then*, according to the *joy of harvest*.'

There are yet two other principles to be borne in mind. (1) There is the principle of identity in kind. There is increase; but it is increase in the same kind. He that soweth tares shall not reap wheat. He that soweth wind shall not reap sunshine. No, nor shall she that soweth wind reap the zephyr. It shall be in kind and increase in kind—'They have sown the wind, and they shall reap the whirlwind.' Whatsoever a man soweth, that also shall he reap. (2) There is the principle of proportion. The return may be manifold; still, it is in proportion. 'He that soweth sparingly shall reap also sparingly; and he that soweth bountifully shall reap also bountifully.' 'Therefore, be ye steadfast, unmoveable, always abounding in the work of the Lord; forasmuch as ye know that your labour is not in vain in the Lord.' Amen.

NOW DARKLY:
THEN FACE TO FACE[1]

*For now we see through a glass, darkly; but then face to
face: now I know in part; but then shall I know even as also
I am known.*—1 Corinthians 13:12

T HIS antithesis—this memorable, pointed contrast—may
have a fourfold application. It may be regarded as discriminating between our present and our future knowledge,

I. Of God.
II. Of ourselves.
III. Of a Christian friend.
IV. Of the whole Church of God.

**I. Now we see GOD through a glass darkly; but then face to face: now
we know him in part; but then shall we know even as also we are known.**

There are two drawbacks on our present knowledge of God. It is
circuitous; and it is partial. An intervening instrumentality is needed;
and a partial result merely is attained. We do not see God directly—
only 'through a glass,' and that 'darkly.' And we do not know God
completely; we know only 'in part.' We behold 'as in a glass' the glory
of the Lord: no man hath seen God himself at any time. It is his own
solemn utterance, 'There shall no man see me, and live; my face shall
not be seen.' So it is 'now.' But 'then'—face to face.

---

[1] [From *The Family Treasury of Sunday Reading* (1866), p. 229ff.]

The 'glass' in which we see God here is the Word—his verbal revelation of himself. This is very beautifully shown in that very communion of the Lord with Moses, in which the vision of his 'face' is so peremptorily denied. In answer to his servant's ardent supplication, 'I beseech thee, show me thy glory;' the Lord said, 'I will make all my goodness pass before thee, and I will proclaim the name of the Lord before thee; for thou canst not see my face' (Exod. 33:18-23; 34:1-7). The arrangements, indeed, for tempering and shading the bright effulgence of the glory were numerous, and indicated, on Jehovah's part, the tenderest caution and care on behalf of his servant. There is first the 'clift of the rock' taken advantage of to shield the holy prophet from being enveloped in the dazzling splendours of Jehovah's presence: 'Behold, there is a place by me, and thou shalt stand upon a rock; and it shall come to pass, while my glory passeth by, that I will put thee in a clift of the rock.' Then, this alone is not sufficient; the wondrous covering of the Lord's own gentle hand of love is needed: 'And I will cover thee with my hand while I pass by.' And then, thirdly, only as the awful vision vanisheth, and the heavenward-moving van-glory hath its face averted and is retiring, can the awe-struck seer be suffered to gaze after it: 'And I will take away my hand, and thou shalt see my back parts: but my face shall not be seen.'

The real vision that Moses had of God was in the proclamation, in the name, in the word: 'And the Lord passed by before him, and proclaimed, The Lord, the Lord God, merciful and gracious.' This was the true, the abiding vision; faith's vision. Now 'faith cometh by hearing; and hearing, by the word of the Lord.'

Thus the vision is 'through a glass, darkly;' through the intervention of the Word. And necessarily it is but partial; it is but parts, and these the 'back parts' merely, that are seen. So it is 'now.' But 'then;' the Word, the intervening glass, the mirror into which the light of the knowledge of the glory of God is cast to be reflected—into which, also, it descends often as through a troubled clouded atmosphere, and is seen by only partially anointed eyes, by powers of vision at the best but feeble—the darkling 'glass' will be withdrawn; the shading 'rock-clift' will be dispensed with; the covering hand of God will be removed; the glory will not 'pass by,' but stand revealed in fullness of the beatific and transforming vision. 'I shall see thy *face* in righteousness: I shall be satisfied when I awake in thy likeness.'

A superficial reading of Holy Scripture brings out some apparent contradictions of our text. A brief discussion of these will disperse all semblance of real disharmony, and only aid us the better in understanding our theme. Thus God is often said to lift upon his people, even now, 'the light of his countenance;' to shine upon them with his reconciled 'face.' And 'we all,' says Paul, 'behold the glory of the Lord with open face.' Job exclaims: 'I have heard of thee by the hearing of the ear, but now mine eye seeth thee.' And even of Moses it is expressly said, 'The Lord spake with him face to face, as a man speaketh to his friend.' Now the explanation is that all these statements are *comparative*, not *absolute*, and the particular explanation in each case turns on the consideration of what the things are that are compared, and what the point of the comparison. Thus:—

1. In the *first* place, if we compare the vague, impersonal, abstract knowledge which unaided reason may attain of a supreme power, with the direct, adoring, inter-communing 'acquaintance'[1] which spiritual faith attains with the Father, through the incarnate Son, and by the Word and Spirit, the latter may relatively or comparatively be called—seeing God, seeing his face. By unaided intellect 'no man hath seen God at any time.' Said Jesus to the unbelieving Jews, 'Ye have neither heard his voice nor seen his shape.' But Jesus declares the Father. By his incarnation and by his cross, the Son makes manifest the sin-avenging justice and the sinner-saving love of the Father; and by his Spirit he shines in the heart, and gives the light of the knowledge of the glory of God, in the face of Jesus Christ.

2. *Secondly*, if we compare the relatively dark and shadowy disclosures of God given in the Old Testament economy with the fullness of manifestation under the New, the latter may be called a 'face to face' revelation. Thus the obscurity of 'the law' which 'came by Moses,' when viewed in relation to the fullness of 'grace and truth' which 'came by Jesus Christ,' is illustrated by the veil which Moses put upon his face

---

[1] 'Acquaint thyself with him, and be at peace' (Job 22:21).

when he came down from the mount of communion with God. The revelation he was chosen to convey was a veiled and shaded one. The full doctrine of redemption, and of the divine glory therein, was to a great degree shrouded and concealed under typical observances. And it is relatively to this that Paul says, 'We all,' under the new economy, 'behold as in a glass the glory of the Lord with its face unveiled.' Comparatively we see God face to face.

3. *Thirdly*, comparing the believer's dark times, in spiritual experience, with his bright, the latter may be called a seeing of the face of God. Spiritual darkness and desertion are frequently in Scripture called the hiding of the face of God, or, rather, the result of that. 'Why hidest thou thy face from me?' 'I will wait for the Lord that hideth his face from the house of Jacob.' When the Lord visits in loving kindness and relieves his waiting people, he is then said to reveal his face, to lift the light of his countenance upon them. He answers their earnest prayer, the thrice-repeated holy refrain (Psa. 80:3, 7, 19), 'Turn us again, O Lord God of hosts: cause thy face to shine: and so we shall be saved.' Saved; for their conscious salvation is in the shining of God's face. Thus also in the similarly threefold refrain (Psa. 42:5, 11; 43:5), in which the soul thrice invokes itself thus, 'Why art thou cast down, O my soul; and why art thou disquieted in me,' it is 'face to face' communion that is longed for and anticipated: 'I shall yet praise him for the help of his countenance' (verse 42:5); first, *his* countenance; and then, the second and the third time, 'I shall yet praise him who is the health of my countenance' (verse 42:11; 43:5); first, *his* face to me in 'help;' then *my* face lifted up to in 'health;' his to me without a cloud or frown; mine to him without a 'spot'[1] or fear. Our communion shall be face to face then, as when a man speaketh with his friend. Oh, when shall it once be? And how shall I attain to it? 'Send forth thy light and thy truth.' *Then* shall I praise him for the help of *his* countenance, and for the health of *mine*.

Here, then, is a rising scale of contrasts; *first*, the contrast between nature's glimmering, profitless knowledge, and that contained in revelation; *second*, the contrast between the scanty dawning light of

---

[1] 'For then shalt thou lift up thy face without spot' (Job 11:15).

Mosaic revelation, and the full sunshine that came by Jesus Christ; *third*, the contrast between spiritual depression or desertion, and the joyful consciousness of fellowship with a reconciled Father. In each of these cases the two sides of the diversity or antithesis may be spoken of in terms which represent the brighter side as a full and face to face disclosure. But now;

4. There is a far higher rise in the scale still remaining. Take the fullest joyfulness of fellowship with God to which the Christian can attain on earth, and compare with it the beatific vision that remaineth; we must still employ, *we can only employ still*, our familiar vocabulary of comparison; and, casting the highest reach of all spiritual percep-tion possible on earth into the shade, we say with Paul, 'Now we see through a glass, darkly; but then face to face: now I know in part; but then shall I know even as also I am known.'

How could we, by our present means of knowledge, know God otherwise than 'darkly' and 'in part'? We have to piece together the portions of the Word—bit by bit; we have to think of one attribute, and then another, and another, and another, and as we think of one, the preceding, even with the faint and partial impression we may have had of it, is in danger of fading out of view. With what laboured effort, at the very best, and in its highest estate of holy, apprehensive, appreci-ating action, does the believing mind take in even one memorial, 'The Lord, the Lord God;' (the very language seems to labour in uttering the idea; how much more our feeble spiritual sense in apprehending; it!)—'The Lord, the Lord God, merciful and gracious, longsuffering, and abundant in goodness and truth, keeping mercy for thousands, forgiving iniquity and transgression and sin, and that will by no means clear the guilty.' Who does not feel that he is but spelling, 'as a child,' the golden letters of this glorious name? Verily, this is emphatically but 'in part.' By such means truly we can but 'know in part;' for this is but 'prophesying in part.' 'When I was a child, I spake, as a child, I understood as a child, I thought as a child:' therefore God prophesied to me, as to a child; he spake unto me as I was able to bear it.

Gather out of Holy Scripture all the names and titles of the Lord Jesus, from the beginning of Genesis to the close of Revelation—from 'seed of the woman' to 'the bright and morning star'—and by Christ's names and titles we are taught to know the Father, for 'he that hath seen me hath seen the Father,' says the great Revealer—and who shall be able to contemplate them all, with intelligence, at once, in all their full-orbed, perfected, and mutually completing glory? Ah! it is but a little of the glory that the 'glass' can bring into the serviceable focus of undeceiving vision at a time. But when this means of vision is removed, and the very Saviour Lord himself is seen; when we shall see him not merely as spoken of, but as he is; not as the word, by little and by little, by line upon line, line upon line, here a little and there a little, sets him forth to us; but in one all-perfect vision as he is; when that which is perfect is come, and that which is in part is done away; then not darkly as in a glass, but face to face shall he stand disclosed, and we shall know even as also we are known.

For it is not merely the down-toning intervention of a medium, at the best most inadequate, that now limits our spiritual perceptions of God; but the 'glass,' moreover, is darkened from the clouded atmosphere in which it has its place; and our vision blurred, besides, from the sin that dwelleth in us. But when we shall see him as he is, we shall be like him. Our vision shall be purified from the intermingling action of gross sense, and from the darkening power of sin. On the one hand, the method of the revelation shall be direct, immediate, finally complete; and, on the other, the powers with which we shall apprehend it, shall be heavenly and perfect as the vision itself is. 'I shall see thy face in righteousness; I shall be satisfied when I awake in thy likeness.'

Yes! The vision perfect; and the perception of it perfect, and perfectly transforming! The vision perfect; and the perfect seer conformed to it!

When Ezekiel sees the cherubic throne, and him that sits upon it, brighter than the dazzling amber and the mysterious self-infolding flame, he will not fall upon his face beside the river of the water of life. His own face shall shine as the sun in the kingdom of his Father; and in glowing gladness shall it bear the glory and radiate back a richer golden sunshine for beholding it. Isaiah, when he sees the Lord seated on his throne, shall not exclaim, 'Woe is me!' but shall himself speak freely in adoration's harmony with the seraphim; 'Holy, holy, holy, Lord God Almighty.' Elijah shall not wrap his face in his mantle. Moses shall not bow his head to shade his countenance. John shall not fall at his feet as dead, but lean upon his bosom above as he did here below, and look into his face of grace and glory. And they shall all walk with him in white, for they shall be worthy 'then;' worthy, and capable, of seeing him as he is. 'Then, face to face.'

But we close our meditation on this head; and we do so, oppressed with the sense of an utter inability to do justice to it. Yet, is not that inevitable, since we can see even this contrast itself only through a glass darkly and understand it only in part? Ere we pass from it, however, let us pause to rejoice in that, though our knowledge of God is indirect and incomplete, it is nevertheless reliable and true. 'For we know that the Son of God is come, and hath given us an understanding, that we may know him that is true, and we are in him that is true, even in his Son Jesus Christ: this is the true God and eternal life' (1 John 5:20). Take two marks of true knowledge: first, obedience; 'Hereby we do know that we know him, if we keep his commandments;' second, love; 'He that loveth not, knoweth not God, for God is love.' But if we can obey, and obey in love, then in the glass of the word, in private study, and in public ordinances, let us hope to see God as he may be seen till the shadows flee away. 'O God, thou art my God; early will I seek thee; my soul thirsteth for thee, my flesh longeth for thee in a dry and thirsty land where no water is; to see thy power and thy glory, so as I have seen thee in the sanctuary.'

II. The comparison—the antithesis—is applicable to our knowledge of ourselves. Now we see ourselves only, as it were, through a glass, darkly; then shall we be face to face with our own souls: now we know ourselves only in part; but then shall we know even as also we are known.

The very duty of self-examination proceeds upon the fact that we do, and in this life can, know ourselves only in part. Not that it is impossible to know ourselves truly, even so as to make our calling and election sure. God forbid. Says the apostle John, 'We know that we are of God, little children.' Says Paul, 'I know whom I have believed.'

And Job had said, long ages before, 'I know that my Redeemer liveth.' Blessed be God, we may understand God's dealings with us in grace far better than his dealings with us in providence. In providence he asks an implicit faith in him; in his grace he gives intelligible and satisfactory explanation. 'Eye hath not seen, nor ear heard, nor have entered into the heart of man, the things which God hath prepared for them that love him.' True. 'But God hath revealed them to us by his spirit, that we may know the things that are freely given us of God.' And 'the secret of the Lord is with them that fear him.'

Still, even of the conscious believer, of him who knows that he is in covenant with God, it is true that he knows himself only in part. The heart is deceitful above all things and desperately wicked; who can know it? And it is believers, 'holy brethren, partakers of the heavenly calling,' who are warned against 'the deceitfulness of sin' (Heb. 3:1, 13). Hence the prayer, 'Search me, O Lord, and try me, and see if there be any wicked way in me, and lead me in the way everlasting.' Hence also the command concerning the celebration of the Lord's supper, 'Let a man examine himself, and so let him eat.' So it is 'now.' But 'then'— the faithful shall sit down to the marriage supper of the Lamb with no note of mournful caution ringing in their ear; with no preparatory self-searching exercises needed; with unbounded brightness of the full assurance of worthiness; for they shall be surely like Jesus, because they shall see him as he is.

This is not attainable here. Even Paul not only says, 'With me it is a very small thing to be judged of man's judgment;' he adds, 'Yea, I judge not mine own self, for I know nothing of myself: yet am I not hereby justified; he that judgeth me is the Lord.' What, indeed, are all upright appeals to the omniscient Lord himself—like that of Peter, 'Lord, thou knowest all things; thou knowest that I love thee'—but acknowledgments that our own judgment of ourselves may possibly be wrong, in the very act of rebelling mentally against the idea that it is wrong; acknowledgments at least that our judgment of ourselves requires to be countersigned by one who cannot err? Thus 'now.' But 'then'? Will any one 'then' think of saying, 'Lord, thou knowest all things; thou knowest that I love thee?' The very grief with which

Peter uttered these words was an admission of the somewhat mournful truth—above which the best cannot rise here—that we know but in part even our own very selves. How could it be otherwise in the Christian warfare? It is otherwise in the wars of the world. Laying aside the unwonted circumstance of spies in the camp, the enemy are all before the united band of patriots. In the Christian warfare, the enemy, partly, always is within. The Lord spreads a table for his people in presence even of enemies within, as well as enemies without; and commanding deliverances for Jacob—as when all Israel convened to Jerusalem's peaceful feasts, and no foe dared invade a land which a wall of fire unseen defended—he gives it to the weary, way-worn, war-worn sufferer to rest a while beneath his shadow with great delight. But still he is a soldier that is enjoying this repose. He is forbidden to ask for tabernacles, as on the mount of Transfiguration. He drinks of the brook in the way; but he must rise and fight again, and lay account with yet again crying out of his wounds, 'O wretched man that I am! who shall deliver me from the body of this death?' He can believe in the fullness and finality of his justification by faith; and he can enjoy peace with God, and access by faith into the grace wherein he stands; crying, 'Who shall lay anything to the charge of God's elect? it is God that justifieth; who is he that condemneth? it is Christ that died; yea, rather, that is risen again; who is even at the right hand of God; who also maketh intercession for us.' He can believe also in the perseverance—the perseverance because the preservation—of the saints; and he may be able to take up the other triumph, 'Who shall separate us from the love of God which is in Christ Jesus our Lord?' He may thus, by spiritual, appropriating faith, enter into the eighth chapter of the Romans. But also he may be able with equal sympathy to read on into the ninth; 'I say the truth in Christ, I lie not, my conscience also bearing me witness in the Holy Ghost, that I have great heaviness and continual sorrow of heart.'

But 'then;' when he hath kept the faith, and finished his course, and received the crown of righteousness—*then* shall he wholly know himself as wholly free both from sorrow and from sin. And, O the bounding joy of seeing himself wholly as he is, and of trusting himself wholly; of knowing that, as all around there is nothing that can enter to defile, so all within there is no root of bitterness to spring up and trouble—that in all this manifold heart there is no fold unrevealed, no tangled knot, no plaited wrinkle, nor any such thing! Here you often feel, O child of God, that you neither know yourself wholly, nor are wholly known by others. Your worst certainly is not known; and that makes you sometimes ashamed to accept the esteem and love of those who in holy charity would seem to take you as if always and entirely at your best. Your best possibly is not known; and capabilities of intensely-loving, confidential friendship that slumber within give a feeling of deepest pain and weariness, and longing wistfulness—a mournful echo as from an aching void—for want of being called forth by others, trusted to, drawn upon, exercised, gratified. Often, also, it is only through a process of self-examination and prayer—self-examination most humiliating, and prayer perhaps prevailing by a conflict in which the thigh is out of joint, and some halting follows afterwards even to the grave—only thus that you can reach, in some present crisis of affliction, the assurance that the whole river of God's pleasures is yours for consolation; only thus that you can reach, in some impending great responsibility, the assurance that, through grace, you can trust yourself to meet it. And when it comes; to keep the under-current of your faith in Christ, in whom you must be trusting, if you are in any right sense to trust yourself—to keep the undercurrent of your faith in harmony with the uppercurrent and flow of necessary action—who that has known it does not know the painfulness and difficulty of it?

But 'then;' when I know even as also I am known; when I know myself; and absolutely and wholly, through grace become glory, can trust myself; when I need no more to say, 'I judge not mine own self,' or, if I do judge myself, can say with Christ, 'I know that my judgment is true;' when bright and undimmed intellect takes in the whole meaning of what my Lord appoints; and joyful consentient will leaps up to acquiesce, and more than acquiesce, in the appointment; and moral sense adoringly owns its rectitude; and finest moral sensibility appreciates the beauty of its holiness; and gratitude responds to the perception of its goodness and blissfulness to me ward; and trust in my

Father's wisdom anticipates the grand result I know must follow; and no inward foe disputes the ground, no halting thigh has to be dragged on the heavenly mission, no adder haunts the heavenly path;—I shall do the will of God as the angels do in heaven, hearkening to the voice of his command and excelling in my strength to do his pleasure

But it is not so yet. 'Now' I see myself only as through a glass, darkly; scarcely face to face with my own soul; having to summon it, as from a distance, ere I can get explanations—as when I have to ask, for instance, Why art thou cast down, O my soul?

Still, while this is partial, it should be progressive too. And there are two great means, or instruments of progress—faith and works. First, *faith*; a believing contemplation of the character of God. 'We all, with open face, beholding as in a *glass* the glory of the Lord, are changed into the same image from glory to glory, even as by the Spirit of the Lord' (2 Cor. 3:18). Second, *works*; the dutiful obedience to the word. 'For if any man be a hearer of the word, and not a doer, he is like unto a man beholding his natural face in a *glass*: for he beholdeth himself, and goeth his way, and straightway forgetteth what manner of man he was. But whoso looketh into the perfect law of liberty, and continueth therein, he being not a forgetful hearer, but a door of the work, this man shall be blessed in his deed' (James 1:23-25).

III. This antithetical maxim has its verification in our knowledge of the brethren. Now we see each other through a glass, darkly; but then face to face: now we know each other in part; but then shall we know even as also we are known.

I do not speak of the misunderstandings that frequently occur through mutual infirmity, and which occasionally become inexplicable and therefore inextricable too. But even in kindliest brotherhood, what sensitive mind is not painfully aware of manifold inevitable causes ceaselessly in operation to set limits on reciprocal knowledge? Even in the brief and blissful love of David and Jonathan, one can see elements that might have painfully embarrassed their communion had it been much prolonged on earth. Perhaps it was well for its blissfulness that it was brief— that the beauteous bud was broken off to bloom where no chill wind can blight its beauty. Would Jonathan always have understood: 'David and all his afflictions'? Would he have always stood true, both to righteousness and David, in all David's sins? 'Very pleasant hast thou been to me, my brother Jonathan!' Yes; but pleasanter far now is thy friend, O sweet Psalmist of Israel! You both have higher thrones than Immanuel's earthly land conferred on one. You both have sweeter harps than earthly Zion-hill re-echoed. And you sway your thrones and sweep your harps while face flashes upon face a mutual knowledge all unbounded, each face shining with the fullness of a love that is purer than the snow, and brighter than the sun in his strength!

We know each other 'now' only 'in part.' And little wonder. For if we know ourselves only in part, we can hardly think our knowledge of each other could be more complete. We are not indeed to judge others with the severity and jealousy which we are to apply to ourselves; nor are we to demand in a friend's case the same amount of evidence without which we ought not to be satisfied even tremblingly about our own. Our text occurs amidst the matchless praise of that charity which 'beareth all things, believeth all things, hopeth all things, endureth all things;' and all these special actings of the love which is born of God were impossible save on the ground that our knowledge of each other is in part. We know each other's disposition, experience, trials, fears, hopes—only in part. Above all, we know each other's Christian conflict only in part. In the great general features, no doubt, marvellously does your own conflict answer to your Christian brother's, even as face answereth to face. But in particulars, how very different may be your cases! And how little able may you be reciprocally to understand them! The principalities of darkness against which you wrestle are legion; their wiles are manifold; and their drift may be exactly to engage you on far distant sides of the field and shut you out from each other's sympathy. May you not have had experience of this very device of the enemy? Ah! there came a blessing doubtless; and you were shut up more fully to the sympathy of Jesus as alone unlimited and perfect. But you yearned to see more truly eye to eye to speak more freely and more frequently 'face to face' with your friend. And yet it might not be. 'David arose and departed; and Jonathan went into the city.'

Yes; the manifold discipline of providence varies with different souls wondrously; and sometimes it removes Christian friends from each other's full intelligent sympathy. Peculiarity of trial may carry you, or seem to carry you, outside the range of all experience but your own. The effort to profit may but pain your sensitive spirit sorely. The well-meant proffered comfort may but extort the cry, 'Miserable comforters are ye all.' And you may be doomed to feel that you neither 'know' nor 'are known' as ye would.

But the conflict ends at last with all the faithful. The toil-worn warriors meet, no longer each engrossed greatly with the single portion of the field assigned to him to keep, or with the special onset of the foe given him to sustain. No unintelligible aspect of anxiety rests now on any brow among them all, as it often was on earth while every man had his sword on his thigh by reason of fear in the night. The righteous all have dominion in the morning. And the unmingled joy with which they clasp hands in mutual congratulation tells that they are meeting truly 'face to face' now—that 'now' they 'know as they are known.'

Meantime, however, let us guard against disparaging the value of Christian brotherhood on earth because of its present imperfection. Let Christian brethren whom Providence brings into special fellowship cultivate each other's confidence in all honourable and holy affection. Let 'the fear of the Lord' be imperatively demanded in all mutual interchange of spiritual experience. 'Come, all ye that fear God, and I will tell you what he hath done for my soul.' Be not unhandsomely inquisitive into the experience of your friend. Abhor being loquacious as to your own; and err, in these weighty things that are divine, rather by defect than by excess. Remember that the Lord is between you, according to your oath implied if not uttered; and think upon his name which is great and dreadful. But when observant of these simple rules, take the comfort of that which was spoken by the prophet (Mal. 3:16), 'They that *feared the Lord* spake often one to another: and the Lord hearkened, and heard it, and a book of remembrance was written before him for them that feared the Lord, and *thought upon his name.*' Great, even 'now,' for mutual help and blessing, are the resources of the communion of saints: and very easy oftentimes is obedience to the command, 'Let each esteem other better than themselves,' partial though mutual knowledge, here and 'now,' may be. 'Jewels' are such friends to one another even 'now.' And 'then'—'in the day when the Lord maketh up his jewels'—how fully shall ye be revealed to one another! when the weak shall be as David and David as the angel of the Lord; when every David and his Jonathan shall be locked in an embrace of love glorified by light on their faces from the jasper walls: and very pleasant shall ye be to one another, your love to one another wonderful!

IV. Now we see the church as through a glass darkly; but then face to face: now we know the Church of God in part, but then shall we know even as also we are known.

How infinitesimally small is our knowledge of God's glorious catholic Church here and now! We pray indeed for Christ's kingdom—for all that in every place call on the name of their Lord and ours. But how poor is the ideal that stands before the mind's eye in doing so! When we pray saying, 'Thy kingdom come,' how very much do we pray as in the dark! In your closet, praying for the Church, how 'darkly' do you see it 'as in a glass'!

Even your own branch of Christ's Church, with your own congregation, and with her numerous assemblies worshipping with you in our own land, and her many gatherings in many lands, some of them indeed as in the day of small things, yet here and there dotting the globe well-nigh from the rising to the setting sun; her home mission labours; her large colonial fields whitening to the harvest; her families of sons and daughters to the Lord rescued from the horns of the idol's altar and bound a loving sacrifice with cords to the altar of the cross; her sons of Israel, her daughters of Jerusalem, brought into captivity to Israel's King;—O how faintly we see in vision this one portion of the Church which is in our hearts so specially to live and die with her! And when we try to take into our embrace of thought and love all faithful brethren in all communions, alas! our minds faint within us in the weakness of our apprehension of the glorious vision of the kingdom. But if we yet further try to gather into one—as at last they shall be gathered into one assembly—all pilgrim-patriarchs, psalmists, prophets; all seers, apostles, martyrs, confessors of the olden times; all elders who obtained a good report, and the countless hidden ones whose report is only in the remembrance-book of God; all Christians also of the new dispensation hitherto; and the millions in the bright millennial days, numerous as the dew drops from the womb of the morning—all as they shall stand around the throne of Shiloh when to him shall the gathering of the people be—ah! we are seeing but through a glass very darkly.

But when all the vast assembly congregate on Zion Mount above; when from their numbers without number the hymn of heaven ascends, 'Worthy is the Lamb that was slain, for he was slain for us;' when the whole family find themselves at home—at home with the Father, and with the Elder Brother, and the Spirit of glory glorifying them all, the oil of gladness gladdening them all—and the table is spread in the presence of no foe, now that they dwell in the house of the Lord for ever; looking round on the wondrous hierarchy of kings and priests, and with vision large and clear to see and know them all, will not each be ready to exclaim, How darkly in yon dark world we saw what now we see face to face! how small the 'part' we knew of what we now know fully even as we ourselves are known!

And is it true that this Church of the living God—this Bride of the Lamb that was slain—will suffer me, a sinner, now to cry, 'Entreat me not to leave thee, nor to return from following after thee'? Is it true that I hear her answering me with myriad voices crying, 'Come thou with us, and we will do thee good'? Is it true that 'the Spirit and *this bride* say, Come'? Amen.

HEAVEN: THE SCENE OF CHRIST'S PRIESTHOOD[1]

First Sermon

We have such an high priest, who is set on the right hand of the throne of the Majesty in the heavens.—Hebrews 8:1

THE particular doctrine concerning our Lord's priesthood which the apostle asserts in these words is, that the locality or scene of that priesthood is heaven. All that he has hitherto said on this exalted theme runs up into this, that heaven itself is the adequate and true home, scene, or sanctuary of the priesthood of Jesus. He sums up in this the various statements he has already made concerning the suitableness, efficiency, permanence, and value of this gracious office, which Christ as our Redeemer executes. He carries us gradually, step by step, through the appointment, ordination, sacrifice, and success of Christ in the priestly office, till he shows us the Son of God exalted, as the High Priest of his people, to the highest throne of heaven; nor is he content to lay down the pen of inspiration on this lofty topic till he has placed it before our view in the glorified person of the Priest himself, shining in the glories of the immediate presence and manifested majesty of the living God.

But he pauses now. Now he looks back on all that has passed under our review, and he says: Of the things which we have spoken this is the sum: 'We have such an high priest, who is set on the right hand of the

[1] [From *The Family Treasury of Sunday Reading* (1867), p. 170ff.]

throne of the Majesty in the heavens; a minister of the sanctuary, and of the true tabernacle, which the Lord pitched, and not man.' Many precious and wonderful statements he has made concerning this priesthood. He sums them all up in the doctrine that the scene or locality of its permanent ministrations is heaven.

The doctrine or fact thus asserted throws a very powerful light on various of the attributes or characteristics of Christ's priesthood. We select the following:—

    I. Its reality.
    II. Its effectiveness.
    III. Its perfection.
    IV. Its permanence.
    V. Its exceeding glory.

I. That the scene or the home of Christ's priesthood is heaven demonstrates the reality of the priesthood of Christ.

The inspired reasoning of this epistle goes on to show this. 'For' says the writer in the 4th verse of this chapter, '*if he were on earth, he should not be a priest*;' his priesthood in that case would be illusory, superfluous, and unreal. Had he continued 'on earth' for the alleged purpose of carrying on the functions of his priesthood here; or had he, on ascending to heaven, abdicated or abandoned the office altogether; had this world been the native home and exclusive scene of his sacerdotal office, it would have evacuated the office itself of all reality. For, in that case, he could have taken rank only with the priests of the tribe of Levi; seeing that 'they are the priests'—the only recognized and consecrated priests—'that offer gifts according to the law.' For such a priesthood on the part of Jesus, there was no necessity. Neither was there any scope for it. For 'it is evident that our Lord sprang not out of Levi, but out of Judah, of which tribe Moses'—who was charged with all the appointments relating to that priesthood—'spake nothing concerning priesthood.' And, furthermore, it is matter of history that our Lord never performed one service of that priesthood—never offered a single sacrifice according to its rules, nor lifted the veil of its holy place, nor burnt incense, nor touched with one finger any of its priestly ceremonies. Such procedure in his case, with reverence be it spoken, would have been Uzziah's sin repeated, for 'it appertained not unto him;' and 'no man taketh this office upon him but he that is called of God, as was Aaron.' It was to another species of priesthood that Jesus was called when God glorified him, saying, 'Thou art my Son, this day have I begotten thee:' 'Thou art a priest for ever, after the order of Melchizedek.' The functions of the Levitical priesthood were confined to this world. The earth was the scene, the only and adequate home and locality, of that priesthood. Aaron was no more a priest when he died. He carried not his priesthood with him into heaven. He was expressly, and by special divine arrangement, stripped of his priestly robes, and left them behind him; for he left his office behind him. And the reason was, that the whole government and kingdom with which his priesthood stood connected was an earthly government, arbitrarily appointed by God, on a limited scale, confined to Israel, and designed to last but for a time. That government, in which God was King in Israel, and Moses his cabinet minister, was not the universal, necessary, and eternal moral government of God—in whose one and all-embracing sweep Jehovah doeth among the armies of heaven and the inhabitants of all the earth according to his pleasure. For that universal government he could not arbitrarily set up at the mere good pleasure of his will, for it is of necessity and not of grace. Nor could he limit it to Israel, for it is necessarily universal. Nor could be abdicate and set it aside, for of necessity it endureth for ever. Among Israel he erected under himself a sovereignly-appointed, special, limited, and local government—temporary also, and inserted as a mere parenthesis into the history of his one moral government of the race. The scene of that government or kingdom was Judea, 'Immanuel's land.' Offences against that government—such as being unclean by touching a dead body or a bone—might be expiated by the services of a priesthood which, in correspondence with the kingdom, was an earthly, local, and temporary priesthood. The scene of its functions was earth, and earth alone. All its procedure, relations, and effects were confined to earth; and when its priests were translated to heaven they were Levitical priests no more. To this priesthood Christ did not belong. He was descended from another tribe in Israel than they. And if earth were the only adequate home and scene of his priesthood, not having their priesthood, he would have had none whatever.

But he had a priesthood, and a real one; and its reality is illustrated and proved by the heavenly home and seat of it, at the right hand of the throne of the Majesty in the heavens.

For Christ's priesthood appertains to that universal and eternal moral government which God from his throne in the heavens exercises, not over the twelve tribes of Israel, but over all responsible agents. The sin which Jesus came to expiate was offence against the moral law and moral government of the Most High. The offence which Aaron and his priests could expiate were against merely 'the law of a carnal commandment'—the merely arbitrary transgressions, such as any king on earth may please to say he will not tolerate in his court. Various things, in themselves indifferent, so far as the moral law is concerned—God, as King in Israel, was pleased to say were intolerable to him as tabernacling in the camp of Israel, and in the holy place of his kingly court and temple—worship there. And the shedding of blood, that 'could not put away sin' or moral defilement, he was pleased, by the ministry of an earthly priesthood, to appoint for the putting away of these offences that were not moral. In such humble priesthood and its services he that came down from heaven had no share. And had his priesthood never been carried into heaven, he could really have had no priesthood at all. But sin, as against the everlasting moral law, is committed against, not the temporary King of Israel, but the everlasting God of heaven, considered as the King whose kingdom ruleth over all. To expiate this, Jesus became a priest after the order of Melchizedek; and though he died on earth, because the scene of sin's occurrence must be the scene of sin's expiation, the reality of his priesthood is illustrated by the fact that in heaven—the palace of the moral universe—he is a priest for ever, at the right hand of the throne of the Majesty above.

II. The fact that heaven is the native home and scene of the priesthood of Christ illustrates its effectiveness or its success, but what consists the effectiveness of priesthood?

Priesthood is designed for reconciliation; for removal of obstructions to communion or fellowship; for the conduct of acceptable worship. But the worship of a king is around his throne. Access, therefore, to his throne must be secured by priesthood, if priesthood is to be effective or successful

When Jehovah was pleased to erect his theocracy in Israel—to become for a time the national king in Jeshurun, with Moses as his prime minister of state, entrusted with the whole administration and executive—he erected in Israel his palace, which was his temple also; and in its sacred penetralia[1] he set up his sacred throne. The mercy-seat was Jehovah's throne in Israel. The glory dwelt between the cherubim; a sensible and earthly manifestation, as the whole government was earthly, that Israel's Shepherd-king was among them. Concerning this throne in the holy place, Jehovah said: 'There I will meet with thee, and I will commune with thee from above the mercy-seat, and from between the cherubims' (Exod. 25:22). And Israel was wont to say: 'Give ear, Shepherd of Israel, thou that leadest Joseph like a flock; thou that dwellest between the cherubims, shine forth. Before Ephraim and Benjamin and Manasseh stir up thy strength, and come and save us' (Psa. 80:1, 2).

If Israel's priesthood was to be truly efficient—if their service and ministry were to be successful—if they were truly to 'accomplish the service of God,' if they were not utterly to fail in the whole object and design of their office, it behoved them to secure access into the tabernacle, and unto the very throne of their king. On the great Day of Atonement they did so unto the uttermost. Theirs was, within its own limits, and in its own adequate and native scene, an efficient and successful—thoroughly efficient and successful within its own sphere. Its sphere was not the universal moral government of God; and it is impossible that the blood of bulls and of goats could take away sin— sin, which is transgression of that moral law by which the universal

---

[1] [The innermost parts of a building, i.e. the Holy of Holies of the temple.]

moral government of God is carried on. But within its own legitimate sphere in the limited, and national, and temporary theocracy
among the chosen people, it was strikingly and perfectly successful.
Would it not have been a very poor type of Christ's priesthood, had
it not been so? But it was effective and successful. On the great day
of atonement the blood of the appointed victim procured entrance
for the high priest within the veil. The innermost penetralia of the
temple; the most sacred, most secret dwelling of the King; his most
immediate presence; his very throne became accessible to Israel in the
person of Israel's high priest. Israel's Divine King unveiled his glory
to his people. He shone upon them from between the cherubims. He
lifted up on them the light of his countenance. He proclaimed his
good pleasure in them, his blessing, and his love. He answered the
prayer of their inspired liturgy: 'God be merciful unto us, and bless
us; and cause his face to shine upon us: that thy way may be known
upon earth, thy saving health among all nations' (Psa. 67:1, 2). And
this was through the efficiency and success of the priesthood he had
established in Israel.

Within the limits, the scope and sphere of this priesthood, even
Jesus, the Son of God, had he partaken of its office and ministry, could
not have been more successful. That priesthood, indeed, he was not
endowed with. But the priesthood into which he had been called, must,
if successful, have a similar index of its success. It was a priesthood
that stood related to the everlasting and universal moral government
of God. The throne of that government is pitched in no worldly tabernacle made with hands. It is not fixed upon the earth, but high above
all heavens. Clouds and darkness are round about it. No created glory,
as between the cherubims, flames upon it; no representative material
splendour is enthroned there; but the King eternal, immortal, and
invisible, personally sits upon it, and ten thousand times ten thousand, and thousands of thousands, wait upon him, hearkening to the
voice of his commandment. It is access through all the ranks of the
holy ones there, which a priest, ministering in what pertains to moral
law and universal moral government, must secure for his brethren, if
his priesthood is to be crowned with success. Its clients must obtain

admission there, if their priest can manage and minister efficiently in their cause and service. They must be able to say: 'Who shall lay anything to the charge of God's elect? It is Christ that died; yea, rather, that is risen again; *who is even at the right hand of God.*' They have reason and right to say so. Their priest has been successful in his priesthood. 'We have such an high priest, who is set on the right hand of the throne of the Majesty in the heavens.'

III. It is a continuation of this line of thought to remark that the heavenly home of Christ's priesthood illustrates also the perfection of that priesthood.

The first covenant was not 'faultless;' and its want of faultlessness was illustrated by the fact that it had but 'a worldly sanctuary' (Heb. 9:1). Its priesthood was imperfect; and it could not possibly be otherwise, seeing its only scene was this world. 'Perfection,' it is strongly asserted, 'was not by the Levitical priesthood' (Heb. 7:11). 'The law made nothing perfect' (Heb. 7:19). Meats and drinks, and divers washings, and carnal ordinances—being all merely the beggarly elements of the world—could only keep men in a certain bondage, never lifting them above the realm of which they were themselves the elements. These 'were but a shadow of good things to come'—not even rising to the character of 'the very image of them' (Heb. 10:1). They were 'weak' and 'unprofitable.' They did not 'profit,' for they did not 'perfect' them that were exercised in them. They 'could not make the comers thereunto perfect' (Heb. 10:1). They 'could not make him that did the service perfect as pertaining to the conscience' (Heb. 9:9). For the conscience asserts man's relation to higher interests than those of earth, and binds him to a government of larger sweep and longer duration than any special government that God established among the seed of Abraham after the flesh. It testifies his relation to the universal moral government of the God of heaven, and no earthly priesthood can minister or mediate to its satisfaction or perfection.

But the eternal Son of God is a Priest—from the bosom of the Father—and the heir of all things. Perfection is largely and variously affirmed of his priesthood. He was himself 'made perfect through suffering' (Heb. 2:10); and 'being made perfect, he became the author of eternal salvation' (Heb. 5:9). 'The law made nothing perfect, but the bringing in of a better hope did, by the which hope we draw near unto God' (Heb. 7:19), now that our priest hath entered as 'the forerunner into that within the veil' (Heb. 6:19), even 'to the right hand of the throne of the Majesty in the heavens.' This perfection he reached in the triumph of his holy sacrifice; and it is proved by his inauguration on his Father's throne. 'Behold, I do cures today, and tomorrow, and the third day I shall be perfected.' As every one shall be perfected as well as his Master. For by his one offering he hath for ever perfected them that are sanctified, seeing that this man, when he had offered one sacrifice for sin, for ever sat down at the right hand of God.

The priesthood of Levi was effective in its own sphere; its sacrifices 'sanctified to the purifying of the flesh.' But it rose not beyond the sphere of earth—it acted by 'the law of a carnal commandment.' It could not penetrate with its virtue, and efficiency, and powers, to 'an endless life.' It could not bring its services and functions to bear on a man's deepest relation to God, and his position as a subject of his eternal moral government. There was a great sphere of influence, interest, and relation, from which it was necessarily excluded. On man's prospect and position in that sphere it had no bearing whatsoever. Dimly it might shadow forth great truths belonging to that sphere, but it could not rise to its elevation; it could exert no influence on its interests. It could keep the Israelitish kingdom from falling to pieces; it could accomplish the service and fulfil the conditions on which the continued residence of the divine Shechinah among Israel depended; and it might restore to the lapsed and unclean worshipper the privilege of returning into Israel's camp, and re-engaging with acceptance in Israel's ceremonial worship. But it could not satisfy the demands of the moral law; it could not obliterate the guilt of sin as the transgression of that law; it could not glorify God as a moral ruler, nor pacify the conscience of man as a moral agent, concerning the forgiveness of sins; it could not re-admit apostate man to the family of heaven. It could admit him no further than into a 'sanctuary made with hands, which was but the figure of the true' (Heb. 9:24).

But Christ's is a perfect priesthood. It appertains to no limited sphere, and no temporary interests, and no arbitrary and local kingdom. It appertains to the universal government of God. It deals with *sin*. It magnifies the moral and eternal law. It pacifies and purifies the conscience of man, not as an Israelite, but as *man*—as a moral agents or subject of the one all-embracing government ranging over heaven and earth, and that grasps every moral being by 'the law of' no 'carnal commandment,' but in 'the power of an endless life.' It hath left no demand of universal and eternal justice unsatisfied; it hath neglected —or passed over unnoticed, unshielded, or eclipsed, or injured—no requirement of God's eternal kingdom that ruleth over all. It hath left no attribute of God's nature unglorified, and no elements of man's nature unrectified; no element of man's ruin unretrieved. It hath knit with eternal firmness the broken bond, by the disruption whereof man was set adrift from heaven, an alien and an outcast from God. It hath poured the splendours of 'glory in the highest' around God's character, and established, by the power of things immutable, the purity of man's character, the peace of his conscience and his hearty, and the blessedness and joy of his destiny. Its virtues prevail to reach unto the highest heavens, and to save from going down unto the pit even those that are worthy of the lowest hell. It sweeps sin away 'as far as the east is distant from the west;' and 'as far as the heavens are higher than the earth, so far doth it remove our iniquities away from us.' Its sweet savour fills the souls of believing men on earth with tranquillity, and the soul of God in heaven with rest. To Jehovah it is 'a savour of rest;' and to those that believe it gives admission into the rest of God. It is perfect. It is absolutely final and conclusive. It seals up into a fearful looking—for of vengeance and fiery indignation those who reject its love and ministrations, shutting with the key of David the hell of the unbelieving, and no man can open; and it seals and perfects into a hope most sure and steadfast those that humbly trust to its mediation, opening heaven for them by a new and living way, and giving them boldness to enter in.

All this is true. And all this is most obviously true by the fact that its ministrations are conducted, as in their rightful native home and sanctuary, at the right hand of the throne in the Majesty in the heavens.

The central throne of God is the scene of this priesthood, a terrible place of testing and of peril to a priesthood that were not perfect; for there, on that stainless seat of holiness and tenderest moral sensibility, any thrill of imperfection, unprofitableness, deficiency, or fault arising anywhere in all the universe, would vibrate and tell with the power of many thunders, and manifest itself with worse than the lightnings and the darkness of Sinai, the mountain that might be touched. But no; there is the rainbow of the covenant, round about the throne. *There* no jarring sound of disharmony or derangement beats to tell of something still unsettled or left unhealed. The storm of Divine wrath is past, and no clouds return after the rain. 'For this is as the waters of Noah unto me: for as I have sworn that the waters of Noah should no more go over the earth; so have I sworn that I would not be wroth with thee, nor rebuke thee. For the mountains shall depart and the hills be removed; but my kindness shall not depart from thee, neither shall the covenant of my peace be removed, saith the Lord that hath mercy on thee.' For this man, continuing ever, hath an unchangeable priesthood; able to save to the uttermost all that come unto God by him, seeing he ever liveth to make intercession—such an high priest indeed becomes us, holy, and harmless, and undefiled, separate from sinners, and now made higher than the heavens. 'For the law made nothing perfect, making men high priests that had infirmity; but the word of the oath maketh the Son, who is perfected for evermore' (Heb. 7:28).

IV. **Our thought runs on, without a break, into our fourth channel of remark—namely, that the heavenly locality of Christ's priesthood illustrates its permanence.**

Its permanence, indeed, necessarily results from its perfection. When that which is perfect is come, then that which is in part is done away; but the perfect, which replaces the partial, is not itself done away—it abideth. The priesthood of Levi was imperfect; for the priests were men that had infirmity, and 'they were not suffered to continue by reason of death. This man, because he continueth ever, hath an 'unchangeable'—an intransferable—'priesthood,' and 'ever liveth to make intercession.' In the virtue of his one perfect and perfecting sacrifice, he *for ever* sat down at the right hand of God. The priesthood of Levi, even if Aaron could have lived through all its dispensation, was, for other reasons, so imperfect, that it could not but pass away. It had no moral virtue or value in its ministrations to establish an ever-lasting covenant, and it could not operate upon the conscience and the heart of Israel, to keep Israel true to their King. For, in itself, it never reached the realm of conscience; it could not make them that did the service perfect, as pertaining to the conscience; and it could not renew, and regulate, and control their wills. It could only 'sanctify, to the purifying of the flesh.' Hence, it was not faultless, and its covenant could not be eternal. They brake it, and the Lord 'regarded them not.' He introduced a new covenant; but from the moment that he uttered the words, '*a new covenant*,' he made the first old. 'Now that which decayeth and waxeth old is ready to vanish away,' and the covenant and the priesthood vanished simultaneously; for they are so bound together that the fall of the one entails the fall of the other. If there be a change of the priesthood, there must be, 'of necessity, a change also of the law' (Heb. 7:12), or constitution, or covenant, under which its provisions were arranged and its ministrations were conducted. But it vanished in a manner not to be regretted. Its believing worshippers had all along fled to it, professedly as an interim arrangement. They got them to the mountains of its sacrifices and its spices of incense, only till the day should dawn and the shadows flee away. For the law had but 'a *shadow* of the good things to come;' and when the day dawned the shadows fled unmourned, for the substance was of Christ.

The covenant which his blood sealed, and in which his priesthood ministers, is a 'faultless' one, 'established on better promises;' cancelling the guilt and the remembrance of sin, providing the regeneration, the obedience, and the final perseverance of its clients. It is an everlasting covenant, ordered in all things and sure. The redemption he obtained ere he entered into the heavenly sanctuary, was an 'eternal' redemption, fulfilling on the cross all conditions of the Law, and rendering any further claims on its part impossible; trampling death into the dust of death, and making death's reappearance or recurrence as impossible for ever. From the highest heights unto the lowest depths it swept, with victorious power, through all realms where evil could dwell or opposition rise. The triumphing reach of it is 'high as heaven: What canst thou do,' O sin and unbelief? Its penetrating force is 'deeper than hell:' How can ye 'prevail against it,' ye 'gates of hell'? 'The measure thereof is longer than the earth:' 'Look unto me, all ye ends of the earth, and be ye saved.' It is 'broader than the sea:' be it your confidence, all ye 'that are afar off upon the sea.' It cannot be excelled, it cannot be supplanted, it cannot be replaced; and, in token thereof, it is at the right hand of the throne of the Majesty in the heavens. It is final, conclusive, eternal. Priesthood now can receive no higher promotion; it cannot any more be brevetted;[1] it can rise to no loftier rank. No step in the peerage of the kingdom now awaits it; no brighter coronet can sit upon the head of the priest upon his throne; and no more august title in celestial heraldry remains to dignify the name that is above every name. Continuing ever, his is an unchangeable and everlasting priesthood; and the song of angels and of men which celebrates the worship of the Lamb of God rejoices in the enraptured recognition of its eternity. 'Worthy is the Lamb that was slain to receive power, and riches, and wisdom, and strength, and honour, and glory, and blessing.' And the high refrain sounds forth again,—'Every creature which is in heaven and on the earth, and such as are in the sea, and all that are in them, heard I saying, Blessing, and honour, and glory, and power, be unto him that sitteth upon the throne, and unto the Lamb, for ever.' *For ever*! It is perfect, permanent, eternal.

V. That heaven is the home, and heaven's high throne the adequate and native seat of this priesthood, illustrates not only its reality and effectiveness, its perfection and its permanence, but also its exceeding glory.

There is glory in all real priesthood. I am not very sure but an investigation of Scripture might prove that the profound idea which revelation conveys by the mysterious word *glory,* is chiefly, if not uniformly, suggested in connection with priesthood, and as flowing from it and secured by it. Certain it is, that when the Priest came to

---

[1] [brevetted = to be promoted up a military rank.]

earth, the heavens rang with the angelic anthem, '*Glory* to God in the highest.' And, doubtless, it is safe to say, that where sin hath been, glory cannot come, save by priesthood; for the antagonist of glory is shame, even as death is the opposite of life, and priesthood's function is to turn sin, the occasion of shame into the counter-occasion of exceeding glory.

How great then, is that glory! How great the glory of priesthood finally and perfectly triumphant, so as even to be seated on the right hand of the throne of the Majesty in the heavens! Even Aaron's priesthood was glorious. Its garments were formed, by divine command, 'For beauty and for glory.' But if that which was done away with was glorious, much more that which remaineth is glorious!

But the glory of this priesthood is beyond searching out. We must have felt already that we have been bordering on the limit where our powers of speech and meditation are baffled and arrested. Let it suffice to say, that the principle concerning the glory of the priesthood, as seated on the throne of God, is this, that it is intrusted of God, in the hands of his own Son, with all power and dominion, in heaven and in earth, for the furtherance and completion of its ministrations of love and of saving power among the sons of men. To our great High Priest in the heavens every knee doth bow, and every tongue confess. Every region of the universe is subject to him in his priesthood. Honour and majesty are before him; strength and beauty are in his holy place within the veil, where Jesus hath entered, as the forerunner appearing in the presence of God for us. 'The Lord said unto my Lord, Sit thou at my right hand, until I make thine enemies thy footstool,' and until 'these whom I have given thee be with thee, that they may behold thy glory, which I have given thee, for I loved thee before the foundation of the world.' 'The Lord hath sworn, and will not repent. Thou art a priest for ever, after the order of Melchizedek' (Psa. 110:4).

Suffer two closing appeals.

1. To the unbelieving. You cannot but feel, I trust, that these meditations bear down, with accumulated, and, I should hope, through the blessing of God, with resistless force, on the folly, and infatuation, and offensiveness of your neglect and unbelief. What think ye of Christ

in his priesthood? Or rather, what think ye of the unbelief that despises him in the functions of an office, in the execution of which the Most High God has thought him worthy to sit 'at the right hand of the throne of the Majesty in the heavens'? If a dull despondency, beneath the guilt and power of sin, has paralysed you into the unbelieving neglect of your salvation, I call upon you to contemplate the real efficacy, the permanent and perfect power, and the illimitable glory of Jesus, in the very office on which salvation from sin so entirely hinges. And if consciousness of defilement, and unworthiness, and shame, cause you to shrink away from the High Priest, by how much the more he is glorious in his office—as if, with Peter, you would say, 'Depart from me, Lord, for I am a sinful man'—I beseech you to consider that his office can have no play nor power, no fruit nor glory, no vindication and no meaning, save as it deals with sin—to put away its shame and its defilement, to rob it of its victory over you, and to quench all its fruits and power for ever. Therefore, put your case, with faith and confidence, into his hands, however evil it may be; and his own right to the throne of the Majesty in the heavens is periled, if, from deficiency, either in power or compassion, he fail to deal with it successfully.

2. To you who believe on his name. How steadfast should your faith be! 'Seeing that we have a great High Priest, that is passed into the heavens—Jesus, the Son of God—let us hold fast our profession.' How believing and expectant your supplications! 'Let us, therefore, come boldly to the throne.' How spiritual your worship and how heavenly, freed from all carnal ceremonies and all beggarly elements of this world, seeing that your sanctuary is not, as of old, a 'worldly' one, but heavenly, within the veil, and in the very presence of God! And how safe is your position, and how sure your prospects! Contemplate habitually the great responsible agent and minister of your salvation, as a priest at the right hand of the throne of the Majesty in the heavens. Behold him bringing all the influence and power with which he is there endowed to bear on your full deliverance from sin, and full attainment of holiness and blessing. There is no backsliding into which you have fallen, from which his intercession cannot recall, and relieve, and restore you; no sin for which he cannot procure your forgiveness;

no corruption which he cannot obtain for you supplies of grace to subdue. There is no blessing which he cannot confer, and no enemy which he cannot destroy; nor is there any possible conjuncture in the affairs of your salvation which he does not foresee and provide for—indeed, arrange rather, and manage, by his own love and power. He sitteth in the central throne of majesty and might; and in all the universe there is no power of evil which, from that central seat of influence and glory, he cannot charm or crush into helplessness, and no power of good which he cannot awaken and evoke into your loving interest, and the promotion of your welfare and salvation. Are ye not complete in him who is the Head of all principality and power; having redemption in his blood, by whom were all things made, whether they be visible or invisible, thrones or dominions, or principalities and powers; and who now, as the High Priest of Zion, hath in all things the pre-eminence sitting 'at the right hand of the throne of the Majesty in the heavens'? Amen.

HEAVEN: THE SCENE OF CHRIST'S PRIESTHOOD AND, THEREFORE, OF THE CHURCH'S WORSHIP[1]

Second Sermon

We have such an high priest, who is set on the right hand of the throne of the Majesty in the heavens.—Hebrews 8:1

WE have formerly contemplated the doctrine or fact, that heaven is the locality and home of Christ's priesthood— the permanent scene of its gracious ministration. We attempted to show how this doctrine illustrates the reality, the efficiency, the perfection, the permanence, and the glory of that priesthood. There are certain inferences naturally following from the doctrine, and so precious, that we can scarcely pass from the subject without directing attention to at least the more important of them.

I remark, therefore, in the first place—

I. That if heaven is the scene of the priesthood of Christ, it is thereby also the scene of the Church's worship.

The priesthood of Christ and the worship of the Church are so connected, that they stand or fall together; and the scene or locality of the one must be the scene or locality of the other. All our worship of God hangs on the mediation of Jesus in the execution of his sacerdotal office;

[1] [From: *The Family Treasury of Sunday Reading* (1867), p. 358ff.]

and he who is unacquainted with the great leading truths concerning Christ's priesthood cannot intelligently nor acceptably worship God. No worship is acceptable to the Father, no ascriptions of praise and glory, and no supplications and prayers, can come into his presence, save through the hands of the one Mediator between God and man. And this does not merely imply that, on the one hand, God has regard to the sacrifice of Jesus, and that, on the other, the worshipper directs his faith to it also. There is more implied in it than that. For the sacrifice of Christ cannot be regarded as something that has passed out of his own hands, so as that benefits may be solicited and bestowed on the ground of it, the continual personal and living intervention of Christ himself being unnecessary. No: not only does the Father dispense the blessings of the covenant on the ground of the satisfaction rendered to divine justice on the cross of Calvary; but when he does dispense those blessings, it is only through the perpetual ministry, the gracious personal intervention, and the very hands of the living High Priest himself. And not only does the acceptable worshipper proffer his faith, and love, and service through the merit of the great propitiation, but his right to do so with acceptance he recognizes as dependent on his making use of the ministry and service of the High Priest, as he personally and officially presents them at the throne. When we are invited to come boldly to the throne of grace, our privilege is rested on the twofold ground: *first,* that we have 'a new and living way into the holiest by the blood of Jesus, and by the rent veil,' which is to say, his flesh: and *secondly,* that 'we have a great High Priest'—the risen Saviour himself, as the leader of our worship—'over the house of God.' And assuredly no one will rise to the purity of a true heart, and to the privilege of the full assurance of an unshaken confidence, whose faith does not embrace the completeness of this double warrant for drawing near to God.

All our worship is dependent on the priesthood of Christ. Our worship, in fact, is nothing else than our communion with Christ in his priesthood. Our whole worship hinges on that priesthood: takes its colour and character, its spiritual life and substance, from it; gathers round it, and revolves about it. Inevitably the scene of his priesthood is the scene of our worship.

It is written in the opening statement of the chapter succeeding that from which our text is taken: 'Then verily the first covenant had ordinances of divine service, and a *worldly* sanctuary.' And the contrast which the apostle is carrying out between the old covenant and the new, suggests, by antithesis, the sure and implied counterpart or correlative truth, that the second covenant has ordinance of divine service, but a *heavenly sanctuary* as the scene of them. And this truth is either expressly asserted or implicitly involved in repeated statements throughout this epistle. When in the fourth chapter we are called on to hold fast our profession, on the ground that we have a great High Priest who has passed into the heavens—Jesus, the Son of God—it is surely the throne of God in heaven to which we are for the same reason invited to 'come boldly, that we may obtain mercy and find grace to help in time of need.' When in the sixth chapter we have a glorious description of the strong consolation which God is willing that the heirs of promise should enjoy in the city of refuge into which they have fled, it is a heavenly refuge-city—heaven itself—into which their hope is seen to carry them, or into which their souls, in the power of hope, are spiritually carried out; Which hope 'enters *into that within the veil, whither the forerunner is for us entered.*' When in the tenth chapter we are invited into the holiest of all now pertaining to gospel worship— analogous to the holy of holies under the law—it is manifestly heaven itself into which we are, by this heavenly calling, summoned to enter by faith: 'Having therefore boldness to enter into the holiest by the blood of Jesus, by a new and living way, which he hath consecrated for us, through the veil, that is to say, his flesh; and having a high priest over the house of God, let us draw near.' When in the thirteenth chapter the writer asserts that 'we have an altar of which they have no right to eat that serve the tabernacle,' it is assuredly no earthly altar that he has in view, but one with which a heavenly and exclusively spiritual worship is connected, and in the virtues of which we are to offer no ceremonial material, or sensuous sacrifice, or any worship of earthly pomp, but the pure and simple 'sacrifice of praise, that is, the fruit of the lips.' And more decisive, perhaps, than any of these, is the grand description of our church-state and privilege under the gospel, which he expressly contrasts with that under the law; and in which he makes heaven so palpably the only scene and seat of worship, that readers are continually tempted to fancy that it is the estate of glory he is depicting, though it is manifestly our present condition under the gospel which he has in view:—'Ye are not come unto the mount that might be touched, and that burned with fire, nor unto blackness, and darkness, and tempest, and the sound of a trumpet, and the voice of words; but ye are come unto mount Sion, and unto the city of the living God, the heavenly Jerusalem, and to an innumerable company of angels, to the general assembly and church of the first-born, which are written in heaven, and to God the Judge of all, and to the spirits of just men made perfect, and to Jesus the mediator of the new covenant, and to the blood of sprinkling, that speaketh better things than that of Abel.'

Yes; as the holy place in the innermost recesses of Israel's temple was the recognised scene of Israel's worship under Aaron's priesthood, heaven is the scene of our worship under Christ. We enter there, indeed, in this life, only by faith. But faith's entrance is real. Faith's entrance is not fanciful, but true. We enter by no effort of imagination, but by an effort and exercise of faith; and faith has the warrant of the word, and the call of the Father, and the quickening of the Spirit, and the ministry and priesthood of the Son to proceed upon, when it enters there. And when our case is called, and our petition to be considered—if reverently we may speak of these great mysteries in terms borrowed from the procedure of men and courts on earth—and if the question is put: Who appears on behalf of these petitioners, and in support of this petition? the answer is: 'Christ hath entered into heaven itself, there to appear in the presence of God for us.'

In the grateful remembrance of this great truth—that God's heaven of glory is the real sanctuary and scene of our unpretending gospel worship—with what perfect satisfaction, with a mind how calm and equal, may we be contented to resign all the grandeur and pomp of a ritualistic worship, and cleave to the simplicity of our Presbyterian order! We are but preferring heaven to earth when doing so. And though our forms may be accounted bald, and tame, and unimpressive, it can only be in the judgment of those that are comparatively carnal, and who in default of spiritual ability to appreciate the heavenliness of New Testament worship, would lay *earth* and *sense* under contribution, where *heaven* and *faith* should rule. The truly spiritual worshipper, sensitive to the difficulty of maintaining his spiritual mindedness, will be jealous of everything fitted to appeal to sense. To such, the grave sweet melody of Zion's psalmody will be a congenial vehicle for spiritual feeling; while the artistic sounds of instrumental music thrilling the ear, awakening bodily sense to energies conflicting with those of the spirit, precisely where most of all the spirit should be free from all such conflict, will be felt intuitively as a great impurity, and a fundamental violation of the great principles of gospel worship. It is remarkably confirmatory of these remarks to remind you that, in point of fact, the tolerating or desiring of such innovations and impurities in the worship of God, always goes hand in hand with false or defective views of the priesthood of Christ. A ritualistic worship is found to be historically connected with notions of an earthly priesthood. When the ministers of the gospel are accounted priests, as in Popish and Puseyite worship, the earthly house of prayer—and not heaven—comes to be regarded as the scene and sanctuary of worship; its observances, in default of heavenly and unseen beauty, are decorated with materials of earthly splendour; and inasmuch as it is a principle of reason that the worship of God should be glorious, and priesthood and glory stand intimately related, the priesthood being on earth, the glory sought is an earthly pomp and glory too. The doctrine of Christ's exclusive and celestial priesthood puts ritualistic worship to flight. And the believing worshipper, seeking in spirit to enter heaven, rejoices to resign every beggarly element of the world, which can only chain down his spirit, too prone to cleave unto the dust, and hinder his entrance within the veil.

I need scarcely remark, in this connection, that it is manifestly the deep appreciation of doctrine—a large, and sound, and rich theology, once highly valued in Scotland, when every peasant could confound the prelates—that will alone protect and conserve among us the worship and government of the Church of God according to his will.

Doctrine, in all things, takes the lead in the Church; doctrine, held fast in the grasp of a living faith, a deep spiritual intelligence, and a loving, cordial appreciation. And where doctrine becomes corrupt, or shallow, or inefficient, neither the worship nor government of the Church can long be safe from the follies of human wisdom, and the corruptions and impurities of human inventions. Nor is there any doctrine more distinguishing and glorious in Christianity than the many-sided and exalted doctrine of the priesthood of Christ. You will always find those deplorably ignorant of it, who desiderate or would welcome innovations and ceremonies in our worship.

II. A second and very valuable inference from our present doctrine is this: That Christ's priesthood, as exercised in heaven, is the bond of an intelligent sympathy between the portion of the Church that is in heaven, and that which is on earth.

The redeemed Church of Christ in heaven and earth is one. 'For this cause I bow my knees unto the God and Father of our Lord Jesus Christ, of whom the whole family in heaven and earth is named.' Neither faith nor the instincts of spiritual feeling and love can brook the idea of any essential separation—any sore dislocation—any effective gulf of disjunction between them. Yet, if the celestial priesthood of Christ be removed, it will be difficult to see how the Church in heaven is other than most effectually dislocated and isolated from the Church militant below. Consider this from both the points of view. Contemplate the two cases: *first*, that of the Church above, in its interest and sympathy with their brethren on earth; and *secondly*, that of the Church on earth, in our interest and sympathy with our brethren in glory. And see how it is on the continued execution of Christ's priestly office in heaven that all intelligent sympathy on both sides must depend.

First, consider the Church in heaven as interested in the affairs of the Church on earth. We cannot imagine that they take no interest in the condition of their brethren here below. We can scarcely believe it to be a part of the perfection of 'the spirits of just men made perfect,' that they have ceased to take an interest in the spiritual affairs of

Christ's people on earth, and in the progress of his kingdom amidst the trials and conflicts of its militant estate. That could hardly be. Many of them, doubtless, felt unceasingly, while on earth themselves, that one distressing element of their imperfection consisted in the very difficulties they felt in grasping largely the interests of Christ's spiritual kingdom on earth; in compassing any large acquaintance with its condition, and maintaining that constant and lively and supreme interest in its progress, which its glorious character and issues demand of the believer's heart. We can scarcely, then, believe that their admitted condition of perfection now shuts them out from an intelligent acquaintance, or from the means of intelligent acquaintance, with what is passing in that kingdom of Christ in its progressive warfare with the powers of darkness. Nor can we believe that their glorious, and serene, and immediate insight into the condition of the Church in heaven, could make up for the deprivation of their knowledge of the estate of the Church on earth. For there is a special glory acquired by God in carrying his Church on earth safely through its conflicts and dangers—a glory such as does not accrue to him from maintaining its unassailed peace and glory in heaven. The history and conduct of the Church triumphant is—if I might use a familiar term for illustration—'plain sailing;' plain sailing, as compared with the administration and protection of its endangered interests on earth. Its preservation, and progress, and triumph, in this dark world of sin and opposition, where Satan's battle-field is, and his chiefest powers are put forth, illustrate the wisdom and grace and power of God, in such wonderful display as heaven can afford no scope for in the same kind at all. And that our glorified brethren, through faith and patience now inheriting the promises, should be debarred from the knowledge of that manifold wisdom of God which by the Church on earth is afforded to angelic principalities and powers in heavenly places, is what we cannot be prepared to believe. I know that on such a theme it is dangerous arguing from what we are prepared to expect or not expect in God's dealings with his translated saints in heaven; yet no small reliance may surely be placed on the intuitions of spiritual faith when these fall into harmony with the general analogy of God's more largely revealed procedure.

And when they find a footing, as in this case they do, in some, though it may be even small and vague, indications of Holy Scripture, they seem worthy of no small confidence being reposed in their dictates.

It is true, we have no ground for believing that the spirits of departed believers return to earth, or revisit the scenes of their former sojourning. They 'depart, and are with Christ.' That they are ever present in the Church below, witnessing directly its history and movements, we have no reason to believe. With the angels indeed it is so, as the Scriptures plainly reveal. They are the immediate spectators of the Church's worship—'I charge thee before God and the elect angels, preach the word.' What bands of these glorious spirits may be present in our worshipping assemblies is hidden from us; but we are commanded to preach the word as under their immediate inspection, as well as that of God himself. Nor are they mere spectators of the Church's history and worship on earth. They are servitors, as well as witnesses. Yea, 'are they not all ministering spirits, sent forth to minister to them that shall be heirs of salvation?'

It is true that no such relation as this subsists between the Church on earth and the redeemed spirits of just men in heaven. Our glorified brethren, we have no reason to think, are immediate spectators of our worship now; nor have they any ministrations to discharge towards the heirs of salvation, as the angels have. But it does not follow that they are therefore uninterested or unintelligent as to the Church's militant estate. It does not follow that they are excluded from the knowledge of the spiritual condition, the progress or reverses, the conflicts and prospects, of their brethren below. That there is nothing whatever in their present heavenly state fitted to debar them from such knowledge, is conclusively demonstrated by an express instance—as good in this case as many—namely, that of the martyred ones of Christ, whose 'souls' are seen in vision 'under the altar,' and heard crying with a loud voice and saying, 'How long, Lord, holy and true, dost thou not judge and avenge our blood on them that dwell on the earth? And white robes were given unto every one of them; and it was said unto them, that they should rest yet for a little season, until their fellow-servants also and their brethren, that should be killed as they were, should be fulfilled.' Here we see no small knowledge of what is going forward in the Church on earth possessed by souls in heaven; and it can scarcely be a too great refining on the passage if we remind you that these intelligent souls—intelligent not only in heaven's history and services, but in earth's present history and sorrows too—are represented to us as 'under the altar'—the chiefest symbol and instrument of priesthood—as if to shadow forth the truth that it is on that priesthood that their intelligence in some way depends. But what I more immediately ask you to notice is, that these souls are not unaware of the aspect of affairs here below. They know that their own blood is not yet avenged. They know the slow and tardy steps of justice, as it is guided by the wisdom, and restrained by the long-suffering, of God towards their persecutors. They have intelligent confidence in that justice in the long run; but they are aware of its present delay. Nor are they checked of God for expressing their information; but rather soothed and quieted, and have their information still more enlarged.

Now, it is very true that, so far as this instance goes, it indicates only knowledge of a very limited matter; but then it is in circumstances which surely argue, among the redeemed in heaven, knowledge of earthly affairs to a far more unlimited extent. Shall the redeemed in glory see the dark side of things—the triumph and temporary impunity of the wicked—and shall they not know the brighter side, and the prosperity, and prospects, and progress of the righteous? Shall they see enough of the Church's estate to understand its bearings on their own past history and wrongs, and on their own rightful claims and vindication, and shall there be withholden from them an insight into its larger and grander bearings upon the claims and the wrongs of Christ—its bearings on his glory—on his seeing of the travail of his soul, and being satisfied? Is it consistent with the spirit of heaven that the redeemed should see the present Church on earth merely in relation to their own personal interests, and not in the more generous and enlarged conception of its relation to God and his anointed One? And when the glorified are seen to have real and true intelligence of what passes here below, is not the question, in all that appertains to the principle of it, finally settled, and the mere *extent* of their knowledge after the fact of it is evident, a matter of comparatively easy solution?

It is manifest, then, that the Church above has intelligent acquaintance, and therefore inevitable sympathy, with the Church on earth. And I think it must be plain that the great medium or organ of their knowledge is the execution in heaven of Christ's priesthood at the right hand of the throne of the Majesty there. Nor is it possible to conceive a medium more satisfactory, effective, and complete. In the eighth chapter of Revelation we have a very grand description of our Lord, in the fulfilment of a portion of his duties as our celestial High Priest. We are told that 'another angel'—manifestly the Angel and Mediator of the covenant—'came and stood at the altar, having a golden censer; and there was given him much incense, that he should offer it with the prayers of all saints upon the golden altar which was before the throne.' That the spirits of just men made perfect, though not present in our assemblies and closets below, nor immediate spectators of our worship here, are present around that altar before the throne—spectators of our worship as it appears there—that is, as God sees it—we know. And it is surely easy to believe that the advantage they thus possess for understanding the condition of the Church is not less, but greater, than if they revisited it here in its militant condition. By the mediation of Christ we see them made intelligently aware of 'the prayers of all saints.' They become cognizant of these prayers in their combined and united fullness; not by any laboured effort of their own to piece together ten thousand isolated portions of their own knowledge of them, but after they are combined, with no omissions and no perversions, by the ministering hand of our glorious High Priest before the throne. But the 'prayers of all saints' at any moment are the very best reflection and exposition of the affairs, and dangers, and prospects of the whole Church at that moment. Nothing so embodies the successes or failures—the joys and sorrows—the conflicts and conquests of the Church, as her prayers. Her history is mirrored in her prayers with perfect accuracy. Give me 'the prayers of all saints,' and I will tell you the condition of the Church—far more accurately than if, with the swiftness of the angels' wings and of the lightning flash, I had coursed through all her assemblies, and witnessed with eyes of flesh the estate of all her families and all her members. Give me the prayers of all saints, and I will write you a Church history such as historian never wrote.

This advantage the redeemed in heaven have by being present while the angel of the covenant offers before the throne the prayers of all saints. And if to this we add that his intercessions are with infinite accuracy grounded continually on the ever-varying estate of his people on earth, and every individual of them, we will see that the priesthood of Christ in heaven is, if I may so speak, a kind of divine dial, on which the whole history of the Church on earth may, with perfect accuracy, be read off at every moment by the redeemed brethren in heaven.

Thus much on the one side of this noble theme. And turning now to the other side, or the correlative and supplementary truth, it will be equally plain,—

Secondly, that the priesthood of Christ in glory is the medium of intelligent sympathy for the Church below with the interests and worship of the Church above than they from us. We cannot know by what varied means God might make up the removal of such a medium or organ of knowledge to them; but we do know that there is nothing in our whole estate here below that could remedy such a loss to us. Were the worship of our departed brethren in heaven altogether dissociated from the priesthood of our Lord, we must be aware from our own experience that we could form no conception of its elements or nature, and consequently could have no real sympathy with them. Direct acquaintance with the infinite, eternal immensity of God, and direct access to communion with God therein, we cannot have. No man cometh unto the Father but by Jesus—by Jesus in the execution of his priesthood. Through the medium of that priesthood we know the aspect in which the divine nature reveals itself to us, to be adored and trusted in—to be glorified and enjoyed. We know the satisfied perfection of its infinite justice, and the satisfying and ever-ready communications of its infinite favour and fatherly and gracious complacency. We know most expressly the revealed and stipulated blessings which we may ask and expect, and the whole terms of peace and grace in which, in our unworthiness and helplessness, we may nevertheless stand towards the great God of heaven and earth. For they are laid down in a covenant, which could not more clearly or explicitly embody them than in its exceeding great and precious promises; and with sufficient spiritual light we may understand our relation and intercourse with God, and his with us—I will say far more satisfactorily, and profoundly, and convincingly, and with far less scope for error, than our relation and intercourse with one another in any of those ties whatsoever that bind us to each other here.

It is in this self-same everlasting covenant-sealed and ministered by the self-same priesthood of our celestial High Priest—that the redeemed in glory worship God. Their spiritual light and insight into their covenant with God far exceed ours. 'We see through a glass darkly;' they 'face to face.' Here 'we know in part;' they 'know even as also they are known.' But what they know fully above, is what we know also truly, though partially, if we have the Spirit's teaching, here below. What they see face to face is the same that we see through a glass darkly—by the help of the Word and the medium of ordinances in the Church militant. Their worship is, in all its constituting elements, in its materials and its spirit, identical with ours. We are not cut off from intelligent sympathy with saints in heaven—our brethren of whom we have been for a time bereaved. The elements of their joy and worship are the very elements of our own believing consciousness here below. Their use of Christ in his priesthood is identical with ours. Their mode of access to the throne in glory is our medium of access to the throne of grace; the themes of their thanksgiving and praise are ours; and the covenant which encompasses and guarantees onto eternity all their joy is ours too; for though our house be not so with God as theirs is, he hath made with us the self-same covenant, ordered in all things and sure, and the High Priest at his right hand for ever protecteth its validity.

> *Take comfort, Christians, when your friends*
> *In Jesus fall asleep.*

They are not carried beyond the compass of your communion, nor rapt away to a realm and exercises defying your comprehension and baffling your sympathy. Your own conversation—your citizenship—even while here, is in heaven. You are not strangers and foreigners, but fellow—citizens with the saints and of the house-hold of God. Ye are come unto Mount Zion, unto the city of the living God, to the heavenly Jerusalem, to the spirits of your beloved departed ones made perfect. They have the deepest sympathy with you; and only earthliness can shut you out from sympathy with them. Your relief against every tendency to earthliness is in the sympathy and services of the High Priest in heaven; and by that priesthood at the right hand of the throne the children of faith on earth and of glory in heaven are knit together in one communion, and the angels of God do service to them. For in the glorious ministrations of the heavenly priesthood of Christ we see heaven opened, and the angels of God ascending and descending upon the Son of Man.

And now, laying our hearts open by faith to the soothing and exalting influence of divine revelations such as these, what force should we not find in the consentient voices of apostles, psalmists, prophets, as they call upon us saying,—'If ye then be risen with Christ, seek those things which are above, where Christ sitteth on the right hand of God. Set your affection on things above, not on things on the earth. For your life is hid with Christ in God.' 'He that dwelleth in the secret place of the Most High shall abide under the shadow of the Almighty.' Come, my people, enter into these your celestial chambers; and when Christ, who is your life, shall appear, ye also shall appear with him in glory. Amen.

CHRIST'S OWN HOUSE[1]

Christ as a Son over his own house.—Hebrews 3:6

HAS Christ a house, or church, or kingdom on the earth? If so, is it distinct from every other kingdom? Is Christ its only head?—and, Is it free?

The Free Church of Scotland answers, yes, to each of these questions; and thereby announces Principles of which, in the providence of Christ, she has been made a special conservator and witness.

I. Has Christ a house or kingdom on the earth?

He has. He has a house, as the text affirms. He has a house that has been given to him by his Father; and his prerogative concerning it is in some sense implicated with his Sonship. He is a Son over his own house. It is a house that has been committed to him especially because of his eternal Sonship. His relation to it is fitted to elicit the evidence, and illustrate the meaning, of his Sonship. For the history of that house will be such as to draw upon the resources of his Sonship;— upon its fullness of grace and truth; its glory as of the only-begotten of the Father; its riches of love and interest, of acceptability and prevailing advocacy, with the Father. Not without scope given for bringing into play all resources of his eternal Sonship shall his great work of reconciliation and adoption be achieved. Intimately is his possession of this house bound up with his being a Son. Christ is a 'Son over his own house.'

[1] [Originally published as a pamphlet: *Christ's 'Own House'* (London: T. Nelson and Sons, 1859).]

This house is not in heaven, but on the earth. 'Whose house are we,' says Paul. 'We;' not disembodied spirits made perfect in glory, but men in flesh and blood, treading still this lower world; pilgrims and strangers on the earth, yet fellow-citizens with the saints and of the household of God—this house over which God presides in the person of his Son.

We are this house of his. We constitute a house. We are not isolated units. Such is not the condition into which we pass when we come forth from the world and are separated unto God. We are compacted together as an house for the Lord. We are not merely disintegrated one by one from the world. We enter into a kingdom of God. Our deliverance from the power of darkness translates us into the kingdom of God's dear Son. When brought forth from the house of the strong man, we are introduced into the house of one stronger than he, 'whose house we' now 'are.' And his house is visible on the earth—visible even as 'we are.'

Many would allow to Christ an unseen kingdom—his invisible Church: 'the whole number of the elect that have been, are, or shall be gathered together into one under Christ the head thereof.' But that he has a visible Church—a visible, organized kingdom of his own on the earth, 'consisting of all those throughout the world that profess the true religion together with their children,' they seem entirely to deny, or at least consistently should deny, to justify their opposition to the principles which we are this day considering.

But their crude unchristian fancy cuts deeper, and goes a greater length, than they imagine. It goes to heathenize the earth hopelessly and for ever; to give the world as a whole to Satan.

We are accustomed to believe that the world does not belong to him; that however his terrible and still subsisting relation to it may be stated, it is a relation mightily affected by the Son's redeeming work upon the cross,—that cursed tree, yet true triumphal car, in which he spoiled principalities and powers, and made a show of them openly. We bear in mind that the tenure by which the prince of darkness held the world—the 'handwriting' on which with subtle malice he pleaded, was taken out of the way and nailed by the Seed of the Woman to that cross by which he bruised the serpent's head. And we have good warrant to maintain (1 Cor. 3:22) that the world is ours if we are Christ's, and not his whose works Christ came to destroy. For Christ is 'the Saviour of the world' (1 John 4:14).

But I know of no sense in which he can be the Saviour of the world if he has, and is to have, no visible kingdom here. Nevertheless, it is expressly said, 'He came not to condemn the world, but that the world through him might be saved.' He came to dethrone and cast out the world's prince; and contemplating in immediate anticipation the crisis of his great work, he said, 'Now is the judgment of this world; now shall the prince of this world be cast out.'

But grant to the Lord Jesus a headship merely over the Church invisible, and all this language is evacuated and falsified. Christ is not the Saviour of the world if all his kingly rule is exerted and exhausted in regenerating his elect, preserving them in grace while here, and then withdrawing them one by one to heaven. And the god of this world is not conquered and cast out if this is all the reprisal that Messiah the Prince makes upon his territory. History, assuredly, will not own him as the saviour of Italy who shall come merely with compassion and a strong hand to carry off in safety some Italians to another land, effecting their escape for them one by one, however numerous the fugitives, or to howsoever blest and free a commonwealth and territory elsewhere he may translate them.[1] And he shall not be styled the conqueror of Italy's real tyrant, sitting on the seven hills, who shall only rescue from his grasp a portion of his victims, leaving him the fair land he has blighted, and the unhumbled throne of iniquity he has erected there. He only is the saviour of Italy and the victor of Italy's tyrant, who casts the tyrant from his throne and secures 'Italy to the Italians.'

Not any more is he 'the Saviour of the world' whose whole work consists in simply conveyancing away from it certain of its inhabitants, leaving, however, the world itself as a whole doomed and abandoned to Satan still. The prince of this world is in no sense dethroned, and the world itself in no sense saved, on such a scheme as that!

---

[1] [The references in this paragraph appear to be to the contemporary events of the Second Italian Independence War of 1859.]

But such is not the Saviour's scheme. He has denounced and doomed the god of this world as a usurper. By his cross he has undermined his reign, and spoiled him of all the weapons whereby he could prevail; to make it good he has erected his visible Church or kingdom on the earth; and he is progressively urging back and hemming in the great adversary for a final and exterminating blow. This world is not given over to Satan. The earth God hath given to the children of men. The Son of man, in name of the sons of men, hath claimed, and conquered, and gained it.

The world is ours by birthright. A tyrant hath usurped it and oppressed us. But we look not round in vain for a deliverer, for a Prince to head our rebellion, our revolt, our revolution. 'To us a child is born, to us a Son is given; and the government shall be upon his shoulder: and his name shall be called Wonderful, Counsellor, The Mighty God, The everlasting Father, The Prince of Peace. Of the increase of his government and peace there shall be no end, upon the throne of David, and upon his kingdom, to order it with judgment and with justice from henceforth even for ever. The zeal of the Lord of hosts will perform this.' And the time will come when,—the Church being visible in all the earth, and the Lord's name great among the Gentiles, from the rising of the sun unto the going down of the same,—it shall be seen that the world is not lost, but saved; not abandoned to Satan, unto the verifying of his boast and the triumph of his malice, but rescued by 'righteousness and strength' from his fell usurpation, and saved by the Son of man to the Father's glory; while the tyrant is for ever flung out of it, and none are given over to perdition but those who perish in his gainsaying—accomplices with him that hath mined them, and enemies to him who came to save.

If Christ has no visible kingdom on the earth—and one, too, that shall have its legitimate and final triumph over all the earth—then men may be saved individually; but the world as a whole is lost. Moreover, on this scheme, Satan is the acknowledged prince of this world still; Messiah, in particular, has no ostensible interest nor standing ground, nor camp, nor banner within its borders; those that perish with Satan, perish for being faithful to the actual and only reigning monarch; while Messiah's ransomed ones, the god of this world may scorn, as some rebellious subjects of his own, that have been surreptitiously abetted in their rebellion, and secretly enabled to escape. But give me Christ's visible kingdom on the earth; let me hear proclamation made by the God of heaven, 'I have set my King upon my holy hill of Zion;' let me see his standard set up, even Shiloh's, and to him let the gathering of the people be, even those that have made a covenant with heaven by sacrifice,—a sacrifice that has broken their covenant with hell, and spoiled the principalities of darkness, making rebellion against Satan both legitimate and possible, because Satan has himself been judged;—then the ransomed of the Lord are not a band of secret conspirators or refugees—rebels after whom their undethroned prince can send forth any 'handwriting' or writ of apprehension. They are the loyal subjects of the reigning monarch who sitteth on the throne of his father David; no one perishes for being faithful to the actual prince in power; traitors only perish with the outcast serpent; and the world is saved to the glory of God.

That the house over which Christ presides as a Son is a visible society, is plain from the antithesis and contrast instituted between it and the sacred commonwealth presided over by Moses as a servant. 'Christ as a Son over his own house was faithful to him that appointed him, as also Moses was faithful in all his house' (verses 6 and 2). But it was an outstanding organized society of which 'Moses was king in Jeshurun, when the heads of the people and the tribes of Israel were gathered together' (Deut. 33:5). Their entire polity had been framed, their whole government instituted, all their rites and practices enjoined, at Sinai; when the Shechinah—apparent, first, in Israel's interest, in the humble burning bush—*nec tamen consumebatur*[1] —had flamed up in terrific glory to the mountain peak where the Lawgiver's throne was set—a typical ascension. And the 'chariots of the Lord were twenty thousand, even thousands of angels: the Lord among them, in Sinai, in the holy place. Thou hast ascended on high, thou hast led captivity captive: thou hast received gifts for men; yea, for the rebellious also, that the Lord God might dwell among them' (Psa. 68:17, 18).

---

[1] [Latin: And yet it was not consumed.]

So speaketh the Spirit expressly, concerning the inauguration of the Old Testament Church—indisputably a visible kingdom. Is it not remarkable that the very language is transferred over to express the constitution of the New Testament Church also, when Paul makes its formal inauguration to hinge on the ascension of our Lord—the true Shechinah: 'When he ascended up on high, he led captivity captive, and gave gifts to men. And he gave some, apostles; and some, prophets; and some, evangelists; and some, pastors and teachers: for the perfecting of the saints, for the work of the ministry: for the edifying of the body of Christ' (Eph. 4:8-12). Is the one kingdom thus inaugurated less visible than the other? The New Testament Church, indeed, is more simple and spiritual,—catholic also, and cosmopolitan—for the middle wall of partition is removed, carnal ordinances abrogated, sacred places set aside, national distinctions disowned. But the enlargement of Christ's house is not, surely, its annihilation; and its government, if less carnal, ceremonial, confined, is only more efficient, and expansive, and free. And to this agree the words of the prophets; as it is written: 'After this I will return, and will build again the tabernacle of David, which is fallen down; and I will build again the ruins thereof; and I will set it up; that the residue of men might seek after the Lord, and all the Gentiles upon whom my name is called, saith the Lord who doeth all these things' (Amos 9:11, 12).

II. Is Christ's house—his visible Church, which is his kingdom on the earth—distinct from all other kingdoms?

It is. It is 'his own house,'—emphatically, peculiarly, distinctively 'his own.' It is as distinct from other kingdoms as the house of Moses or commonwealth of Israel was distinct from the kingdom of Egypt, or the nomadic hordes of Amalek, or the nations of Edom and Moab. Nay, by how much the more spiritual and cosmopolitan Christ's kingdom now is in gospel times, by so much the more manifestly is it distinct from every other kingdom, and its power distinct from all other power.

Nor is it from other kingdoms, considered merely as heathen or ungodly, that Christ's visible kingdom—his own house—is distinct.

Even when 'all the ends of the world shall remember and turn unto the Lord, and all the kindreds of the nations shall worship before him,' the distinction will remain. The kingdoms of this world shall then become the kingdoms of our Lord and his Christ. But they will be the 'kingdoms of this world' still—though Christ's; they will not be 'the kingdom of heaven.' And they will be many—'kingdoms'—not Christ's 'own house,' which is one. And being many, they may be of diverse constitutions, too: monarchies, empires, republics; for all these forms may consist with their being the kingdoms of Christ. In every light clearly they will not be the one kingdom of heaven—the visible Church which, with its many branches, is one household of faith, and in which the presiding Son hath given—no sword, but—the keys to his faithful stewards.

For this is the one great abiding mark of distinction between the power that is in the Church, and all other power,—namely, that it is wholly spiritual, dealing exclusively with the consciences of men. The power of civil magistracy deals with men's persons and properties, their liberties and lives. His is the power of the sword. The Church has no such power. She has neither power nor right to inflict punishment on men's persons, nor to control their liberties, nor to dispose of their property, far less of their lives. Her power can only act upon their consciences. And if it can abridge them in anything, it is only in what the kingdoms of this world can neither give, nor remove, nor restore— privileges wholly spiritual. Hence the weapons which the Church has received to wield are not carnal—not the axe girt round with rods, emblem of the Roman lictor's office,[1] the axe indicating the extreme power of life and death, the rods symbolizing minor inflictions for minor crimes,—not the sword, to recur to the Scriptural figure. The Church, indeed, is a power in the world—nay, an aggressive power. She is in the field. And she is militant. And she needs armour and weapons of war. But the strongholds she assails are the hearts and consciences of men. The walls and bulwarks she levels with the ground are the dark thoughts of mansoul, the prejudices and proud imagi- nations which darken the character of God and defy his will. And

[1] [A lictor was a bodyguard to the magistrate in ancient Rome.]

the captives which she binds in triumph to her advancing car are the thoughts and affections of men brought into sweet captivity to the love and obedience of her King. 'The weapons of our warfare are not carnal but mighty through God to the pulling down of strongholds; casting down imaginations, and every high thing that exalteth itself against the knowledge of God, and bringing into captivity every thought to the obedience of Christ.' 'And thanks be unto God which always causeth us to triumph in Christ, and maketh manifest the savour of his knowledge by us in every place.'

Great is this power. And it shall prevail. But it is utterly diverse from all other power; insomuch, that from its very diversity it never can come into conflict with any legitimate power whatever, whether civic or political, military or imperial—any power of any kind that has any right to be. Nay, all righteous power—all power that has right, in reason and in nature, to be—the progress of the Church's power will tend indirectly to confirm. Can the friends of civil order object to that? All unrighteous power—power founded on mere might, and having no right to be—the progress of the Church's power, which is light and truth, will tend indirectly to overthrow. Can the friends of civil liberty object to that? Shall this blessed sunshine be blamed if it has in store a sun-stroke for beasts of prey, and if then it lights the eagles to their gathering together?

Great is the power in the Church. For it is the power of the truth, and of the Spirit that beareth witness to the truth. Its sphere is the conscience of man; and its weapon is the Word of God.

'Pilate therefore said unto him: Art thou a king then? Jesus answered, Thou sayest that I am a king. To this end was I born, and for this cause came I into the world, that I might bear witness unto the truth.'

III. Is Christ the alone head of this house?

He is. Even as a 'Son over his own house.' He can have no rival, no vicar, no colleague. He is alone the head and king—the Only-begotten Son over his own house. And we shall hang upon him all its glory.

The sole headship of Christ, and the leading prerogatives implied in it, will be manifest, if we reflect that from Christ alone the Church has—1, her existence; 2, her organization; 3, her action; and 4, her efficiency.

1. She has her *existence* from Christ alone. 'On this rock,' says the Son, speaking concerning his own house, and one of his many relations to it,—'on this rock I will build my church.' It is the Lord that doth, build up Jerusalem and gathereth together the dispersed of Israel, 'I am the Lord your Holy One, the creator of Israel, your king: this people have I formed for myself; they shall show forth my praise.' The formation of the Church is a divine work. Every house is builded by some man; but he that built all things is God. And this man—this God-man—is worthy of more glory than Moses, inasmuch as he who hath builded the house hath more honour than the house. It is Christ that builds the Church,—and it is the visible Church, I again remind you, which is here treated of, and here declared to be his building. The visible Church hath its existence from Christ.

2. Simultaneously with existence the Church derives *organisation* from Christ. For she cannot exist save as organised. The Church as a kingdom is an organised society. The Church as a body is an organism.

Listen to the remarkable terms, applicable only to a living organism, in which the Spirit writes of the Church. 'Holding the head, from whom all the body by joints and bands having nourishment ministered, and knit together, increaseth with the increase of God' (Col. 2:19). And again, 'Speaking the truth in love, we grow up into him in all things which is the head, even Christ: from whom the whole body, fitly joined together and compacted by that which every joint supplieth, according to the effectual working in the measure of every part, maketh increase of the body unto the edifying of itself in love; even until we all come in the unity of the faith, and of the knowledge of the Son of God, unto a perfect man, unto the measure of the stature of the fullness of Christ' (Eph. 4:15, 6). Nor are these remarkable expressions to be applied to the Church invisible. They refer to that 'body of Christ' for the 'edifying' of which Christ has just been said to give apostles, and prophets, and evangelists, pastors, and teachers, for the 'work of a ministry,' Whose existence alone, were it nothing else, makes the Church a visible society. And mark how, in that singular chapter (1 Cor. 12) in which, more than anywhere else in Scripture, the Church is treated of as a living organism—'God hath set the members every one of them in the body as it hath pleased him; and ye are the body of Christ, and members in particular;'—mark, I say, how the apostle indicates that it is the visible Church which is the subject of his theme throughout, when he closes his train of thought thus: 'And God hath set some in the church, first, apostles; secondarily, prophets; thirdly, teachers.'

From all which we gather—*first*, that this organism has all its organisation from Christ; and, *secondly*, that its organisation as a kingdom is vitally implicated in the appointment of its ministers or stewards by Christ himself.

For he himself gives office-bearers to his Church. He did so in the Old Testament Church. He appeared to Moses in the bush, and commissioned him there as a servant; and 'Moses was faithful.' He gave directions for the setting apart of Aaron to the priesthood; and—'Aaron's rod blossomed.' Also, 'no man taketh this honour upon him, but he that is called of God, as was Aaron.' In the days of his flesh he selected his twelve apostles. And when one of them fell from his apostleship, the eleven appealed to their King, now in heaven, to show whom he had chosen to fill his place. From heaven he appeared in his glory, calling Saul the persecutor to be his apostle to the Gentiles. And the apostles, acting under Christ as ministers of his will, as stewards, or factors, or commissioners in his house, appointed in his name and by his authority other office-bearers, everywhere, as the progress of the Church required.

In all these instances it will be admitted that Christ himself gave officers to his Church.

But he does so still. And nothing in any kingdom ever known is more regular or wisely regulated than the ordinary procedure in which validly appointed office-bearers in the Church come to be invested with their office. To be validly an office-bearer in the house of Christ, a man must be endowed with the gift or faculty suitable to the nature, and requisite to the exercise, of the particular office. This in the first instance. And such gift is from Christ alone (Eph. 4:7; 1 Cor. 12:6). Inwardly he must have a desire to serve Christ in that office—a desire that must come from Christ's own Spirit. And outwardly he must be guided and directed to it in providence, the movements of which are all in Christ's own hands. Further, he must be called and welcomed by Christ's flock; and he must be approved and ordained of Christ's ministers—men already clothed with the same office themselves. There is no place here, in all this procedure, or any stage of it, for the interference or intervention of any power or authority external to the Church itself. And all power exercised in this matter within the Church is directly and solely from Christ.

For any authority of civil courts or earthly kings to interpose, is, at least, as unwarrantable and offensive, as if a foreign potentate should dictate to this city in the selection of your civic magistrates, or dictate to this nation the succession to the crown; or as if a stranger interfered in the government of your family, and presumed to chastise your child. In the one case, the foreign power might enjoin the appointment of the very magistrate or monarch, whom the city or the nation intended to elect; nevertheless, his interposition would be repelled by the indignation of an insulted people. And in the other case, though the stranger might punish your offending child, exactly to the measure of what you had purposed to inflict, you would proceed against him notwithstanding, on the ground that infliction of pain by him upon your child was not correction, but a crime—not chastisement in his hand, but assault.

Even when office-bearers have been given by Christ, and are validly and truly his, they do not in any sense rule the Church as lords, or kings, or heads, or co-ordinate coadjutors with Jesus. He remains the only Head and King. They have no legislative functions. Their functions are exclusively administrative. They are ministers of Christ. They administer; they set forth, enforce, and apply his laws alone—his laws as written in his word. They are stewards, not lords. And 'it is required of stewards that a man be found faithful' (1 Cor. 4:2).

3. From Christ alone the Church has all her *action*. Her existence is an organisation. Her organism is designed for action.

Now, all the action of the Church takes place within the limits, and by the rule, of ordinances. These ordinances are exclusively from Christ. And they are prescribed and defined in his Word.

The Church has the Sabbath from Christ, the Son over his own house—even the Son of man, who is Lord also of the Sabbath. And by divine right she can demand all civil liberty which the nature of the case requires, to secure for her the actual enjoyment of this boon, to prevent this gift from her Lord being either nullified or impaired.

To the Church belong the oracles of God, for they constitute 'the law of the house,' the charter of the kingdom. The ordinance of united prayer is hers also; 'My house shall be called an house of prayer for all nations.' A standing ministry is likewise hers from Christ, as all her ordinances are; and it implies her right to assemble her members for the public worship of God, and to listen unmolested to the preaching of his gospel. The sacraments are given to her only by her heavenly King; he only has a right to say who shall receive and who shall be denied them; his own officers alone can minister them; his word alone guides them in doing so; and to him alone they are responsible in dispensing them.

The ordinance of the ruling eldership the Church also has from Christ. By his Holy Spirit he giveth her elders and overseers;—'Take heed to the flock over which the Holy Ghost hath made you overseers;'—that, by their service, purity may be preserved within her pale; offences purged away; censures inflicted on scandalous members and removed from penitents; the health of the body preserved; and divine displeasure averted. And this ordinance implies that the Church has right to call and to conduct such councils, synods, and assemblies, as may be needful for the right ordering of the affairs of Christ's house, and under his presidency to transact whatsoever his word may direct there anent.

I have spoken of privileges belonging manifestly to the Church as considered as visible,[1] as an organised, outstanding society. Ordinances,

[1] The intelligent reader will see that this point is not unadvisedly insisted on throughout these pages. For, unquestionably, the Cardross case shapes itself finally into this issue: Has Christ a visible church? We confess we shrink from fashioning the question into its other form: Is Christ to be permitted to have a

indeed, in their very nature, imply the visibility of the Church; and the headship of Christ is manifestly implicated in them all. They are the limits, and the forms, within which the living organism of the Church is ordained to act. And they are all from Christ.

4. The Church has all her *efficiency* from Christ.

Her very being is an organism. Her action is efficient. It is not as the action of one that runneth uncertainly, or that beateth the air. It is guided by spiritual intelligence, sustained by spiritual strength, replete with results that are spiritual and everlasting.

But all this efficiency is from Christ. All blessing on her ordinances—all benefit in the enjoyment of her rights—all prosperity and spiritual health in the exercise of her functions, are from him alone. By his presence only, and the working of his Spirit, can any real work be done in the visible Church, or any real issues result from her operations. If Christ be not present, presiding as a Son over his own house, in the assemblies of his people, and in the councils of his stewards, no church work is done at all. His people are not enlightened, refreshed, sanctified under ordinances, save as Christ, by his Spirit, is present in the midst of them. His officers and stewards are doing no work of his, unless Christ is guiding them by his own heavenly wisdom, and working in them to will and to do of his own designs. For the keys that he hath given them open nothing, save as he opens the door of faith and penitence; and can lock no soul out from spiritual blessing, save as he sanctions, and, indeed, himself effects the exclusion. The sanctuary is not Bethel, unless the goings of the King be there; and the courts of the Church are the most insignificant and inefficient assemblies on earth, unless the Lord be there himself to rule and overrule—to guide, and sanction, and effectuate their decisions.

But when the Only-begotten which is in the bosom of the Father is present, presiding as a Son over his own house, or any faithful branch of it; and his servants, like Moses, are faithful in all his house, receiving

---

visible Church? [The Cardross case was a famous case in the ecclesiastical courts of the Free Church of Scotland. A minister who was deposed by the church for behaviour unbecoming the office, appealed to the civil courts in an attempt to overturn the decision of the church courts, effectiviely rejecting the right of the church to rule on ecclesiastical matters.]

the word at his mouth, and ministering in the wisdom and will of the Lord; how far-seeing is the intelligence with which mortal men may then be found endowed, and how efficiently transacted the work which the Spirit prompts them to essay and achieve! For the Son in this house hath all power given to him in heaven and in earth. By his almighty Providence he seconds what, according to his will, his ministers of state have decided must be done in his kingdom. And he binds in heaven what they have bound on earth.

Now, if a house, or body, or kingdom, have its existence, organization, action, efficiency, all from Christ, must not Christ be her only head?

IV. Is the house of Christ free? Or, rather, now the question comes simply to be: what is the nature, and what the limits, of the freedom which, manifestly, such a house must have?

Is it a claim of right on her part to do simply what she pleases? It has been perpetually thus misrepresented, and ever will be so by those, who, through spiritual blindness, have no perception of her connection with Christ,—who can see nothing in the visible Church but a voluntary society of their fellow-citizens exercising their civil liberty to unite for religious objects. Having no spiritual perception of the fact that Christ is the Creator of this society; that Christ is its indwelling Lord and king; that Christ confers office on all its lawful officers; that Christ presides gloriously over all its legitimate assemblies,—presides efficiently by his Word and Spirit, even as the word and spirit of no earthly monarch surrounded by his ministers of state can be efficient; that Christ sitteth Counsellor alone, and only wise, in its councils, and countersigns with heaven's signet-ring all its legitimate decisions; and that then he girds his sword upon his thigh, and putteth forth the arm of his might to carry these decisions forth into accomplishment:—blind utterly to these spiritual wonders,—to the wall of fire that is round about, and the glory that is in the midst—as the prophet's servant was blind to the chariots of fire and horses of fire that encompassed the mountain and safe-guarded his master, they have, in all ages, scorned the Church's claim of independence, as if it were equivalent to an assertion of her right to do whatever she may please. The Church challenges no such freedom. Her claim is exactly what Jehovah asserted on behalf of Israel: 'Let my son go free that he may serve me.' The freedom of the Church is freedom to obey her king,—to hearken to his alone voice in his word, and execute his will alone. With this freedom the 'Son over his own house' hath made his own house free. And 'if the Son hath made her free, she is free indeed' (John 8:36).

Such freedom, for generations, the Church of Scotland had—protected by the State; furthered also, as she was, by the State in temporal things for the more abundant discharge of her spiritual functions. Her connection with the State she never understood as trammelling her independence as the servant and steward of the King, bound to be 'faithful as a servant, as Moses was in all his house.' And when a construction was put on the terms of her establishment which introduced between her and her Lord another—as that construction glaringly and abundantly did—she disrupted herself from the State, and came forth, as from Egypt, to be free. To the eye of faith her exodus was glorious and good; for by the power of faith it was calmly and nobly done; orderly and edifying; and no mischance was in it. Her King went before her, and her King was her rearward. He smiled on her fidelity. He seconded and manifestly carried out into accomplishment all her leading decisions at that great epoch of her history. And, with all her unworthiness since, he is not utterly withholding from her tokens that he remembereth her and the love of her espousals, when she went after him in the wilderness, in a land that was not sown.

Doubtless she doeth well to commemorate that transaction this day, and to recall to—on liberal thoughts intent—the sufferings her faithful pastors underwent, and many of them still undergo, as witnesses that Christ is 'a Son over his own house' in Scotland,—even Scotland's historic Church, national and free. For assuredly the sacrifice your pastors made, was made in the service of the Christian people, and in defence of their Christian rights. And while in readiness to sacrifice for a cause so holy, your pastors may rightly be expected to be ensamples to the flock; in this, as in all things else; yet the people, whose cause it is, equally with theirs, ought to shrink from demanding at their hands a proportion of that sacrifice excessive, undue, and burdensome. Rather should they so unite with them in bearing it, that it may not fall undue anywhere.

Finally: rejoice, brethren, in the completeness and catholicity of your principles as a Church. As on the platform of Scotland—they are national, not denominational. As on the platform of the world—they are cosmopolitan; suitable in all lands alike. And, as testified unto the whole visible Church—they are not sectional, but truly catholic; unitive,—so far as they shall prevail within the Church,—to her, alas! too scattered, ranks; protective, also,—so far as they shall prevail in the world—to her, alas! too endangered, rights;—for they cover no narrow interest of ours, but proclaim what is the glory and the birth right of all branches of the Church—being simply this: that the visible church is Christ's own house; and, as such, is free. Amen.

SERMON 10

THE MANIFESTATION OF
THE SON OF PERDITION[1]

*The following sermon was preached by Hugh Martin at
Panbride on 23rd March, 1845, as appointed by the Commission of the General Assembly of the Free Church of Scotland.
The church was alarmed at the spread of Tractarianism, and
the rise again of Papacy in the United Kingdom, especially
in Ireland, and desire to call 'the attention of the people to…
the progress of the Man of Sin… and for solemn and earnest prayer to God,' because of it. Martin later preached the
sermon in Free Holburn Church, Aberdeen on 9th April,
1845, and then subsequently published it. This is one of the
earliest extant records of Martin's ministry, having been
preached when he was just 22 years old.[2]*

---

[1] [Originally published as a pamphlet: *The Manifestation of the Son of Perdition:
A Sermon, Preached in the Free Church, Panbride, on March* 23rd, *in Accordance
with the Recommendation of the Commission of the General Assembly, and in the
Free Holburn Church, Aberdeen,* on April 9th. (1845) George Davidson, Aberdeen.]

[2] [The earliest sermon available is: Hugh Martin *The Sabbath Made for Man:
a Sermon Preached in the Free Church, Panbride, on February 2, 1845, in Accordance with the Recommendation of the General Assembly.* (Dundee: M'Cosh, Park
and Dewars, 1845). This sermon is available for download online from the Yale
University Library (Beinecke Rare Book and Manuscript Library), Call number:
College Pamphlets 1474 13.]

*That man of sin shall be revealed, the son of perdition, who
opposeth and exalteth himself above all that is called God,
or that is worshipped; so that he, as God, sitteth in the
temple of God, showing himself that he is God.*
—2 Thessalonians 2:3-4

THE last and boldest stroke of the arch-enemy, in his temptation of our blessed Lord, was when he 'took him up into an exceeding high mountain, and showed him all the kingdoms of the world and the glory of them, and said unto him, All these things will I give thee, if thou wilt fall down and worship me.' But this had little effect on him whose is the earth and the fullness of it, the world and they that dwell therein; so little, indeed, that, in his answer, the Saviour passes by all notice of the bribe, as indeed worthless and ridiculous, and speaks merely of the condition that the devil had impiously connected with it: 'Get thee hence, Satan, for it is written, Thou shalt worship the Lord thy God, and him only shalt thou serve.' And it is briefly added, 'the devil leaveth him.'

That Satan retired from the unequal conflict, in deepest mortification, is not to be doubted. He knew that on this struggle was periled the problem of his own continued reign, as the god of this world and the prince of darkness. He had seized the very first opportunity, after Christ had, by the outpoured Spirit, been consecrated to the ministry of his grand achievement; and ere Jesus was yet emboldened (so to speak) by any evidences of success, the roaring lion waylaid him, and dared him to the battle. Defeated in these circumstances—the die cast against him, in such fearful odds, in his very first adventure on this diabolic and blasphemous game of his,—we may well conceive him retiring from his overthrow, and returning to his nether regions, and to the companionship of his fellows in rebellion, with the marks of such discomfiture upon his countenance, as would read forth to them more forcibly than speech the fact of his thorough and unmitigated failure. But, even if his own infernal hate had not accomplished it, his terror for the failing of his character in the eyes of those whom he had seduced from their God, would soon have dissipated from his brazen contour the evidences of his late defeat, and no doubt it was not long ere the council of hell was assembled, to devise the plan of a second best attempt.

If asked what the character and features of that second and subsequent plot of devils might be, we would have no hesitation in saying that it could be nothing else than the origination of the man of Sin, the Son of Perdition, the hell-begotten Antichrist, the Papacy. By boldly scheming out this mystery of iniquity did Satan contrive to mar the beauty of that Church, which he had vainly essayed to crush in the person of its Founder. The temple was founded amidst the songs of angels and the chorus of all heaven's holy ones, and its foundation Satan could not overturn; from the bold and blasphemous attempt he retired, in shame and failure and disgrace and wrath. But conscious disgrace and consequent rage are fearful inventors of the diabolic, and, while Satan stood aside to let the building advance, he schemed it so that ere long he should introduce such pollutions within it as should make it the presence chamber of the wicked one, rather than the temple of the living God. The external fabric must go up, notwithstanding all his efforts, but the internal arrangements are still open for him to defile and degrade by his iniquity; and thus, if the building must advance, he will at all events be revenged, by changing it from the honourable residence of Deity into the out-court and antechamber of hell.

True, a little delay must be tolerated; he must keep aloof for a while—the 'stronger than he' keeps his house at the present time, and, if he enter now, he will overcome and bind him. But let matters take their course, and ere long he may advance even to the inmost secrecies and sacrednesses; he will depose and dispossess the present proud proprietor, and set there his own vice-regent in his stead, and then 'the Man of Sin shall be revealed.' Nor will it need the device of some new and novel bribe to induce this future ambassador to take the post of honour. The spurned bribe to the Lord of Glory, though useless once, may yet, nay *will* yet, stand Satan in good stead; and the scarlet-covered Antichrist of Rome shall, in his very origin, earn well his name of Antichrist, by being successfully tempted by the offer of that throne and that glory of the nations, which the Jehovah God of all nations had indignantly rejected. He will take him to the 'pinnacle of the temple,' and show him there as God. In the interval, the fires of hell and the band of their prince inhabitant had transmuted the spurned crown into the gladly-seized tiara.

But if this was Satan's rapid reserved device, his Divine opponent was beforehand with him; for, while the wrath not of men only but of devils shall praise God, it is previously seen through and provided for. The text is a proof of this. His very plot is here minutely predicted and described, and we seem to be reading rather a description of something than merely of what he had prospectively designed. Indeed, while we expound this prophecy, we do in fact bring forth all the features of the embodied character and accomplished deeds of the Man of Sin, and do indeed pass in review before us the several acts of that tragedy of iniquity which Antichrist, in his allotted time, has been permitted to work out.

Let us, in dependence on promised aid, attempt to discover the mind of the Spirit speaking through the Apostle in these words, and we will find that the character and doings of the Church of Rome are the most complete commentary and fulfilment of their meaning.

'That Man of Sin shall be revealed, etc.' What, then, are the chief features of this apostasy? Let us address ourselves to this question, and we will find that the answer to it will bring out the object of this day's lecture.

I. This gigantic evil and apostasy is manifestly not an extended or a prevalent infidelity. It is not towards infidelity and the denial of a God that our fears are directed.

Indeed, all Scripture treats infidelity in a far more summary and unceremonious way than to give it the honour of so creditable a reference. It is looked upon as ridiculous and unworthy of creating a single fear. It is denominated folly, and the abettor of it a fool. 'The fool hath said in his heart there is no God.' Awful as the height of blasphemy is to which the infidel carries his audacity, it bears with it so much of its own refutation as to be worthy of no regard but that of unmitigated contempt, and so *pithless* a device is it, that Satan had to try a deeper trick of iniquity than this, ere he could succeed in injuring the Church of the living God sufficiently and to his mind.

Besides; this apostasy, this mystery of iniquity is looked upon as thoroughly systematized, and is set before us with a representative at its head, on whom all its character and all its guilt are collected and concentrated. 'That Man of Sin.' 'That Son of Perdition.' Such an honour as this, no one ever thinks of ascribing to infidelity. The scattered ranks of infidels present the opposite of anything like system or arrangement or co-operation. They never could collect their forces; they never could acknowledge a leader; they never could effect anything as a body. Why should they have a system—why should *they* have a governor—who deny that there is any government or any system in the universe? But concerning this iniquity, it is very different. It is represented by an individual. It is embodied in one man and his successors. It is a visible and a tangible something. It is not 'an airy nothing, but has a local habitation and a name.' It has a head. One not ashamed to show himself. One who 'sits in the temple, showing himself that he is God.'

And here is another proof of the same position. 'He sitteth in the temple.' He reverences religion. He acknowledges the claims of sacredness—the obligation of the ordinances. He maintains the order of God's house. He is not an open opposer of the truth. He assumes the character of the friend of truth. False he is to all intents and purposes; but it is the falseness of the traitor and the hypocrite, not that of the open foe, which belongs to him. His name has a reference that brings this distinctly before us. He is called the Son of Perdition, the very name given to the false-hearted disciple who betrayed his Master with a kiss. He is in the very citadel of religion's strength, and no weapons of opposition are in his hand. He copies his father, not so much in the character of the 'roaring lion,' as in that of 'the angel of light.' He has his place within the very Jerusalem of God's Church itself. See him, with cautious step and wary but false-hearted glance, daring to wield the very means of grace themselves, but doing it as some used the Scriptures, wresting them to his own and others' destruction.

Nor is it merely the religion of Deism to which this Son of Perdition pretends. It is not Infidelity, or the absence of all religion—it is not the religion of Paganism—it is not the religion of Nature—it is not even the religion of Deism, which this great apostate professes. It is nothing less than Christianity itself; the very religion of Jesus! that religion, namely, which confesses existent sin, and provides an existent atoning Saviour. It goes a far way on the right road, this iniquity. This Man of Sin does not pass by carelessly or contemptuously, in neglect or in derision, the base of the hill of holiness. He ascends the mount of God, even to its summit. But here, in saying anything apparently good of him, we must stop. Here the mysterious iniquity begins. For what purpose has he gone all this length? For what purpose has he so far reverenced the true religion, and so far ascended the hill of God? Is it that he may bend in reverence before him who sitteth on its summit, clothed in all the glories and the majesty of Godhead, controlling, by his simple will, ten thousand times ten thousand worlds? Is it to prostrate himself before the Creator of the ends of the earth, and acknowledge his divine and eternal and just and benevolent supremacy? Nay; that were no mystery of iniquity. But he ascends to the summit, to the very pinnacle of the temple, and seats himself there, showing himself that he is God. He does not deny a God. Oh! no. Far from that; he claims to be himself God. This is the mystery of audacious and blaspheming iniquity. He is no infidel, this Man of Sin. Not at all. There is a God. There is a God on earth, and the honour and the worship of him he claims as his own. This is the true meaning of his title Antichrist. Not an opposer of Christ, but a pretender to be the Christ. Infidelity is an opposer of Christ—Heathenism is an opposer of Christ—pure Deism is an opposer of Christ; but none of them on that account can properly be called an Antichrist. And so this Antichrist is something different from any and from all of these. They all deny a Christ; this acknowledges a Christ, but claims to be that Christ, and aims at the possession of his honours.

This is a most important and a most vital point. I wish you to attend well to it. Antichrist not merely impugns Christ, but claims to be Christ; not merely aims at dethroning him, but does so with the ulterior view of assuming his place. A king may have many foes; but among them there may be one who, besides being a foe, is a rival for his throne. Every enemy of a sovereign does not oppose him on the plea that he, the enemy, is the rightful sovereign. There may be many foes, but among them all there may be no anti-king. Take a historical illustration: The race of Stuart had a stern and a deadly and successful foe in Cromwell; but he never pretended to the throne, he resisted the offer of kingly power. He derided the hereditary right of sovereigns; he refused the emblems of royalty as his. He was an opposer and an enemy, but nothing more. The race of Guelph, on the other hand, had a quick and a ready and a fiery foe in Charles the pretender; but besides an enemy, they had in him a rival—a pretender to their right, and a claimant to the throne on which a nation's decision had seated them. This was an enemy risen up against them, but he was also an *anti-prince.* And so Infidelity may be an enemy of Christ, but the Papal power is all *Antichrist.* Cromwell typifies the opposing character of Infidelity; Charles, the pretender, symbolises that of the Papacy.

Thus, then, this mystery of iniquity is manifestly not a powerful or a prevalent spirit of Infidelity. Infidelity is not so much to be honoured as a source of dread; but rather to be treated with utter contempt. Infidelity never has been systematised or brought into embodied form and arrangement; whereas that which is the subject of investigation, is set before us as in a condition of complete and wondrous organisation. Still farther, this is manifestly an outward form of religion—and still farther, a form, a pretended and reverential semblance, of the only true religion, Christianity itself; and a Christ is honoured, though it be for the purpose of introducing a subsequent blasphemy, in the pretence of being the Christ. This is the origin and meaning of the title Antichrist, as something distinct from, and in advance of, a simple opposer of Christ. Now, the whole of this matter looks as little like a rampant Infidelity as we could conceive; indeed, if we be permitted the sarcasm, it is a great improvement upon Infidelity.

II. This is not a powerful secular or civil authority.

This follows very naturally in the train of thought which we have been prosecuting, and is evidently supported by an examination of the passage. As we have already said, this is manifestly a religious dominancy—an ecclesiastical and spiritual despotism, subordinating civil authority to its own power. 'He opposeth and exalteth himself above all that is called God, sitting and doing this in the temple.' Civil magistrates and rulers and princes were often called in eastern language 'gods;' and in this sense it is true that 'there be gods many and lords many.' Now, when it is affirmed that this Man of Sin opposeth and exalteth himself above all that is called God, it is manifestly implied that he subjects to himself the authority of those magistrates and governors whom God hath appointed for the benefit of his people, as the ministers to them for good, and to whom he hath solemnly delegated, as it were, a portion of his own sovereignty and dominion, and charged them to use it well, as they shall be responsible to him. But to the Church he has never made them responsible. Certain duties to the Church they assuredly owe, and, by the appointment of God, the Church ought to look for the performance of these duties, and present and enforce her claim if they are not voluntarily yielded to. But the idea of compelling their performance is manifestly absurd, from the position in which God has placed the civil authority, a position involving at once independence and responsibility—independence, as far as man in his religious prospects is placed—responsibility, towards God, and towards God alone. If the civil magistrate refuse his duty, and spurn the Church's claim, upon himself be the shame and the guilt, and unto God must he answer on the day when the secrets of all hearts shall be revealed. Of this guilt the Church is clear when she appeals and protests against it. Farther than this she has nought to do. To enter the domain of civil things is clearly forbidden. The civil and the spiritual are utterly distinct in their very essence, and are most carefully discriminated and separated in the Word of God. They are utterly heterogeneous, and what God hath separated let no man join together.

Now, on this Man of Sin and Son of Perdition, is fixed the charge of amalgamating or uniting these two. He exalteth himself above all that is called God. He not only assumes a lordship within the Church, but, under pretence of his spiritual authority—under covert of his religious character, and what he fancies his religious dominion—in short, as sitting in the temple—he drags within his domain all things civil, and the authority of all terrestrial government; and, though the Lord of glory refused to be a judge and a divider in matters earthly, this Antichrist, his opponent and his rival, seats himself on the mount of God, with the sword of civil power buckled on his thigh, and the keys of spiritual authority tied to his girdle, and when questioned of his right so to reign, spurning all control, he rises up, and defying men and blaspheming God, he impiously dangles the keys in one hand, and unsheathes the sword with the other.

This is one grand distinctive feature in Popery, sufficient in itself to settle the reference of this passage to the Papal power. We search the annals of the world in vain for another exhibition, another practical embodiment, of this iniquity. Popery alone hath grasped and gripped the secular under the arm of a spiritual despotism. Popery alone, with the gorging power of Aaron's rod, hath swallowed up the sceptres and the swords of earthly governors. Popery alone, in virtue of its spiritual authority, hath dared, as history tells, to kick the diadem from a prince's forehead! Popery alone hath made a head that wore a crown bend that the lips thereof might kiss its feet, and taste the dust upon its sandal! Popery alone hath commanded the hand that should have held a sceptre to hold a stirrup, that it might mount a beast better and nobler far than the beast that purposed to bestride it! We know no rival that Popery can have for the claim of this honour—unless, indeed, it be *Moderatism*. Moderatism hath combined under one the *civil* and the *spiritual*. But the rivalry is a failure, for Popery had the most difficult and the most noble task to do. To subject the civil to the ecclesiastical was Popery's work—but to subject the civil to the ecclesiastical went against all the probabilities and all the natural tendencies of things, as well as all the precedents of history. Moderatism hath taken a lower field—hath tried a more ignoble plan of uniting them. Moderatism has yielded up the spiritual at the demand of the *civil* and the *secular*. It was easily done, this. It was a downward, unopposed movement, it exhibited cowardice, not vigour. Moreover, it was a natural movement. 'The world knoweth its own.' We place the abettors of Moderatism far lower in the scale of talent and ingenuity than those of Popery, and yet we accord them their wretched claim to originality, in changing the method of the combination.

III. But we have not exhausted the full meaning of 'exalting himself above all that is called God.'

God maketh himself known by the legislative and the ruling authority which he delegates to the secular magistrate. But this is not all 'that whereby God maketh himself known.' We have still the whole domain peculiar to the Church itself, with all the ordinances which God hath established therein, to cause his name to be remembered; and all this the Man of Sin opposeth, and above all this he exalteth himself. The holy Word, the worship of the living God, supplication and prayer, and the sacraments—these are the institutions of God within the Church, which is his own house, and these are to remain for ever, as he has settled them; and to God, for the right use of them, man is responsible, and to him alone.

But Antichrist hath risen up, as Lord of the conscience, commanding and demanding obedience to its own prescribed forms in the use of these, under the impiously denounced penalty of exclusion from the mystical body of the living God, in which alone the true Spirit is. Rome hath added thereto, and taken away therefrom, and hath taught for doctrines the commandments and traditions of men. Rome hath dared to abrogate and annul and alter and modify what Christ hath appointed as the order of his own house and family. Rome hath taken the blessed word of God, and refused it to the common people of her communion, or given it tantalizing only (as long as she dared maintain the practice) in a language which the people cannot understand. She hath wrapped this brightest gift of God to men (brightest next to the gift of him who was the Word made flesh)—hath wrapped it within an impenetrable covering, and hath sealed it fast from vulgar gaze; and if questioned of the impression of that impious seal, our answer is that it exhibits the mark of the beast. Rome hath taken the worship of God, and nullified it likewise, by performing it, or parts of it, in an unknown tongue; and to let the besotted worshippers know the proper intervals for their prostrate genuflexions, a miserable bell is tinkled by a more miserable bellman, as if the beings within this pretended temple of God were unconscious brute beasts, incapable of being addressed in the articulate language of humanity. Rome hath nullified and worse than nullified the use of all prayer, and hath conjoined with the name of the living God, as worthy of equal honour, the names of various of his creatures, whom she calls saints, but the saintship of many of whom is of rather worse than equivocal character. And, as if to address the souls of departed men were not enough, pictures and statues and crucifixes, and pretended pieces of the cross, and, as in Germany at this very moment, pretended coats of Christ, are reverenced and addressed in prayer. All this, by the decreets[1] of the councils of Rome, as if the Papacy were in haste and panting to realize the very character described in this verse, and in mortal terror lest, while she was rapidly approaching, another should reach the goal before her.

And of the sacraments, by which God so emphatically makes himself known,—how shall we speak of how Rome opposeth and exalteth herself above them, and blasphemeth him who instituted them? What shall we say of her boldness, in daring to multiply their number? What shall we say of her audacity, in keeping back an essential part of the elements? What shall we say of her outraging common sense, in declaring the bread and wine to be very flesh and blood, nay, the very flesh and blood of the actual body of Jesus, miraculously multiplied, and renewed of course continually, as if the glorified body of the 'Man who continueth ever,' were, by every act of communion on earth, riven asunder, and the portions torn away from the throne of the living God, where he sits for ever, unchanged and unchangeable? What shall we say of her impiety, in declaring that baptism by her priests is the very securing of the Spirit, and the actual salvation of the soul, and the true cleansing of it from all sin? All this

[1] [Scots Law: final judgment.]

Rome does, in the fulfilment of this prophesied opposition and coun-
ter exaltation of herself against all that is called God. The place of a
living faith in the Lord's dealings with the soul is of course derided,
and, instead of it, there is the blind and implicit belief demanded,
the ignorant and unintelligent submission of the whole man into the
hands of a consecrated blasphemer; and then, as if by some magic
spell, some curious and unconscious process or virtue, some jargon
contemptible, or manipulations unintelligible, some legerdemain[1]
applied to souls, this besotted worshipper is passed onwards through
the fingers of his deluding spiritual despot, and through the proper
door of the chapel or consistory, where he gives a triumphant dip of
his finger in the holy water, and a gleesome and complacent bend of the
body to the picture of the Virgin; and away again into all the iniquity of
the world, under the horrifying conception and belief that his priest has
made him infallibly a child of God, and that, die when he may, he will
go to heaven by the nearest route, without check or question from men,
or angels, or the Godhead.

**IV. But this brings us to the confines of the last act of blasphemy. He,
as God, sitteth in the temple of God, showing himself that he is God.
This of course is the very climax of iniquity, beyond which impiety,
however mysterious, cannot go.**

That Papal Rome answers this description is quite undeniable. The
very first tenet of the Papacy is that the Pope is infallible, and of course
this is an attribute belonging to 'the only wise God alone.' Then again,
another dogma is that the Pope is the head of the Church, a function
which belongs only to the living and Divine Saviour.

And yet, though we cannot conceive of anything worse in guilt than
this, there are things vastly more contemptible for absurdity. Popery
appoints a head, who is also a member of the Church, a portion of the
ecclesiastical polity. The Popish Church, head and members of it, is of
the same material throughout. *Moderatism* sets up a head, of another
material; no member of the Church—an extrinsic power, not ecclesiastical, or a portion of the Church, but a different substance altogether, an

---

[1] [legerdemain = deception.]

entirely foreign and discordant element. Popery is a real improvement on Belshazzar's image. The head and the members are not of different material. Moderatism is an exhibition of absurdity far more deplorable than that incongruous and unstable statue. It is a Belshazzar's image inverted; the head of clay, and the legs and the feet of more noble substance. Moderatism is a display of far less talent and consistency than Popery. Of course, however, both are but statues, cold, dead, worthless; neither of them possesses a living head.

Then, again, this Man of Sin showeth himself that he is God, by his violent lordship over the conscience of the members of his corporation, and his assumption of the power to forgive sin. I need not run over the history of Papal blasphemy, and tell you how the Pope's legates traversed Europe as peddling venders of indulgences, bits of parchment which they sold for gold, and the possession of which they taught their blinded votaries secured pardon for all past iniquities, however numerous, and exemption from punishment of all future transgressions, however horrible.

I need not tell you how 'this wicked one was revealed, whose coming was after the working of Satan, with all power and signs and lying wonders, and with all deceivableness of unrighteousness in them that perish, in whose train there came strong delusion, so that men believed a lie, so that all such were damned who believed not the truth, but had pleasure in unrighteousness.' The heart sickens at the detail of such blaspheming audacity, and acknowledges what else could scarcely have been conceived, that, with an awful literality of truth, Antichristian or Papal Rome hath fearfully earned the right to be identified with that Son of Perdition who is here prophesied of as sitting in the temple as God, showing himself that he is God. This is a result that we may well ascribe to the working of Satan, with all deceivableness, and to the diabolic plot devised by him, while he writhed under the agony of conscious disgrace and defeat, and meditated fell and terrible revenge. He has indeed achieved his masterpiece. He has indeed brought out his grand drama on the seven-hilled stage of Rome. And there, by his puppets of popes and cardinals and bishops and long-robed priests, and by the aid of his scenery of holy pictures, and with the dim religious light of Rome's favourite glimmering tapers, and applauded by the congregated dupes of almost a world-wide delusion, hath the god of this world enacted a scene which we may well believe he had previously rehearsed in his nether regions by the aid of his cleverest demons, whom, having taught them well their varied parts, he had sent for a time to inhabit the bodies of the various actors, himself to remain as general prompter behind the scenes, till the accursed tragedy in all its acts should itself be fully realised.

Upon this tragedy the curtain hath not yet fallen. The mass is still said. Holy water is still sprinkled. The host is still carried on the stage in solemn procession, and impiously worshipped and adored. Holy bells are yet rung, whose sound prostrates the hearer in a blind and senseless awe. The drama still goes on in full force; the full complement of impious actors ever and anon presenting themselves right readily to take their parts.

Some years ago, and the doors of this accursed theatre seemed almost ready to be closed, and its attractions to lose their power, and its fame to be upon the wane. But, alas! the end had not come—a tame scene only was being enacted to give performers breathing time for a better effort. New reinforcements have arrived. New stars have arisen to give brilliancy to the coming season. New attractions blaze forth upon the world. In a dark hour, Puseyism has been begotten, twin brother to the Papacy, and the two are about to club their means to produce a grand and a brilliant demonstration. Woe to the southern Church of our land, which permits so large a number of its priests to tamper and coquet with the scarlet-covered wretch of Rome! Woe to the Church which retains within its pale thousands who are drinking of the wine of that harlot's fornications! Woe to the Church which, by such permission, is virtually serving itself heir to the very qualities of that Man of Sin who starved the servants of the highest in the dungeon of pollution, or outraged humanity in the broad light of day, by burning their flesh in the roaring flame!

And woe to the nation and the government which proposes to support and enrich a nursery for training actors for that theatre on whose stage there parades a rival to the very God of gods, and a claimant to be the Christ of the living God on earth. Woe to the government calling itself Protestant, and writing on its current coin beneath its sovereign's name, this inscription (is there not sarcasm in it?) 'defender of the faith,' if it dare to give that coin in thousands for the aggrandisement of Antichrist—a coin, too, wrung out at present into its exchequer almost from the life's blood of its labouring and well-nigh enslaved population—a population to which that government hath sworn to be 'the ministers of God to them for good'! Woe to that government which, in a time when we have but barely emerged from a period of almost unexampled commercial difficulty and distress, and which therefore calls loudly for pious gratitude and solemn pondering of our ways, and as loudly rebukes a reckless and an impious audacity—a time which, for aught we know, may yet have a futurity of gloom before it such as should terrify the statesman of talent and of virtue from putting a rude hand to venture an adjustment of the disjointed state of affairs—a crisis which, with all its yet unsolved problems, and all its yet unsettled difficulties, and all its yet unalleviated distress, may well 'make the boldest hold his breath for a time'—a crisis in which none but the reckless and the godless would expose their country to an additional risk of the threatened judgments of the Almighty, so manifold are the provocations which Jehovah has already met with at our hands—a crisis in which even common prudence tells that a thoughtless touch of the helm of the vessel of the state will dash the bark with all its mal-governed crew irretrievably upon the rocks of a barren and a foodless shore. I say woe to the government which, in such a time as this, shall coolly stretch out to the scarlet-covered Antichrist of Rome the hand of friendship, filled with its sorely-gotten and its sorely-needed gold! And woe doubly, and shame doubly, if history shall have to tell that it was the same government which, in 1843, disendowed and disestablished *Presbytery in Scotland*, that in 1845 dared to outrage the feelings of the Scottish heart by establishing and enriching *Popery in Ireland*!

May God yet avert from our nation the guilt of such a national crime, and the subsequent and necessary national judgments. The

Lord knoweth we have crimes enough already to answer for, without perpetrating this one, and judgments sufficient hanging over us without serving ourselves heirs to the character and the plagues of him 'whom the Lord shall consume with the spirit of his mouth, and shall destroy with the brightness of his coming' (2 Thess. 2:8). Arise, O Lord, and let thine enemies be scattered; let them that hate thee flee before thee. Arise, O Lord, and build up thy Zion.

But if this abandonment of the truth is now to advance, what, my Christian friends, is your security against being dragged away in the vortex of apostasy? Will the *enlightenment of the age* save you? The enlightenment of this enlightened age—will *that* keep you true to your God? We question very much the truth of this cry anent *enlightenment*. Men often walk amid a shower of sparks, of their own kindling, and then, in the proud spirit of Nebuchadnezzar, turn round, and exultingly exclaim, what a blaze of light we cast around us! Our posterity, however, will be better qualified than we to tell whether or not our age was an enlightened one, and assuredly it were considerably more safe, and considerably more modest, to leave the decision to them, than prematurely to sound the trumpet of self-praise so loudly, as will doubtless cause them wonder at the startling triumph of the song, compared with the meanness and the meagre nature of the victory which it was designed to celebrate. But be that as it may, to depend for our security on our enlightenment is unquestionably the delusion of him who is the prompting and the master spirit of Antichrist, and is in good keeping with the doings of him who 'transformeth himself into an angel of *enlightenment*.' My brethren, knowledge will not save you; knowledge will not give you security in the hour and the power of darkness; knowledge is not pardon; knowledge is not faith; knowledge is not *life*. In paradise there were two trees; the one, the tree of knowledge, and, entirely diverse and apart from this, with no necessary or even casual connexion stood the other, called the tree of life. Nay, still farther, so distinctly disjoined were the two, that the history of Eden tells of a transaction in which the partaking of the one blocked up all access to the other.

Nothing but a heaven-gifted and a heaven-bringing faith can keep you steadfast;—a faith which, spurning, as alike infantile and impious, the jargon of a self-efficacious sacrament, a transmitted priesthood, an apostolical succession, a human headship, a mortal infallibility, will look, even in the darkest night of persecution, to the unmingled righteousness of a living and a kingly Saviour, even as, during the horror of thick darkness, Abraham's faith caused him keep his sacrifice free from the touch of the polluting birds of prey;—a faith which makes the soul in which it lives a very portion of the fullness of the living Jesus,—an essential part and element and member of the spiritual body of the crucified I AM. Ah! there is no danger of such a soul apostatizing. He who has such a faith as this need not fear. He is a portion of the body of the blessed and unchangeable Immanuel, and if 'no man ever hated his own body, but nourisheth and cherisheth it,' surely for this reason, as for many others, 'Jesus, having loved his own from the beginning, will love them even to the end.' Amen.

ESSAYS

CHRIST'S VICTORY OVER DEATH[1]

THE most scientifically accurate treatment of this question resolves itself ultimately into an exposition of that *locus insignis*, Hebrews 2:14, 15: 'Forasmuch then as the children are partakers of flesh and blood, he also himself likewise took part of the same; that through death he might destroy him that had the power of death, that is, the devil; and deliver them who through fear of death were all their lifetime subject to bondage.' There are one or two passages, such as Hosea 13:14, 'Death, I will be thy plagues; grave, I will be thy destruction;' and again, the well-remembered exultation of Paul in writing to the Corinthians, 'Death, where is thy sting? grave, where is thy victory?' But the value of these is chiefly rhetorical. It remains that the theology of this singularly interesting and indeed very glorious topic is laid up in the verses of Hebrews which we have quoted. And to these verses we propose devoting a somewhat careful consideration. Like the gold-dust merchant, with covetous eye and greedy hand, we would fain gather up the most minute particles and finest fibres of thought on a topic so immediately affecting the official glory of the Son of God, and so directly bearing on the eternal destinies of his holy universe. The Church flickers in her divine life, and becomes shallow in her divine knowledge, when she thinks she has ascertained all that is implied in the death of Christ. Not without its being the dictate of infinite wisdom did the Redeemer require his Church to 'show forth his death until he shall come again.' She ought to be filled with a habitual and holy astonishment in her daily believing contemplations of 'that

[1] [From: *The British and Foreign Evangelical Review* (1880), p. 669f.]

wondrous cross on which the Lord of glory died.' And if we now seek to penetrate a little further than is usually attempted into one of the more immediate effects of the death of Christ, may it not be without somewhat of that light and reverence which he whose office it is to testify of Christ is so willing to supply!

In that remarkable theological utterance of Holy Scripture there are two effects ascribed to the death of Christ—or, more properly, there are two works which Christ, through his death, is said to have accomplished. There is a work of destruction, and there is a work of deliverance. On the one hand, there is the destruction of him that had the power of death, that is, the devil; on the other hand, there is the deliverance of them who through fear of death were all their lifetime subject to bondage.

Here also there is a tyrant (that is, the devil); and his slaves (that is, the children, partakers of flesh and blood). The tyrant wields the power of death; the slaves tremble under the fear of death. All the power of the tyrant is included, substantially, in the power of death; all the subjection and misery of his slaves may be run up ultimately into their liability to death and their fear of death. It is clear, also, the death of which the one has the power and the other the dread is the self-same death. In either case it is that unknown and unfathomed abyss of misery of which God spoke when he said: 'In the day thou eatest thereof thou shalt surely die.'

This death constitutes the whole power of the tyrant and the whole dread of his slaves. It is, in fact, the entire bond in virtue of which this relation subsists between them—this relation of tyranny on his part, of subjection and bondage on theirs. Against this bond—this death through which the tyrant triumphs, and through the dread of which his miserable subjects tremble—against this bond a Destroyer of the tyrant, a Deliverer of his victims, must manifestly direct his efforts. Against this bond—this death—Christ, in destroying the devil and delivering the children, does direct his efforts: and that in a most singular way. 'Through death he destroyed him that had the power of death, that is, the devil, and delivered them who through fear of death were all their lifetime subject to bondage.' He effectually destroys him that had the power of death, and he does so through death: he delivers them who through fear of death were all their lifetime subject to bondage, and he does so through death. And as we have seen that the death of which the one has the power and the death of which the others have the dread are the same, it seems probable, even at first sight, that the death which Christ dies, the death of which the devil has the power, and the death to which (and to the fear of which) the children are subject, are all three the same. It is, in fact, in their being all three the same that the unloosing of this awful knot is accomplished. By dying that self-same death of which Satan had the power, and to which sinful men were liable, he destroyed him that had the power of it, and delivered them that had the dread of it.

Let us contemplate, then, this death of Christ as, first, a work of destruction; and then, and therefore, a work of deliverance.

I. Through death Christ destroyed him that had the power of death.

Two preliminary explanations are here called for. *First*, when the 'power of death' is thus assigned on Scriptural, that is divine, authority to the devil, it is not meant to acknowledge that he possesses any lawful, judicial, and sovereign power of life and death. 'God is judge himself.' God is supreme sovereign. In his hands, as the blessed and only potentate, are life and death. 'I kill, and I make alive.' At his appointment, as the only judge, are the sentences of life and death. It is he that saith, on the one hand, 'Do this and live;' on the other, 'The soul that sinneth shall die.' Meantime, mankind having become, through their sin, liable to the sentence of death, are by that penal infliction cast out of the household and kingdom and care of God, into that domain of darkness and death of which Satan is the prince. Finding us, by complicity in his own revolt from God, lying under the guilt of death, Satan, the spirit of greatest subtlety and power in the ranks of the fallen—being allowed of God, for his greater punishment, and that of all who hold with him, to exercise dominion as the leading principality of the powers of darkness—malignantly, yet, alas! effectually enough wields against us the liability to death, which the righteous curse of God's law inflicts. The very righteousness of that penalty then becomes Satan's strength and stronghold. In virtue of that penalty, he claims us as under the curse of God, abandoned of God, exposed helplessly and hopelessly to his power. As in the language of the Psalm (71:10, 11), 'They that lay wait for my soul take counsel together, saying, God hath forsaken him: take and persecute him, for there is none to deliver him.' Thus much for the sense in which Satan has the power of death.

The *second* explanation refers to the sense in which the devil is, by Christ's death, 'destroyed.' It cannot, of course, be supposed that the substance of his being is annihilated, or that his supremacy, as within his own kingdom, is abolished. Personally, he still remains; and he still remains the prince of the devils and the lost. But as having the power of death (in the sense explained)—to that extent, and as one might say officially and in that capacity—he is destroyed. The guilt of death on the children's part is the sole ground of the 'power of death' over them on Satan's part. Remove that guilt of death on their part, and the power of death on his part is destroyed; or he himself, as wielding that power of death, on his part, is destroyed. As for any influence, any interest, he can assert or maintain in that direction any longer, Satan is as good as annihilated.

Now this Christ achieves 'through death.' 'Through death he destroyed him that had the power of death.' And a careful examination of the facts of the history, and the implications of the doctrine, reveal these two truths—

1. That, before dying, Christ defeated him that has the power of death.

2. That by dying he destroyed him.

Before dying he conquered and routed him; *by* dying, he pursued and destroyed him. Before dying, Christ in the conflict and victory proved that Satan had no power over him; and by dying for *others* he took away the power of death that Satan had over *them*. The *first* of these achievements was the *defeating* of him that had the power of death and driving him from the field. The *second* was pursuing and *destroying* him.

1. First, then, Christ before he died defeated him that had the power of death.

Our blessed Lord was not brought to death by him that had the power of death. Vanquishing and overthrowing Satan's power, he went voluntarily to death. Christ did not meet death passively—with any one overpoweringly pressing death upon him as a doom which he could not evade—exercising over him the power of death. But he met death voluntarily, actively, by his own positive deed. This great truth has of late almost lapsed out of our theology, insomuch that not a few are quite conscious of the feeling of novelty and astonishment when it is vigorously put before their minds.

Jesus died voluntarily, not by being overpowered. Nay, that is not enough to bring out the doctrine of Scripture. He actively offered himself to God. He was not a slain Lamb only; he was an active—the acting—Priest.

Thus when the hour appointed of his Father was near—the hour and the power of darkness—Jesus said, 'Henceforth I will not talk much with you, for the prince of this world cometh, but hath nothing in me. But that the world may know that I love the Father, arise, let us go hence.' The prince of this world—the god of this world—that wicked one in whom the world lies, and who wields over the wicked world the power of death—he 'cometh;' cometh now as if he had never come before, cometh to his fullest, his fatal, his final assault But he 'hath nothing in me.' In what sense had Satan nothing in Christ? Manifestly in reference to that death which Jesus is now about to die. 'He hath nothing in me by means of which, or by reason of which, he might inflict death on me, and make me his victim. I shall indeed be a victim; but it shall be the Father's victim: an offering of a sweet-smelling savour unto God, all holy to the Lord; no atom, no hair's-breadth in me of that plague-spot by reason whereof Satan might insert his influence, or make good his claim, or wield his power of death.' 'By one man sin entered into the world, and *death by sin.*' 'By sin' does death enter, and the power of death. But in Jesus was no sin. He was holy, harmless, undefiled, and separate from sinners. 'Such an high priest became us.' Mark that—an *high priest.* We needed a Lamb, and a holy Lamb no doubt. But this Lamb was in the moment of his offering up to be a Priest. He was to be offered by himself. And as there must be no sin in the Lamb to be offered, there must also *a fortiori*[1] be none in the Priest. For in the offering up of the dying Lamb the Priest must be living. But sin is death. By sin death entered. But sin had never entered the holy, holy, holy person of Jesus. He had done no violence, neither was guile found in his mouth. Nothing by which death might enter, or by which the power of death might be fastened, could Satan find in Christ. 'He hath nothing in me.' He cannot lead or drive me to death. If he could—if he could drag me as a victim to his altar—little proof would I then be able to afford of love to my Father, love to my Father's commandment, love to my Father's eternal covenant, love to my Father's covenant people. But I go to my Father's altar: I go to my cross freely. By my own choice, by my own act, I go. And I go out of love to my Father. Yea, 'that the world may know that I love the Father, arise, let us go hence.' And he went forth with the eleven across the brook Cedron.

But if Christ had no sin of his own, had he not the sins of his people? True; but still Satan had nothing in Christ. Surely it was nothing of *his* that Christ bare his people's sins in his own body on the tree! Surely it was nothing of the devil's that Christ died, the just for the unjust, that he might bring us unto God! It was not a sin in Christ to be made sin for us! It was at an infinite remove from all that is of Satan. It was holiness. It was the most brilliant holiness the world had ever seen. It was holiness burnished bright in the fires of a furnace seven times heated. Ay, it was holiness in him to be made sin for us. It was love to us. It was love to the Father. It was love to the Father's government. It was love to the Father's law—in both tables of it in one. It was love to the Father's honour, and purpose, and sovereignty, and grace. It was love to the Father's will. 'Lo, I come to do thy will:' 'by the which will we are sanctified through the offering (not merely the sufferings) of the body of Christ once for all.' It was love, love, love; infinite, eternal, and unchangeable love, which many waters could not quench, and the floods could not drown; and it was lovely in the Father's sight. 'Therefore doth my Father love me, because I lay down my life for the sheep. No one taketh it from me; I lay it down of myself.'

[1] [Latin: for a stronger reason.]

Still, did not this commandment of the Father, and this position as sin-bearer for the children, require that he should die? Yes indeed. But they required that he should die, in the way of 'laying down his life,' not of leaving it in the power of him that had the power of death. This substitution of himself in the room of the guilty required that he should 'offer himself without spot to God;' not that he should resign himself to Satan. The price he should pay as our ransom should be paid, not to Apollyon, the malignant and misanthropic enemy of God and man, saying, 'God hath forsaken him, persecute and take him;' but to the righteous judge, to the philanthropic God, saying, 'Save him from going down to the pit, for I have found a ransom.'

If Jesus could not secure this—if he could not baffle, defeat, and put to flight him that hitherto had had the power of death, and, with the field thus clear, secure triumphantly the opportunity of freely, unembarrassedly, and by active and positive deed of his own giving himself in death an offering and a sacrifice unto God—it is clear he must have been baffled and defeated by him that had the power of death; for Satan's whole aim was to prevent him from securing this. But it was to secure exactly this that Christ offered up supplications with strong crying and tears. These supplications he offered up 'unto him that was able to save him from death;' and we are told, 'he was heard'—and *was* saved therefore—and saved 'in that he feared.' But in what sense was he saved from death except in this—that in the conflict with him that had the power of death he was strengthened to defeat him—that he was saved from the dominion and power of death—that he was saved, not from dying, but in dying—that though not saved from dying. He was saved from dying *perforce*—that though not saved from dying? He was saved from death, that is, from being passively overpowered by death—that he was strengthened, through the Eternal Spirit, voluntarily, actively, powerfully to die—and so to die as in dying to offer himself an infinitely acceptable and delightful offering unto God.

This voluntariness and activity in his death, Jesus, in the tenth chapter of John, asserts with great frequency and carefulness; anxious, almost sensitively anxious, if one might say so, to put this truth in a clear and forcible light. 'I am the good shepherd; the good shepherd giveth his life for the sheep.' 'As the Father knoweth me, even so know I the Father: and I lay dawn my life for the sheep.' 'Therefore doth my Father love me, because I lay down my life that I might take it again' (John 10:11, 15, 17). And then, stating the doctrine yet more power-fully, assiduous to prevent the very possibility of misunderstanding, he continues: 'No one taketh it from me, but I lay it down of myself: I have power to lay it down, and I have power to take it up again. This commandment received I of my Father' (John 10:18). Thus the very commandment which he received of the Father—that 'will of God' of which he said, 'Lo, I come to do thy will, O God,'—turns upon the voluntariness and activity of his death. He receives a commandment from the Father, not so much to die—not to die—but to lay down his life; to lay it down of himself; to suffer no one to take it from him; not for a moment to suffer it to lapse out of his own power, but so to retain supreme power over it in all circumstances, and so to lay it down at last of himself, as to retain and exercise the power of taking it up again. And his Father's love to him in the discharge of this work and office turns on this self-same aspect of it 'Therefore doth my Father love me;' not so much because I die; not at all because I die; but, very specially, 'because I lay down my life for the sheep.'

Satan had no objection to make to the proposal that Christ should die; but great objection to Christ laying down his life. Great was the difference between these two things; and, to the view of both the combatants, there clearly turned upon it the question of which of them should take command of the great transaction that was in progress. Satan had no objection to assume and exercise over Christ the power of death, and to see Christ die. For Christ thus to die would have been the proof of Christ's weakness and Satan's power. But for Christ, of his own accord, and of his own deed, 'to lay down his life'—that was a *toto caelo*[1] different thing; that was a defiance and defeat of Satan—a demonstration of Satan's weakness and defeat, not his own; and on Christ's part, nailed as he was to the cross, an act of transcend-ent power and triumph. Satan's whole policy was to assume into his

---

[1] [Latin: by the whole extent of the heavens: utterly.]

own hand the active and positive power of the cross, and to take command of it himself. He would have been delighted to turn Christ into a passive sufferer; to make Christ, in the coarsest sense of the term, a victim—a mere victim. Christ's priesthood, in that case, would have been destroyed; for it is not the part of a priest passively to suffer, but actively to offer—to offer a sacrifice to God. No doubt Jesus suffered; deeply did he suffer. He suffered from the rage of men, from assaults of Satan, and from the wrath of God. But even under the wrath of God, which was unspeakably more for the blessed Son to bear than all the efforts of men and devils, he fell not a passive victim. Patiently, positively, powerfully, as a priest fulfilling his course, he presented himself to all that it was appointed to him to suffer; and having defeated all the assaults of Satan, and drunk all the cup of his Father's wrath, there was the triumph of a mighty conqueror in the cry that burst from his lips, 'It is finished!' and there was the consciousness of voluntary action and mighty power in consummating the sacrifice when he exclaimed, 'Father, into thy hands I commit my spirit.' Manifestly he was master of his own life when he thus spake. No one was taking it from him; he was laying it down of himself: he was offering himself to God, presenting his united soul and body to the sword of justice to separate them in death; and in testimony of this it is added that, having thus spoken, 'he gave up the ghost'—he dismissed his spirit.

Evidently the dark cloud was gone before Jesus died, and he died in the light. The conflict was past, the enemy defeated, and he died in power and victory.

It lies at the root of all sound views of the sacrifice of Christ to keep clear sight of this element of active and positive triumph in the Saviour's death. Christ, in his death, was both the Lamb and the Priest—the Lamb of God, bearing away the sin of the world; and the Priest, acting with God in our name, offering a slain Lamb—the Lamb of God—himself—for a sacrifice and an offering of a sweet-smelling savour. He by himself purged our sins (Heb. 1:3), himself Priest and Lamb in one. The Godhead and the humanity united in one person rendered this amazing combination in his own personality possible; for, as Scripture puts it, the Eternal Son, because the children were partakers of flesh and blood, himself also likewise took part in the same, in order that by death he might destroy him that had the power of death, that is, the devil. The natures were twofold; but the Christ, the person, was one. Having assumed human nature—that is to say, a united human soul and body—into union with his Godhead, he had power over the union of that soul and body with each other. He had power to maintain and prolong it. He had power to abandon it if he chose; though he never did, and never will. He had power to suspend it; and, if suspended, he had power to restore it. While maintaining, suspending, or restoring this union of his soul and body with each other, he maintains unbroken, all throughout, the union of each of them with his Godhead. By his own priestly act he himself offered up himself: he, himself, a divine person, a glorious, powerful, and acceptable Priest, offered up himself—an infinitely worthy slain Lamb. An eternal, inviolable, omnipotent, divine person, having voluntarily taken our nature, having voluntarily taken our sin—holily acquiescing in and approving of the penalty of sin, which is death (that very death of which the children had the dread and the devil had the power), he goes forward in love, reverence, and obedience unto death, to his Father, the righteous judge; and in virtue of his rights and power over the body which was prepared for him, and in the spirit in which he assumed it ('Lo, I come; I delight to do thy will, my God'), he presents himself to his Father's sword, for the separation from each other, but of neither from his Godhead (i.e. of neither from himself—for in his Godhead is the eternal seat of his personality), of that soul and body, through which in death, in their separation from each other (his own power over each of them still abiding intact), he thus actively and livingly offers himself to God.

This is the sacrifice for our sins. Not Christ's life taken away by force, but laid down of himself. Halleluiah! *Gloria in excelsis!* This is the offering of the sweet-smelling savour unto God. Christ's whole self, in the separation from each other of his soul and body, which is the death of his human nature (a rather incorrect expression by the way, for it is of a person that you predicate death; but the expression is intelligible, and not fitted to mislead), in the separation from each other of his human soul and body, in which he was the slain Lamb—yet separated in his own sacrificial offering of himself unto God, by his own act, in the performance of which he was while a slain Lamb a glorious Priest also—not dead even in death—not a dead Priest, but living—at once a slain Lamb and a living High Priest. This, this is the sacrifice for our sins. It was the whole person in the eternal life of the Godhead that was the Priest. It was the whole person, in the separation in death of the parts of the humanity that was the Lamb. And the whole person abode undiminished, undivided, even in death. Neither his soul nor his body was separated from his Godhead, nor therefore from himself; for it is in his eternal Godhead *that* the seat of his unchanged and eternal personality rests for evermore. Had either his soul or his body—still more, had both his soul and his body, that is, his humanity—been separated from his Godhead, that would have been his falling under the power of death. That would have been death reiving[1] away his soul and body from himself; asserting over them a greater power than his own, a power to seize and remove away from him what he had not power to retain. They were separated from each other, and that was death; but not separated from him, Jesus died according to the Scriptures. But neither his soul nor his body was separated from his Godhead, nor (of course therefore) from himself. In virtue of his Godhead, and by the power thereof, he kept them, each of them, still in union with himself, though he offered them (and, of course, himself in them) to divine justice. When he offered them to the Father's sword to separate them from each other, he so offered them, by his priestly act, to death, that he offered them therein, and himself therein, in death, to God. He did not throw away his soul or his body; he did not suffer either of them to lapse out of his own power; for he did not suffer either of them to lapse out of union with his own person. He could not have offered them to God in death, if he had therein allowed them, or either of them, to fall out of union with himself. How could he have been offering them unto God in death, if death had been removing either of them from himself? or, if we should imagine death to have parted them, or either of them, from his person, and he had, simply by the power of his Godhead, laid hold of them in that state of separation from himself,

[1] [Scots: robbing.]

and offered them to God, as by his divine power he might lay hold of and offer anything, yet how should that have been an offering up of himself? But it is of the essence of his sacrifice that he offered himself without spot to God.

See you not, then, how glorious was the triumph here achieved over him that had the power of death? Christ has evidently defeated him. Bearing the sin of the world, and dying a vicarious death, weighted with the agony of the cross, with all its shame and woe; dying beneath the wrath of God and the curse of an all-holy law—a Lamb against whom the Father has been saying, 'Awake, sword, against the man that is my fellow; smite the shepherd;' dying thus, he nevertheless prevails, though nailed to his cross, to defeat his foe. This Priest even in dying—yea, very specially in dying—is a Priest after the power of an endless life. This death of his is no victimising of him. He is living in it, living through it, living more powerfully than ever while he is dying it. This death is the most livingly active work he has ever yet 'accomplished' (Luke 9:31). It is the grandest act of his priesthood, instinct with the most vital, and what will prove to ten thousand times ten thousand, and thousands of thousands, the most vitalising and quickening efficiency.

It would have been the death of his priesthood, it would have been the destruction of his priesthood's life and energy, had he failed to defeat him that had the power of death. Like the priests under the law, he would not have been suffered to continue by reason of death. He would have died out of his priesthood. As it was, he died in his priesthood. He died, with his own will, in the very forth-putting and mightiest exercise of the endless life of his priesthood. Ay, he died into the perfection and reward and eternal life-giving glory of his priesthood. The word of the oath made the divine Son a priest for ever; was, then, the fundamental act of his priesthood to destroy his priesthood's chiefest glory—its ceaseless activity—its quenchless, endless life? That fundamental act was the laying down of his life, that life which was his in virtue of the vital union of his soul and body with each other. But in the very shrine and sanctuary of inviolable Godhead, into which Satan in vain sought access, the divine Priest transacted, in the power of an endless life, this voluntary death-defeating death of his, this laying down of his life of himself, this offering of himself unto God! In the most secret, sacred shrine and inmost sanctuary of Godhead—in the bosom of the Father, into which his soul had been afresh committed—Satan standing without, baffled and afar off indeed—Christ himself 'accomplished his decease' at Jerusalem—master of his life to the last moment, no man taking it from him, but laying it down of himself; none able to help, none able to hinder; himself offering to the devouring sword's judicial power of separation that soul and body which were his own, which were himself, in virtue whereof he was the Son of Man, and in which he was the same one only person he had been from all eternity—the Son of God, and daily his delight, rejoicing always before him, rejoicing also in the habitable parts of the earth. His delights being with the 'sons of men.' Yet all the while he was retaining them in union with himself, neither of them in the power of any other person, because neither of them beyond his own power, and neither of them disjoined from his own person; himself offering them in their peculiar union with himself—so peculiar, and yet still so perfect, that in offering them he was offering nothing less and nothing other than himself unto God. 'Christ through the Spirit offered himself without spot unto God' (Heb. 9:13, 14).

And as it was himself that was offered, so it was himself that was buried. When the lifeless body of the Son of God was carried to the grave, it was as much in union with the Godhead as when, by the word of his lips, he raised Lazarus from the dead. That body was not his mortal remains, as we speak. It was himself. It was Christ. It was the Son of God. It was the Holy One of God. It was not separated from his person—his divine person—as in death our bodies are separated from our souls. It was not Christ's mortal remains that were buried. 'Christ was buried; and rose again'—not merely was raised—'according to the scriptures.' What saith he himself on this point? Addressing the Father, to whom he alike offered and committed himself in death, in the hope of his resurrection, he saith, 'Thou wilt not leave my soul in the state of the dead'—this much concerning his soul. And what concerning his body?—Neither wilt thou suffer my remains to see corruption? No. 'Neither wilt thou suffer thine Holy One—neither wilt thou suffer myself—to see corruption.' The person was one and undivided (is Christ divided?—1 Cor. 1:13); the Priest was living, triumphantly discharging his office; he was a divine, undivided, living person and Priest; though as to his humanity he was dead. There was in this person, this Priest, the power of an endless life—a life never for a moment suspended—never more powerful and vigorous than in the epoch and instant of death on the cross; vigorous thereafter in maintaining in union with himself both soul and body in their separation from each other, the soul in paradise, the body in the tomb, gloriously vigorous again in bringing them into mutual union once more when he rose from the dead. For not merely was he raised from the dead. But he raised himself. 'He rose again according to the scriptures.' Thus he had power to lay down his life, and he had power to take it again. The commandment he had received from the Father embraced the one as much as the other. Satan was manifestly defeated. He was obviously deprived of the power of death. In that respect Christ defied, baffled, and defeated him. Such was his defeat.

2. But Christ not only defeated him that had the power of death, but destroyed him.

Christ did more than defeat his adversary; that he evidently did before dying, and the *voluntariness* of his death proves it. He defeated him before he died; but in dying, he destroyed him. The *vicariousness* of his death proves that.

When Satan was defeated and repulsed, all that was proved was that he had no power of death over Christ; and this was proved before Christ died. But though Satan fled defied and defeated, he carried with him the power of death, which he held over the children, and it was only through death that Christ pursued his routed enemy into the depths of his own domains, and there spoiled and destroyed him— spoiled him and made a show of him openly. Christ died voluntarily; and hence the proof that Satan had no power over him, but had fled and left both the victory and the field to Jesus. The life which Jesus was now about victoriously to lay down was hereby evidently seen to be vicariously laid down—was seen to be laid down wholly and exclusively for the sheep—no one taking it from him; he was laying it down of himself, and laying it down for them. The bond of death under which they were subject to bondage Christ had taken on himself, and now cancels by fulfilling it. That same bond formed the legal instrument by which alone Satan held the power of death. Founding on the righteousness and consequent certainty of our deserved penalty, he wielded it to all effects as a charter granting him the power of death over his miserable slaves. In vain he essayed to wield the same over their great Deliverer. The prince of darkness and the king of terrors Christ repulsed before he died. They had no power over him; but by dying, by filling up and thereby blotting out the handwriting of ordinances, the charter, the dark diploma of death, he pursued the enemy, mightily entered his peculiar dominions, pressed his triumphant way to the very heart and citadel of them, overthrew in reigning righteousness the foundations of his power; and when Satan looked upon the handwriting of ordinances which condemned the children to death, after Christ's death had been recorded there he saw that that once irrefragable document was clean obliterated—that the death it had formerly denounced amidst thunder and lightning, and the tempest, and the voice of words, was all executed, endured, and gone; that the only plea on which he had been accustomed to rest his malignant power was thus torn from his grasp; that the whole and very death by the power whereof the tyrant tyrannised, and in the face whereof the children trembled, was annihilated, while the Conqueror, who had endured all that death, was in death itself living in the power of an endless life, traversing the realms of the dead in the power of the life everlasting.

O most blessed and glorious scene of triumph! To breathe the air of it is immortality. Before Christ died, death and he that had the power of death fled from the field to their own dark domains, leaving Christ's human nature still living on the cross. Thereafter, not subject to their power, and relieved even of their presence, free and unembarrassed, and of his own proper will and power he offereth himself in death to the Father. And thus by his own living energy offering up his soul and body in death, yet retaining them in union with himself—as with his soul in one hand and his body in the other—master of all that was his own, of all that was *himself*, by the gates of death he enters the realm of death; in the power of his unvanquished, undivided, undiminished, mediatorial divine person, he traverses all its range from east to west, from north to south; tramples down all its power, carries its captivity captive, spoils and destroys its prince,—through death destroying him that had the power of death,—through death lighting up with life and glory the region of the shadow of death—his victorious, majestic, divine person being at once the dismay and destruction of the tyrant; 'O death, I will be thy plagues; grave, I will be thy destruction'—and the joy and deliverer of the bond-slaves, 'Rise up, my love, my fair one, and come away; I will ransom thee from the power of the grave, I will redeem thee from death: for lo! the winter is past, the rain is over and gone, the flowers appear on the earth, and the time of the singing of birds is come. Arise, my love, my fair one, and come away.'

II. Thus the train of thought merges into the second doctrine of our theme, namely, that Christ 'through death delivers them who through fear of death were all their lifetime subject to bondage.'

And this follows at once from the great, all-pervading truth that Christ's people have union and communion with him by faith. Bring in this principle of union with Christ in the matter and epoch and victory which we have been considering—bring in the principle and import of your union by faith with Christ, as in the very instant of his voluntary, vicarious, victorious death,—you are entitled to realise yourself as having fellowship as in the very moment and in the whole import of that victory. Is it not said by the Spirit concerning the believer that he is dead with Christ, that he is crucified with Christ, that he is raised up together with Christ, watching with Christ in his temptations, sitting with him in heavenly places? Come, then, and join yourself on with Christ in his peculiar act of, through death, destroying him that had the power of death. You may do this, and do it now, though that victorious act of his was completed so many centuries ago. It was a victory so complete as to be not transient, but perfect and permanent. Satan felt the full meaning of *despair*, the eternal impossibility of ever having a chance again, when he heard the conquering cry, 'It is finished.' 'Tis a grand distinguishing peculiarity of the Messiah's work, this permanence. The present tense—the perpetual present—applies to it more appropriately than any other. 'It is finished'—so finished, so perfected, as to be always fresh and new, and presently powerful, exactly as in the instant of its first transacting. His blood cleanseth now precisely as in the moment of its being shed. In like manner this victory of Christ over death was in the power of an endless life, and it liveth and abideth for ever. Christ adopts you into the participation of it now by faith, precisely as if in that very moment he had carried you with him in his triumphal entry into the realms of death. Would you have been afraid *then*? There is no more reason for being afraid or subject to bondage now.

Jesus draws near to you in the preaching of the Cross and the call of the Gospel (both of which, to them that believe, are the power of God and the wisdom of God unto salvation). He sets himself forth to you therein very specially, as manifestly crucified. Altogether unlike the 'Scotch Pulpit' (so-called) of the current day, in which, to the indignation and astonishment of all Christian readers, Christ is not set forth—or to say 'manifestly crucified,' but not even perceptibly in that aspect at all. All Gospel divine dealings with your soul for its salvation point first of all, and last of all, and throughout all, to Christ and him crucified. He deals with you, chiefest of all, exactly anent his crucifixion and his death. He will have you meet him and strike hands with him exactly here—at his Cross—or not at all. Precisely as if he were this moment about to 'accomplish' that decease at Jerusalem, he draws near and says, 'O my brother, partaker of flesh and blood as I am, I am going to pursue yon routed host—death, and him that hath the power of death, and the principalities of darkness: wilt thou go with me? Wilt thou cast in thy lot with me, and die with me? See how different a thing this dying is when you find it in me—not falling under the power of death, but conquering death, destroying him that hath the power of it. I go not as the victim of death, but as the mighty Conqueror of death. Wilt thou seize the opportunity and go with me? Thou mayst have thy physical pain, my brother, thou partaker of flesh and blood—thy pain, hard for flesh and blood to bear. But seest thou not how in this also I have fellowship in thy suffering, as thou hast in my victory? For because the children were partakers of flesh and blood, I also myself likewise took part in the same. And now, seeing I am death's plagues and death's conqueror, do thou also thyself likewise take part with me in the same—in the same victory and endless life. Behold, I descend as the life everlasting into the valley and shadow of death; and even there—there very specially—I am the light of life, shedding light and glory over all the realm; and even there, therefore—yea, very specially there—if thou go with thy Lord, even there thy Lord shall be thine everlasting light, and thy God thy glory. Seize this instant—the instant of my victorious descent into the realm of death—for examining what to thee, in fellowship with me, the valley and the shadow of death will be. And as I go down into that dreaded realm, and pour the floods of light and glory round all its dark domains, and trample down all its boasted power and dominion; and as thou seest all shades of terror put to flight, all principalities of tyranny stripped of every shred of energy, and trembling in dismay and in fastly coming conscious rottenness; and as thou tracest to my person, standing here, all the light and glory and triumph and endless life that are quenching the power of death in death's own domain, bear in mind concerning the place where I now am, and concerning the just effect of my being there, that if any man will be my disciple let him follow me, and where I am, and as I am, there and so shall my servant be. Very specially, concerning my descent into the realms of death, 'Follow me'! To thee, in that case, these realms of death are the path of life, the gate of heaven, and the very vestibule of glory.' Just as for malicious apostates there remaineth no more sacrifice for sin, so for humble believers there remaineth now no more death, but only a sleep in Jesus. It is enough. Halleluiah! for the Lord God omnipotent reigneth, and reigneth to keep his people's souls alive even in famine. Where is thy sting, death? Begone, thou helpless, stingless, toothless shade! We shall not die, but only sleep—

> *Asleep in Jesus! blessed sleep,*
> *From which no soul awakes to weep.*

We shall be satisfied when we awake in thy likeness, O Lord our God. Even now our cup runneth over. Christ hath abolished death, and given us the morning star. Goodness and mercy shall follow us all the days of our life, and we shall dwell in the house of the Lord for ever. μ.

CHRIST'S DEATH:
WHAT WAS IT?[1]

W HAT was Christ's death, physically? It was the separation from each other of his soul and his body. Death was to the man Christ Jesus what it is to any other man—separation of soul and body.

But even in death, neither was separated from his Godhead. His Godhead held his soul in union with itself, and thereby in union with his Divine Person. So, also, his Godhead held even his dead body in the grave, in union with itself, and thereby in union with himself, the same Divine Person, the Son of God, the very God, Second Person of the Godhead.

If this is not correct, then, say that the soul of Christ crucified was not in union with his Godhead, and let us look at the consequence.

Either his soul, when separated from his Godhead, was a person, or it was not.

Say that it was not a person. Then what was it? Was it a thing? It could in that case have no duties, no obligation, no graces, no virtues, no enjoyments, no sorrows, no consciousness. Was it a corruptible thing, such as silver and gold! Then it was not by giving his soul a ransom that he redeemed his people; for 'they are not redeemed with corruptible things such as silver and gold.' Besides, if this thing was not in union with his person, by what right, or unto what end, did he give it more than he had to give, or had in view in giving, any other soul, any person's soul? He was not in the one case giving himself any more than in the other.

[1] [From: *The British and Foreign Evangelical Review* (1880), p. 451f.]

If it was not a thing, but still what we call a soul, whose soul was it? It was not his soul by any specification or propriety. It became his soul when he took it to himself—when he took a true body and a reasonable soul into union with his Godhead—took them to himself, the Second Person of the Godhead, the Son of God. When that union should cease then that soul (as well as body) should cease to be his. And then whose should it be? Whosesoever soul it was, not being his, still less could it be he. And in giving it he could not be giving himself. This follows from thinking it not a person.

Suppose it was a person. Then what person was it? It was not the Christ. The Christ of God is in such union with Godhead as to be entitled to be called God; but what union this soul, this person, once had with Godhead is cancelled, by what we must call our present vicious supposition. And this person, whatever he may be called, cannot be called God, or the Son of God; for the one only distinct idea that we seem able to form concerning him is, by the original supposition, the negative one, that he is separate from God. There are now therefore two distinct natures, and two distinct persons, instead of two distinct natures and one person for ever.

It is as far from being true that his body was separated from his Godhead. While it lay in the grave it was his body, not the body which had been his; but, then and now, his body, yea, himself: 'He was buried.'

If not his, whose was it? Was it nobody's? Was it a cast-away? Was it a body for the morgue, or for the deadhouse, for friends to look after, and identify, and claim? Was it anybody's? Who shall dare to claim the body which we have been accustomed to call the body of our Lord? The soul of the Lord Jesus has no hold upon it; for he is really dead. The meaning of his being dead is that his soul has no hold upon it, no more connection with it, or power over it, than over or with any other dead body. His Godhead has of course almighty power over it, but exactly as, and no otherwise than as, over any other dead body;—not at all as over his own body; for that it is not, being separated from the Godhead, and therefore from his person, the seat of which the Godhead is.

These reasonings are irresistible; and where do they necessarily land? They necessarily land in this, that by the supposition of either the soul or the body of Christ being separated from his Godhead, the Incarnation is undone and reversed; the Atonement nullified and obliterated; and the death of Christ becomes not a laying down of his life, but a succumbing to death; not a breaking of his body ('my body broken for you'), but an abandonment of it; not a giving of his soul, a judicial and victorious giving of his soul a ransom for sin, but a physical relinquishment of it.

But it is certain that as he will not cease through all eternity to be the Son of Man, so he did not cease upon the cross, or in the grave. He died—not in semblance, but in truth. But for the man Christ Jesus to die in truth required nothing more than for any other man truly to die—that is, to have his soul and his body separated from one another. Every case of death that has hitherto occurred in the human race has been this and (physically) nothing more. There never, till this moment, had been a case in which either a soul or a body could be separated from the Godhead; and now, in the very worst case of its possibility, it is impossible to affirm its necessity. There could be no necessity, no requirement; it could not possibly be called for; and assuredly it was not realised. The Son of God was in his Godhead still united to his body, so that not only was his body crucified, not only was his body dead, not only was his body buried; but he was crucified, he died, he was buried. The Son of God—to wit, our Divine and infinitely precious Saviour— the Son of God, in his Godhead, was in union with his soul, so that the Son of God, our Divine Redeemer, committed himself, in dying, to his Father when he committed his soul; saying, 'Into thy hands I commit my spirit' (Psa. 31:5).

While, therefore, he was a dead man, he was a living, powerful, almighty Christ; so a living Christ, that even in dying he livingly offered up himself—a slain Lamb, but a living Priest. Living! of course, he was: this is the true God and Eternal Life. How could Life die? especially Eternal Life? Did he become—did he require to become— incarnate a second time? Was his resurrection a second incarnation? Was the Word twice made flesh?

In taking Christ's body, therefore (of course, by faith), in the Lord's Supper, we take himself. We take himself; for his body, though broken, being indivisibly connected with his Godhead, in taking his body we necessarily take his Godhead; and in taking his Godhead we take himself, his Person, for in the Godhead is the seat of his personality. Moreover, in taking his Godhead we cannot fail to take his soul, which is indissolubly connected with his Godhead. Thus we take all of Christ, whole Christ, when we take Christ in his death: i.e. his Godhead, his soul, and his body also—his soul and his body in their separation from each other. That is, we take Christ and him crucified. Him, not his soul only; not his body only; nay, not his human nature only; for, aside from his Godhead, that human nature is not a person, and certainly not he—not this person—not the Christ. For he is the Son of God, just the person from whom this human nature is, by this supposition, supposed to be both distinct and separate. Nor, separate from his Godhead,—and therefore from him,—can this human nature be the Son of Man. For the Son of Man is unquestionably a person (no doubt the same person as the Son of God is). The Son of Man, we repeat, is a person; and that cannot be his human nature as separated from his Godhead, for that was not a person. In his human nature, separately and by itself alone, he was not a person, because in his human nature separately and alone he was not. In his Godhead it was that he was the Son of God, not in his manhood. In the manhood, no doubt, he was the Son of Man; but if he had not been the Son of God in the Godhead, he would not at the same time have been the Son of Man. For a human person he was not; and never would have been even a man, save for being God and the Son of God. There was no place in the universe, no standing in the race of human beings, for a person called Jesus, except on the ground of that person (Jesus) being, not a new and newly introduced person, but the Eternal Son of God (no doubt, in his person, newly constituted), but just the Eternal Son of God, the same yesterday, today, and for ever, whose goings forth have been of old, from everlasting.

The following inferences flow from the doctrine now maintained:—

1. Jesus Christ was at once a slain Lamb and a living Priest.

2. He was buried: not his remains. The Son of God, the Second Person of the Godhead, lay in the grave. This is the carefully asserted doctrine of Scripture: 'and that he was buried' (1 Cor. 15:4). And while no doubt the phrase 'my flesh shall rest in hope' is used as quite correct so far as it goes, it is of the person that that other proposition is affirmed, 'Thou wilt not suffer thine Holy One to see corruption.'

3. Neither his soul nor his body was for one moment in any one's power but his own: 'I have power to lay it down; and I have power to take it again.' This, indeed, was the special ground of his Father's wondrous love to him: 'Therefore doth my Father love me, because I lay down my life, that I might take it again.'

4. This was his defeat of him that had the power, and his deliverance of them that had the fear, of death. And while death's work was done, not in semblance, but in reality, on Christ's person; and while it could not possibly be said that death was cheated—it is nevertheless true that in being successful, death failed; that Christ's person, by being in the grave, was death's grave—that in separating Christ's soul from Christ's body, these separated twain became the mill-stones of omnipotence, between which, triumphantly dying, Christ ground death to powder, and, in the instant of death's success, proclaimed death's eternal failure, and poured through earth and hell the insulting cry, 'O grave, where is thy victory? O death, where is thy sting?' Hallelujah!

5. Not merely was he raised by the glory of the Father, and according to the Spirit of holiness, and by his own Divine power; but he rose. Not merely did he raise himself, as he might by Divine power raise another—Lazarus, for instance, but in all the literality and exactitude of the expression—he rose.

6. Christ is not less whole Christ for being crucified: 'Is Christ divided?' (1 Cor. 1:13).

7. The person of Christ constitutes the same check, or limit, on death's work and power in our case, as in his own. As he himself in his Godhead, in which is the seat of his personality, was a bond of

connection between his soul in paradise and his body in the grave, so that, even while truly dead, he was in heaven, and he was in the grave: so the souls of believers are at death made perfect in holiness, and do immediately pass into glory, and their bodies, being still united to Christ do rest in their graves till the resurrection. Thus Christ's person is a bond of union between glorified souls and their respective dead bodies—to that extent checking the separation which death makes, and delivering them who, through fear of death, were all their lifetime subject to bondage; just as the like wonderful issue concerning Christ himself—the permission of separation of the parts of his human nature, consistently with the undividedness of his person—defeated him that had the power of death. This was the Death of Death in the Death of Christ: and Christ abides to say, 'I am the Resurrection and the Life.' 'Believest thou this?' μ.

THE EXCHANGE OF PLACES [1]

THE juridical procurement, righteously and consistently with divine honour, of redemption's grace to guilty and spiritually dead sinners; and the actual administration and bestowal of it; proceed upon the all-embracing and most simplifying covenant arrangement of an *exchange of places* between the Redeemer and the redeemed. It is nowhere stated in the general theorem, as distinguished from a particular case (to use the language of geometricians), more beautifully than in 2 Corinthians 8:9: 'For ye know the grace of our Lord Jesus Christ, that, though he was rich, yet for your sakes he became poor, that ye through his poverty might be rich.'

The words announce to us the splendid and wonderful arrangement made for enriching us with the blessings of everlasting salvation. That arrangement proceeds upon the principle of an exchange—an exchange of places between Christ and his people. Originally Christ is rich, and ultimately his people are made rich. They are made rich by sharing Christ's riches: but the intervening process calls for adoring admiration. The holy angels indeed share in the riches of Christ; he is their Creator and their Lord, and their portion for ever. But being holy, harmless, and undefiled, they have ever since their origin been rich, directly drawing from the full riches of the Father, Son, and Spirit, having nothing but what they have received—yet receiving continually, freely, without let or hindrance, without money and without price; also without any difficulty to be overcome; without any special arrangement being needed.

[1] [From: *The British and Foreign Evangelical Review* (1882), p. 46of.]

It is very far otherwise with the redeemed from among men. They indeed share the riches of Christ; and ultimately they become rich even as originally he is rich. But a very peculiar arrangement was needed.

Not all at once, without obstruction, and easily, as with the angels, could fallen men be adopted into the participation of the riches of God's Eternal Son. Angels are poor as creatures; men are poor as sinners. As creatures, angels are dependent; and, owning their dependence, the Lord meets them with the free, full treasures of his love and blessing and support. As sinners, men are cut off from the fountain of holiness, and life, and blessing: and how shall the sin-hating God again admit them to his riches?

Most blessed scheme! Most wise and gracious arrangement! The Son of God exchanges places with them. He assumes their place and poverty; he transfers them into his place and riches. Though rich, he becomes poor; they, though poor, become rich; though rich in his own riches, he becomes poor in their poverty; though poor in their own poverty, they become rich in his riches; and it is through his poverty they become rich.

In the first place, we shall illustrate this arrangement in several particulars or details. The terms 'rich' and 'poor' are highly general: they are inclusive of a vast variety of particulars; and the principle of this exchange may become more obvious, and faith may be aided in acting on it, if we fill up the general statement by a variety of details.

Let us say, then, that Christ was rich in righteousness, in life, in blessing, in strength, in glory. And in these five cases let us trace the steps of the exchange.

1. Say that by riches we mean *righteousness*. The corresponding poverty then is sin; and then the proposition reads thus: 'Though Christ was righteous, yet for our sakes he was made sin, that we might thereby be made righteous.' Thus, it is but a particular case of the great principle when Paul says elsewhere, 'He that knew no sin was made sin for us, that we might be made the righteousness of God in him' (2 Cor. 5:21).

In this respect how very rich was Christ! how poor were we! How poor, for our sakes, did he become! how rich do we become in him!

He was rich in righteousness originally, as the Eternal Son of God, co-equal possessor of all the righteousness of Godhead. It is a fundamental and primary conception of God, that he is holy. There is none holy as the Lord. He is emphatically '*the Holy One*.' He is 'the high and lofty one that inhabiteth eternity, whose name is Holy' (Isa. 57:15). Sin is infinitely repugnant to his will, infinitely distant from his nature. Perfect, eternal, inviolable righteousness characterises the Godhead. Oh, with what resplendent righteousness the sacred Three-in-One have from everlasting dealt with one another! And when, in unity of council, they turn to deal with creation, 'the judge of all the earth cannot do but what is right' (Gen. 18:25). 'There is no unrighteousness in him' (Psa. 92:15). The saints give thanks at the remembrance of his holiness. Of all this, the Son is co-equal possessor with the Father and the Spirit. He is the Holy One and the Just. As God, he is holy and righteous infinitely. This divine person, our Lord Jesus Christ, is in his Godhead infinitely righteous.

Was there any unrighteousness in his becoming man, so as to render the God-man less righteous than God? Did he become less righteous by becoming man? Is Immanuel, God manifest in the flesh, less righteous than the Eternal Son? If he were, he would not be God manifest: he would be God misrepresented. Yea, he could not possibly still be God. The righteousness and holiness of this divine person are not altered by his incarnation—not diminished or deteriorated: they are disclosed. The Holy Ghost prepared a human nature for him, itself so holy, and pure, and stainless as to be a mirror, infinitely, absolutely accurate, in which his Godhead's holiness should shine. The Eternal Son, incarnate in our flesh, the man Christ Jesus, is holy as God is holy—perfect as his Father in heaven is perfect. Immanuel is rich in a divine, unimpaired, eternal, inviolable righteousness. In this, indeed, our Lord Jesus Christ is pre-eminently rich—'*Jesus Christ the righteous*.' For our sakes he became poor—'was made sin' (2 Cor. 5:21). The Father laid on him the iniquity of his people. He bore our sins in his own body on the tree. He became the Lamb of God, bearing the sins of the world. The Father made him to be sin. Constituting him the substitute of sinners, he imputed their sins to him accordingly; and held him responsible for the dishonour they had done to God, *obnoxious*[1] to the wages and penalty of sin—and the wages of sin is death.

How amazing the exchange—from highest riches to deepest poverty: from righteousness, the most glorious of all riches, to sin, the most profound and degrading possible style of poverty!

Isaiah saw him in his riches, in his holiness, upon his heavenly throne, and the myriads of the holy ones he heard crying, 'Holy, holy, holy is the Lord Almighty; the whole earth is full of thy glory.' But the exchange takes place. No more is he on the throne, shining glorious in holiness, but on the footstool, laden with sin; on the altar, suffering for sin; yea, expelled without the camp; standing in the place of the guilty, the base, the poor.

But where is now his righteousness? Is it gone? Is it overborne, extinguished, annihilated by the sin? How is it affected? Is it diminished? Is it absorbed? Where are his riches of righteousness?

Mark that though he became poor in our poverty, he was so rich in his own riches that he never became bankrupt. Ah! if he had, how could he ever have made us rich? In his poverty, assumed for us—and, indeed, assumed *from* us—he yet remained rich. He drew not on his riches: he claimed them not: he used them not. He might have drawn upon them. In his righteousness, he might have demanded the presence and services of twelve legions of angels (Matt. 26:53). But he voluntarily consented to be poor: yet his riches, his righteousness, abode: and in due time the poverty, the sin, passed away, and the righteousness remained as before—righteousness eternal, infinite, invincible: proved to be so because it had withstood the *run*, the draft, the drain upon it caused by our poverty, our sin.

But mark now, how, through this poverty, we are made rich; how, through this sin-bearing, we are made righteous. The righteousness has borne our sin, and borne it all away. The sin has not extinguished the righteousness, but the righteousness has extinguished the sin: and we, the poor, the sinful, have this righteousness now for ours. Our poverty has been his, and still he abides rich. Our sin has been his, and still he abides righteous. As he was poor and a sinner not in himself

---

[1] [obnoxious = exposed or liable to harm.]

but in us, we are rich and righteous, not in ourselves, but in him: the whole arrangement is infinitely useless and foolish if now poor sinners are not rich and righteous in him.

Oh, most blessed justification, without works, freely by faith, by his grace, in the very righteousness of God! Come, O believer, and enter afresh into all the deep perfection and precision of this exchange. Bring your sin, else there can be no exchange at all. Bring your sin and poverty, else you are not profiting by this arrangement at all. Bring your sin, and obtain freely perfect righteousness. The Lord requires you not to bring righteousness, but to bring sin. Sin you have: bring what you have. Righteousness you have not: come and receive what you have not. The grace of our Lord Jesus Christ exempts you from having to bring righteousness: exempts you from being paralysed by the terror of having nothing but sin: exempts you from the despairing task and toil of finding any righteousness of your own: exempts you from finding any ground of peace with God yourself: from constructing any justifying reason for peace with God yourself: from drawing up any terms or covenant of peace yourself: from extinguishing or putting away your sin yourself: from bringing in any righteousness yourself. At one grand stroke the Lord settles all for ever. Jesus Christ, the holy one, the righteous, receives you, a sinner! He puts himself in your place: he puts you in his: and his is a place of righteousness still, even though he is in your place of sin: for, in your place of sin, he puts away sin by the sacrifice of himself; abiding righteousness for you, and you the righteousness of God in him! Most profitable, most liberal, most gracious barter or exchange, profitable unto you a sinner, for you give sin and get righteousness—the righteousness of God. And as the righteous God can have no quarrel with the very 'righteousness of God,' God verily can have no quarrel with you. For if the righteous God is at peace with his own righteousness, with you also he must be at peace: 'for he hath made him that knew no sin to be sin for us, that we might be made the righteousness of God in him' (2 Cor. 5:21).

2. Say that by riches we mean *life*. The corresponding poverty then is death; the proposition then reads thus: 'He who is the Living One, yet for our sakes died, that we through his death might live for ever.'

Our particular poverty in this case is death, and we are released from it, and enriched with the opposite riches, even eternal life, by Christ, the Living One, dying for us.

The Godhead is the fountain of life. 'With thee, God, is the fountain of life' (Psa. 36:9). This prerogative the Eternal Son shares with the Father and the Spirit. Proceeding by eternal generation from the Father, he has life in himself, and is a fountain of life to whomsoever he will. This life is self-existent, independent, indefectible, unalterable, unfailing. It is from all eternity. It never was not, and can never cease.

This life was not diminished or injuriously affected by his incarnation. It was manifested: 'The life was manifested, and we have seen it, and bear witness, and show unto you that eternal life which was with the Father, and was manifested unto us' (1 John 1:2). The fullness and fountain of eternal life was deposited in human flesh, when the Word was made flesh. The Father gave us eternal life, and this life was in his Son. 'In him was life' (John 1:4).

This rich one became poor—for our sakes he became poor. Rich in independent possession of infinite, eternal, infallible life, he became poor unto death. He humbled himself, and became obedient unto death. He poured out his soul unto death. For 'the wages of sin is death' (Rom 6:23), and being made sin, he shunned not the righteous doom whereby it comes to pass that by sin death enters—'Sin entered into the world, and death by sin, and so death passes on all that are accounted sinners' (Rom. 5:12). It was our death he assumed: it was our death he died. 'For if one died for all, then were all dead, and he died for all that they might not live unto themselves,' which is just a species and special element of death, 'but might live unto him that died for them and rose again' (2 Cor. 5:14-15).

Now consider *this* poverty and its effects upon the original riches of Christ. Was he rendered bankrupt as to life? did he fall under the power of death? God forbid. For how, then, should *we* live by him? He wholly died our death: he died it truly, he died it all: he died it once, and once for all and for ever: and he rose again. The lost, who have refused to live his life, and preferred to die their own death, are ever dying it, and it is never done. Jesus died it all. He is not dying our death now, and never will or can die again. 'I am he that liveth and was dead; and, behold, I am alive for evermore' (Rev. 1:18). In death itself he was living—the Living One,—his divine person abiding unconquerable and triumphant: in the living power of his Godhead offering himself a sacrifice in the death of his human nature—by death destroying him that had the power of death: abiding in the field as the Eternal Life manifest and now victorious: with the field swept clean and clear of the second death for ever. That is the death of the Living One. Come, you who are spiritually dead, arise and come. Come, for you have not far to come. Christ has come to meet you; and how far has he come into your place? You have no farther to come than into your own place—recognising that Christ is in it—Christ dead and alive again. But now his life is theirs for whom he became poor in death—not his own only now, but theirs for whose sake he died. 'They are crucified with Christ; nevertheless they live; yet not they, but Christ liveth in them.' 'Because I live,' says Jesus, 'ye shall live also' (Gal. 2:20; John 14:19). He adventured his own life against their death. He made their death his, and now his life is theirs. 'He that hath the Son hath life' (1 John 5:11, 12); 'he shall not perish, but have everlasting life.' Surely he 'abolished death, and brought life and immortality to light' (2 Tim. 1:10). And this life is in himself. For 'as in Adam all die, so shall all in Christ be made alive' (1 Cor. 15:22).

Come, then, you poor and needy—so poor as to be pining, dying, perishing—come, and in respect of life, life inviolable and eternal, be made rich in Christ. Shun not to feel your poverty pressing your soul; shun not to feel the power of death—yea, the sentence of death—in yourself (2 Cor. 1:9). But come with it to the glorious exchange; come; and as Christ the Living One has taken up his place in your place, in your person, and in your death, assume now your place in his person and in his life. Let your assumption of his life be as true, clear, resolute, business-like as his assumption of your death. There was nothing fanciful, sentimental, imaginary, shrinking, tentative, dilettante, incomplete about his descent into your poverty. There was everything terrifically real in his entrance into your death. Enter then with equally intense reality into his life. He brought his life into your place, your death: and his life abolished death, and abode life undiminished—abode, and abode *there*. Bring your death into his life: you have not far to bring it: and let it be there abolished for ever. Shun not to own yourself dead under sin, but admit with Paul, 'We have the sentence of death in ourselves, that we may not trust in ourselves, but in him that quickeneth the dead' (2 Cor. 1:9). And do this actually in him: 'Reckon yourselves dead indeed unto sin, but alive unto God by Jesus Christ' (Rom. 6:11). 'Know ye not that as many of us as have been baptized or engrafted into Christ, have been baptized into his death? Therefore we are buried with him by baptism into death; that like as Christ was raised from the dead by the glory of the Father, even so we also should walk in newness of life' (Rom. 6:3, 4).

In the light of these thoughts, how luminous are many passages of Scripture! And to get or give any help to such luminosity is the very delight of Christian souls, and that the more they may have been tried with and have suffered from spiritual darkness. How true, for instance, is that wonderful word—'To me to live is Christ'!—with all its intensity and apophthegmatic[1] brevity: a kind of watchword at the gates of death. And again, in this light—

> *I shall not die, but live, and shall*
> *The works of God discover;*
> *The Lord hath me chastised sore,*
> *But not to death given over.*

How literally true, also, it is in the case of all believers, that it is none less than the very 'life of Jesus that is made manifest in their mortal body' (2 Cor. 4:11). And how reviving is it that 'the last Adam is a quickening spirit' (1 Cor. 15:45). Yes; we see how the 'Son quickeneth whom he will' (John 5:21). Is he not the bread of life also? and how precious the discourse in which he took occasion of that figure of speech to put on record for us! (John 6:30-40). And seeing he became life to us by exchange of places, even unto death, even the death of the cross, the death of juridical sacrifice, how intelligible are even those verses! (John 6:52-58).

---

[1] [apophthegmatic = terse or pithy.]

3. Say that by riches we mean *blessing*. The corresponding poverty is the curse; and the wondrous theorem of exchange then reads, 'He, though he was the Blessed One, for our sakes was made a curse, that we might thereby receive the blessing.' The particular element of detail in our poverty is, in this case, the curse of God: and we are relieved from it, and enriched with the corresponding and contrary riches, namely, the blessing, by Christ the Blessed One being subjected to our curse. Thus it is but another case of the same great general fact when Paul says: 'Christ hath redeemed us from the curse of the law, being made a curse for us, that the blessing of Abraham might come upon us' (Gal. 3:13). Here again is the principle of the exchange. In this element, then, in this particular variety of his riches, how rich was Christ! How poor were we! It is essential to our conceptions of the persons of the God-head to regard them as blessed, infinitely blessed. 'Blessed art thou, O Lord; teach me thy statutes' (Psa. 119:12); 'Jehovah is the blessed and only Potentate' (1 Tim. 6:15). Of this infinite blessedness the Son is the co-equal sharer with the Father and the Spirit; and besides his possession of the fullness of the Godhead, his relation and intercourse, in the Spirit, with the Father as the Eternal Son, must be necessarily replete with fathomless and inexpressible blessedness. He is God's only-begotten Son (John 1:14, 18; 1 John 4:9; John 3:16,18): he is the Son of his love (Col. 1:13). Again and again the Father bore testimony to him: 'This is my beloved Son, in whom I am well pleased' (Matt. 3:17, 17:5; Mark 1:11, 9:7; Luke 3:22, 9:35; 2 Pet. 1:17). Oh, who can enter into the boundless depths of joy in the fellowship of the Eternal Father and the Eternal Son in the Eternal Spirit! We hear the Son himself essaying to put us in possession of some idea of his infinite blessedness in the bosom of the Father, ere yet the worlds were: 'The Lord possessed me in the beginning of his way, before his works of old. I was set up from everlasting, from the beginning, or ever the earth was. When there were no depths, I was brought forth; when there were no fountains abounding with water. Before the mountains were settled; before the hills was I brought forth. While as yet he had not made the earth, nor the fields, nor the highest part of the dust of the world. When he prepared the heavens, I was there: when he set a compass on the face

of the depth, when he established the clouds above: when he strengthened the fountains of the deep: when he gave to the sea his decree, that the waters should not pass his commandment: when he appointed the foundations of the earth: then I was by him, as one brought up with him: I was daily his delight, rejoicing always before him; rejoicing in the habitable part of his earth; and my delights were with the sons of men' (Prov. 8:22-31). Oh the blessedness of God's dear Son, basking in the eternal sunshine and joy of his Father's blessing! 'I was by him as one brought up with him. I was daily his delight, rejoicing always before him.'

How happy preachers of the gospel ought to be! Yes, and how happy they really are, if they truly preach this Christ! And how careful the Church ought to be in maintaining the doctrine of the Eternal Sonship! How much that truth has fallen out of sight! How neglected Treffry's glorious book has become![1] How otherwise could Dr R. S. Candlish's volume on the 'Fatherhood of God' have been so much misunderstood? The title, no doubt, was not well chosen; the book might better have been called, 'On Adoption'—a specially favourite topic of Dr Candlish's very rich and gracious ministry.[2] But it was a degenerating age, surely, that had so little thanks to give him for it. It was an age not familiar with Treffry's glorious and immortal work. How shall Christ's blessedness ever be rightly estimated, if his Eternal Sonship be forgotten? 'Daily his Father's delight,' eternally in his Father's bosom, not properly leaving it—(a most miserable but common idea)—even when made flesh and

---

[1] R. Treffry, *An Inquiry Into the Doctrine of the Eternal Sonship of Our Lord Jesus Christ* (London, Mason, 1837).

[2] [In addition to his Cunningham Lectures, *The Fatherhood of God* (1865), previously mentioned, R. S. Candlish also published a stunning volume of sermons on adoption: *Discourses Bearing upon the Sonship and Brotherhood of Believers, and other Kindred Subjects* (Edinburgh, Black, 1872). Although Candlish and Martin would not have agreed in the church courts over several key issues of the day, Martin was devastated by his death. See: A. Auld, *Life of John Kennedy* (London: D. D. Nelson, 1887), pp. 163-4, and preached a funeral sermon for Candlish in Dingwall Free Church. See: *The Chariot of Israel and the Horsemen thereof: a Tribute to the Memory of Robert S. Candlish, D.D.: being Sermon preached on Sabbath 2nd Nov. 1873, in the Free Church of Dingwall, in the absence of Dr Kennedy in Canada* (Edinburgh: MacLaren and MacNiven, 1873)]

born in Bethlehem. Always from eternity to eternity *there*, how near to the Father! What an inconceivably glorious reconciler! And what an unfathomable necessity there was that our salvation should take the form of a 'reconciliation'!

For, while *he* is eternally in the bosom of the Father; as for *us*, each of us was as one cut off from him; cast out from his presence, wrapped up in his own curse. Even thus poor did Immanuel become for us; thus cursed did the Blessed One submit to be. For into our place, though it was ominously distinguished as the dwelling-place of the curse, Jesus, in his love, consented to come; and his Father's wrath became then his portion. Then he became 'acquainted with grief' (Isa. 53:3). The Blessed One became 'a man of sorrows.' Anxieties, cares, hunger, thirst, wounds, stripes, agony, bloodshed, a cursed death, accrued unto him. His Father, far from helping him: concealing his love from him: hiding his countenance: appearing against him, armed with an offended judge's indignation: forsaking him to the malignity of men and the onset of principalities and powers of darkness: drawing against him the sword of justice: calling on the sword to awake and smite and slay him (Zech. 13:7)—such was the inexpressible exchange which Jesus made when he took our curse upon him to bear it. 'He indeed *suffered* for sins, the just for the unjust' (1 Pet. 3:18).

Most marvellous exchange! Who can tell the joy and felicity of the Blessed One? But who can tell the sorrows of the curse? 'Behold, and see, was there ever sorrow like unto my sorrow?' (Lam. 1:12). His soul was in the curse of travail (Isa. 53:11). His body was crucified in the curse upon the tree.

Now, *surely* for our sakes he thus became poor. 'Surely he hath borne *our* griefs and carried *our* sorrows: ... he was wounded for our transgressions, he was bruised for our iniquities; the chastisement of our peace was upon him: and with his stripes we are healed' (Isa. 53:4). And how gloriously are we healed! How fully are we blessed! Come again, and exchange with Jesus. He receives your curse, and renders back to you the blessing. For though he bore the curse, the blessing was never injured. He remained the Blessed One, even when the curse lay heavily upon him. The curse was *on* him, but the blessing was in him. Yea, he was the blessing, and the Blessed One. 'Therefore did his Father love him, because he was laying down his life for the sheep' (John 10:17). Therefore did his Father rejoice over him, as one who was his infinite delight, even in the very instant when he was bearing sin and abolishing the curse. And the curse—our curse—being now gone, oh how blessed may we be in Christ! Yea, 'in thee, and in thy seed, shall all the families of the earth be blessed' (Gen. 12:3; Psa 72:17; Jer. 4:2). 'He hath redeemed us from the curse, that the blessing of Abraham might come upon us' (Gal. 3:13-14).

Again I say, how blessed this exchange for us! Cursed and outcast we enter into this most marvellous arrangement; and we find it never fails us. In terms of its glorious procedure we are blessed and accepted of the Lord. We find grace in his sight: we have acceptance in the Beloved (Eph. 1:6). We are God's dear sons (Eph. 5:1); we are daily his delight (Isa. 62:4); rejoicing always before him (Deut. 12:12). For into Christ's riches of nearness to the Father, of joy with the Father, and of the Father's joy and love in him—into all this we are adopted: in all this we are enriched: 'blessed with all spiritual blessings in heavenly places in Christ Jesus, according to the riches of his grace' (Eph. 1:3).

4. Say that by riches we mean *strength* or power. The corresponding poverty then is weakness; and the particular case of this intensely gracious arrangement is,—'He, though he was strong, yet for our sakes became weak, that we through his weakness might be made strong.'

Here also how profound and amazing was the exchange Jesus made with us! How rich is he in strength! How poor and weak did he become! He is indeed 'the strength of Israel' (1 Sam. 15:27). 'Who among the sons of the mighty can be likened unto the Lord?' (Psa. 89:6). 'O Lord God of hosts, who is a strong lord like unto thee?' (Psa. 89:8). 'Thou hast a mighty arm; strong is thy hand, and high is thy right hand.' Is anything too hard for the Lord? With God all things are possible. 'The Lord strong and mighty; the Lord mighty in battle' (Psa. 24:8). By God's dear Son—whose grace this marvellous exchange demonstrates—were all things made, whether they be things in heaven, or things on earth, or things under the earth. By him do all things consist: upholding all things by the word of his power. Meditate upon the strength of the everlasting hills, upon the power of the angry ocean, upon the weight of the solid globe which by his hand he has hung upon nothing, upon the might of the Lord, so great that it brings Orion in his season, and that it guides Arcturus with his sons, and by which not one of heaven's countless multitudes of suns and systems fails, for that he is strong in power, and calls them all by names, in the greatness of his might. And bear in mind that these are but limited effects of Immanuel's power, which itself is limitless and infinite. And you may have some impression of the truth that he was rich in power. Yet for our sakes he became weak. Weak! I should say so—a frail babe in Mary's arms: a wearied man on Jacob's well: a prostrate sufferer stretched upon the ground in the garden of his agony: anon fainting beneath the weight of the cross on which he was about to suffer: crucified (the Holy Spirit tells us) in weakness. Ah! how very poor in this respect did he become! How deeply self-denying, as he refrained from drawing on his divine almighty power: himself the mighty God all the while; yet in no respect drawing on his omnipotence as God while suffering in weakness as a man—for that would have been to counteract and renounce his incarnation. Not merely that his human nature was weak—that is plain. But *he*, this divine person, was weak: and the weakness of God was stronger than man; and by his very weakness, to the infinite shame of mighty principalities and powers, he spoiled them on the cross in the depth of his utmost weakness. He made a show of them openly, when they put forth all their power, by wholly eschewing his own, and consenting to be crucified in weakness.

It was 'for our sakes' he thus became weak—for he stood in our place, and it was one of weakness indeed. Ours was indeed a weak position. We were emphatically 'without strength,' when, 'in due time, Christ died for the ungodly' (Rom. 5:6). We were 'not sufficient even to think one thought as of ourselves' (2 Cor. 3:5). We were helpless as an infant cast out into the field, 'in his blood to the loathing of his person' (Ezek. 16:5). But through his weakness, we are now made strong. We bring *our* weakness to his weakness, and join on the one to the other. And well we may bring ours to his—for his was just ours, assumed by him in his love. And as, in union with him, and with our weakness identified with his, we see his pass away, and leave his strength unimpaired, it is our weakness that thereby doth pass away—all pass away—and we abide strong in the Lord, and in the glory of his power. 'My strength,' says Jesus, 'is made perfect in weakness' (2 Cor. 12:9). How intensely, how singularly, how profoundly true! 'I can do all things, through Christ that strengtheneth me' (Phil. 4:13). 'They that wait upon the Lord shall renew their strength' (Isa. 40:31, 41:1).

5. Say that by riches we mean *glory*. The corresponding poverty then is shame; and the noble theology of the exchange then reads thus: 'Ye know the grace of our Saviour Jesus Christ, who though he was glorious, yet for our sakes he was clothed with shame, that we through his shame might attain to glory.'

Who shall speak of his original glory—the glory which he had with the Father before the world was? What is all the excellence and grandeur of created things? What is all the moral loveliness of the ten thousand times ten thousand of the stainless seraphim to the infinite glory of the living God? 'Great is the Lord, and greatly to be praised; and his greatness is unsearchable.' 'I will speak of the glorious honour of his majesty. Honour and majesty are before him, strength and beauty are in his sanctuary.' Not an attribute of Godhead but is a source of glory and excellency infinite; and the infinitely excellent and perfect combination of them all constitutes the inconceivable glory of the Lord.

This glorious God in our Immanuel stooped to suffer shame. It is his own testimony: 'For thy sake I have borne reproach; shame hath covered my face' (Psa. 69:7). It is his holy protestation of the willingness with which he suffered shame for his people; 'I gave my back to the smiters, and my cheeks to them that plucked off the hair; I hid not my face from shame and spitting' (Isa. 50:6). 'Thou hast known my reproach, and my shame, and my dishonour; reproach hath broken my heart' (Psa. 69:20). Again and again we are told he was dealt with as a shame-covered man. 'He was despised'—think of it—the God of glory!—the rich become exceeding poor!—'He was despised and rejected of men, a man of sorrows and acquainted with grief; and we hid as it were our faces from him: he was despised, and we esteemed him not' (Isa. 53:3).

Remember the scene of his trial. 'Then did they spit in his face, and buffeted him; and others smote him with the palms of their hands, saying, Prophesy unto us, thou Christ, who it is that smote thee? (Matt. 26:67). And yet again, 'They stripped him, and put on him a scarlet robe. And when they had platted a crown of thorns, they put it upon his head, and a reed in his right hand: and they bowed the knee before him, and mocked him, saying, Hail, king of the Jews!' (Matt. 27:28, 29). Remember how he was overwhelmed with insult, with calumny, with charges of blasphemy, rebellion, imposture, conspiracy with devils. They said, 'He casteth out devils through the prince of the devils' (Luke 11:15). Remember how he was crucified between two thieves, and even one of them railed upon him, as if he had sunk to a lower depth than they, and even thieves might afford to look down upon him. Think of it! The Lord of glory, laden, clothed, broken in heart with shame!

And this was 'for our sakes,' for he came into our position, and ours was a shameful position. The position of a sinner is full of shame. Shame followed sin into the world immediately (Gen. 3:8). And till redemption is absolutely perfect in glory, shame still abideth. Even the body of redeemed, regenerated man is sown in dishonour. It shall indeed be raised in glory, while the wicked shall arise to shame and everlasting contempt.

But he that believeth shall not be ashamed. United with Christ, his shame shall be lost and swallowed up in Christ's shame, which was itself lost and swallowed up in glory. For 'he despised the shame:' bearing it all, till it passed away, and his glory again shone out. In this sense, while exclaiming, 'I hid not my face from shame and spitting,' the suffering, humbled Saviour also adds: 'The Lord God will help me; therefore I shall not be confounded: therefore have I set my face like a flint: and I know that I shall not be ashamed' (Isa. 50:7). No; the glory broke forth in its resistless splendour. The vindication came, like as the sun shineth in his strength. And it is now a shame-destroying glory in which his people are glorified with him. He gives them pure raiment, clean and white, that the shame of their nakedness appear not (Rev. 3:18). He clothes them with beauty and with glory, with excellency and with comeliness. He says to his engrafted members, 'Your shame be mine! The dishonour done to me, Immanuel, the Lord of glory, let that be reckoned for your shame, and that being now passed away, my glory now be yours.' 'Father, I have given them the glory which thou gavest me' (John 17:22), 'Since thou wast precious in my sight, and I loved thee, thou hast been honourable' (Isa. 43:4), 'The king's daughter is all glorious, her clothing is of wrought gold' (Psa. 45:13), 'And beholding as in a glass the glory of the Lord, we shall be transformed into the same image, from glory to glory, as by the Spirit of the Lord' (2 Cor. 3:18).

Behold then the unsearchable riches of Christ in righteousness, life, blessing, strength, and glory! Behold how for our sakes he becomes poor—made sin, subjected to death, loaded with the curse, crucified in weakness, clothed in shame; and all in order that we guilty, dead, cursed, weak, and shameful sinners might have righteousness, life, blessing, strength, and glory. In all these particulars, and in every other in which he was rich and we poor, he who was rich for our sakes became poor, that we through his poverty might be made rich.

What then shall we say of this grace of Jesus? 'Ye know the grace of our Lord Jesus Christ, who,' etc. What love! How condescending! The love of him who was so rich. How self-sacrificing!—the love of him who became so poor. How sovereign and free!—to us who were ourselves so poor in ourselves. How fruitful and advantageous!—making us so rich in him. Herein is love! Herein is the matchless and excelling love of Jesus.

Two great gospel duties are suggested and enforced by this arrangement. *First*, the duty of being poor in spirit. *Second*, the duty of being rich in Christ.

I. The duty of being poor in spirit.

'Blessed are the poor in spirit, for theirs is the kingdom of heaven' (Matt. 5:3). 'To this man will I look, even to him that is poor.' 'I am poor and needy, yet the Lord thinketh upon me' 'I will leave in the midst of her a poor and afflicted people, and they shall trust in the name of the Lord.' 'The Lord heareth the poor.' 'Thou, O God, hast prepared of thy goodness for the poor.' 'I will satisfy the poor with bread' (Psa. 132:15). Always, in Scripture, it is the poor whom the Lord encourages—the poor in spirit.

And it is not difficult to see why it should be so. The poor in spirit have a spirit suitable to the truth. They are poor in fact; destitute of righteousness, life, blessing, strength, and glory; plunged in guilt, death, curse, helplessness, and shame. They are poor in fact—and if not poor in spirit, they are of a false spirit, a spirit which denies the reality of their condition.

All pride is falsehood—anti-fact. God desireth truth in the inward parts. Oh how far off the unhumbled spirit is from God! 'Thou sayest, I am rich, and increased in goods, and have need of nothing, and knowest not that thou art wretched, and miserable, and poor, and blind, and naked' (Rev. 3:17).

Am I in danger of falling into this terrible falsehood? Am I ever inclined to fancy I am rich? The Lord points me to one who was truly and infinitely rich, and shows me how inexpressibly poor he became, and—O wonder!—he became poor for such as me. And in that poverty of the Rich One, let me learn to see my destitution. For I cannot be left to feel in myself, unrelieved, all my own poverty, without collapsing and sinking for ever under the terrible experience. The Lord, in his mercy, does not suffer me to learn my own poverty by forsaking me to discover or experience all its depths. Of his great forbearance he does not suffer my guilt, my death, my curse, my helplessness, my shame, to overwhelm me. He stays his hand: he stays his rough wind: he deals with me in measure: he is long-suffering. He does not strip me bare and leave me destitute. And therefore—alas! therefore—I am in danger of abusing his long-suffering, and saying, 'I am rich.' Did he leave me to reap, and learn all the destitution of my position, I would know that I was poor; but I would sink eternally under the discovery. But he points me to Jesus. He tells me that he took my position and my poverty, and in him I may learn what my position and poverty are. He showed no long-suffering to him. Sheer and exact, unrelieved, my position and poverty did Jesus take. In my own person God forbeareth and is long-suffering; and I abuse this to conceal from myself how very poor I am. In the person of Christ my position and poverty come all clearly out to light; and I have not where to lay my head: I have nothing but sin, as I see in that sin-bearing Lamb—and death, as I see, in that dying Sacrifice—and curse, in that cursed tree—and weakness, in that fainting Sufferer—and shame, in his deep confusion and reproach. All these were mine, if he became poor for me. All these I own as mine, if I would not repudiate him and deny that he became poor for me. If he took my position and my poverty, I read my position and learn my poverty in him. For he did not become needlessly poor; he did not become more poor than I. There was indeed neither need, nor room, nor possibility of *that*.

And did, then, my poverty reduce the Rich One—him who was rich—did it reduce even such an one to such humiliation? He was so poor he had not where to lay his head: he had not a friend to comfort him: he had not a smile from his Father: he had not a garment: he had not a grave.

And is this my poverty—even mine? Will I disown it? I disown Christ if I do. Is this my poverty? And am I proud? Do I thank God I am not as other men? Do I resent God's call to humiliation and contrition? Do I feel as if the Lord were asking too much when he asks me to abhor myself in dust and ashes?—to own that I am wretched, and miserable, and poor, and blind, and naked? He refrains from showing me my poverty fully in my own person, for it would eternally destroy me. He shows it to me in Christ, and asks me to behold the truth. He shows it to me in Christ bearing it for me—bearing it away; and still do I quarrel with the truth? Do I still say, I am rich? Do I still refuse to break down, and own that I am poor—and be accordingly poor in spirit? Then how can God deal with me after this? Can he find a better way of teaching me that I am poor—of training me to be poor in spirit?

Oh! let me not resist God's wondrous method; let me not charge God foolishly with making the Rich One poorer than was needed, poorer than was true of those for whose sakes he became poor. This is my poverty: I am a guilty, dead, cursed, helpless, shameful thing. O my God, 'I am poor and needy.'

II. 'But the Lord thinketh upon me.'

For the self-same plan enforces, with equal power and relevancy, the duty of my being rich in Christ. Every thread and fibre of this great thought is crying, on the part of Christ, 'I counsel thee to buy of me gold tried in the fire, that thou mayest be rich.' And I am bound to be rich. I am not merely at liberty: not merely have the right, the opportunity, the privilege of being rich: but I am under imperative and overwhelming obligation. Guilty though I be, I am bound to be the righteousness of God in him. With the sentence of death in myself, I am bound to arise from the dead and have life eternal. Cursed for continuing not in all things written in the law to do them, I am bound to have the blessing in all its fullness. Weak and helpless, I am bound to be strong in the Lord. Covered with shame, I am bound to glory in the Lord, and to be glorious in the eyes of the Lord. 'For he who was rich yet for our sakes became poor, that we through his poverty might be made rich.'

And I am shut up to acquiesce in this arrangement, and responsible, in my own case, for seeing to it, that this arrangement does not fail of its issue. I dare not face the guilt of making it, in my case, void. Jesus looks to me, to you, to each one of us, for his vindication, for his satisfaction, for his reward. He became poor. He who was rich became poor. Am I prepared to say that I will stand out and render this arrangement void, without effect, useless? I *do* make it, in my case, useless, if I am not poor in spirit. But I also make it useless, ineffectual, superfluous, if I do not by faith in Christ become rich. That is the fruit designed and contemplated by divine wisdom, love, and purpose. Save for making the poor rich, it fails and is dishonoured. Dishonoured, in fact, it shall never be. The Father's purpose must prevent it. Its own inherent character must prevent it. But my responsibility is not affected by the secret decree. I am called upon to come, and, by faith in Christ, receive, through his poverty, the destruction of my poverty and the enriching of my position and person before God for ever. It must be offensive to Christ if I affect to be rich when I am so poor. It must be offensive to Christ if I continue to be poor, when I may be so rich. I am constrained—necessity is laid upon me—to give effect by faith to this arrangement—to gratify and glorify Christ by giving effect to it.

He having entered into my position and poverty, I am bound to enter into his position and his riches. Had he merely proposed to become poor that I might become rich, I dared not have rejected his proposal. But it is no mere proposal: he who was rich for our sakes became poor: and now I have no alternative, but at once by faith to become rich. I see in his poverty how poor I am—for his poverty was for my sake, was for me, was mine. And if I would not stamp his wonderful arrangement with the brand of stupidity, and folly, and failure, I must follow out the design of his becoming poor, even this, namely, that I might become rich. By all the riches of glory in the highest heavens from which he stooped, and by all the depth of poverty as in the lowest hell to which he descended; and by all in Christ found anywhere within the range between that highest glory and that deepest shame, I am pressed in spirit to acquiesce in this glorious exchange, that it may not be of none effect; that I may have all my need supplied according to his riches in glory; that I through his poverty may be made rich; for better put it cannot be than in these sacred and ever-memorable words.

And thus, most marvellously, I am bound to be poor in myself to the utmost depths of poverty—and rich in Christ to the highest heights of the heavenly places: and I am bound in both these obligations, by the one inexpressibly splendid and inexhaustible arrangement by which 'he who was rich for our sakes became poor, that we through his poverty might be made rich.' Oh! poor and needy soul! As a magnet passes over iron filings and attracts them, you cannot escape from being drawn into the riches of Christ. Yours is the kingdom of heaven. You are pressed, constrained, shut up into it. The Spirit moves you to gratify him whom your soul loves—to gratify him by causing him to see of the travail of his soul—to see of the fruit of his poverty.

Come, therefore, to this glorious exchange. Be distinct, be special, be detailed, in transacting it. Jesus put himself in full detail into all your poverty. Bring your poverty in all its details, and find special, exact, countervailing riches. What is your poverty at this hour? what is your desire? Righteousness? Life? Blessing? Strength? Glory? Grace in thy Father's sight? Nearness to God? Peace? Joy? Comfort? Can you not find it in Christ's riches? in the unsearchable riches of Christ? and did he not suffer the very poverty from which, out of his riches, you desire relief? Is it your desire, for instance, to be near to God? and you feel that you are poor in that you are far from God? He who was rich in being near to God, in the Father's bosom, became poor, far-off, forsaken ('My God, my God, why hast thou forsaken me?') that we through this poverty might be made rich, might be brought nigh. Come only with your own poverty by the way of *his* poverty, and you shall find yourself, ere ever you are aware, standing amidst the full riches of Christ—acceptable in the Father's sight; alive for evermore; blessed with all spiritual blessing in heavenly places in Christ Jesus; strong in the Lord and in the glory of his power; changed into the same image from glory to glory—the faithful Lord fulfilling in this wondrous and charming method his all-comprehending promise, 'The Lord will give grace and glory' (Psa. 84:11), according to the riches of his own grace, and according to his riches in glory by Christ Jesus. For, in every respect wherein Christ was rich, he became poor; that, in every respect wherein we were poor, we might be rich. μ.

ESSAY 4

JUSTIFICATION [1]

T HE justification of a sinner is a Divine transaction full of wonders. It is emphatically and eminently 'the doing of the Lord,' for 'it is God that justifieth,' and 'it is marvellous in our eyes.' Nor can it be understood with that spiritual intelligence which calls forth our admiration and gratitude and praise, without our being led to see, as a first principle—(what is three times stated in the compass of a single verse, Gal. 2:16)—that 'a man is not justified by the works of the law.'

The justification of an unfallen, ever-dutiful creature and holy subject of God is an act most simple, involving not the slightest moral difficulty, and illustrating no marvellous or peculiar principles. It consists simply in judicially declaring the obedient and righteous one, whose case is to be disposed of, to be what he really is—obedient and righteous. It acquits of all blame or charge him who by stainless purity and innocence has incurred none; and it pronounces to be worthy of reward, or entitled to the promise, him who by his own merit and service, according to the stipulated condition, has earned his right and title and reward to the full. Nothing can be more simple in its procedure, or more obvious in its principle, than justification in such a case as this. The innocence of the innocent is investigated and admitted: the righteousness of the righteous is brought to light and acknowledged and rewarded. The just is pronounced to be just, and accepted and dealt with as such. The just is justified.

---

[1] [From: *The British and Foreign Evangelical Review* (1880), p. 393f.]

But when we pass from the justification of the holy and unfallen to contemplate the justification of the sinner, it immediately becomes clear that if such a thing is not an utter impossibility—if it is not, as reason would at first sight pronounce, a contradiction in terms—it must be through the introduction of other principles—principles otherwise unnecessary and inadmissible, and indeed altogether new and astonishing.

For, let it be observed that justification in this case, precisely as in the other, is to consist in a judicial announcement that the party is free from blame and righteously entitled to reward. This is to be the import of the act performed or privilege conferred—a full acquittal from all charge or condemnation, and a full acknowledgment of a perfect right and title to all honour, inheritance, and life eternal. This is to be the deliverance from the tribunal of the Holy One—the tribunal from which no error can proceed, and from which no appeal can be taken; and this deliverance, accurate, final, irresistible, is to be anent a sinner—a sinner guilty before God and his mouth stopped—declaring that sinner, notwithstanding that he is such, to be free from blame and entitled to favour and blessing and heaven.

Here, we again repeat, is a marvellous thing; and the marvel is that it is not an impossibility, an unrighteousness, a contradiction. To save it from being such, it is requisite that certain principles be introduced, unknown in the simple transaction of justifying the holy and unfallen.

These principles are three—namely, Grace, Suretyship, and Faith.

We shall, in the first place, notice the manner in which they are introduced, rendering the justification of a sinner possible, holy, and real; and, in the second place, we shall show how each of these three principles excludes the presence and influence of works or merit from this same act of a sinner's justification—thus demonstrating the thrice repeated declaration or doctrine of Galatians 2:16, that 'a man is not justified by the works of the law.'

I. In the first place, we propose to give a sketch of the manner in which these three principles, unnecessary and unknown in the justification of the innocent and obedient, become requisite and indispensable in justifying the ungodly.

1. And *first*, Grace must appear, else the sinner lies unpitied, unrelieved, beneath the sentence due to his iniquity; for 'cursed is every one that continueth not in all things written in the book of the law to do them,' and 'the wrath of God, is revealed from heaven against all unrighteousness and ungodliness of men.' Hence grace must interpose.

In justifying the holy and unerring, grace is not required nor admissible. 'To him that worketh is the reward not reckoned of grace, but of debt.' Omniscient accuracy in examining his work or obedience, and then inflexible justice announcing and rewarding its faultless perfection,—this is all that is required where the law has been fulfilled and its reward been earned. Justice, simple and alone, rules this simple case. But where the subject is a sinful man, confessedly rebellious and apostate, alienated by an evil heart and by wicked works from God, and worthy of the Divine abhorrence and wrath,—if the penalty, righteously incurred, is nevertheless to be remitted, and the reward not earned is nevertheless to be conferred, this result must accrue from the grace of God; and the grace thus coming into action must obviously be absolutely sovereign and free. For the sinner, having broken a law that is holy and just and good, is in the hands and at the disposal of an offended righteous lawgiver; justice awards to him the wrath of God and the second death; it does so with unimpeachable righteousness. There can be no principle of holy government traversed, no rights in God's whole creation violated, no rightful claims dishonoured or neglected, if this guilty and condemned transgressor be forsaken to the doom he has incurred. And the Sovereign Lord is in the position therefore—a position standing out in bold relief against the dark background of the sinner's dreadful doom, strongly and sharply delineated in the light of unanswerable justice as it fills the court of heaven and discloses the rectitude of the sinner's condemnation and the terrors of the sinner's peril,—the Sovereign Lord is in the position to vindicate his pure sovereignty and the free good pleasure of his will, and to declare that 'he will have mercy on whom he will have mercy; he will have compassion on whom he will have compassion.' Any dislike to his sovereignty, any appeal against his mere sovereignty, in such a case, is an infatuated retreat into the hands of justice, as it is offended by our sin, and demands our death. The one door of hope here, in this valley of Achor, is the good pleasure of the will of God—the introduction and inbringing of singular, signal, sovereign grace; the only grace, free, sovereign, and unfettered, that can be seasonable, or suitable, or sufficient for the crisis. The grace of God must appear, bringing salvation. For while the sinner stands condemned, shut up to the righteously deserved wrath of God, sovereign grace holds the key of the position, the key of David that openeth and no man shutteth, and shutteth and no man openeth. Save for the introduction of grace, the sinner must go down into the pit.

If you are saved from going down into the pit, if you are acquitted and accepted notwithstanding your demonstrated and acknowledged guilt, if after lying in the hands of Divine justice you nevertheless appear at liberty again no more condemned but justified of God, most obvious it is that you are justified freely by his grace. In proportion to the force with which you realised the fact and the righteousness of your former condemnation, must you now be ready with the deeper emphasis to say, 'According to his mercy he saved me, that being justified by grace, I might be made an heir according to the hope of eternal life' (Titus 3:7). Thus all throughout Holy Scripture the sinner's acquittal from guilt and acceptance as righteous are attributed to the grace, the mercy, the free love of God. 'According to the good pleasure of his will, to the praise of the glory of his grace, wherein he hath made us accepted in the Beloved. In whom we have redemption through his blood, even the forgiveness of sins, according to the riches of his grace' (Eph. 1:5-7). Expressly, indeed, to illustrate the existence, in the glorious depths of his own nature, of this lovely attribute of grace, does God justify the ungodly, revealing at the same time its unsearchable riches, its infinite fullness, its absolute all-sufficiency, which can meet the case of literally the chief of sinners. He willeth to make known the riches of his glory in the vessels of mercy. His heart is set on demonstrating the boundlessness of the mercy he hath kept in store for them. Yea, and his grand design is not merely to show his grace in this life and in this world, during the ages of this world only, or to the inhabitants of this world only, but that in the ages to come, and unto the principalities and powers in heavenly places; in coming ages and in other worlds; he might show the exceeding riches of his grace in his kindness towards us through Jesus Christ (Eph. 2:7). Hence, while we were yet without strength, while we were ungodly, while we were enemies, guilty and condemned, God commendeth his love to us, in that he made provision to save us from wrath, to justify us freely, to reconcile us to himself as righteous and pleasing in his sight. And herein 'God is rich in mercy, even for the great love wherewith he loved us, when we were dead in trespasses and in sins: for by grace are ye saved' (Eph. 2:4, 5).

Hence, the saints in Scripture, in seeking relief from the sentence of condemnation and the sense of sin, are found betaking themselves to the mercy, the grace, the loving-kindness of God. 'Hear me, God; for thy loving-kindness is good: turn unto me according to the multitude of thy tender mercies' (Psa. 69:16). 'Remember, Lord, thy tender mercies and thy loving-kindnesses; for they have been ever of old. Remember not the sins of my youth, nor my transgressions: according to thy mercy remember me, for thy goodness' sake, Lord' (Psa. 25:6, 7). 'Where is the sounding of thy bowels and of thy tender mercies towards me?' (Isa. 63:15). 'Have mercy upon me, Lord, according to thy loving-kindness; according to the multitude of thy tender mercies blot out my transgressions' (Psa. 51:1). And having found relief, to this attribute of God and this principle in his procedure towards them, to the sovereign and free introduction of this principle of grace, of gratuitous compassion, of unclaimable, unexpected love, they uniformly attribute all the glory. 'O give thanks unto the Lord, for he is good: for his mercy endureth for ever. Let the redeemed of the Lord say so, whom he hath redeemed from the hand of the enemy' (Psa. 107:1, 2).

Thus in the justification of the ungodly, Grace is conspicuous. It is a free gift that comes upon sinners unto justification of life; abundance of grace and of the gift of righteousness. And under the reign of grace alone could the ungodly be acquitted or accepted as righteous. But this principle of Grace has been introduced, to the praise of the glory of

God, and in a measure of full sufficiency for every hearer of the gospel: for 'where sin abounded, grace did much more abound' (Rom. 5:20).

2. But, *secondly,* it is just as clear that some other principle still must be introduced, though it were only to justify the introduction of this first principle of Grace. It cannot be supposed that the sovereignty wherewith this grace of God in the very nature of things must act is a mere arbitrary resolution on the part of God to do anything whatsoever, whether that might be worthy of himself or not. Grace, though sovereign, cannot possibly be an arbitrary principle of procedure, carrying out its purpose at all hazards, whatever damage might accrue to the interests of holiness, or whatever dishonour to the character of God. In justifying the ungodly, it must proceed on some basis of action, some understanding, some ground or reason, sufficient to justify itself. For, if some sufficient ground to which sovereign grace may have regard be not brought forward, it is impossible to vindicate or justify the grace of God in justifying the ungodly. Grace, in proposing to reverse the sentence of condemnation, must be able to justify itself to justice,—that justice which pronounced the sentence now about to be reversed. Nor can the wisdom, the faithfulness, the immutability of God be redeemed from sore aspersion, unless a new ground be brought forward sufficient to account for this change of procedure towards the guilty.

For, to condemn at one moment and justify the next, however the first may have proceeded from justice and the second from grace, must be an anomaly in government, utterly inexplicable, unless the Judge hath, in so changing and reversing his sentence, admitted into consideration or calculation a new and another principle, confessedly regarded as absent when the sentence of condemnation was pronounced. Save for this, the change must be absolutely arbitrary, reasonless, groundless; either the former sentence of condemnation, or the new sentence of absolution, must be unjust; they cannot both, proceeding on the same ground or basis, be righteous; and on the supposition that the offender had been righteously condemned, his acquittal now must be unjust and unholy. It matters not to reply that it is an act of grace; the question is, how Grace, in achieving this act, can justify herself to Justice, whose acknowledgedly righteous sentence Grace thus presumes to set aside and to reverse.

Now in reply to this the answer is, that there is another ground introduced for Grace to recognise in justifying the ungodly—a ground or basis or foundation of procedure additional to any that Justice had under consideration in condemning; and that therefore, although the sentence of the one is diametrically opposed to that of the other, still they come not at all into collision or contradiction. Grace can vindicate her own decision or deliverance, maintaining its righteousness as resting on this new element, this new foundation.

This second principle thus brought forward is the Suretyship of Christ, the introduction of a mediator, a substitute, a surety. An atoning surety, satisfying divine justice and redeeming from the curse, himself being made a curse for us, places the work of Grace on a sure, a righteous, a holy foundation. The representation of the sinner at the bar of God by One altogether able to appear in his room, doing so of his own will, and appointed by supreme and sovereign authority to do so—one who is holy, harmless, undefiled, and separate from sinners; a divine person moreover, having his life in his own power as none but a divine person could have, able therefore to lay it down of himself, in the room and stead of others, able also to expend it in obeying in the room and stead of others, thus bringing in a righteousness available for them; the blood of his ransom, likewise, being the pricelessly satisfying and all-purchasing blood of God, and his righteousness the righteousness of God; a representative and substitute such as this, releasing his clients from the death which he bears in their room and name, and releasing them from needing to achieve the title which by his obedience he secures on their behalf, may well justify the grace of God in justifying the ungodly, and demonstrate that the reversal of the condemning sentence of justice will secure the approbation of justice itself, yea, will be the very dictate and demand and doing of justice now.

We are justified freely by his grace: but it is through the redemption that is in Christ; and Grace reigns through righteousness. We have redemption, even the forgiveness of sins, through his blood. Yea, we are ʻjustified freely by his grace, through the redemption that is in Christ, whom God hath set forth to be a propitiation through faith in his blood, to declare his justice in the remission of sins, to declare at this time his justice, in that he is both just and the justifier of him that believeth on Jesus' (Rom. 3:24-26).

Introduce this as the meritorious ground—the obedience, namely, and blood-shedding of the Lamb of God, standing in the room of his people, the responsible Head and Husband of the Church, appointed to be so by the offended Lawgiver himself the Sovereign God,—himself God's dear Son, acquiescing of his own accord and with much delight in the position, and sustained in it by the infinite sufficiency of the Eternal Spirit;—and divine grace, having respect or regard to such a ground of procedure, appears no more an arbitrary, reasonless thing, choosing to say the opposite of what justice had solemnly said; but reasonable, righteous, and holy, itself even providing this very surety, and seeing to it that in him all the deliverances of justice shall be justified and executed, all the demands of justice owned and satisfied; providing, also, that through this holy and righteous channel, through the channel of the law made honourable and magnified in the cross and righteousness of God manifest in the flesh, a salvation free and rich, sovereign, triumphant, and unchallengeable, shall accrue to the poor and needy, without money and without price.

Such is the meritorious cause or justifying reason of justification by grace. Grace is the originating cause of justification, but the death and obedience unto death of a qualified and willing substitute is the meritorious or procuring cause. Sovereign grace is the free source, imputed righteousness the valid ground. The Father's grace is the fountain; the Son's righteousness is the foundation. The justified transgressor tastes the sweetness of the fountain, tries the security of the foundation. He tastes that the Lord is gracious, unto whom coming as unto a living stone, a foundation elect and precious, he is built up a lively stone, a member of a spiritual house, an acceptable royal priesthood.

Thus we are justified freely by his grace, but we are justified through the redemption, the propitiation, the righteousness of Christ. And thus the sovereign Lord secures his honour, declares his righteousness, vindicates and justifies the holiness of his grace, and establishes for ever the security of his gracious procedure in justifying the ungodly that believe on Jesus.

Here, then, are two principles in the justification of a sinner, altogether new, and unknown in the justification of the unfallen,—(*first*), Grace, sovereign free grace and love, justifying where mere justice must condemn; and (*secondly*) the surety-righteousness of Christ, making it as thoroughly just and righteous for grace to acquit and accept as for justice to condemn and disown.

And these two principles, the grace of God and the suretyship of Christ, singularly support each other. For it is grace that in seeking to justify the ungodly has provided the suretyship as a ground of justification. And it is this suretyship as the ground of the sinner's justification which justifies grace in justifying the sinner that believeth.

3. Observe, 'the sinner *that believeth*.' For there is manifestly a third new principle required, in order that this justification by sovereign grace through imputed righteousness may take effect, may actually take effect in each separate instance. The whole world is not justified *en masse*, simply because there is a source of justification in the grace of God and a ground of justification in the suretyship of Christ. Personally and individually, one by one, each for himself, must sinful men come under the operation of these principles if they are to enjoy actual justification before God. And what, it may be asked, is it that brings one and not another, that brings some and not all,—what is it that brings any into contact or connection with the grace which is the origin of this privilege, or the righteousness which is the foundation of it? Evidently there is necessity for some third new principle, not requisite, and indeed inadmissible, in the justification of the holy and unfallen. It is the principle of Faith:—Faith, by which, as an act and habit of the heart, the sinner appeals to the grace of God; by which, as by a mental spiritual instrument, the sinner appropriates the righteousness of Christ.

And it is evident that this personal and appropriating faith on the sinner's part is required on God's part not by a mere arbitrary decree, any more than his own act of grace is a mere arbitrary and groundless deliverance. In the very nature of the case faith is requisite in order that this justification by grace may actually take effect. For it must take effect and terminate in the sinner's own conscience. It must so transpire and be enacted there, as that he may be free from guilt in his conscience,—free from all sentence, prosecution, and condemnation there. But a justification thus taking effect in the inmost spiritual being of an intelligent responsible subject of the divine government— the first condition and commencement of his intelligent friendship with God—cannot possibly accomplish its own design, save where it is understood and acquiesced in, where it is embraced and rested on, where it is intelligently appreciated, appealed to, and appropriated by the individual. But to do this is the very office of faith. Without faith therefore it is impossible to be justified before God, impossible to please God, or be pleasing and accepted in his sight. Without faith, transferring the soul and all its confidence to the new foundation laid in Zion, to the atoning, accepted substitute, it is impossible to have any personal interest in the new righteousness of justification. Without faith confiding in the grace and free promise of God, it is impossible to lean on the new righteousness, which is itself the provision and the gift of grace. Without faith, the sinner stands alone, and aloof from the Lord our righteousness; and not being in him as the Lord his righteousness, the imputation of righteousness to such an one on God's part would be a mere fiction or mistake: he remains, therefore, destitute of righteousness, unjustified, condemned. So indispensable is faith as a means of bringing the sinner into the grace of justification, and under the ministration or imputation of its righteousness.

Here, then, is the *third* principle introduced, namely, Faith; securing the connection of the individual with the ground of justification, which is the righteousness of Christ, and with the source of justification, which is the grace of God.

Here we may pause with advantage, and notice in the light of these remarks the different senses in which Holy Scripture attributes our justification to three different causes,—distinct yet conspiring— distinct and therefore conspiring.

1. In the *first* place, we are said to be justified by the grace of God, as in Romans 3:24: 'Being justified freely by his grace.' For being, as sinners, under the righteous wrath of God, our justification in such circumstances must be an act of eminent and singular, of free and

unfettered grace. Its very origin must be in grace. Its very possibility, its very idea or conception, presupposes grace. We are justified by grace as the *originating* cause.

2. In the *second* place, we are said to be justified by the righteousness or obedience of Christ, including of course his death, as the most eminent act of his obedience, as in Romans 5:19: 'By the obedience of one shall many be made righteous.' For, being destitute of all righteousness ourselves, and justice demanding a perfect satisfaction and impregnable title ere it remit the sentence of death, and confer the reward of life, and Jesus in our room bearing the curse, and bringing in the righteousness to which God has regard in justifying us, we are thus justified by the righteousness of Christ as the *procuring* cause.

3. And, *thirdly,* we are said to be justified by faith, as in Romans 5:1: 'Being justified by faith, we have peace with God,' or in Galatians 2:16: 'A man is justified by the faith of Jesus Christ;' and the reason is that faith as an instrument embraces and pleads the righteousness of Christ, and appeals and gives glory to the grace of God. We are justified by faith as the *instrumental* cause.

Thus do these three causes—the originating cause, the procuring cause, the instrumental cause—conspire, each in its own place, and for its own end, to put us in possession of a merciful and holy, a pleadable and sure justification. We attribute all to the grace of God alone, as its source. We rest all on the righteousness of Christ alone, as the sure and sufficient ground. We hold all in actual possession by faith, and faith alone.

Thus much for the sketch we proposed to give of the three principles inevitably introduced into justification, if it is to be the justification of one worthy of death.

II. And now, secondly—which may now be comparatively a brief work—let us consider how each of these three principles necessarily excludes the presence and influence of 'works.'

Nay, rather, let us show—from Scripture of course, our only source of knowledge—how the introduction of works, even in any measure, must subvert at once the grace of God as the origin, the righteousness of Christ as the ground, and the exercise of faith as the instrument, of our justification. So that by works (1) the grace of God is frustrated, (2) the death of Christ made in vain, (3) faith itself made void.

1. If you introduce the element of works at all, in any measure, into the question of your acceptance with God, and the ground of your peace with God, you immediately fetter and thereby frustrate the grace of God. From this—from frustrating the grace of God—from such guilt, Paul shrank back affrighted. 'I do not frustrate the grace of God,' said he. It is as with a cry of agony that he flees, affrighted, from such guilt. And how that fearful guilt may be incurred, he shows is by resting our acceptance on our own obedience, or expecting righteousness or justification to come by the law. 'I do not frustrate the grace of God; for if righteousness come by the law, Christ is dead in vain' (Gal. 2:21). And again, in warning the Galatians against resting anything of their acceptance with God upon the law, or imagining circumcision necessary to their justification, he cries out to them with peculiar solemnity in one of those passages in which, Luther said, Paul thundered rather than spake: 'I testify again to every man that is circumcised, that he is a debtor to do the whole law. Christ is become of none effect to you, whosoever of you are justified by the law; ye are fallen from grace' (Gal. 5:3, 4).

'Ye are fallen from grace:'—'Ye have frustrated grace.'

And let it be remarked, we 'fall from grace'—we 'frustrate grace'—not merely by excluding it altogether, but by admitting works to any rivalry or co-ordinate share of influence with it, even in the least degree. For if it is of works at all, it is no more grace. For, argues our apostle, 'To him that worketh is the reward not reckoned of grace, but of debt; but to him that worketh not'—to him who in this matter, and for this end, absolutely worketh not, worketh nothing, abstains from working, obtrudes or introduces no works at all—but simply 'believeth on him that justifieth the ungodly, his faith is counted for righteousness' (Rom. 4:4, 5). Otherwise righteousness could not be imputed to him. He could not be justified. It is his entire cessation in this matter from all works that can alone admit the action of grace. To trust in works and distrust grace are more than conjoined. Self-righteousness and unbelieving dislike or suspicion of grace are indeed identical.

Let me appeal to those whom it may concern, and ask them to examine their own hearts. Why is it that you do not take your entire and trustful and hearty appeal to the free, unfettered, sovereign grace of God? Why is it that you are not content and delighted that God should be altogether sovereign in showing mercy? Why do you feel as if something grated harshly on your ear, or your heart or hopes, when the voice of the gracious Lord is heard, 'I will have mercy on whom I will have mercy, and I will have compassion on whom I will have compassion'? Why should *that* give you pain, or give you pause? It would not do so if you felt that you have not, and can never have, any righteousness of your own. You imagine that God, in declaring he will have mercy on you simply and only if he please, is overlooking and dishonouring some claim which you possess upon his mercy, some hold upon his pity which your goodness or repentance or anxieties and prayers have given you. Oh! if you would believe it, sovereign, free mercy is much more large and unbounded—much more safe and sufficient—in its perfect freedom, which you never can bring under constraint to you, than all your fancied claim could be, though it were ten thousand times stronger than your fondest imagination can conceive. Free grace is unsearchably rich. It hath multitudes of tender mercies; and it *acteth 'according* to the multitude of its tender mercies.' Free grace, in virtue of being utterly unfettered and free, is precisely the grace that can omnipotently and all freely move and sway, in answer to your need; the helm, answering in the darkest night and the utmost tempest—'though the waters roar and are troubled, and the mountains shake with the swelling thereof.' Free grace, most sovereign, acting on the lead, and following second to no claim or work or righteousness of yours, following second to no power in earth or hell or heaven, owning no power higher than itself, but triumphing in the absolute and inde- pendent power of its own sweet royal will, reigning on its throne—its 'throne of grace,'—at which let no sin-stained soul ever dare to unfold his offensive claim of right, and no contrite sinner ever dread to tell his tale of woe in deep and full confession,—free grace, most sovereign, is that alone that can suffice for you, for it is that of which alone it can be said, 'Where sin abounded, grace hath much more abounded.' Why will you not leave the grace of God to be free and independent, royal and sovereign indeed? Why will you produce any worth or works of yours, and wield them as an instrument to arrest and constrain and fasten down this grace of God? Why will you seek to tie up the hands of love? Why not acquiesce in the free and sovereign reign of grace?

Even *sin* hath reigned: 'Sin hath reigned unto death:' sin hath reigned with your own consent. It hath spurned control and brooked no interference with the freedom of its reign. Sin, in you, hath had the field unhindered, to itself. This is the real ground for any anxieties anent death and eternity and God. Sin hath reigned; and you have allowed it. And will you not allow Grace to reign?—to reign over you, and in you, and for you, unto your salvation and eternal life? Will you not allow it to reign, that by its own free and kingly and unhampered and triumphant action, it may justify you freely, and make you also free and kingly and unhampered and triumphant in the liberty wherewith Christ by free grace makes his people free? Your self-righteousnesses are but chains you forge wherewith to bind this king a captive for your service. Will he stoop to the infinite degradation? No: he will sit free on his own royal seat, his 'throne of grace,' and acting from thence, he will save in his sovereign reign and pleasure, or not at all. If you yield not to the reign of grace, you are a slave beneath the reign of sin, and sin shall reign over you unto the second death. Why, then, will you not shake off every dependence on your own righteousness and works? Say not that you have really done so, unless you be content to rest on sovereign grace; and unless, being content and really resting, you find in that rest and that contentment some of the repose of soul which rest and contentment are sure to bring.

But if not yet content with sovereign grace alone, it is because you have not yet resigned every other hope; because you cling to something you have done, or still expect to have power (or even help from God) to do; because you desire to have something of your own by which to secure your salvation yourself, by which to tie and bind the Lord and his mercy. You cannot bear the thought of leaving God free; with all its absurdity, you would rather lay some train that would necessitate and force the action of grace. And then it would be grace no more: its very nature would be subverted, and its action frustrated. 'But,' says Paul, 'I do not frustrate the grace of God.'

2. The introduction of works equally overthrows the suretyship of Christ. In that case Christ is made of none effect to you. Christ is dead in vain!

What an impeachment of the righteousness and wisdom of God!—to pursue any line of action, thought, or feeling, which, if right, must naturally tend to show that Christ is dead in vain, fruitlessly, uselessly, unnecessarily! But if by some works or worth of yours you can entitle yourself to the justifying grace of God, then God himself cannot be justified in requiring the satisfaction and atonement of Christ to vindicate his grace in justifying you. He, in that case, demanded a sacrifice and subjected his own Son to suffering which you undertake to prove might have been dispensed with. Away with the vain and blasphemous attempt! But how away with it? Only if, resigning every rag of righteousness, every plea and claim, we (in the first place) justify God in thus condemning us,—and this we do when we say from the heart, 'Against thee, thee only, have I sinned, and done this evil in thy sight, that thou mightest be justified when thou speakest, and be clear when thou judgest;' and if (in the second place) we justify God in calling in the death of his Son as the only ground of our justification, and this we do when we flee to Christ as our refuge, counting all things but loss that we may gain Christ, and be found in him, not having our own righteousness, which is of the law, but the righteousness which is through the faith of Christ,—the righteousness which is of God by faith.

3. For, thirdly, as resting on our own works subverts justification, both as originating in the grace of God, and as founded on the suretyship of Christ, so thereby also is 'faith made void;' for 'if they which are of the law be heirs, faith is made void, and the promise,' to which faith looks, 'is made of none effect' (Rom. 4:14). And the reason is, that faith leaning in any measure on our works—looking to a promise suspended or conditional on our righteousness—a fallible, faltering, failing condition—faith, in that case, falters and fails too. Let faith rest on sovereign, unconditional grace, on a righteousness already finished and eternal, on a promise not suspended on any condition,

but absolute; then 'it is of faith, that it might be by grace, to the end the promise might be sure to all the seed' (Rom. 4:16). And thus, faith, claiming God's free love, in Christ's sure, and perfect work, on the warrant of God's absolute, unfailing word, abides fully 'persuaded that what God hath promised he is able also to perform; and therefore it is imputed to us for righteousness' (Rom. 4:21, 22). Every reason for suspicion of insecurity is cleared away; every gate by which danger might enter is closed; the glory shines forth as belonging wholly to the Lord; the covenant stands impregnable as the everlasting and blessed home of our weary and waiting souls: and 'being justified by faith, we have peace with God, through our Lord Jesus Christ; by whom also we have access by faith into the grace wherein we stand, and rejoice in hope of the glory of God.' μ.

CONSCIENCE AND
THE BLOOD OF SPRINKLING[1]

A VERY strong argument for the strictly substitutionary, propitiatory, justice-satisfying character of the sacrifice of Christ may be presented and pressed from the fact of his blood being called the 'blood of sprinkling,' and spoken of, as it is so often in Holy Scripture, as having such bearing on the conscience—the peace, the purity, and the health of the conscience.

Such argument is, in these days, assuredly not unnecessary, as must be known to all who are acquainted with the lines on which modem theological speculation runs. In the earlier decades of the century the Socinian view of Christ's death as an example—an example of patience under suffering—was almost the only theory antagonistic to the Westminster doctrine of propitiation which the Church was called on to contend against. And very noble and satisfactory were her contendings. Nor are they yet to be dispensed with. For that such a doctrine is eminently and fatally destructive of the truth as it is unto salvation we need scarcely say; and poorly equipped, indeed, for the office of the ministry must that unfortunate man be, who has not a heart-hatred for Socinianism, and a quiver well filled with deadly arrows against its soul-destroying errors, and especially this fundamental one. For no intelligent theologian can hesitate to give us his hearty concurrence when we say that in view of this leading tenet, Socinianism is even worse than Popery itself. Roman Catholicism has never abandoned the great leading truth of Christianity. Many even of

---

[1] [From: *The British and Foreign Evangelical Review* (1882), p. 258f.]

her perversions of the truth are built on the great leading doctrine that the sacrifice of our Lord Jesus Christ was truly a propitiation for the sins of mankind. The very Mass itself might be mentioned as a testimony to this great truth. And while many of her tenets are fitted with diabolical ingenuity to make it void, still it is there, rendering these perversions themselves unintelligible without it. So much so is this true, that no intelligent Christian, if shut up to make a choice between Romanism and Socinianism, could have a moment's difficulty; because while by a simple combination of grace and providence, though born and brought up under the influence of Romanism, it might be possible to throw off the super-incumbent mass of Romanising perversions, and find and feed upon the catholic truth of Christ and him crucified, there is nothing in Socinianism to favour the 'precious redemption' of souls at all. We trust to meet in a better world with many who have lived and died in the communion of the Romish church,—a hope which the entire ignoring of anything to be called real 'reconciliation with God' on the part of the votaries of Socinianism renders simply impossible.

And, indeed, Socinianism is, and ever will continue to be the Church's most deadly antagonist. Notwithstanding the more fascinating aspects in which the Broad-Churchism of these later decades has succeeded in presenting a negative theology of *'example'* even when 'self-sacrifice,' and 'martyrdom,' and 'fidelity amidst suffering,' are contended for, the notion of 'example' is, after all, the essence of every view of the Cross which fails to present it as a substitutionary sacrifice to satisfy Divine justice, and reconcile us unto God. In whatever fresh and constantly changing forms anything less than that chooses to present itself, it will uniformly be found that radically and at bottom it is really nothing more than a Socinian evasion of the idea of atonement, propitiation, substitutionary and juridical sacrifice. The arguments that suffice to overthrow Socinianism overthrow Broad-Churchism too. There are, indeed, these two alternatives, and no more—the orthodox 'sacrifice to satisfy Divine justice,' and the Socinian interpretation of 'example.' In all cases it is towards Socinianism that the natural man inevitably gravitates, because the other passes a severer condemnation upon himself than he can bear. He is content, from his want of conviction of sin, to take up with any view of the Cross that allows him to escape without assenting, and (especially) consenting, to those juridical views of sin in which the conviction essentially consists. Is 'sin any want of conformity unto or transgression of the law of God'? Does every sin, as such, 'deserve God's wrath and curse, both in this life and in that which is to come'? Then, without entering into any moral philosophy of the nature, origin, and function of conscience, enough to say that conscience is that faculty which consents unto the truth of these things: and if so, there is, staring us in the face, in point of fact, a juridical case already, calling for juridical redemption such as we have in view when, in the language of every Calvinistic church on earth, we say: 'Christ executes the office of a priest, in his once offering up of himself a sacrifice to satisfy Divine justice, and reconcile us unto God; and in making continual intercession for us' (*The Shorter Catechism*). The whole truth set forth in the Westminster standards, which is the catholic doctrine of sin and sacrifice-for-sin—wrath as sin's desert, and reconciliation as the result of such sacrifice—is seen to hold beautifully together. The same thing is true of a correct representation of sin and of Christ's sacrifice for sin. The desert of sin must correspond with his design of sacrifice for sin. If the real nature of sin be denied, as violation of necessary and truly moral law; and if (consequently) the righteousness of God's wrath and curse fail to be recognised;—if, on the contrary, the notion be that sin is a calamity or a disease for which the adequate attitude of the Divine mind must be compassion, wrath or curse would then only be synonymous with hatred and grudge—cruel hatred and degrading grudge, or rage;—in that case, the only existing or tenable pre-supposition of holy, justice-satisfying, or reconciliatory sacrifice is altogether absent; and defence of the Westminster doctrine of the Cross becomes impossible.

Our views of sacrifice-for-sin must be determined by our views of sin itself, and these again by our views of moral law. Where moral law is assimilated to laws of nature, and transgression of it to transgression of them, in the very nature of things sin becomes more a calamity to be deplored than a criminality to be condemned, and place cannot be found in men's minds for the idea of a propitiatory sacrifice. If a man cannot say, 'Against thee, thee only, have I sinned, and done sin in thy sight; that thou mightest be justified when thou speakest, and be clear when thou judgest,' then how can he be willing to add, 'Purge me with hyssop, and I shall be clean; wash me, and I shall be whiter than snow'?

There is a passage in the Epistle to the Hebrews (9:13, 14) which may at this stage be somewhat carefully examined, with advantage to our argument:—'If the blood of bulls and of goats, and the ashes of an heifer sprinkling the unclean, sanctifieth to the purifying of the flesh; how much more shall the blood of Christ, who through the eternal Spirit offered himself without spot to God, purge your conscience from dead works, to serve the Living God?'

It is evident that it contains one central and absolute and supremely important proposition: 'The blood of Christ purges the conscience to serve the living God.' The proposition, however, is not put forward in this gaunt and naked form. It is set off and enriched by a twofold rhetorical method. There is, *first*, the use of a comparison drawn from the Old Testament ordinances, according to the use and wont of this archaic and beautifully variegated epistle, and followed by an argumentative 'how much more?'—enforcing the still more obvious certainty that Christ's sacrifice for sin is efficaciously such as is being pleaded for. Into the nature, design, and results of those ancient and divinely appointed ordinances, with their certain action and unquestioned efficacy, we need not now enter, farther than to notice these two essential points;—(1) that they were not matters of will-worship, but indeed appointed by Divine authority; and (2) that they carried with them undoubted efficaciousness for the ends for which they were instituted. Poor types or illustrations of the sacrifice of Christ they would have been had they not, but of the fact that 'the blood of bulls and of goats, and the ashes of an heifer sprinkling the unclean, sanctified unto the purifying of the flesh,' thoroughly removing in God's own way all disability for, access to, and engagement in, the worship of God as instituted and maintained in Israel of old, there could be, and was, no doubt whatever. And that the assertion of this undoubted fact was entitled to be followed by the 'how much more?' when asserting the efficacy of the sacrifice of Christ is equally plain; while the otherwise absolute and somewhat bald-like statement of what is really the leading and invaluable proposition (concerning the efficacy of Christ's sacrifice) is, as we have said, both rhetorically enriched and argumentatively sustained.

But apart from this equally striking and powerful comparison, there is a whole galaxy of considerations, rendering to the great central proposition the same service, in the words, 'The blood of *Christ*, who, through the eternal Spirit, offered himself without spot to God.' None of these considerations—and we find four of them, all equally conclusive—enter grammatically into what we called the great fundamental proposition which the inspiring Spirit is desirous of teaching us. That proposition is complete at once in point of grammar and logic and rhetoric without them. But that various really enhancing and enriching considerations are presented to our notice by these accessory statements, it may be important to tarry long enough to show.

First, thus, as bearing vitally upon the efficacy of the sacrifice, we are called to remember that he who offered it is the 'Christ;' no private individual, engaging in a private and non-official transaction, but 'the Christ' of God, divinely appointed by supreme Divine authority, and anointed and qualified by the Divine Spirit (Luke 4:1) for offering a powerful, public, priestly, and efficacious atonement

Second, we have the great thought that he was personally and perfectly holy: which he required to be—both the spotless Lamb of God, if he would take away the sin of the world (John 1:29), as well as a not only duly appointed but adequately furnished high priest; for 'such an high priest became us, who was holy, harmless, undefiled, and separate from sinners' (Heb. 7:26). And in close alliance with that holiness, which 'became' at once the object of worship (Heb. 2:14), the offerer and the client (Heb. 7:26), and which is so often adverted to as essential to 'the Christ' who would redeem us, both as an acceptable Lamb of sacrifice and the efficacious high priest of our profession, we are taught to regard his Resurrection and ascension, when, without either a break or a pause in his statements, the writer to the Hebrews goes on to tell us that he is now 'made higher than the heavens' (Heb. 7:26, 27).

Thirdly, it would be an unpardonable mistake to omit pointing how powerfully discriminated and distinguished from all merely typical sacrifices that of Christ is, by his being priest as well as sacrifice,—a consideration never forgotten or omitted by the Spirit of truth—'He offered up himself,'

And, *fourthly*, the efficaciousness, acceptableness (to the Father, of course), and unsearchable perfection and glory of this sacrifice of Christ, are all affirmed in the strongest possible manner when it is declared that he achieved and presented this Sacrifice on the Cross in the utmost that even the eternal Spirit could enable him to do, by filling his person and action with all the moral excellency and glory that he could create and impart to his person—'He through the eternal Spirit offered himself without spot unto God.'

Each of these four considerations enters vitally into the reality, efficacy, glory, and acceptableness to God, even the Father, of the propitiatory sacrifice for us which Christ offered on the Cross. And we might descant almost to any extent on each of them, if our intention was to give a full exposition of the passage of Holy Scripture in which the *insignis locus*[1] and this illustrious congeries of statements occur.

But after all that we could say—and there is scarcely any end to what might relevantly, forcibly, and with advantage be said on these great themes of theology—it still remains an indubitable, and to any clear-thinking mind it is, in point of fact, an undoubted truth that the grand thought is independent of them, and sufficient by itself alone to engross attention: 'The blood of Christ purges the conscience from dead works to serve the living God.' And what possible meaning such language can have on any supposition anent the sacrifice of Christ which traverses the great truth that it is propitiatory, atoning, satisfying Divine justice, and righteously reconciling us to God, to a justly angry God, cleansing our persons also even unto the utmost depths of conscience from all imputation of sin both in God's sight and our own, the moment we concur with him, and have conscience with him in our case as it really stands in his view, and as it ought to stand, and does

[1] [Latin: pre-eminent truth.]

stand in our own, if we have due conviction of sin,—it is impossible to see. Our argument will be strengthened by a careful examination of these great words.

'Dead works' are works done in a state of spiritual death. A man's works are as the man himself is: if alive unto God, his works will be living; if spiritually dead, so also will his works be. Dead in trespasses and sins, the unconverted and uncalled sinner cannot present a living sacrifice. The very 'ploughing of the wicked is sin' (Prov. 21:4). Cut off from God personally, so also are his works, and therefore 'dead.' It is the great principle that Christ himself pleads for: 'Make the tree good if you would have the fruit good;' 'An evil tree cannot bring forth good fruit, neither can a good tree bring forth corrupt fruit.' So also, 'In that a man liveth, he liveth unto God.' For he is the 'Living God,' and, as such, the effectually called and truly believing serve him. They 'serve the living God.' Naturally we do not consider God for any practical purpose as the 'living God.' The man whose works are 'dead,' or who has not been 'purged from dead works,' does not consider his God as 'living.' He is himself spiritually dead, and his works are as himself. The moment he becomes spiritually alive, he liveth unto a living God, the fountain of his own new life. He has living fellowship with a living God, and his works are service to a living personal being. He no longer serves 'the great first cause,' or 'virtue,' or 'the moral interests of the universe,' or 'the nature of things,' or 'the dignity of human nature,' or ' the claims of society,' or 'the interest of being,' or any of those substitutes by which men dead to God, yet not altogether lost to thought, shut out from their view the One Living and True God, and the claims which his holy moral administration has upon them and their love. No; but 'the living God.'

Now there is nothing that tends to quicken this service more than an earnest, intelligent, believing dealing with the blood of Christ's sacrifice. And it may serve to make our views more exact and deep if we carry this thought with us throughout the present investigation. For the blood, or blood-shedding, the sacrifice or death of Christ, is not a 'dead work.' It is at the greatest conceivable distance from that. It is the greatest conceivable antagonist to death. 'He, through the eternal

Spirit,' and with such a tide of life as the unction and indwelling of the eternal Spirit could not fail to give, 'offered himself without spot to God' (Heb. 9:14). 'In the blood is the life.' 'Except a man drink my blood, he has no life abiding in him' (John 6:53). 'I am the resurrection and the life' (John 11:25). And no one can have followed the views we lately gave of Christ's death, conquering death, and opening the way for life, and life-giving, without seeing this. 'I am come that ye might have life, and that ye might have it more abundantly' (John 10:10).

No doubt in the Cross you have Christ's death—Christ dying—the separation of the soul and body. But what a tide of life! What an intensity of life! What a living transaction you have! His life is not ebbing away, he is laying it down, he is offering it to God. That is of the essence of the service, the priestly service he is rendering. His life is not ebbing away. The language of the Paraphrase—reminding us by the way of the constant danger to doctrine in those unauthorised hymns—that talks about 'light forsaking his closing eyes and life his drooping head' is most inaccurate; as the old theologians used so vigorously to say, 'abominably injurious' to the glorious fact.

Life did not forsake him: he was pouring it out: pouring out his soul unto death. He was bearing a burden that would have sunk all the angels of heaven. He needed to be the Resurrection and the Life: *and he was*, he was eminently, 'the Living One' while dying; and dealing with the 'Living God' in the most intensely active and living service the universe ever saw. Such living power and amazing glory is there in it, that, because of it, 'God hath highly exalted him, and given him a name that is above every name' (Phil. 2:9); and all holy beings proclaim but a simple fact when they proclaim him worthy to 'receive power, and riches, and wisdom, and strength, and honour, and glory, and blessing' (Rev. 5:12, 13). We know of none who deny that he was in possession of these things when they were ascribed unto him. We know of none in any recognised sphere of controversy so stupid as to imagine that these things were first communicated to him when ascribed. We know of none so thoroughly low in their theology as to suppose that these things never would have been his but for angelic songs which ascribe them. Where, otherwise, could those angelic songs have found their own justification? All those things which they ascribe to Christ in song were his in his dying moments—they were in the 'offering up of himself a sacrifice to satisfy divine justice'—else were the question pertinent: Where did they find them? They were *in his offering up of himself*: and it is somewhat shameful if his Church should require an argument to prove it. Holy heaven, in its worship of him, never did, nor does, nor will *contribute* any of these things; his worshippers simply *ascribe.* They read off what they see: recognise them as belonging to him, and so belonging to him ('power, and riches, and wisdom, and strength, and honour, and glory, and blessing') as to have been especially brought to light—brought into view, because into exercise—in pouring out his soul unto death as the slain Lamb of Sacrifice for sin. 'Worthy is the Lamb to receive power, and riches, and wisdom and strength, and honour, and glory, and blessing.' They are declaring what they see: that is the praise of the enlightened. They are promoting his declarative glory,—no more. And all that they see and celebrate is an action on the cross; and it is seen by faith—by every soul that believeth.

Take any one of these ascriptions—say the 'blessing,' and what of his endurance of the 'curse'? How could he have endured the 'curse,' but for the countervailing 'blessing' being present in its curse-extinguishing energy? In every view it would have been too late had it tarried to be conveyed only with the angelic ascription. And generally, summing them all up in that which they constitute, namely the Life, how otherwise was it that death did its utmost on the cross, and yet was prevented from being victorious? How was death vanquished, if not by Life, that master of the field, destroying death and him that had the power of death? And who should stand and mediate between the living and the dead—the living God and sinful man dead in trespasses and sins? Who, if not the Living One? Oh, what life was that which was in him, and said, 'I was daily his delight, rejoicing always before him' (Prov. 8:30)? What life was that which said—'Father, forgive them, for they know not what they do;' 'Father, into thy hands I commit my spirit' (Psa. 31:5)? We speak of Christ's active and passive obedience; it is inaccurate phraseology. The temptation to use it arises from the fact that he had to be obedient amid extreme suffering. Had there been no suffering, there could have been nothing to be called 'passive obedience.' But we are apt, through a misuse of the phrase, to conceive of Christ's obedience as if, whereas he had hitherto been going about doing good, that came to an end, and he had to do the best he could with his spiritual invisible energies ebbing away, and his whole attitude on the cross gradually becoming 'passive.' The very reverse is true. His activity continued with his sufferings, increased with their increase, and in still greater proportion—so that it was greatest at the close. It culminated and triumphed in the laying down of himself a sacrifice; else never could it have been a sacrifice to satisfy Divine justice and reconcile us to God. It was an active, powerful, living service, when he expiated the guilt of our dead works: and the great end of it was that we also might actively, powerfully, livingly 'serve the living God,' and have consciences in a condition to do so. But that they cannot be, except as the blood of Christ purges them, and that is what we are now inquiring into.

Even the pacifying, purifying, strengthening, and gladdening of the conscience is not the ultimate end of the blood-shedding of Christ. Even these are but means to an end still more important. The blood of Christ purges the conscience from dead works to serve the living God. To this end was he appointed and constituted the Christ. To this end did he offer himself a spotless lamb unto God. To this end did the eternal Spirit fill his human soul to the uttermost with all holy affection towards God and man—zeal towards God's glory, and love for man's salvation; rendering him in the hour of his offering up a sacrifice most acceptable to God—acceptable in its essential and fundamental character as a sin-expiating, God-atoning, wrath-appeasing, justice-satisfying sacrifice: and, being in this character a living sacrifice, satisfying God, magnifying his law, it satisfies the conscience of the sinner the more fully the more it is enlightened, and purging it from dead works to serve the living God.

It 'purges the conscience.' Yes; but not to be sent adrift as a pardoned criminal may be, to whom a monarch, in a relenting fit, may have extended his pity in an hour when his compassion may have been awakened. For here is the difference: The human mercy may have been granted from relenting in a fit of imbecility, or mental weakness. With God, it is unto the illustrious forth-showing of his glory ('his glory is made great in the salvation wrought by him') The human mercy may have been flung to the wretch from some doubt about the evidence, the pardoner merely stretching a point. Or it may have been contemptuously flung at his head. But here is *expiation*. In the one case, the wretch hugs himself in his good fortune, being nearly as much a wretch as ever. Here all is on honour. Specially is it so on God's part. The sovereign Lord God, instead of giving his law a wrench, hath magnified it and made it honourable—ascribing sovereignty unto it, and compelling universal recognition of it. 'I have sworn by myself, the word is gone out of my mouth in righteousness, and shall not return: Unto me every knee shall bow, every tongue shall swear. Surely, shall one say, In the Lord have I righteousness and strength' (Isa. 45:23, 24). All is on honour on our part also when we believe. The offending subject of a truly most holy, moral administration, glorified as that of God is by the Cross, cannot (simply cannot) understand, and consequently cannot appropriate, this pardon—can neither assent nor consent—without being on honour. 'They shall look on me whom they have pierced, and they shall mourn' (Zech. 12:10). The believer, on his own part, becomes free from guile when God frees him from guilt. Not from punishment or penalty merely, but—what is infinitely more and better—from the liability to punishment: not from punishment only, but from guilt—the desert of punishment. He becomes ashamed, yea, even confounded, and opens his mouth no more, when God is thus righteously pacified towards him. He becomes profoundly peaceful and pure; and his peace is not now marred by his mourning over his iniquity. This is, indeed, essential to his now being honourable with God, ('Since I have loved thee, thou hast been honourable.') And his forgiveness, being the fruit of love, as well as brought into an unexpected and glorious consonance with justice, instead of being the solitary privilege he obtains, after the obtaining of which he might drift away from the loving God, as if God should say, 'Now you may go.' No: God forbid. He is accepted and kissed, and clothed, and feasted; yea, and adopted, and the one grand motto of the complete transaction is, 'This my son was dead, and is alive again; was lost and is found,'—found, to be lost again no more. This is, indeed, the jet, or edge, or joy, of his being 'found.' Instead of drifting away again, he is 'found' so as to make that impossible any more. With all his heart, rather, will he henceforth serve the living God. 'The love of Christ constraineth us; because we thus judge, that if one died for all, then were all dead (themselves and their works too): and that he died for all, that, living, they might not henceforth live unto themselves, but unto him that died for them, and rose again' (2 Cor. 5:15).

There are three things that this sacrifice of Christ procures for those interested in it, and which go to render their equipment for 'serving the living God' complete:—(1). By the sacrifice of Christ they obtain a *right* to serve the living God; (2). They procure a *desire* to do it; (3). They procure the *ability* to do it. And these three things are all that can be imagined to be either necessary or helpful. Let the Lord give a man 1. the Right, 2. the Desire, 3. the Power for this service, and, immediately he enters on it, 'tis a case of the right man in the right place; and his language is:—'Lord, truly I am thy servant; I am thy servant, and the son of thine handmaid: thou hast loosed my bonds' (Psa. 116:16).

I. As to the right. It is to be observed that this aspect of the matter turns essentially on the sacrifice of Christ being in its nature atoning.

It is in that view alone that it bears an right, as right,—on the rights of God and of conscience—the being of God as the Moral Ruler of the universe, and the rights, the moral and pleadable rights, of moral creatures over whom he rules. All other views of Christ's Cross fail fundamentally here, because they have no bearing on *right* at all. They never really touch on what in any true holy sense can be called the rights of men, because they do not come into the realm of *right* at all. To the spiritually dead sinner, the Lord denies all right to serve him. 'To the wicked God saith, What hast thou to do to take my covenant into thy lips?' When such persons attempt to come before him with their services God saith, 'Who hath required this at your hand?' (Psa. 50:16; Isa. 1:12). Such persons have no idea that *right* has been violated and must be rectified. But that is the primary and essential idea at the root of all atonement—all sacrifice, propitiation, or expiation. No wonder, therefore, when the fundamental idea gets the go-by, the blossom goeth up like dust. Christ's death as an example, as a proof even of divine love, as a display even of the Divine perfection, as a transcendent instance of self-denial and self-sacrifice, may be fraught with many useful and most instructive lessons; and in all these points of view it may be worthy of most profound study and delighted admiration. But all of these taken together fail to present any bearing upon right—the rights of God, or the claims and requirements and rights of conscience. It is as an *atonement*—satisfying Divine justice, and on that ground reconciling us unto God (who otherwise insists that he is most righteously angry with us every day, and all the day long), that it bears on conscience, purging it from dead works to serve the living God. For it is in that view alone that it magnifies the Divine law, after which conscience craves continually, so long as conscience acts like itself at all, protesting for the honour of that holy law, and never satisfied without its vindication.

For, while not thinking it necessary, in a way of explaining conscience, to do more than indicate the practical correlation between conscience and the law of God,—without tarrying to arrange a moral philosophy of the subject,—it is enough to point out that what we have called attention to is just what is commonly called conviction of sin; and that is intelligible to average readers—learned and unlearned alike—without any philosophical distinctions. It is just conscious guilt; and no moral philosophy can supply it, where it is wanting, or even deepen it where it is present, though defective or shallow. Substantially, it is just honourable and guileless confession. The claims of God's law, the rights of God himself, as the Moral Ruler of the universe, must be satisfied and vindicated, if I am to plead any rights; and before I can, save with consummate and inconceivable impudence, in the presence of high heaven, speak or even think of any rights of mine, or 'rights of man.' Till God's rights are satisfied, man's must be in abeyance, even my rights of conscience must till then be in abeyance—excepting only the rights of my conscience (if it is to be worthy of the name) to call for the vindication of the rights of God—even though that should be in the vengeance due to my own transgression. Here it is that the Cross comes in—satisfying this claim of conscience even in all its awfulness—vindicating the right of the living God to my service even more completely than it would have been by my total and eternal destruction; and vindicating also my right to serve him, though a thousand tempters and a thousand hells should reclaim against it.

Once I had a perfect and undoubted right to serve the living God. Once, in Adam (for 'the covenant was made with Adam, not only for himself but his posterity descending from him by ordinary genera-tion'—*The Shorter Catechism*) I had a perfect right to serve the Lord: and when I heard his voice in the garden in the cool of the day, I had a right to run to him, and to present to him and call his paternal notice to whatever service I had been rendering as a son working in his vine-yard, tilling the happy garden and keeping it. But alas! with Adam I 'sinned in him and fell with him in his first transgression;' and one of the deepest meanings I give to the expression, 'I am lost,' is that I have lost my right to serve the living God, 'God drove out the man' (Gen. 3:24), and drove out me. And while he placed 'cherubim' at the spot where I had lost my right, in proof that a second Adam should regain it for me, he also placed a 'sword' debarring me till then—debarring me till that sword should awake and smite the man that was Jeho-vah's fellow (Zech. 13:7). Blessed be the everlasting love of God, he gave me a second Adam, whose glorious right and power to serve the living God none may question! 'Behold my servant, whom I uphold; mine elect, in whom my soul delighteth; I have put my Spirit upon him: he shall not fail nor be discouraged, till he have set judgment in the earth, and the isles shall wait for his law' (Isa. 42:1). And, blessed be the same sovereign grace of God,—the covenant being made *with* him, but *for* all whom the Father hath given to him, yea, for all who will,—(for all who will, do will because they are made willing in the day of his power),—Christ's willing work of service to the living God was exactly the work of vindicating (by the willing endurance of the curse of the law) God's violated and dishonoured but ever holy right to be served, and man's shamefully surrendered right to serve him. *That* is the sacrifice of Christ. That is the atonement (Rom. 8:3, 4; Gal. 4:4, 5). If it be not *that*, it comes not into contact with guilty and unclean conscience. If it be not *that*, it is not in the sphere either of man's conscience or God's law. Not only does it not purge the conscience to serve the living God, but it could not enter the same sphere as conscience at all. If it be not *that*, then so far as I, the chief of sinners, am concerned, it matters not what it is: it is the vilest, pettiest imposition. I can neither live upon it (John 6:51; Heb. 11:28), nor die upon it (Heb. 11:29). If it be not *that*, it may awaken the admiration of holy angels: so they say; I do not know: it seems to me it would have been merely an *explosion*. Assuredly, it touches not the need, the primary indispensable need, of a guilty man.

But if it *be that*—if in its deepest essence it *satisfies* Divine justice—if the Lord God Omnipotent is well pleased for this substitutionary and sacrificial blood-shedding and righteousness of the Lamb—then not a shadow of a difficulty can there be as to its purging the conscience, and making it whiter than the snow. For purposes of philosophy and learning, more accurate statements concerning the origin, nature, and office of conscience may be necessary than we should ever think of giving here. The continual presentation of the Divine law as moral (not physical)[1] is here enough. Conscience with any life in it will ever respond to that. And again we say, if this law of God have received at the Cross a vindication of those rights of God's government, and, therefore, of man's conscience, which sin had violated, then, on the supposition of my faith, that is, my intelligent assent and consent (Heb. 11:28, 29), not a micrometer hair's-breadth of space can there intervene between it and my unclean conscience, nor an instant of time intervene between my sense (and acknowledged sense) of guilt (Psa. 51:4, 5), and my enjoyment of the peace that passeth all understanding. 'Lo, this hath touched thy lips, and thine iniquity is taken away' (Isa. 6:7). For under the acknowledged and vindicated rights of God I find mine

---

[1] Physical law is merely generalised statement of fact. Moral law is authoritative command, and, failing obedience, condemnation. The juridical is an institution never lost sight of by a people in their simplicity. An efflorescence [flowering] of physical science, however brilliant, will never satisfy a nation, save in their decline and fall. The moral is similarly scientific, it is true; but it is more.

restored, and primarily my lost right to serve the living God. For, how and in what sense can I who was lost be found, if my great right which I had lost be not found? In what sense, or to what effect had I myself been lost, if not in the loss of my right to serve the living God? There, and in that loss, you and I and all of us were lost. And in what sense, or to what effect, can I who was lost be found, if not in that I have found my God again, and found even him only and exactly in finding again my blessed right to serve him?

Nor am I merely entitled, in the name of Christ and of his sacrifice, of Christ and him crucified, to claim this glorious right again, but bound. There is not a nicer point in all the moral government of God from eternity unto eternity than is now found here. Behold my servant! Behold the Lamb of God! Behold him whom you have pierced, and whose wounds reconcile you to heaven and the throne thereof! Will you not have the reconciliation? While justice testifies its satisfaction and smiles approval, be ye reconciled to God. Is it possible you can still have your difficulties, now that the Moral Governor of heaven and earth has none? Is it possible you can still refuse the service of the living God, now that smiling cherubim—emblems of redemption—point the way (Psa. 80:1, 7, 19), and no opposing 'sword' (Zech. 13:7) bars the way to the tree of life or the throne of grace? What inveterate, envenomed enmity to God is this! If now ye will not come unto me that ye may have life, if sin can be, and can do, as *unbelief* in such circumstances has revealed and proved it can do and be, then was not sin altogether such an evil as demanded such a remedy? Who now will say that the divine justice, which Christ crucified has satisfied, was too stern? Who would not now break down and worship him? Who shall not praise and glorify thy name? 'O Lord I will praise thee: though thou wast angry with me, thine anger is turned away, and thou comfortedst me' (Isa. 12:1). Behold Jehovah himself hath become my song, he also is my salvation. I 'look on him whom I have pierced, and mourn,' while in the midst of the freely reconciled Church he 'sings praise' (Psa. 22:22, Heb. 2:12) unto the Father. 'Gracious is the Lord, and righteous; yea, our God is merciful. The Lord preserveth the simple: I was brought low, and he helped me. Return unto thy rest, my soul, for the Lord hath dealt bountifully with thee. What shall I render unto him for all his benefits?' (Psa. 116:5-7, 12). And all freely? All free to me, because they cost dear to him—*him*, Jehovah's Christ. All free and immediate to me, because they cost *him,* groans and wounds and tears, to satisfy Divine justice. And he did it. He *did* satisfy Divine justice, and reconciled us unto God.

It is in this rectification of the juridical—this rectification of right on God's part to be served, right on my part to serve him: it is in this judicial aspect of the Cross, that its primary preciousness consists. And it is in this that faith primarily, first of all, and always, and most of all, rejoices. Without this, conscience will never cease to assert its dissatisfaction and its wrongs. Have I any rights towards God? If I have, it can only be because God's violated rights in me have been vindicated. Can I aspire to say, 'I have found God, the living God'? It must be because he has first found me. For in violating *his* rights, I had lost my *own;* and in losing my God, I had lost myself. Redemption—Redemption—*Redemption*—is the essence of the only salvation I am capable of—redemption of myself, my person—and therewith of my right to serve the living God, founded on the glorifying of God's name in the vindication of his right to my person and service. And that is the vicarious, propitiatory service of the Cross, whereon, through the Eternal Spirit, my second Adam, the Lord from heaven, offered himself without spot unto God, a sacrifice to satisfy Divine justice and reconcile us unto God. And why then should I not instantly, *instantly* serve him? Why not? for a thousand of heaven's loudest trumpets to make all earth and hell resound with that 'Why not?' Receive, then,—call it old-fashioned doctrine if you please,—receive in simple faith (which neither adds unto nor diminishes from the Gospel which it embraces and assimilates) the Cross of Christ as yours, the death of Christ as yours, dying Christ and him crucified as yours; and therein receive and assert before high heaven the rectification of your conscience in its violated relation to the living God, and to the law and service of God. And then stand fast in this liberty of conscience wherewith Christ hath made you free. In fellowship with Christ and him crucified whereunto you are called of God by the Gospel,—claim your right to serve the living God; claim and exercise your right in companionship with Christ himself in this very Cross, as a service of the living God (Isa. 42:1), and his consequent or accompanying right to repel all who would hinder, and to attract all who would help, you in his service. Be one with Christ in that great experience, 'I am crucified with Christ' (Gal. 2:20). Be one with him in that great experience of his in serving the living God. And you shall be one with him in his victory of praise and his banquet of grace and joy, implied in that great historic word of the Holy Ghost concerning him:—'Then the devil leaveth him, and angels came and ministered unto him' (Matt.4:11). For be very sure in your holy conscience-cleansed service of the living God—God will fulfil, and in that service will alone fulfil, to you the promise—

> *I will beat down before his face*
> *All his malicious foes;*
> *I will them greatly plague that do*
> *With hatred him oppose:*

and also that other word:

> *The angel of the Lord encamps,*
> *And round encompasseth*
> *All those about that do him fear,*
> *And them delivereth.*

Have I a right to serve the living God? Oh! how precious it is! How precious in itself, as the reversal and off-lifting of the sentence, 'He drove out the man!'—as that at least! And as the removal of the flaming sword! As the simple presentation of the beautiful and peaceful cherubim, and of him who dwells between them! How precious also as my right to defy the malice of Satan and to claim the sympathy of angels! my right to defy the malice of hell, and to claim the protection of heaven!

And is it possible that, for a few mellifluous phrases, you could barter such a heritage? Rather, as morning dawns upon you, will you not sing of it? And as evening throws its shades around you, will you not return to your song? Will you not keep your views of it ever fresh and lively by clinging to it and crowding the canvas of your history with active 'service to the living God'? For, be very sure that only in serving the living

God can you succeed in resisting the powers of darkness or acquiring and retaining the sympathy of the powers of light. The former will not bate their opposition, and the latter will not waste their sympathy upon you in any dilettante[1] trifling with the cross. No; not in amusement (of which there is none in all the history of your crucified Lord), but only in actual service will they acknowledge the result of justice-satisfying sacrifice; therein will devils own your power, and angels sympathise with your weakness. They will not waste their sympathy upon you in any other light than as sympathy with you in service, nor will they care to shield you for any other end than to shield and augment your service. Nor will you ever make Satan feel your force—or the force of any weapon you try to wield against him,—save as you are wielding it as a servant of the living God. You may quote a whole volume of threats against him and promises to yourself. Not a jot of his opposition will he bate on that account. He can quote Scripture too. But, if with conscience cleansed by the blood of sprinkling;—if with rights restored by that Greater Man in his work of blood-shedding, atonement, and redemption;—and if, in the actual service of the living God, you resist the devil, he will flee from you: and in the joy and elastic freedom wherewith, on his fleeing from you, you return in holy liberty to the service of the living God, it is scarcely possible to tell how much of your blessedness may be the result of angels coming and ministering to you. One thing is clear: your right to his service is undoubted: and your right to be joyous in it equally so. God will not meet you with a 'Who hath required this at your hands?' No: but with that great word of his holy righteousness and joyful delight in his people, 'I will bring them to my holy mountain, and I will make them joyful in my house of prayer: For there will I require mine offerings, saith the Lord' (Ezek. 20:40).

II. It is not the right only that the propitiatory sacrifice of Christ supplies, but also the motive, the desire.

In shedding of the blood, Christ, as an atonement for sin, as a truly justice-satisfying sacrifice, secures, as we have seen, the right to

[1] [dilettante = casual, uncommited.]

serve the living God But if that were all, the right might remain in abeyance, from not being claimed, not being taken advantage of, not being sued out, and urged, and acted upon. But the shedding of the blood of Christ as an atoning sacrifice, as a ransom for sin, is of such perfection and preciousness as shall secure that the right be claimed and enjoyed. It does not admit of the possibility of its being refused by man any more than by God. Refused on God's part it cannot be: for while there are three persons in the Godhead, one of them is the propitiation for our sins. The God-Man, in his mediatorial intervenient position, is surety for both. Both his Father and his people shall see the preciousness of his blood. It does not admit of its being left in abeyance. It secures that those benefited in covenant by its being shed, shall desire to have it *sprinkled*; and shall, in longings of faith, exclaim, 'Purge me with hyssop, and I shall be clean: wash me, and I shall be whiter than snow.' If this, however, is to be, it must have power to quicken the dead; and when sprinkled, to stimulate them to long for the sprinkling of itself. It doth indeed accomplish this sure result, namely, that every soul for whom it was shed shall ask for it, pray for it, receive the answer to its prayers, enjoy it, cry, 'Lord, truly I am thy servant: thou hast loosed my bonds;' find in this a precious reason for its being; live for it, and desire to live for it. And we really give an interest for the first time, an immortal being, intelligently reconciled to its own existence—its own never-ending existence—by the service of the living God, as that on which its existence is to be spent, and that worthily, honourably, unweariedly spent. 'This is the true God and eternal life,' cries out every soul who rightly deals with this precious blood. Thus, when Isaiah had his lips touched with a live coal from off the altar of atonement, and an opportunity of service offered, he longs and is in haste to allowed to engage in it: 'Here am I, send me.' When the bands are truly loosed, as only a divinely-appointed, all-sufficient sacrifice of propitiation with which God declares himself satisfied can loose them—when guilt vanishes from the conscience—in that instant, mysterious, sweet, and inexpressible joy amidst which it is purged from dead works to serve the living God in newness of life, it has a right to serve. Indeed it has. 'In the blood is the life.' The Spirit of Christ never departs from the sacrifice of Christ. The sacrifice of Christ is no more a dead thing than ever it was. It was offered that we might have life, and that we might have it more abundantly. 'They shall look on me whom they have pierced, and shall mourn,' saith the Lord. And why? Because they cannot find the sacrifice apart from the Spirit. 'And I will pour out on the house of Israel, and on the inhabitants of Jerusalem the Spirit of grace and supplication, and they shall look on me whom they have pierced.' And the Spirit shall give such views of the goodness of a state in which the living God is served, as shall inspire with a longing for such service—for enjoyment of such right. And this the sprinkled blood Christ uniformly does. For that blood of Christ is quick with the Spirit of Christ. 'In the blood is the life,' and this life is the Spirit. For 'it is the Spirit that quickeneth: the flesh profiteth nothing.' Now the Spirit—the Eternal Spirit—through whom the atonement was offered or the blood was shed, abides for ever by the blood of Christ. And just as he makes the word the vehicle by which he conveys his mind or meaning, he makes the blood his vehicle by which he conveys his love, his grace, his affectionate regard for the believing sinner, and his gracious power to quicken and renew the soul: and on these combinedly,—enlightening the mind in the knowledge of Christ, and renewing the will till it perceives the amiableness, goodness, beauty, and desirableness of Christ, and of God in him as the reconciled God, the very God of peace and comfort,—the Spirit moves the whole soul with admiration, love, and gratitude towards God which inevitably issues in an effort to 'serve the living God.' Primarily the blood of Christ secures the right to serve God; and the sprinkling of that blood on any conscience in particular gives that conscience nothing less than the exact right, as a nobleman's insignia of order entitle him to demand admission to any meeting of the knights of the special brotherhood, as the case may be.

But more than the right. Through the Spirit—who is the Spirit of light, and wisdom, and love, and of adoption—it gives knowledge of the right, intelligent, spiritual understanding of its preciousness, perception of its holy beauty, its grand condignity, its honourableness, its splendid congruities alike of manliness and godliness. The soul, through this same Spirit through whom Jesus offered himself without spot to God, is joined not by a legal covenant bond outside, but by love to Jesus: offers itself to God with Jesus in the eternal law-magnifying virtue of his blood, and meets with acceptance in the service: sees the blessedness and goodness of the service: tastes and sees that God is good, and that it is good to serve him: and is led to desire and long for, more and more, to engage in and delight in, the actual service of God, for its own sake, as the very zest and joy of life here below, and one of the highest forms under which it can imagine true enjoyment hereafter. Hence the grand brevity of the proposition, 'His servants shall serve him.' Ay will they; that they will. It remains no more a beautiful ideal, that the service of the living God is a valuable estate of being: but the soul, from experience of its delights, goes forth towards it, delights to think that there can, even in eternity, be no ennui[1] to 'souls in serving the living God,' and the escaped bird escapes into no boundless contiguity of shade, but Home! Home, sweet Home! Home into the service of the living God, crying, 'What shall I render unto the Lord for all his benefits towards me?' Nor, seen in the light of Calvary, is this the least, this right to serve. To see it in the light of the word and Spirit of Christ is to desire it. To see it thus is to see that it resembles God's law, 'holy and just and good and spiritual' And, oh! joy of joys! To feel that I am no longer criminal nor carnal, 'sold under sin,' but redeemed! Oh! 'how love I thy law!' The law thus magnified is my legal security for ever! 'I am thy servant; truly I am thy servant;' and 'being delivered out of the hands of thine enemies and ours, we will serve thee without fear, with holiness and righteousness before thee all the days of our lives' (Luke 1:74-75). 'The love of Christ constraineth us, because we thus judge, that if one died for all, then all died in him, that when they live, they should not henceforth live unto themselves, but unto him who died for them and rose again' (2 Cor. 5:15).

Yes: it is living service to a living God that is gained by a dying Redeemer. Returning from death and the grave, he says, 'I am he that liveth and was dead, and behold! I am alive for evermore.' By one offering I have for ever perfected them that are sanctified; death cannot come again. The God whom I reveal—the Father whom you see when you see him that died for you and rose again (for he that hath seen

---

[1] [French: boredom.]

me hath seen the Father), is the God of life and death in every possible sense—the living God, triumphing over death, never so much seen to be the living God as in putting away death for ever; giving you in me everlasting life, a life in which death's finger, death's interest, death's shadow shall never come again unto eternity!' Oh! this is the living God, and you see him as such, and are become fit companions, in a sense, for him as such; citizens of the city of the living God. The Eternal Spirit, through the blood of Jesus, hath given you a longing for the service—a view of it that fills your heart with a sense of its dignity, its joy, its infinite worth to spend and be spent upon. For to spend my strength on this service is to conserve, increase, and renew it. 'They that wait upon the Lord shall renew their strength.' Here you get by giving. 'Give unto the Lord glory and strength,' if you would be mighty and 'sons of the mighty.' 'Make a joyful noise unto the Lord, O ye lands. Serve the Lord with gladness; come before his presence with singing.' The blood of the Lamb gives you the light and the desire. It purges your conscience to serve the living God.

III. If you would thoroughly equip the living and intelligent soul for this service, you must supply not only the right, and the desire, but the power.

Grant that: show a free full fountain of that: and nothing more is wanting. But the blood of Christ supplies that too. It supplies the Divine Spirit without measure to those for whom the atoning blood was shed. 'He hath redeemed us from the curse of the law, being made a curse for us: that the blessing of Abraham might come upon us, that we might receive the promise of the Spirit through faith' (Gal. 3:13, 14). But this is one of those commonplaces of the Christian life of which we need not say more, than that while the old views of the sacrifice show it as providing us at once with the Right, and the Motive, and the Power to serve the living God, we shall have no hesitation in saying,—'No man, when he hath drunk old wine, straightway desireth new, for he saith, *The old is better.*' μ.

THE PROCESSION OF THE HOLY SPIRIT FROM THE SON[1]

THE doctrine that 'the Spirit proceedeth from the Son' has not been affirmed by the Westminster divines in the Shorter Catechism; and hence, perhaps, it has come to pass, that not one in a thousand, even of intelligent, pious people among us, has any idea of the scriptural evidence of the doctrine, or imagines it possible that it can have any important bearings. It seems, also, to be very generally presumed, that it is a doctrine which cannot be handled without entailing the necessity of dealing with a good deal of Patristic and Scholastic lore. And as confessedly it rests on no direct affirmation of Holy Scripture, but is the result of comparison and inference exclusively, while its bearings on spiritual life are certainly not very obvious, it is not to be wondered at that the doctrine has become, so to speak, generally unpopular, and that many intelligent Christians have no believing convictions concerning it. Nevertheless, it is an integral portion of divine truth, which God has been pleased to reveal: the church is, therefore, bound to set it forth in the Confession of her Faith, and to see that it be intelligently embraced and maintained by her office-bearers and members. There is no reason whatever why the discussion of this doctrine should be confined to the writings of strictly professional theologians. And as we believe that it may be presented in an intelligible and interesting light, without alluding to the fathers and scholastic divines,[2] we propose to devote a brief article to the consideration of it.

[1] [From: *The British and Foreign Evangelical Review* (1869), p. 272f.]
[2] The church history of the discussion may be stated almost in a single sentence.

In answer to the question, 'What are the personal properties of the three persons of the Godhead?' the *Larger Catechism* replies, 'It is proper to the Father to beget the Son, and to the Son to be begotten of the Father, and to the Holy Ghost to proceed from the Father and the Son from all eternity.' The *Confession* presents the same doctrine thus: 'In the unity of the Godhead there be three persons, of one substance, power, and eternity,—God the Father, God the Son, and God the Holy Ghost. The Father is of none, neither begotten nor proceeding; the Son is eternally begotten of the Father; the Holy Ghost eternally proceeding from the Father and the Son.'

That the Spirit 'proceedeth from the Father,' we have our Lord's affirmation in terms:—'But when the Comforter is come, whom I will send unto you from the Father, even the Spirit of truth, which proceedeth from the Father, he shall testify of me' (John 15:26). Here we have the explicit assertion that the Spirit of truth proceedeth from the Father. And that this averment, or proposition, is not intended to apply to the Spirit's office in the covenant, or to be descriptive of his mission by the Father and the Son, is most obvious, because that covenant-mission is here described by another phrase—'I will send him from the Father.' These are the terms which affirm his mission, his coming forth from the Father in his office, and according to sovereign arrangement and covenant dispensation. But his proceeding from the Father is affirmative and descriptive of an eternal and necessary personal property, and is, indeed, presupposed as the ground,—the infinitely decorous and congruous reason,—of his coming forth in

---

The doctrine became a much disputed point between the Greek and Western Churches. The Greeks, laying emphasis on the letter of the text John 15:26, maintained simply that 'the Spirit proceeded from the Father;' and thus the article was expressed in the second Ecumenical Council at Constantinople (AD 381) The Western Church, attaching itself to Augustine's speculative deduction of the Trinity, and laying emphasis on the texts, 'Spirit of his Son' (Gal. 4:6), 'Spirit of Christ' (Rom. 8:9), maintained what was called the *filioque*, or the doctrine of the procession of the Spirit from the Father and the Son. With this addition, the Niceno-Constantipolitan Creed was confessed at the Council of Toledo (AD 589). One of the most remarkable discussions of the question, in the interest of the Western view of the doctrine, was published by Anselm. (See also *Zanchii Opera*, tom. i.)

the free interpositions and covenant operations of his grace. In the constitution of the Godhead, there is a prior and everlasting relation between the eternal Father and the eternal Spirit, which renders his coming forth from the Father in time, and voluntarily, and for a special sovereign purpose, a fit and Godhead-honouring arrangement. And that is, that his very subsistence as a distinct person from the Father, while one God with him, is by a mysterious, but glorious, 'proceeding' from him.

Let it be observed, then, that the Spirit's eternal procession from the Father is the divine foundation on which his official mission from the Father in sovereign grace rests. This consideration is of value, in shewing that the Spirit proceedeth also from the Son. To evince this is what now lies before us.

In doing so, we must, of course, admit from the outset, that there is no statement in Scripture so explicit on this portion of the doctrine of the Spirit's procession as on the former. We have no assertion in similar terms—in so many words—that the Spirit proceedeth from the Son. Yet the doctrine, we believe, is contained in Scripture most assuredly, and is, therefore, to be deduced, and believed, and practically improved in the faith, and adoration, and gratitude of the church. For that is divine truth, not only which is expressly set down in Scripture, but that also which may, by good and necessary consequence, be deduced from Scripture.

The direct and positive argument, then, by which the Spirit's procession from the Son may, by good and necessary consequence, be deduced from Scripture, is very brief, and is as follows:—The Spirit proceedeth from the Father. Also, the Spirit is called the Spirit of the Father:—'It is not ye that speak, but the Spirit of your Father which is in you.' And in countless texts,—as, first, in Genesis 1:2,—he is called 'the Spirit of God,' where the name of God is doubtless given to the Father. He is the 'Spirit of the Father:' and he 'proceedeth from the Father.' We have both these assertions explicitly in Scripture; and they must be held to be identical in value or import. They are interchangeable. We infer the one from the other. We explain the one by the other. He is 'the Spirit of the Father' in the special and peculiar sense that he 'proceedeth from the Father.' He is not, indeed, said to proceed from the Son; but he is said to be 'the Spirit of the Son:' 'Because ye are sons, God hath sent forth the Spirit of his Son into your hearts, crying, Abba, Father' (Gal. 4:6). If, however, he is the Spirit of the Father—the Spirit of God—in the sense of proceeding from God, even the Father, then his being the Spirit of God the Son implies that he proceedeth from the Son also. There is not the slightest indication in Scripture, and therefore not the slightest reason to believe, that he is to be regarded as the Spirit of God, even the Father, in one sense or to one effect, and the Spirit of the Son, who is also God, in another sense and to another effect. We have received from himself, in his Holy Scriptures, no reason whatever to believe that he is the Spirit of the Son in any less intense, peculiar, intimate, and unsearchably glorious and ineffable a manner than he is the Spirit of the Father. And if, therefore, he is the Spirit of the Father by a necessary, and eternal, and ineffable procession, he is the Spirit of the Son by a necessary, eternal, and ineffable procession from the Son also.

This is the argument by which it is shewn that the doctrine is implicitly, while not on that account less assuredly, set forth in Holy Scripture; and it is in substance the whole of the argument. It arises from a comparison of two passages of Scripture,—John 15:26, and Galatians 4:6; and these are the two texts which the Westminster divines have appended to each of their presentments of the doctrine, in the *Confession* and in the *Larger Catechism* severally, proving that to their mind the scriptural evidence is educed by the comparison and inference which the above brief argument sets forth.

There are, however, two guards, so to speak, that must be placed on this argument in order to render it unassailable. In the first place, we must see to it that the two expressions, 'the Spirit proceedeth from the Father,' and 'the Spirit is the Spirit of the Father,' are really equivalent; so that if we find either of them applied to the Son, we may infer and believe the other also. And in the second place, the one of them which we do find used with regard to the Son—namely, 'the Spirit of the Son'—we must shew to be applied to the Son, not merely with reference to his Messiahship, but specially with reference to his Godhead.

In the *first* place, then, we may best prove the equivalence of the two definitions of the Spirit's relation to the Father, by shewing that each of them is equivalent to a third definition, which joins on very beautifully to each, and holds a sort of intermediate place between the two,—in verbal expression, that is, for all the three are equivalent in real import. That the Spirit is 'the Spirit of the Father,' and that 'he proceedeth from the Father,' may not appear at first sight to be anything like expressions of identical or equivalent truth. But take a third expression, which varies less in form from either of them than they do from each other, and forms a manifest bond of union between them. In 1 Corinthians 2:12, it is said, 'Now we have received, not the spirit of the world, but the Spirit which is of God.' In the immediately preceding verse, the Holy Spirit had been called the 'Spirit of God:' 'The things of God knoweth no man but the Spirit of God.' Clearly the two persons in the 11th and 12th verses respectively are the same—the 'Spirit of God' and the 'Spirit which is of God;' and the one expression more specifically and exactly defines the import of the other. He is the 'Spirit of God,' τοῦ θεοῦ, in the sense of being the 'Spirit which is of God' τὸ ἐκ τοῦ θεοῦ. At first sight, perhaps, this may not seem to import very much, or to give much additional light. But if we carefully watch the impression inevitably produced on our minds by the two sentences;—he is the Spirit of God; he is the Spirit which is of God;—we will see that the second imparts more exactness, and a limitation, to the first. That he is the 'Spirit of God,' does not necessarily imply more than that, in some vague sense, God hath a peculiar relation to him or possessory interest in him. Or it might mean merely that he is the Spirit whom God gives. But, that he is the 'Spirit which is of God,' implies that he hath his derivation in some sense from God, even the Father. 'Ye are of God, little children,' says the apostle John. He means that these little children have their subsistence, as children, from God; that they do not merely belong to God, but that they have a spiritual derivation from God; that, in a sense, they proceed from God. Their being 'of God' implies a derivation from God consistent with creatureship. The Spirit is not a creature; he is God. But his being 'of God' must imply that he has his subsistence in a way of derivation from God too,—though, of course, such a derivation as consists with the necessity and eternity of his subsistence as a distinct person, who is himself very God. He is, therefore, the 'Spirit of God,' in no vague or general sense, but in the particular sense of being the 'Spirit which is of God,'—which hath his forthcoming, or emanation, or derivation, from God, even the Father. But the scriptural expression for this relation of dependence which the person of the Spirit has on the person of the Father, is his 'proceeding from the Father.' His being 'the Spirit of the Father,' therefore, in its exact, and specific, and well-limited meaning, according to other scriptures, just imports that 'he proceedeth from the Father.' And his being 'the Spirit of the Son,' must, by unassailable parity of reasoning, imply that, in like manner, he 'proceedeth from the Son.'

But, *secondly*, is he the Spirit of the Son in relation to the Godhead of the Son, or only in relation to his Messiahship? This is the question which, rightly answered, puts a second guard upon the argument. We observe, therefore, that when he is called the Spirit of the Son, it is a necessary and eternal relation in the Godhead that is intended, and not a relation dependent on the Covenant or the Mediatorship. He is called the 'Spirit of Christ' times without number; and if that were all, it might imply that he is related to Christ in his office as Mediator; the Spirit whom the Father hath given, not by measure, to the Mediator, and whom the Mediator, according to the measure of his own gift, pours out on his members. His being the 'Spirit of Christ' might imply merely that he has been given to Christ, or that he is given by Christ—either of these truths, or both. But he is called the Spirit of God's Son, which is not a title that Christ hath derived from his office, but from eternal and divine relation. He is God's Son, not in virtue of his Messiahship, but in virtue of being that divine Person which Scripture elsewhere calls the Word of God, which was with God, and which was God. 'The Spirit of God's Son'—which is the *vox signata*[1] on which the Westminster divines rest, is a title given to him from his relation to the Son as God, and would have been his title though the Son of God had never become the Christ or Mediator. He

---

[1] [Latin: sealed word.]

is not officially—by covenant agreement, by voluntary susception, by contingent sovereign arrangement—the Spirit of the Son, considered as Messiah. But necessarily and eternally—considered as preceding all exercise of will in the Godhead, in the order of nature, that is—he is, in the internal relations of the Godhead, the Spirit of the Second Person, even as he is the Spirit of the First. But his being the Spirit of the first person of the Godhead, is defined as implying that he proceedeth from the Father. His being the Spirit of the second person, implies also that he proceedeth from the Son.

Such is the simple, and, we believe, unanswerable positive argument in proof of the doctrine before us. There are several collateral and confirmatory arguments also, each of them, perhaps, not very powerful by itself, but combined, affording no small body of evidence in support of what has been already evinced. We shall put them, however, in the reverential form of questions rather than allege them to be proofs; for the theme is one calling for our most humble and reverent regard. The ground whereon we stand is peculiarly holy ground.

1. In the first place, then, if we conceive of the Son as related to the Father, by being eternally begotten of him, and of the Spirit as related to the Father, by eternally proceeding from him, while we conceive of the Son and the Spirit as not directly related to each other at all, does not our conception of the Tri-unity seem to be deficient in respect of some bond needed whereby the three persons should still be one God?

2. Again: the Son is the brightness of the Father's glory. But is it not an element of the Father's glory that the Spirit proceedeth from him? The Son is the express image of the Father's person. But is it not a property of the Father's person that the Spirit proceedeth from him? Does it not seem, therefore, as if the Son could scarcely be the express image of the Father's person, or the very brightness of the Father's glory, if the Spirit do not proceed from the Son as well as from the Father? May not this be part of what is implied, when Christ says, 'All that the Father hath is mine' (John 16:15)? Yea, is it not somewhat evident that Christ meant expressly to include the Spirit among the 'all' that he and the Father have in common? For he goes on, as an adequate and pointed following up of the claim, 'All that the Father hath is mine,' to give the

promise, 'Therefore the Spirit shall take of mine, or rather to justify himself in giving this promise, 'Therefore, *said* I, the Spirit shall take of mine and shew it unto you.'

3. But farther: the Spirit's eternal procession from the Father, is the prior ground of his being sent by the Father in the economy of grace. But the Spirit is sent by the Son as well as by the Father. Can this be without an analogous prior ground of his being sent by the Son—without his proceeding from the Son as well as from the Father?

It is unnecessary to prove that the Father 'sends' the Spirit. He is called the 'promise of the Father'—the Comforter 'whom the Father will send.' Saith Jesus, 'I will pray the Father, and he will send you another Comforter.' It is as little necessary to shew that the Son is said to 'send' the Spirit, and that in language indicative of as much divine authority and dignity as when he is spoken of as sent by the Father, 'If I go not away, the Comforter, which is the Holy Ghost, will not come unto you; but if I go away, I will send him.' These are the words of the Son himself. In some passages the Spirit is spoken of as being sent by, and as coming from, both the Father and the Son co-ordinately: thus, 'The Comforter whom I will send unto you from the Father;' manifestly implying. You are to receive him as coming from me, for 'I will send him,' and as coming from the Father, for 'I will send him from the Father.' And again, 'The Comforter whom the Father will send in my name.' This is exactly correlative to the former. The 'Father will send him;' and yet when he comes you are to receive him as sent by me, for he comes 'in my name.' I acknowledge, and I share the Father's right and power to send him; for when I send him, I send him 'from the Father.' The Father owns and takes part in my right and power to send the Spirit; for when he sends him, he sends him 'in my name.' Surely the Father's sending and the Son's sending are one.

But now the question is: If even the eternal Father, representing the majesty of Godhead, sends the Spirit in sovereign grace and covenant economy, only on the prior ground, that the Spirit, in the eternal constitution of the Godhead, proceedeth from the Father, shall the Son send the Spirit in the same economy of grace, though there be no such prior ground for his sending him? If the Father send not the

Spirit, except because of a pre-existing foundation for his doing so in his own eternal relation to the Spirit, shall the Son, with equal authority and dignity, send the same Spirit if there be no analogous foundation for his doing so? Shall a contingent and voluntary arrangement with regard to the Son in a created nature and delegated office, be a reason for his exercising a prerogative which the supreme Father does not exercise, save on the ground of a necessary and eternal relation in the Godhead? Shall the position of the Son in the nature of man procure for him a power which the Father, on his part, owns as having its ground, its root and rise, in the depths of the nature of God? Such, in two or three of its various forms, is the formidable question which arises in opposition to the notion that the Spirit proceedeth, not from the Son, but only from the Father. Difficulties, doubtless, are never to be pleaded against a proved truth. But it must be remembered that it never has been, and never can be proved—the attempt, indeed, never has been made, and, from the nature of the case, cannot be made, to prove—that the Spirit does not proceed from the Son. And hence formidable difficulties in the way of our believing on the negative side of the question may be pleaded as confirmatory evidence on the positive side. On the supposition, then, that the Spirit proceedeth from the Father, but not from the Son, let it be inquired:—

1. In the first place: Shall the Mediator, the Father's servant, receive a prerogative concerning the Spirit which the Father even does not exercise save on the prior ground of a necessary and eternal relation between himself and the Spirit?

2. Let it further be inquired: Can the Father confer on the Mediator a power, limitlessly, of sending the Spirit on any ground less than that on which he himself sends him? The eternal relation between the Father and the Spirit is a glorious depth of divine mystery, unfathomable in its deep abyss of shining waters, but having its well-marked channel defined by scriptural assertion. From its unsearchable riches and resources, from its inaccessible depths of glory, there is seen welling up—if one may dare so to speak, in mingled reverence and weakness—welling up, and efflorescing on its current, a covenant relation and arrangement between the Father and the Spirit, bearing blessedly on our salvation. A like relation

and arrangement in covenant—wholly alike, and all but identical, save that the Son is a different person from the Father—we find appearing as between the Son and the Spirit, bearing in an exactly similar manner on our salvation too. Is it possible to doubt that beneath this covenant arrangement and relation between the Son and the Spirit, there is a like fathomless abyss of eternal relational glory, as between the Father and the Spirit? For, can the Father found and form that same covenant bond between the Spirit and the Son which subsists between the Spirit and himself only because the Spirit proceedeth from himself, if it be not true that the Spirit proceedeth also from the Son? Or can the Son dispense, 'give,' 'send,' 'pour out' the Spirit, even as the Father does, unless he be his own Spirit exactly and in the same sense in which he is the Father's?

3. Once more: If the Spirit is sent and cometh forth from Christ as the God-man, without a prior and eternal proceeding from the Son as God, must it not follow that the mission of the Comforter is one, not merely of condescension, but of obedience, and therefore of humiliation? His mission, indeed, is of glorious condescension; but there is and can be nothing of humiliation in it. It is a great and plain truth, that of the persons of the Godhead, the Son alone was humbled. 'He humbled himself.' He was 'made under the law.' He 'became obedient.' And even now that he is glorified, still, in office and in human nature, he is the Father's glorified servant; glorified, yet his servant still: his king and plenipotentiary; yet as he is Mediator, the Father is greater than he. But the Spirit's entire office in the covenant is one, not of obedience, of servitude, of humiliation, but of condescension only, and of great glory therein,—a glory that excelleth. He doth not humble himself, he is not made under the law. He is not subjected to any conditions pertaining to a created nature, or to a servant's work. He is, in covenant arrangement, as in necessary glory, the sovereign Spirit of all majesty and might. But, seeing that undeniably he is 'sent' by the Son manifest in the flesh, if he proceedeth not from the Son as God by a necessary and eternal property pertaining to his person and glory, and indeed, crowning and completing his personal glory, as God, then his proceeding from the Son as God-man, and merely by dispensation and appointment, is a

subordination and subjection—is it not?—of the eternal Spirit to the flesh of Christ: he is made in a sense of no reputation as Christ was; his glory is veiled, and his absolute sovereignty placed in abeyance. If his mission from the Son has its roots only in the Son's Messiahship, while he proceedeth not from the Son as God, then, is it not really and wholly on Christ's manhood that his coming forth from Christ ultimately turns? If Christ as God cannot call all the fullness of the Spirit his, in the same sense in which the Father does, and if as God-man he can, then it is clearly on the strength of his manhood that he can do so; on the strength of his manhood he has received the gift, and bestows the promise, of the Comforter. And if this be so, then is it not a subjection of the Spirit to the humanity of Christ? There is no such result, if the mission of the Comforter from the Mediator has its ultimate and deepest ground and root—its sustaining foundation and justifying reason—in his eternal procession from the person of the eternal Son. He may in that case come forth upon the work of his office, and pass to the discharge of it, through the person of the Son as God manifest in the flesh: but his coming is then in no sense subordinate to the flesh of Immanuel. The light is still sunlight and of heaven, which, passing through a prism of earth's materials and earth's construction, gives forth its beams modified and refracted by the medium through which it reaches us. And even so,—if a comparison between divine mysteries ineffable, and the purest, though still humble, elements of nature be permissible,—the Holy Ghost in his mission may pass to the discharge of his voluntary covenant appointments through the medium of Christ's person as God manifest in the flesh: but it is a mission of condescension only, and not subjection; a mission of sovereign glory unabated and unconcealed. Yea, it is unto the forth shewing of a glory—for it runs parallel with, it flows in the same channel with, and is the outcome of, a glory—which otherwise, it may be, could never have been so conclusively displayed. It is the brightest manifestation, and perhaps the only conclusive proof,—possibly the only adequate medium of proof,—to men or angels, that he proceedeth eternally at once from the Father and from the Son. For if the Spirit proceedeth from the Son as God, then for the Son as God-man to receive the Spirit without measure, is merely this, that his divine and eternal possession of the Spirit is not restrained from him or held in abeyance, but given to him, as he is Immanuel. That is simply accorded to him in the covenant, and as he is God-man, with respect to the Spirit, which eternally appertains to him, as he is God. The prayer is simply answered to the Mediator:—'Father, glorify thou me with the glory which I had with thee before the world was.' And the mission of the Comforter by the Messiah is now no subjection to the flesh of Jesus, but a demonstration of the Son's co-equal glory with the Father, and of the eternal Spirit's identical or analogous relation to both, as proceeding alike from the Father and from the Son.

Such, then, is the scriptural evidence on which the Church of God believes with divine faith, that the Spirit proceedeth from the Son as from the Father. That such a truth should have no bearings, no claims, no practical influence on the living faith, the spiritual reason, and the adoring gratitude of the church, is not to be admitted. Rather must it be maintained, that it is a truth which, throughout the everlasting ages, will be found yielding up to the chosen Bride of the Lamb, treasures of marvellous love and wisdom,—ever growing beams of divine light, as in ever-variegating combinations and diffractions,—in the reflecting whereof she shall growingly be transformed, in endless progression, from glory to glory, as by the Spirit of the Lord. Nor is the practical improvement (as we say) of this doctrine to be left over till the entrance of the Church on her beatific vision. The Church of God has the first-fruits of her beatific vision here. The Spirit himself is the first-fruits of heavenly glory; and that there should be no first-fruits of a divine doctrine concerning his own person and personal properties and relations in the Godhead, is what ought not to be imagined. It is out of place to call this great revealed truth a mere abstract dogma. It is a baseless assumption to aver that it is susceptible of no practical bearings, and replete with no capabilities of personal application to intelligent and reverential believing men. It is not so. Looking even merely to the church history of the doctrine, how can it be thought of no practical importance? A doctrine which divided the Greek and Latin churches from each other, splitting the visible

Christian Church so early by a schism which never has been healed, can hardly be supposed to be a matter of mere abstract speculation; a matter that has no bearings on the spiritual life of the individual or of the Church. In point of fact, the Greek Church, becoming very corrupt and idolatrous, continuing to deny the eternal procession of the Spirit from the Son, has had comparatively little reviving and refreshing from the Spirit's presence and power. The Western Church, on the other hand, has had her great Reformation of the sixteenth century, and her great revivals, through the outpouring of the Spirit, especially in America and Great Britain, both in former days and in the present generation. Is it not very remarkable that the Spirit has incalculably more abundantly manifested his grace and power in that great section of the Church in which the complete doctrine of his Divine Person and eternal relations has been maintained, and comparatively abandoned the other section in which an integral portion of the truth concerning him has been surrendered? Is not this a fact in church history, on a great scale, that may well be held as proving the infinite value and importance of a correct and complete doctrine on the person and relations of the blessed Spirit of God?

It is but a little way that we can profess to go in indicating the bearings of this doctrine on the faith and duty of the church; but there are one or two so clear and powerful that we shall here very briefly ask attention to them.

I. This doctrine has a clear bearing on the faith and duty of the church, as a powerful encouragement to her hope, and stimulus to her faith, in praying continually for the outpouring of the Holy Spirit from on high.

Let it be considered how infinitely willing God must be to pour out his Spirit to act according to the everlasting covenant, seeing that it is by the arrangements, and provisions, and dispensation of that covenant that the most peculiar, and profound, and mysterious glories of the Triunity in Godhead are brought to light. In the infinite wisdom of God, the covenant dispensation and relations are built on the eternal divine relations of the persons; and this is unspeakably the most complete, perhaps the only effectual, means of bringing out to view the declarative glory of these divine relations themselves. Creation and ordinary providence can probably, at the uttermost, be made to go but a very little way in carrying in them traces, or adequate evidence and declaration, of the glory of God as Triune; and perhaps scarcely any token or testimony whatever of the special relations which the Sacred Three bear to one another. But the whole truth anent these relations is embodied,—the archetypal glory of them all is reflected,— the infinitely conservatory energy of them all is committed, and in actual and gracious operation,—in the great fact of the redemption that is in Christ. It is by the Son's mission of the Spirit, the Comforter, that the finishing and all-securing touch is given to the establishment of that redemption, in the enjoyment of its fruits actually in each individual case; and if so great a revenue of specific glory to God as Triune thus accrues to him from pouring out his Spirit, with what confidence may the Church of God continue instant in prayer both for herself and for the world; for the universal effusion of the Spirit on the Church and on the world alike; till the Church be 'endowed with power from on high,' and the world be 'convinced of sin, and righteousness, and judgment.'

II. If our faith, so also our adoration and our marvelling ought to be quickened and called forth by this doctrine.

Nil admirari[1] is one of the most debasing maxims a proud heathenism ever uttered. To admire and marvel, is one of the highest duties and delights of Christianity. God's light, into which we are called, is his 'marvellous light.' And our marvelling cannot fail to be excited, if, with reverent minds, we contemplate the doctrine before us. For how marvellous is that salvation, on the accomplishment of which all the glory, all the divine riches and resources, all the mysterious capabilities of the Triune Godhead, and even of the peculiar personal relations of the distinct persons in the Triune Godhead towards each other, have been embarked and laid out for our own everlasting welfare! It is not merely that the three persons of the Godhead are

[1] [Latin: Let nothing astonish you.]

concerned and concurrent in this great salvation. It is not merely that the First person of the Godhead gives the Second to redeem us, and that the Third person is given to quicken us and put us in possession of the redemption wrought out. It is not merely that three persons, each of them divine—together one in the substance, power, and eternity, of undivided Godhead—unite to effect our restoration to the favour, and image, and glory of God. Not the three persons merely, but the most profound, and peculiar, and mysterious relations in which they stand towards each other, and all that is contained in these relations: this is what is brought forward into action and made, in amazing love and wisdom, to yield various and multiplied elements of gracious and glorious arrangement and operation, combinedly uniting to achieve a result most worthy of the marvellous purpose, and means, and causes that go to achieve it.

1. For, in the *first* place: not merely does the First person of the Godhead act with the original authority and special majesty and power which, as sustaining the honours of the Godhead, may well be expected to shew themselves forth in him; but his being the Father, is a fact fertile in the covenant with richest blessings to us. 'Blessed be the God and Father of our Lord Jesus Christ, who, according to his abundant mercy, hath begotten us again.' He acts towards us as the Father of the eternal Son, and becomes to us in him our Father in heaven. Salvation is of the Lord our God. But our salvation of this God—the God and Father of our Lord Jesus Christ—is, our being 'begotten unto him to be a kind of first-fruits from among his creatures.' We are not merely saved in a way of being renewed in the spirit of our minds, created again unto God; but regenerated unto the Father; begotten of him; and, unto that effect, made partakers of a divine nature,—susceptible, therefore, of the command, 'Be ye perfect, as your Father in heaven is perfect.' Ye are of God, little children.

2. In the *second* place, and in like manner: we are not merely to think of the Godhead of our Redeemer,—the Second person in the glorious Trinity. Truly, his Godhead is the rock on which our salvation rests. 'Surely, shall one say, in Jehovah have I righteousness and strength.' His Godhead gives all their efficacy to his blood and righteousness,

as the infinitely valid grounds of our justification before God, and of the justification of God's own procedure in giving us the Spirit, and all spiritual blessings. But while our Redeemer is God, while he is one person in the Godhead, he is *that* person who is the Word of God, and God's only-begotten Son. And each of these relations is replete, by covenant arrangement, with integral elements of our full salvation. It is his being the eternal Word of the eternal Father which constitutes the foundation of his qualification to be our prophet, to reveal the Father to us. And it is his being the eternal Son of the eternal Father which qualifies him to be a redeemer of aliens and prodigals, and a pledge and bond of adoption to them. His relation to the first person of the Godhead is thus a foundation and spring of sonship to those who are called into the fellowship of the Son; for they are called into his fellowship with certification that he is the Son, and that the Father who calls them is faithful. Whether we regard them as thus enjoying an identity in any sense, or simply an analogy of sonship in their union to the eternal Son, it remains, in either case, that they are conformed unto God's Son, that he may be the firstborn of many brethren.

3. And so, *thirdly*: it is not merely the case that there is a Third person in the Godhead who renews our natures; but, proceeding as he does from the Father, the Father sends him, and our renewal then is our being regenerated unto the Father as his very and his 'dear children.' And proceeding as he does from the Son, the Son sends him, and our renewal then is our union to the Son as sons in him, and our being conformed unto him as our elder brother,—the Spirit of the Son in our hearts, as in the Son's own heart, crying, Abba, Father. And thus, all that is implied in the first person of the Godhead being the eternal Father; all that is implied in the second being the Word of God, and God's only-begotten and eternal Son; and all that is implied in the Spirit's proceeding from the Father, and in his proceeding also from the Son: each and all of these relations of incomprehensible glory, and intercommunion, and love ineffable within the Godhead, is made to yield some element of grace, and intimacy, and stability, some characteristic of specific and distinguishing excellence, some trace and signature, some radiant and ineffaceable mark or token, that

shall shine for ever in that many-sided theme of glorying and praise—the salvation of our own lost souls. Oh! surely a flood of light thus falls, even from the abysmal depths of Godhead's most mysterious relations, on that overwhelming expostulation of a redeeming God, 'What more could I have done for my vineyard that I have not done?' I have offered myself unto you as your portion, not merely in respect of all attributes and glories that pertain to me as being God, but in respect of all the grace and tenderness that are implied in my being the eternal Father. And I have given you not merely a divine person—one person in the Godhead—to be your substitute, and surety, and head; but he is the eternal Son whom I have given you: and whatever his being the Son—my well-beloved and only-begotten can yield towards the greater fullness of grace, and truth, and love, in your redemption, and of greater nearness and stability in your restored relation to me when redeemed, I have not withheld from you. And I have given you not merely another divine person—one person in the Godhead—to quicken you to newness of life; but his procession, in glorious eternal necessity, from the Father, and his procession, in like manner, from the Son, have been founded on to perfect the covenant economy according to the manifold wisdom whereof the Spirit is the irrefragable witness, and the sovereign love whereof the Spirit is the glorious, and final, and securing seal. What more could I have done for my vineyard that I have not done? There is not one remaining fact as to the constitution of the everlasting Godhead, and not one remaining fragment of relationship among the glorious co-equal, co-eternal Persons, to each of whom in Trinity the one substance, power, and eternity of Godhead appertains, which has been left—if we may so dare to speak—which has been left dormant, unrevealed, undeveloped, unapplied, in compassing the salvation of the lost children of men. All, all has been drawn upon,—all has been drawn forth. The deepest depths; the richest resources; all the most specific internal relations in the nature of Godhead;—all have been brought into requisition, into revelation, into action, and into pledged covenant certainty, to compass the salvation of the lost children of men. Oh, the depth of the riches, both of the wisdom and knowledge of God! how unsearchable are his judgments, and his ways past finding out! Who hath known the mind of the Lord? or who hath been his counsellor?

III. And how very glorious a thing, then, must it be to be a saved soul! How very glorious to be a Christian! Doubtless all such are the excellent of the earth. Doubtless they are a peculiar treasure unto God Most High.

Even when translated to the heavenly Jerusalem, and associated with the angelic hosts, the ransomed of the Lord will be distinguished among the morning stars, when all the sons of God, even from all principalities and kingdoms, may congregate for special jubilee or worship. 'Who are these that are arrayed in white robes, and whence came they?'—the occupants of thrones and dominions may be heard to ask with rapturous joy and admiration. Whence came they? for surely they are 'a kind of first-fruits unto God from among his creatures.'

It were a high and noble theme—the very epic poem of a profound subjective Christian theology—to set forth the evidence and the elements of that transcendent superiority that shall place once lost, now saved, sons of Adam in the front rank of the creatures of God; nearer the throne than angels; with holy natures of finer spiritual fabric,—more firmly knit in strength of everlasting loyalty, and more refined and delicate in tenderness of everlasting love,—than angelic natures can exhibit. It would demand a theologian in stature such as Milton among the poets, to set forth all that is involved in the ransomed Bride of Jehovah-Jesus being 'all glorious within, her raiment of needle-work,' awakening the wonder and inquiries of those whose garments, pure as the light, have been unstained since first the morning stars sang. But there is one transcendent dignity that belongs to them, not merely in their peculiarly near relation to God, but in the style, if we may so say, or tone of that spiritual estate into which they have been formed or moulded in the perfecting of grace in their holy natures. And it is this: They bear traces of the glory of Godhead's Tri-unity, such as unfallen, unredeemed beings cannot bear. Who are these that are arrayed in white robes? These are they who are where they are, and who are what they are, only because there is Tri-unity in Godhead, and only because the Son is eternally begotten of the Father, and the Spirit eternally proceedeth from the Father and from the Son. Other creatures may shine with the reflected light of the attributes of God. To the ransomed of the Lord it is given on the behalf of Christ, to shine with the peculiar reflected glory of Tri-unity of Godhead, and of all that the relations of the persons in the Godhead involve of the deepest glories, and love, and joy of their Lord. Yon bright seraph may be a proof that God is good, and wise, and mighty, and faithful, and holy, and full of love: but yon once lost child of Adam, now a king and a priest unto the Father, is a living proof that 'there are three persons in the Godhead, the Father, the Son, and the Holy Ghost; that the Father is of none, neither begotten nor proceeding; that the Son is eternally begotten of the Father; and the Spirit eternally proceeding from the Father and from the Son.' Even this light hath come up upon Mount Zion; this glory of the Lord arisen upon her. Therefore will Jehovah rejoice over her with singing. She shall be a crown of glory in his hand, a royal diadem in the hand of her God. He shall call her Hephzibah, because he delighteth in her. And when myriads of thrones, and dominions, and principalities, and angelic powers in heavenly places, shall be his to choose among. He will, through endless ages, say of the worm Jacob,—'Jacob is the lot of my inheritance.' μ.

THE SPIRIT OF THE FATHER
GLORIFYING THE SON[1]

SUCH is the topic that we mean at present to deal with; and that in a way not of ranging over all Scripture for our materials, but rather of opening up a little of what the Prince of Theologians, the Prince of Peace himself, says about it. 'When he, the Spirit of Truth is come, he will guide you into all truth: for he shall not speak of himself; but whatsoever he shall hear, that shall he speak. He shall glorify me: for he shall receive of mine, and shall show it unto you. All that the Father hath are mine: therefore said I, that he shall take of mine, and shall show it unto you' (John 16:13-15).

I. There are three distinct views to be taken of the glory of Christ, or three different respects in which he is glorified.

These are all beautifully bound up together, as we hope to show, and they are all more or less strikingly alluded to in the amazing discourse with which Jesus closed his earthly ministry.

1. In the *first* place, there is that glory of Christ which he received personally as his reward for his obedience, but which he received also for the benefit and in the name of his Church. Great grace and condescension were revealed and embodied in Christ's consenting at all to rise from the dead. He might have said, 'The ends of my incarnation, and of my humiliation by being exhibited in human flesh, are accomplished. Let my incarnation itself now cease. Let me be done with it. Let the grave retain the body of my humiliation,

---

[1] [From: *The British and Foreign Evangelical Review* (1882), p. 64f.]

while my Godhead's glory shall now be revealed in a manner worthy of Godhead.' But no. It did not satisfy Jesus to be made flesh for a limited time, however long. Being once God-man, 'this man abideth for ever:' and hence his resurrection from the dead. 'Tis with a view to, and in prospect of, that resurrection that he says (John 17:1), 'Father, glorify thy Son:' and again (verse 5), 'And now, Father, glorify thou me with thine own self with the glory which I had with thee before the world was.' Glorify thou him who presents himself before thee in a creature-nature and scorns not creature-duties—(as thus, even now, in prayer); Glorify thou the Son of Man.

This supplication of our Lord began to be answered as soon as his body had lain the appointed time in Joseph's tomb. 'He was crucified in weakness, but raised by the power of God.' And, *eo usque,*[1] he was glorified by the Spirit. For it is written: 'He was declared to be the Son of God with power, according to the Spirit of holiness, by his resurrection from the dead.' True, the glory was but sparingly assumed or exhibited at first. For the Lord's resurrection-body must be shown by 'infallible signs' to be the same identically with that which suffered—the very same, alive again after his passion; and so, lest it should fail to be identified, the glory is at first very much restrained. No dazzling, blinding, brilliancy is emitted from his person like that of the Shekinah when he was trans-figured. Rather it was on this wise,—'Handle me and see, a spirit hath not flesh and bones as ye see me have;' and again, 'Reach hither thy finger;' and again, 'Children, have ye any meat? Come and dine.' And the conviction was complete; they identified their Lord. 'And none of the disciples durst ask him, Who art thou? knowing that it was the Lord.' Yet, evidently, fain would they have asked him after all; they *would* have questioned his identity had the evidence been less than overpowering: but it was not, and they durst not refuse it. Yet it needed overpower-ing evidence; for there was some great change begun in Immanuel's person: the *glory* was begun. Accordingly he does not dwell with them now as he had been wont to do. It is a sudden appearance, and reap-pearance occasionally, and, as it would almost seem, arbitrarily: and again, 'he vanished out of their sight.' There is singular emphasis and

[1] [Latin: until that time.]

meaning in the language used in recording these transient glimpses which the apostles now had of Jesus. '*He was seen;*' simply 'seen.' 'He was seen of Cephas, then of the twelve; after that he was seen of above five hundred brethren at once; after that, he was seen of James; then of all the apostles.' 'He was seen,' in brief and unexpected and miraculous glimpses rather than visits; enough for purposes of witness-bearing by the twelve: but transient, so much so that even Paul does not need to change the expression when he would describe his own view of Jesus in his heavenly glory: 'Lastly, he was seen of me also, as of one born out of due time.'

But, ere Paul thus saw the Lord, that Jesus whom he persecuted had been invested with all glory at the right hand of God. His last, his parting blessing had been given to the twelve; the cloud had received him out of their sight. The Wonderful, the Counsellor, the Mighty God-man, the Prince of Peace, had ascended, with the chariots of God, which are twenty thousand, even thousands of angels, the Lord among them, as in the holy place. 'Thou hast ascended on high, thou hast led captivity captive.' Neither the eye of sense nor of imagination can follow Jesus beyond the cloud which curtained in the view of his disciples. We cannot figure to ourselves with what attire of heavenly, magnificent, majestic state the Man of Sorrows took his way to the throne of his victory and reward. Nor, though we could, would the knowledge profit us. But we have a more sure word of prophecy, and from it we learn that as this triumphing Messiah entered the realms of glory, he ascended through all the high ranks of heaven's holy hierarchy, he rose beyond angels and archangels, far above all principality and power, and might and dominion, and every name that is named; until, all things being under his feet, he was received as a 'priest upon his throne;'—how touching!—in his office of priest, and all because he had loved us and given himself for us!—and the spirit of David beheld what David in Spirit had foretold in song, for 'Jehovah said unto our Lord, Sit thou at my right hand, until I make thy foes thy footstool' (Psa. 110:1).

It is not easy to explain in few words the nature of the glory thus communicated to Messiah. (1) As to his human nature, it is crowned, or, more correctly, in it he is crowned with honour immeasurably beyond what is found in any or all creatures; filled with the everlasting fruition of Jehovah as its—rather, as in it, his—covenant God and head; at once glorified and blessed in the unparalleled prerogative of being constituted the wonderful and willing medium through which—the living, co-operating, ever-blessed instrument through which—the glory of the Godhead has its brightest shining; for in the Word-made-flesh, in the Man that is God's fellow, there is beholden the glory as of the only-begotten of the Father, full of grace and truth. In the face of Jesus Christ, the light of the knowledge of the glory of God shines. (2) As to his divine nature, it is glorified in the sense, that while hitherto it had been veiled and concealed from view in the likeness of sinful flesh, now its perfections and attributes begin to shine forth, no longer restrained and checked beneath the form of a servant, but in the person of One acknowledged to be Lord of all, before all, over all, and in all; no longer hidden in the garb and fashion of a man as in the days of his flesh, but rather declared the more clearly because in human flesh, and through his glorified humanity, with all of Divine glory that is in the nature of things visible, plainly brought to light, and all that is necessarily invisible revealed as it had never been before to spiritual wisdom. To the light of faith, his Divinity is glorified in that the most hidden glory of God is disclosed through the assumption, sacrifice, death, and exaltation of his human nature. His humanity, again, this human nature in such alliance with Deity, hath a glory unparalleled in honour and majesty, as being the real dwelling-place of God, and the perfection of beauty.

And (3) his entire person as Immanuel is glorified, in that as God-man he is the head of all the universe: holding of Godhead, as being himself one of the persons thereof; holding of man, as he was himself the Elder Brother, made most blessed for evermore; made exceeding glad with the light of God's countenance; invested with all right to rule, and all power in heaven and earth to conduct his government; the representative of the Creator to the creature, and reciprocally of the creature to the Creator; the representative of God to man in all that God is pleased to do toward men, and of men toward God in all that man can need from God; the king of angels, prince of the kings of the earth; the fountain of all authority, and wellspring of all beneficence and grace; in whom dwelleth all the fullness of the Godhead bodily; the storehouse of all treasures and unsearchable riches of blessing and power; that we, under his kingly hand, may have protection unto eternal life; may have a safe and sacred place on the platform of God's holy universe in the person and fellowship of the Son, and out of his fullness may obtain grace for grace. On earth he was the God-man as much as now, as much as ever. But then the deep abasement of his humanity almost alone was visible: the unalterable, inalienable glory of his Godhead was retired from view. *Now*, his Divine claims are no longer in abeyance; but all in heaven and earth are called upon to honour the Son (in human nature) even as they honour the Father. His power is no more under restraint, as when on Calvary he was crucified through weakness; he wields the sceptre and holds the reins of universal sway over interests and governments which it would crush the feeble mind of man to have a moment's view of; and all in the interest and for the advancement of our salvation. His all-sufficiency is no longer voluntarily locked up from his own use, as when he was content in Gethsemane to receive strength from an angel; but in the midst of the throne he is seen to be the First, and the Last, and the Living One, with whom is the fountain of life and the fullness of being, and who feeds with endless life and faculty and holy joy the myriads that wait on his service and his throne.

All this glory of the Son of Man is given to him for the Church, in her name, or in her behalf. This revenue of majesty and honour, of strength and beauty, of shining, shielding power and grace and glory, Immanuel hath taken possession of, in his character or capacity as Head of the Church. All whom the Father hath given him are interested in this inheritance on which the Elder Brother hath entered, for they also are heirs of God, joint-heirs with Christ, and they shall finally be brought to share in all that is his, that his love and belovedness, his joy and glory, may be fulfilled in them.

And it is the Spirit of the Father that hath given him all this glory. 'He shall glorify me.' He shall glorify me for the Church!

2. But besides the glory now spoken of, there is also that glory which accrues to Christ in the Church. We have seen that in heaven he is personally glorified for the Church, glorified on behalf of his people. But, in addition to this, he is glorified in his people. To this also express and distinctive allusion is made in his intercessory prayer (John 17:10), 'I am glorified in them.'

There is a close, a vital relation between this department of Christ's glory and the former. Indeed this second glory is none other than the former, in its ever-varying measures, transmitted and communicated from the fountain-head, and now exhibited in the Church,—in believing souls as in its resting-place. 'Tis the glory in the Head revealed as grace in the members, and in them reflected back again as glory upon their living Head. It was in order that he might be thus glorified in the Church, both in heaven and earth, that he was glorified personally in heaven for the Church, in the Church's stead and name. The one is the designed and intended issue of the other. He was glorified for his people that he might be glorified in them: glorified in his saints, and herein most of all admired in all them that believe.

Now *this* also is a rich and fertile theme—the glory of Christ in his chosen,—and only a little of it can be brought under review. You will have some idea, however, of what is meant if you bear in mind that the word of Christ dwells richly in his people, and by its effects in them through the Spirit—by whom alone, and always, Christ is in every light glorified,—it greatly promotes the glory of the Word made flesh. Within his people's souls his eternal and unchangeable word of grace has been lodged by the Spirit more or less plentifully: and having, as it were, taken fire within them (for 'is not my word a fire? saith the Lord'), it is burning up and consuming their dross and corruption, and refining them as silver is refined. Or, having as it were taken life (for Christ's words are spirit and they are life), it is working in them faith and penitence, and comfort, and joy, and holiness. It is no dead letter in their minds or consciences, but the word made alive, quickening and rousing their soul and all that is within them,—powerful, lively, living, life-giving, moving, purifying, acting,—the living word of Christ, traced to him, known and read of all men, in which he himself is directly glorified.

Nor is it enough to say merely that Christ's word is in his people, and that thus they are his representatives and witnesses to an ungodly world in the bodily absence of the Lord himself. Thus, no doubt, he is greatly glorified; and precisely those attributes of God, and that revelation of his glory, which the work of inanimate creation cannot embody, are seen more or less in the written word, as it lives and moves and has its being and free course, and operates and cannot be hid when it transforms the Church into the image of her living Saviour. But we must bear in mind, further, that the very life of Christ, as well as the word of Christ, is in his children, and it is there as a source of wonderful glory to him. Christ dwells in his own by faith: he is in them the hope of glory. Saith the apostle, 'I am crucified with Christ, nevertheless I live, yet not I, but Christ liveth in me' (Gal. 2:20).

The life of Christ in the world, while he tabernacled with men upon the earth, was wonderful. To a spiritual eye, the spectacle of the Holy One having his abode in a corrupted and polluted world like this is passing strange. That holiness itself should have come into such close, continued, painful, and prolonged contact with sin,—should have suffered by sin on all hands for many long and weary years, yet uncontaminated, holy still, harmless, undefiled, separate from sinners, yet without sin,—this is indeed amazing. But when you pass from the life of Christ personal in this fallen world, the life and indwelling of Christ mystical in a fallen and but partially recovered soul, is in some respects a far greater, or, at least, additional mystery. To think of Christ dwelling in one who still has to cry, 'I am carnal, sold under sin;' 'In me, that is, in my flesh, dwelleth no good thing;' 'Oh wretched man that I am, who shall deliver me from this body of death?' Here is Immanuel's life in far closer contact with sin, yet in no fellowship with it: more narrowly hemmed in by the evil, yet never touched or tarnished by it: far more likely to be choked in the atmosphere of uncongenial, contrary, destructive elements; yet living still, because fed from the fountain of eternal blessedness: far more nearly swamped in the waters of ungodliness and iniquity; but still surviving, a flame inviolable, which many waters cannot quench and the floods cannot drown, but which is dissipating and driving off the floods, mightier in its greatness than the noise of many waters: far more closely grappling with darkness, corruption, death; yet evermore holding its own, and proving more than conqueror. Is not this glory to Christ in the highest?

Further, Christ is seen to be glorified in his people when we think that his righteousness, as well as his life, is theirs, and when we think what it procures for them. It was little that for his righteousness' sake the Father should have been well pleased with, and should have justified, the Son. It was a light matter that God should be pleased with Immanuel personally for his righteousness' sake, and should, because of it, admit him to everlasting favour and inalienable honours. Comparatively small was the glory accruing to him when, on his ascending up on high, he was accepted as God's righteous servant, whose days should be prolonged, yea, should last as long as the sun, and to whom there should be divided a portion with the great and a spoil with the strong. There was reserved for him a greater revenue and fund of glory to be derived from his righteousness than this, and it is given to him when he is glorified in his people. For surely it is far more wonderful when it is found that the same righteousness which has already carried God's servant to the throne of glory and acceptance, instead of having its merits or its power thereby exhausted in accomplishing the exaltation of the Son of God, prevails to raise aloft from death to life—from condemnation to favour—from hell to heaven—from a doomed and lost eternity to life, and bliss, and immortality, and confidential fellow-ship with God,—yea, even into the most tender and blessed, and eternal reconciliation with the righteous Father, myriads who lay exposed to all possible evils, most justly shut up to their endurance, but who now, through the robe of Immanuel's obedience unto death, shall pass into the everlasting glory, as they have already passed into the peace of God without all check, beneath the sanctifying gaze, and even with the entire approbation of God, and the universal plaudits of all his holy creatures. That this also should result from his righteousness—that the personally guilty and hell-deserving should be so dealt with for Christ's sake—is surely greatly to Immanuel's glory: herein indeed is he glorified. When he contemplates this primary and fundamental element of his people's salvation, surely he may well say, in the simple and touching words, 'I am glorified in them.' And 'in him shall all the seed of Israel be justified, and shall glory,' when they give unto him the honour of that name whereby he shall be called, 'Jehovah-Tzidkenu,' 'The Lord our Righteousness.'

There are many other views that might be taken of Christ's glory in his people. The Church is the place of his glory, for he dwells in it, and he shall glorify the place of his glory. Zion is the 'perfection of beauty,' because Immanuel has here his desire and his abode; and that perfect beauty is none other than the exhibition of his own glory, when 'out of Zion, the perfection of beauty, God hath shined.' 'Arise, shine; for thy light is come, and the glory of the Lord hath risen upon thee' (Isa. 60:1).

The manifestation of Christ's glory in his people is, as has been said already, the end and issue of his glory for them, as he sitteth at the right hand of power. These stand related to each other as cause and effect, or as means to an end. Never could Christ have been glorified in his people, had he not been glorified for them. Never could he have received glory in their name without causing it in due time to reach themselves in their salvation and holiness, so that he should be glorified in their persons. But it is certain he shall be glorified in them, though it were only because he was glorified for them.

But while we see this very close and beautiful connection between the glory that Christ enjoys for his people, and that which he enjoys in them, it still remains open for consideration: How, or by what means, agency, and process, the glory of Jesus as the Priest upon his throne, in his people's name, serves to produce ultimately a manifestation of his glory in their persons? Because Christ is glorified for them, it does not follow that he is therefore and thereby glorified in them without any intermediate agency or operation. What intervening process is there by which the glory of Immanuel's own person is safely and effectually lodged in the dwelling place designed for it—in his people's persons— and beautifully and permanently manifested there? How do we account for the glory of Immanuel in the land that is very far off ever finding reception and exhibition in the Church and in the Christian in the land of their pilgrimage here?

3. The answer is, that there is a third glory of the Saviour—a third respect in which he is glorified—which comes in between the two already spoken of, efficaciously linking them together, and bringing it about that the glory of Christ *for* the Church on high, as a means, shall surely be productive of glory to Christ *in* the Church as the end in view. And this third glory of Christ is that spoken of in the farewell address when he says, 'He shall testify of me; he shall glorify me; he shall take of mine, and shall show it unto you. He shall not speak of himself, he shall testify of me. All that the Father hath are mine: therefore said I, he shall take of mine, and shall show it unto you.'

The Spirit testifies of Christ and reveals his fullness of grace and glory to the believing soul. This is the intervening Agent; this the intermediate process. It is in this way that the plenitude of grace and truth and glory that is in Christ—received by him as clothed in human flesh when he was received up on high and glorified with the Father *for* the Church, and made the living depository of her blessings, and her blessedness—is made available, and is dispensed to the Church, that he may be glorified in the Church, and admired in all them that believe—Mark the complete arrangement for revealing Immanuel's glory. He is glorified *for* the Church, *to* the Church, in the Church. This is the whole in brief; but it is complete.

First, he is exalted to the right hand of the Majesty on high, endowed with all power, and replenished with all blessing, grace, and glory as the Immanuel-Head of his people. He is glorified for the Church, or in her name.

Secondly, Jesus being thus glorified, the living Spirit, hitherto largely restrained, is freely and richly poured out. Previously he had not been given for this express reason, we are told, namely, because Jesus was not yet glorified. But now that the Christ hath gone to his reward, he sends him: and the Spirit's work is to reveal the gracious Saviour; to open, exhibit, commend Immanuel to our faith, to take of the things of Christ and show them to us; to glorify Jesus before our gaze. Now is Christ glorified to the Church, or in the Church's intelligent and delighted estimation.

And *lastly*, being thus glorified before the reverent, intelligent, believing, admiring gaze of his people, the sure and final consequence is that Christ, already glorified *for* and *to* his people, is now glorified in them—in their pardon, acceptance, reconciliation with God, their peace, and liberty, and joy, and holiness, and full salvation.

Because he has been glorified in heaven above for his people, and in order to his being glorified on earth below in them, therefore is he glorified to them by the Spirit, in the means of grace, taking of the things that are Christ's and showing them to their believing and grateful souls.

Such is the place which the Spirit's work in this matter holds in the economy of glory to God in the highest, through Jesus Christ the Son of his love. The glory is seen issuing from the fountain of Immanuel's glory in heaven—from that exhaustless well-spring or treasure-house of mercy, love, grace, truth, and blessing. The Holy Spirit, if the expression may be allowed, fills his hands when he visits the Church refreshingly; he brings the burden to his waiting people; and through the means of grace, through the word read and preached and heard in faith, and sealed believingly in holy sacraments, he discloses to their faith the meaning, moral beauty, worth, and fullness of the things which are only 'revealed from faith to faith,' because such is their nature that 'eye hath not seen, nor ear heard, and there have not entered into the hearts of men the things which God hath prepared for them that love him; but God hath revealed them to us by the Spirit: for the Spirit searcheth all things, yea, the deep things of God.'

'He takes of the things of Christ:'—of the wounds, the griefs, the sorrows, the curse-bearing, the wrath, the darkness, the desolation and abandonment of Christ, and shows them to the soul. The Spirit of grace and supplication bids the believer look upon Jesus whom he hath pierced; and convincing the conscience of deadly guilt as brought to light by the awful scene, he gives birth to the mournings of repentance and contrition of spirit.

'He takes of the things of Christ:'—of the same death of Christ in another view—of its sacrificial worth, its substitutionary character, its penal pain, its atoning design and efficacy, its sin-cleansing, peace-giving power, as endured by him only because he was a loving substitute, a holy sin-bearer:—not sinful because bearing the sin of others, but therein making sin the occasion of a holiness and holy love which without it the universe could have never seen; and revealing this at the same time, as a fountain of propitiating merit, inexhaustible, and ever full and free, without money and without price, to all who renounce all other merit and approach in faith, he brings into the very heart of contrite mourning that most blessed gift of heaven, the element of peace, the gleam of joy unspeakable and full of glory, which makes the heart yet more tender, and true, and contrite.

'He takes of the things of Christ:'—of his meritorious obedience, his perfect righteousness, the abundance of the gift of righteousness, the everlasting and vicarious righteousness which Jesus brought in for his Church; and opening the understanding to understand its meaning, history, design, and fullness—its necessity, availableness, and perfect adaptation to supply the place of Joshua's filthy garments, that so he may stand before the angel unquailingly, and have places to walk in among them that stand by the throne of God—no mere sufferance, but each his own place,—as righteously his *own*, on the joyful side of justice as that of Judas was his own on the awful side of justice and of vengeance, no mere sufferance, but a legal title to dwell there;—he shows the soul in this a plea for seeking in full assurance of faith all needful grace while here, all boundless glory hereafter.

'He takes of the things of Christ:'—of his power and strength, and victory and triumph, and shows *them* also to the weak, the weary, the wavering, the worn with the long conflict with sin and Satan and temptation. He shows them that the prince of this world is judged; that Messiah grappled with the foe of man, and spoiled, and crushed, and trampled on him, flinging him down like lightning from heaven, to be devoured and engulfed in hell as the lightning is engulfed in the swiftly-following darkness for ever. He shows Immanuel's mastery over the believer's enemies, and cheers him on to keep his spiritual weapons still in constant, vigorous use, in the full assurance that victory is unfailingly the lot of those who hold on to the end. He shows the full fountain of Immanuel's endless strength and victory; its free availableness and perfect suitableness to the weakest and most weary soldier in Immanuel's army; and how gently it will be given him; and how by the Spirit's grace he will be enabled to wield it, infinite and almighty in itself though it be. 'And a bruised reed will he not break, and the smoking flax will he not quench, till he bring forth judgment unto victory' (Isa. 42:3).

But it were impossible to give an exhaustive description of the Spirit's work as he glorifies Christ to the believing estimation of his people. One would have to speak of all the perfections of Christ, of all his work, of all his offices, and of the faithfulness and love of the Spirit in pouring his illumination over that love and these offices, and every part of all his action in them. Time would fail to tell how he shows to them the unsearchable riches of the grace of Jesus—his manifold wisdom,—and his love which passeth understanding. By his gracious spiritual work upon the soul, somewhat is rightly known of the mind, and will, and truth, and thoughts of God—of the hidden treasures, wisdom, and knowledge that are laid up in Jesus—of the love, mercy, tenderness, compassion, sympathy, and care of the good Shepherd of the sheep—of his brilliancy and splendour as the Morning Star—of his quickening, life-giving, life-sustaining beams as the Sun of Righteousness—of the comely beauty, order, harmony, and holiness of that government which he maintains as the King of Zion—of the honour, the very peculiar honour, which is seen upon him as a Royal High Priest, a priest upon his throne, dispensing righteous mercy and holy sanctifying pardon to the guilty;—in short, of the power, and riches, and wisdom, and strength, and honour, and glory, and beauty, and blessing which are due unto the Lamb that was slain, and are ascribed to him by all that are around the throne, and by all here below whom the Holy Spirit hath enabled joyfully to join in the celebration of his power, and say—'Unto him that loved us, and washed us from our sins in his own blood, and hath made us kings and priests unto God, even the Father, to him be glory and dominion for ever and ever. Amen.'—Christ Jesus, the Son of God in human nature, is glorified for, to, and in the Church.

There are, at this point, three emerging questions—(1) Would you know whether Christ has been glorified for you? (2) Would you have Christ glorified to you? (3) Would you have Christ glorified in you?

1. Would you know whether Christ has been glorified *in* heaven *for you—for you*? Then you must have Christ glorified to you, i.e. in your enlightened and believing estimation. There is no other proof that the glory Christ received was in your behalf, and in your name,—in your stead, as your own Head and Redeemer—except a present spiritual insight by the Spirit into his glory. And the delightful consideration is, that infinite wisdom and grace have arranged that you cannot see his glory without by faith claiming himself; and further that that you cannot do without having the claim duly, divinely honoured, 'My beloved is mine, and I am his;' 'As the apple tree among the trees of the garden, so is my Beloved among the sons;' 'Whom have I in heaven but thee, and on earth there is none besides thee; my heart and my flesh fail, but thou art the strength of my heart and my portion for ever.' We take out no other extract from the registers of heaven to prove that the honoured Messiah at his ascension took possession of his glory in our name, than the thankful reception in our own souls of the gifts he ascended to give; and first of all, and as the fountain, pledge, guarantee, and author of all, his own adorable Spirit—the indwelling of his Spirit and the consequent views which we may receive of the grace, loveliness, love, love-worthiness, and glory of our exalted King. Jesus is glorified by the Spirit to all those for whom he was glorified.

2. And would you have Jesus glorified to you? Would you have your desire to see the King in his beauty gratified? Would you see the glory of God in the face of Jesus Christ? To enable you to look upon and appreciate such a sight is a work to which none but a Divine Person—the Holy Spirit—is competent. You cannot do it for yourself. Ministers cannot do it for you. 'The Spirit,' saith Jesus, 'shall glorify me.' He, and he alone. How diligent, then, ought we to be in praying for his coming, for he is given to them that ask him. How dutiful and diligent should we be in plying the throne of grace for one of those pure 'revivals' with which he alone can enrich the Church! 'For if men, being evil, know how to give good gifts unto their children, how much more will he give the Holy Spirit to them that ask him?'

What a hold upon himself he hath given us, in assuring us that he hath redeemed us from the law for this very purpose, that we might receive the promise of the Spirit! And how careful should we be to avoid all that would grieve or quench the Spirit—for this brings darkness and blindness upon us, both as it injures our faculties, and as it grieves away the only agent that can savingly enlighten them. How precious, moreover, should the Word of God be to us, read and preached, seeing it is the only glass into which the Spirit casts the glorious image of our Lord; yea, in which, intently gazing as 'with open face, we may behold as in a glass the glory of the Lord.'

3. Would you have Christ glorified in you? Would you reflect his glory? Would you be transchanged into the same image from glory to glory? Still the answer is the same. You must have the Spirit glorifying Christ *to you*. There is no other proof that he has been glorified *for you*. There is no other possibility of his being glorified *in you*. 'Tis by beholding as in a glass the glory of the Lord that you are transformed into the same image from glory to glory. Faith must be in lively exercise. 'Said I not unto thee, If thou wouldest believe, thou shouldest see the glory of God?' And thus being strong in the faith, thou wilt give glory unto him. The hidden glory will be taken by the Spirit of glory and of God, and held up to your admiring view; and being seen in the very same light as the one intellect of Godhead, of the Three-in-one, and specially of the Holy Spirit, sees it, it will impress its living likeness on your souls, and now for the first time you will be unable to avoid knowing that seeing is believing, and believing is receiving, and that to see Jesus by the Holy Ghost is to see him as consciously your own. Seeing the glory of Immanuel in the Spirit, you will see it in him *for* you, to give sure salvation; while reciprocally, he will behold it again in you, to the praise of the glory of his grace.

Here, then, is the entire amazingly beautiful arrangement: Christ glorified now *to* you, and in your delighted admiration of him, the only evidence you can have that he was glorified *for* you: Christ glorified for ever *in* you, in your beauty and bliss and holiness, the sure result if glorified *to* you by the Spirit.

II. But this glorifying of the Son has its relation to the past purposes and present intervention of the Father as well as of the Spirit.

For the very first beginnings of personal Christianity have relations with the Trinity, closer far than it is customary to give due consideration to. The ever-vital doctrine of Trinity comes out in Holy Scripture, not as an abstract mystery, but as invaluable truth bearing incessantly on the well-springs, and the familiar and great principles of all true spiritual religion. If there be not three persons in the Godhead equal in power and glory: one of them—the Second Person, the Eternal Son himself, in his person, not in something that he has done, and which would of course have its limits, but in his person, which is infinite in being, resources, and glory—the propitiation for our sins, and our endless peace with God; another, the Third Person, the Holy Spirit, infinite in being, grace, and power, pledged to see us united in our person and being to Christ; while the First Person is a Father, and knows all a father's feelings and love unquenchable—if all this be not true, then what hath the righteous done? But if it is true, then when is it time for a believer's despondency or fears?

Now this, in connection with the origination and first up-springings in us individually of Divine light and life, is nowhere more beautifully brought out than by Jesus himself in this same farewell discourse. And the words are peculiarly rich and deep: 'All that the Father hath are mine: therefore said I, The Spirit shall take of mine, and shall show it unto you' (John 16:15). By this one step of reasoning, the Prince of Peace, who is the prince of theologians and logicians too, vindicates his having given the promise of the Spirit to testify of him, to take the things of Christ and show them unto us. 'All that the Father hath is mine:' that is, 'To me there belongeth essential Godhead, with all its inalienable prerogatives, rights, and possessions. Not only am I, as the Eternal Son, equal in power and glory with the Father, as I have been from of old, from everlasting; but now, as Mediator, the God-man, Immanuel, though in that capacity the Father's servant, still to me as Mediator, as your advocate, propitiation, and high-priest, your living head and sympathising friend—to me belong the same exhaustless and unsearchable perfections, prerogatives, and possessions as to the Father himself who sends me. I am secluded, as Mediator, from the possession, declaration, employment, or use of no powers, counsels, designs, judgments, claims, or excellencies which are mine in Godhead as the Father's fellow—daily his delight, rejoicing always before him. As Mediator, I still possess them all, to reveal, employ, communicate them all, as their respective natures may admit, as my will and honour may suggest, or your necessity and advantage require. 'All that the Father hath is mine.' And that is the ground and reason and justification of my promise of the Spirit, the Comforter, to reveal them: 'Therefore said I, The Spirit shall take of mine and show it unto you.'

It is very striking that in each of the three views or relations that Christ gives us of his glory,—his being glorified for, in, and to his people,—in each and all he is careful in the same manner to identify his own glory with the Father's.

1. When he prays that he may be glorified for the Church, he does so on the ground that originally, in his Divine person, he is equal in glory with the Father; and that for less than that to be apparent now in his Immanuelism,[1] would be a punishment instead of a reward. 'And now, O Father, glorify thou me with thine own self with the glory which I had with thee before the world was' (John 17:5). 'Let nothing that was mine, as I was with thee as one brought up with thee, be restrained, secluded, or withheld from me now that, as thy righteous servant, as thy holy child Jesus, as the Man who is thy fellow, I return, righteous Father, my work complete, my sheep redeemed, thy name declared, thy glory made great in the salvation wrought by me: glorify thou me with the everlasting, incommunicable glory, that the world may know that thou hast sent me, and that the Church may know that all that the Father hath is mine.' Thus, when glorified for his people, Jesus rejoiceth to remember and assert that 'all that the Father hath' is his.

2. When Jesus speaks of his glory in his people—'I am glorified in them' (John 17:10)—still he speaks of that glory as common to him with the Father; and this consideration he employs as a plea in interceding

---

[1] A phrase peculiar, I think, to my late beloved and lamented friend, Dr Samuel Miller of Glasgow. A very few of us Disruptionists will be left by and bye, with the touching lament, 'The flowers of the forest are a' wede awa.'

with the Father for them, and praying that he would keep and sanctify them. The Redeemer has three arguments in pleading for his people:—

The *first* argument is that they are his own—his own by his Father's gift. They have been given him by the Father himself; and on this ground he would be encouraged to pray the Father for them, seeing he is but following out the Father's own purpose of eternal love: 'I pray for them: I pray not for the world, but for them which thou hast given me' (John 17:9). 'I am praying only for those for whom, holy Father, thou hast already manifested thy love in giving them to me; "thine they were, and thou gavest them to me."'

The *second* argument urged by Jesus for his people is that they are the Father's. 'I pray only for thine own. I seek blessings, O righteous Father, for none that are outcasts from thy love, or family, or councils.' 'I pray for them, for they are thine' (verse 9).

A *third* plea Jesus has with the Father in praying for his people, and this perhaps is more exactly the point in hand. It follows the other two (in the 10th verse), reiterating and re-impressing and combining them: 'And all thine are mine, and mine are thine, and I am glorified in them' (verse 10). This is not a pleonasm, or an empty repetition of the former arguments, as if it merely re-assured us that the elect are Christ's and the Father's also. Such is not our Lord's meaning; nor is the slip-shod ever a feature in his reasoning, for this, indeed, is not said of persons at all, but of things, as being true of all things, or all possessions of whatsoever kind, no doubt true of the elect also, but not spoken here in that narrow sense, but in the same large and all-comprehensive sense as in his vindication of the promise (John 16:15), and which implies that all necessary possessions and prerogatives of his are coeval, co-equal, and co-extensive—yea, identical—with the Father's. And this marks the pressing urgency and force of the plea which Jesus founds upon it: '*First*, I pray for my people; they are my own that I pray for; those whom thou didst commit to me and my care: yea, *secondly*, I pray for them, O righteous Father, because they are thine. And, *thirdly*, I pray for them because I am glorified in them; and this cannot be but that thou also wilt be glorified, 'for all mine are thine, and thine are mine.' My honour and excelling glory in their salvation, purity, and peace, and protected holy blissful estate of grace and glory, are thine honour and thine excellency also, O righteous Father. 'Therefore I pray for them, that I being glorified in them, thou also mayest be glorified. And this cannot fail to be, since all of "mine" that shall become visible upon them, is simply "thine" seen upon them, "for all mine are thine."'

3. And now, as in speaking of his glory *for* the Church and his glory in the Church, Jesus is thus careful in both instances to identify all that the Father hath with his own, claiming for himself an unlimited possession of the boundless 'all' that Godhead claims and holds, shall it be thought wonderful that again, the *third* time, when it is presented to our notice in this department of it, namely, as revealed by the Spirit to the Church, in order that the same Jesus who has been glorified *for* the Church may now be effectually glorified in it, the same rule is maintained, the same holy policy observed, *ex expresso* and *in terminis*,[1] identifying his glory with the Father's? Nor may it be at all mysterious, or even unexpected, if he should rest on this ground the reasons why he desires the manifestation of what is thus to be manifested to the Church: 'All that the Father hath is mine, *therefore* said I, he shall take of mine, and shall show it unto you.'

Let us address ourselves to the delightful task of pointing out some of the many sides, evolving some of the various lines of force of this argument—this beautiful argument of the Prince of Logicians—himself the Logos of Jehovah. There is absolute storage of electric force and light in this 'therefore.'

I. This 'therefore' holds good in respect of our Lord's possession, jointly with the Father, of the Spirit himself.

'All that the Father hath is mine, *therefore* said I, the Spirit shall take of mine, and shall show it unto you.' For among the all that the Father hath, is the fullness of this glorious spiritual agent, the holy and loving Spirit of grace and power. He proceedeth from the Father and *from the Son*; 'therefore have I a right to arrange in covenant what the Spirit shall do, and as the Logos of God, the Eternal Word, to say or foretell the same. He is given without measure, restraint, or

---

[1] [Latin: in explicit terms.]

modification to me, in my mediatorial person and work; and when I go away I will send him. It is true I have told you that the Father will send him; but even then it shall be in my name, it shall be as my Spirit, as the Spirit of the Christ, the anointed, that he will come unto you—the Spirit of the Son crying Abba, Father. For what possession and control the Father hath over the agency of the glorious and co-equal Spirit, the same also have I. As the Father sent me, and I came to testify not of myself, but him—even so will I send the Spirit; and exactly thus he shall testify not of himself but of me. As the Father's official servant in this high economy of grace and salvation, I speak not of myself, but what I have seen and heard, and in words which the Father gave me. And thus also, as my special servant, to apply and complete the high achievement, will my Spirit come to you in like manner; to speak not of himself, but whatsoever he shall hear, that shall he speak. And just as my word is not mine, but his that sends me, so his word is not really his, but mine that sends him; and he shall take of mine and show it unto you. On this ground I vindicate my great master-promise, as one which I am fully able to fulfil: "I will send the Comforter" and truly he is mine to send; for "all that the Father hath is mine, therefore said I, the Spirit shall take of mine and show it unto you.'"

II. Our Lord's 'therefore' is of force in a second respect—in reference, namely, to the grandeur of the things to be revealed, and the consequent necessity of the Spirit to reveal them.

'It is all the Father hath that is to be revealed unto you; and there-fore I said that the Spirit would do it. What you are to see is not only mine, but the Father's. When you receive of mine, remember it is the Father's. The truth you are now to understand is the name, and counsel, and inner intellect, the free thoughts, and purposes, and love of Godhead, the profound designs and hidden wisdom of the only wise Jehovah. The grace you are to experience, to be subdued by, to be sanctified by, to enjoy and delight yourselves in the abundance of, is to be straight from the overflowing fountain of the Divine nature, the deepest love of God, the covenant mercy, the sovereign grace of him that is past finding out,—a love the existence of which in the searchless depths of Deity, was never dreamt of by highest archangel till it was voluntarily revealed in me, the Son. The wisdom you are now to follow in many of its beautiful and precious arrangements is the wisdom which reconciles the extremes of damning justice and pleading love, of divinest glory and deepest shame, in the person, humiliation, and sacrifice of the Son of God; which has accomplished harmonies and comely order where discord and disorder reigned; built up the things that cannot be moved, out of what was moral wreckage and seemed eternal ruin, and made sin itself the occasion of God's brightest declaration of his holiness.[1] The promises you are to receive, and the spiritual gift thereby to be conveyed, are such as only the Divine being could give, and the Divine nature yield; and in every respect the disclosures that I provide for you, and now invite you to expect, are such as an insight into Divine manifestations alone could afford. Wonder not, then, that you shall need, as your teacher, an Agent of unfathomable wisdom, of boundless power, of exhaustless and untiring grace, of glorious spiritual efficacy to reveal and communicate marvels such as these. You will indeed require that Sovereign One who worketh in every one severally as he will; who, being in creation the father of the spirits of all flesh, shall adapt and prepare your spirit to receive, and understand, and profit by the disclosure, even as he alone can dispose of, and divide out to, every one sovereignly and severally as he will. None but the Spirit can wield and handle these mysteries and weighty gifts of God. None but he may dare to intromit[2] with them. None but he can with right or with success enter into the counsels of Godhead. For who else hath known the mind of the Lord? Who but he hath been his counsellor? Who but he, being God, can by searching find out God? It is he that beareth witness: and he is qualified, for not only is he the Spirit of truth, but intrinsically and essentially, the Spirit is truth. With him is the fountain of light, and in his light shall you see light.

'It is on this ground that I vindicate my promise of the Spirit to be your teacher. You will indeed require his aid, and you shall have it. "All

---

[1] Our students were better furnished when they used to read so plain but valuable (or rather invaluable) a book as [William] Bates on the *Harmony of the Divine Attributes*.

[2] [intromit = enter.]

that the Father hath is mine; therefore said I, the Spirit shall take of mine and show it unto you.'"

III. The argument is good in reference to the inexhaustible and all-satisfying nature of the things to be revealed, and these as offered to be a substitute, and more than a substitute, for our Lord's continued bodily presence.

'All that,' etc.—that is to say, 'I have promised you the Spirit, the Comforter, that his presence and spiritual action in you and on your behalf may more than counterbalance the disadvantage of the want of my bodily presence. Do you say that none can be a substitute for the absent Jesus?—that you can think of none and will hear of none but myself? Be it so, beloved children; the Spirit shall fully gratify you. He shall not speak of himself, it shall be all of me. "He will take of mine and show it unto you." "He shall testify of *me*." "He shall glorify *me*." Do you reply, that it were better still to have me with you: that present vivid sight were better than any remembrance, any rehearsal, and any anticipation that the Comforter may give, let them be ever so bright; and that whatever may be the power of memory, and howsoever whetted by the Spirit (the master of man's spirit) to make you live over again once more the days you spent with me, and cause you to feel again as in my presence in the days of old, yet they must ever be inferior to continued personal intercourse with Jesus? There might be truth and reason in this, were it only your old views of Jesus that the Spirit shall revive and unfold again. But it is not so. What you have seen of me is but very limited indeed; and it will be the Spirit's work to give you greatly enlarged views of that Jesus whom you would detain among you that you might know him better, but who will go away that you may know him better far. As yet it is little more than his humanity and his humiliation that you have known. You have been familiar chiefly with his deep abasement. But in Jesus, your faithful friend, there are other things to be disclosed which you little know of, which when you see you will rejoice that I have gone to the Father, and you see me no more with eyes of flesh. And these things the Spirit will reveal unto you. I have many things to say unto you through him. Now you are not able to bear them. You have indeed been unable to avoid knowing that I came out from God. Ye have seen and thought rightly of Jesus, even that he is the Christ, the Son of the living God. But, ah! how little of the mercy and glory which this involves has opened out to your view! How little of the illimitable compass of this truth have you discovered! How little spiritual power does it exert upon your understandings, your characters, your wills! Alas! so little, that in a few brief hours, thou, Peter, wilt deny me, the rest of you forsake me and flee. Behold, the hour cometh and now is, when ye shall be scattered every man to his own, and shall leave me alone. You have indeed seen little of the Jesus whom I admit you unfeignedly love. You need yet to see in him precisely what the eye of sense can never see—the all things of the Father, which are his also. The Spirit will show you this. The Spirit will teach you that the fullness of the Godhead dwelleth in your friend, though he shall be emptied[1] by and bye on Calvary; that almighty, boundless, creative power is his—the power of him who fainteth not, neither is weary—though he shall be crucified in weakness on Calvary. Hitherto ye have known me chiefly after the flesh. You will never know me rightly till ye know me thus no more, till ye know me spiritually and after the Spirit. Hitherto I have been revealing among you little else than what I have in common with the brethren, with whom, because they are partakers of flesh and blood, I also took part in the same. But when the Spirit is come, far greater things than these shall ye see, because I go unto the Father, and ye see me no more; for besides those things which I have in common with the brethren, ye shall see those things which I have in common with the Father. Ye shall then understand how all power in heaven and earth that is my Father's is mine also—your friend's, your brother's, your mediator's. Knowing not this, ye have hitherto asked nothing in my name, for the boundless compass of my power is hid from you; but at that day ye shall ask what ye will, and it shall be done unto you. You shall then know me as possessing all that the Father hath—as being myself over all, and above all, and in you all, who am before all, and by whom all things consist. You shall have disclosed unto you the fullness of the

[1] [As given in the *'Revised Version'* translation of the Holy Bible, (1881).]

Godhead dwelling in me bodily, that ye yourselves, in comprehending my love with all saints, may be filled with all the fullness of God. The living Spirit whom I will send shall do all this for you. He shall so irradiate your minds with light and glorious revelations, that the Jesus who can send you such an Agent to perform for you such a work, you shall clearly understand to be himself reposing in the light that is inaccessible and full of glory. Your own blessed consciousness under the informing guidance of the Comforter, shall then tell you that the Father hath loved the Son and given all things into his hands. At that day ye shall know that I am in the Father, and the Father in me. At that day ye shall give acknowledgment that you know that in me which is worth knowing indeed: for ye shall say, 'We know that the Son of God is come, and hath given us an understanding to know him that is true; and we are in him that is true, even in his Son, Jesus Christ. This is the true God, and eternal life' (1 John 5:20). 'All that the Father hath is mine; therefore said I, the Spirit shall take of mine and show it unto you:' and surely, in order to know these things, 'it is expedient for you that I go away: for if I go not away, the Spirit will not come unto you; but if I go away, I will send him.'

Yes, beloved,—we may hear Jesus in conclusion adding,—'it is no inadequate return ye shall receive for parting willingly with Jesus. Ye shall know him better far then than now. Ye shall see him from everlasting the heir of God, possessing all that the Father hath, and yourselves joint-heirs in him. It is this that emboldens me to say that the Spirit's advent will be better than my abiding. Otherwise I could not say it, I could not trifle or tamper with your feelings. But as it is, I tell you the truth. It is the truth I tell you when I say, 'It is expedient for you that I go away,' and that precisely on the same grounds on which you dread my departure—in reference exactly to your future prospect of knowing me better. Do you not see it yourselves, since 'all that the Father hath is mine?' And do you not see it as flowing inevitably from the fact, firstly, that all that the Father hath are mine; and, secondly, from my consequent determination that his Spirit shall take of mine and show it unto you?'

IV. Our Lord's logic and argument—his striking and fertile 'therefore'—are good in another point of view;—in reference even to those things that are Christ's, and not the Father's—yea, very specially with regard to those things.

There are many such. There is a whole wonderful class of peculiarities in our Lord's person and history, and the entire essence of the Christian faith turns upon them. There is the incarnation, the humiliation, the blood-shedding of Christ—the propitiatory sacrifice—the human sympathy and fellow-feeling, the reign in human nature and by the Holy Ghost, the expectancy till all his enemies be made his footstool, and thereafter his headship in our humanity over all the universe—the resurrection, the ascension, the reward, the intercession,—there are all these things which belong to Jesus and not to the Father. Is it imaginable that his logic refers not to these? Impossible! It must refer to them by way of eminence. It cannot be supposed that he permits and overlooks them, and makes no arrangement for revealing them in grace and in spiritual power to his elect. This were to make void his glorious gospel utterly. And there is no ground in his careful, rich, and pointed language, for such a thought. For it is not said, 'All that the Father hath is mine, therefore said I, the Spirit shall take of his and show it unto you.' But 'shall take of mine.'

For indeed the things which the Son hath, and which the Father hath not, are worth your knowing only because all the Father hath are his. Under the Spirit's guidance you shall consider him who endured such contradiction of sinners against himself, lest ye be weary and faint in your minds. 'And ye shall look on me whom ye have pierced, and mourn and be in bitterness. Yea, and all that ye have known of me and my sojourn among yourselves, the Spirit shall bring to your remembrance, interpreting and irradiating more brightly than before. And whereas there was great fragmentariness before, there shall be no reserve now. In his light shall you fully see light; and truly Christ shall not be divided. But consider: while these things that are peculiarly and exclusively mine, and not the Father's, are not excluded from the sphere of the Spirit's revelations, on what ground is it important that these very things should be known by you? Why do I look for great results from the spiritual revelation of my humanity—ingemmed[1] as it is in words of the Holy Ghost's teaching, and these more especially shone upon by him, 'A body hast thou, Father, prepared for me.' Why am I so solicitous that the Spirit should reveal to you, as he only can, my humanity, my humiliation, my covenant-obedience and suffering, my sacrifice—my propitiation and peace-making, my sympathy and intercession, and every peculiarity which is mine, and not the Father's? Solely because, while the Father hath not these things as the Son hath, yet are they imbued with infinite, exact suitableness, availableness, and grace, and ready worth to you, by being in indissoluble union with all that the Father hath.

It is this in reality which gives them all their power, all their preciousness, all their peculiarity so grand and unapproachable. There have been other sufferers, other martyrs, other sympathising brothers, ere ever Jesus came into the world. But because 'all that the Father hath is mine,' there have been, and can be, none like me. You have heard of the sufferings and patience of Job, as well as mine; of the blood of Abel as well as mine; of Jeremiah's generous tears as well as mine; of Elijah's ascension as well as mine.' But who save Jesus was ever in circumstances to say, 'All that the Father hath is mine? Therefore said I unto you, the Spirit shall take of mine and show it unto you.'

It would, indeed, be wrong, as it is groundless, to call this *the* enlightening work of the Spirit, as if there were no enlightenment in that prior work of reproving or convincing, which is set forth in so orderly and, indeed, philosophical or scientific arrangement in this same chapter (John 16:8-11). The reverse is the case. There is much of heavenly light in the Holy Spirit's reproof. Especially it must be so when the reproof ranges over so wide a moral field as 'sin, righteousness, and judgment.' There must be light in such a case; and light in no small degree. Indeed, in all true and honourable reproof there is light, and especially is this true when reproof is allied with conviction—when reproving is well-nigh identical with convincing or convicting. Light must precede and accompany true conviction, and is presupposed by it. Proof must precede re-proof. Reproof—by the very construction of the

[1] [ingemmed = set as a gem would be.]

word—is reduplication of proof. It is proof, addressed as proof to the understanding, reiterated as conviction or re-proof on the conscience. *Reproof* is a reproduction in the conscience of what was simply science (knowledge) or *proof* in the understanding. The man who attempts or professes or pretends to reprove me without prior proof (proof suitable to the case or circumstances),—i.e. who attempts to reach my conscience otherwise than through my understanding—cannot possibly convince me, and does not really reprove me. He does not reprove: he simply rages. He dishonours one of the noblest parts of my nature, and insults me.

Now God cannot do that. He never insults any of his creatures. Perhaps one of the finest and most irresistible arguments for the Inspiration and thorough Divineness of the Scriptures might be based on the fact, that much as they have to say to guilty sinful men, they never insult even the chief of sinners. Much as God speaks to me in his word, and terrible as some of his utterances are, he never insults me. He is too honourable to do that. If he re-proves, he first *proves*. Proof irresistible precedes his re-proof. As even grammatically it ought to be, his reproof is true reduplication on his proof. He 'proves you,' before he reproves you. And if you only suffer him thus to prove you, 'he will do you good in your latter end.'—In particular, in the reproving work of the Spirit, eminently he will do you good:—

1. He reproves you of sin—the sin of *unbelief*;—the proof being, that the object of faith is worthy of all acceptation, and that you are bound by Divine authority to receive the gift of God.

2. He reproves you of *righteousness*;—the proof being that Jesus has gone to the Father, and we see him no more. For no more do we need to see him here below, his work of atoning righteousness being perfected on earth and accepted in heaven; and him the heavens, therefore, must righteously retain till the righteous restitution of all things.

3. He reproves of *judgment*;—the proof being that the prince of this world is judged; not merely that Satan personally is judged; that to me is but a small matter, however solemn, and exemplary, and instructive, and impressive it may be. But, as the 'prince of this world'—the leader of this evil and apostate state of things in which I am immersed,

and which has such paralysing hold upon me—in that character or capacity Satan is judged. In other words, the very life-centre and nerve-centre of the evil and apostate world-power that paralysed me, and made my return to God hopeless and, indeed, impossible, is itself smitten with paralysis, insomuch that I am this moment absolutely and wholly free, simply if I will; and, escaping from the judgment, like Lot from the cities of the plain, and taking hold by faith of the righteousness and victory of this conqueror of the world-power and its prince, I may stand fast in the liberty wherewith Christ makes me free.

This is the Holy Spirit's convincing or reproving work, all built on proof preceding the *reproof.* Let me only accept honestly the proof, and it reappears as re-proof; it appears now in the very depths of my inner man as a repetition, a re-duplication, a re-presentation of the very transaction in that cross of Christ which, firstly, so loudly calling for faith, condemns unbelief; which, secondly, so clearly revealing righteousness, calls to holy reconciliation with the Father, and justification of life eternal: which, thirdly, so terrifically spoiling the spoiler, sets every captive free who simply will. All this is re-proved—proved a second time; reproduced—when I accept the Spirit's proof and reproof. And in this very acceptance of his proof I prove him and see. I get experimental proof that his reproof is an excellent oil which does not break my head, but heart—an unction from the Holy One: and being once willing, giving up my will to God's will, I prove what is that good and acceptable and perfect will of God. But this is the will of God, that every one that seeth the Son, the glorious object of faith, the Lord our righteousness, now with the Father, the conqueror of the world's power and the world's prince, should have everlasting life, and Christ shall raise him up at the last day.

There is enlightenment, therefore, in the Spirit's work of gracious conviction and reproof. But when it is successful, the Spirit goes on to give more and more light. Enlightenment now becomes pre-eminently of the very essence of what the Spirit now goes on to do. For when contritely accepted in his reproving work as an excellent oil, this 'unction of the Holy One,' this anointing that ye have received of him will abide in you, and the same anointing will teach you all things, for it is truth (personally and essentially truth) and no lie, even as it hath taught you, as it hath already taught you—taught you the enormous guilt implied in not believing on so glorious an object of faith, taught you to apprehend by faith the perfect righteousness—taught you to defy in faith the sin-power, the world-power, the devil-power, all the power of him who is the author of sin and the prince of the world. There is, indeed, no limit now to what the good Spirit of God will show unto you. 'When he, the Spirit of truth, is come, he shall guide you into all truth; for he shall not speak of himself, but whatsoever he shall hear that shall he speak; and he shall glorify me, for he shall receive of mine and shall show it unto you.'

We are chargeable with great ingratitude to the good Spirit of truth, the Comforter. The very faithfulness with which he executes his office lays him open through our infirmity to be ungratefully dealt with. He is, if I may reverentially say so, so unobtrusive of himself, so wholly replenished, in his teachings and revelations, with the Son, and with the all things which being the Father's are the Son's also. His own equally divine and glorious personality is kept all the while in the background. 'He does not speak of himself.' 'He does not testify of himself.' 'He does not glorify himself.' 'He glorifies Christ,' 'testifies of Christ,' 'speaks what he hath heard the Father speak with Christ, and Christ with the Father;' 'he takes of the things of Christ and shows them to us.' All the while he keeps himself in the background, not presenting his own personality—simply doing his work, and that work to make Christ glorious in our eyes; to glorify the Son, and the Father in the Son. And *therefore*, alas! having the provocation, the temptation, the opportunity, the scope for being ungrateful, we embrace it; with fatal certainty we turn the risk into a reality; we forget our obligations to him, and because he does not protrude himself and his claims, but Christ and Christ's glory, therefore, alas! *therefore* we are unthankful. We are taken up, or think we are taken up, with the Christ of whom he testifies, the Christ whom he glorifies, and we forget that Christ without the Spirit would be no anointed One, no Christ at all to us. We forget *him* without whom we would never see Christ nor the Father; never hear Christ's voice nor the Father's word; never have that word abiding in us. How base is this ingratitude! How dark-hearted is this requital! Ah! we will never glorify our Lord till we deal more righteously with his promised Spirit. 'He shall glorify me,' saith Jesus. And only in the communion of the Holy Ghost, whose office alone it is to glorify Christ, and who alone hath competence and power to glorify him—only by being led to fall into the concert and communion of the Spirit, as he glorifies the Son by taking of the things that are his and showing them to our souls—only thus shall we ever glorify our Lord himself, or the Father in whom the Son is glorified, and who is glorified in the Son. μ.

A GREAT DOXOLOGY[1]

T HERE is a doxology of Paul's, under which it were well if Christian men would glorify God every day of their lives. It is recorded in Ephesians 3:20, 21: 'Now unto him that is able to do exceeding abundantly above all that we ask or think, according to the power that worketh in us, unto him be glory in the church by Christ Jesus throughout all ages, world without end.'

It is, as we have said, a doxology; there is a devotional ascription of glory to God: 'Unto him be glory.' The locality, or scene, or sphere of this ascription, or ministration, or offering up of glory to God, is the church; the company of the elect or redeemed; the whole family in heaven and earth; the higher principalities (it may be) taking part in this ministering, but secondarily, as being adopted into and embraced by grace among the redeemed from among men: 'Unto him be glory in the church.' The responsible, supreme, and ever acceptable minister of this glory to God, he by whom it is proffered and presented with acceptance, is the Lord Jesus Christ, the minister of the true tabernacle which the Lord pitched and not man: 'Unto him be glory in the church by Christ Jesus.' And the duration of this service, this ministration of glory to God, is eternal; it is no secondary, temporary, parenthetical, or transitory worship; it is no interlude or episode occurring in the middle of some nobler theme, thrown in to grace the onward march to something better, something more nearly final, more worthy to be permanent. It is itself the terminal and everlasting issue, to the enhancement whereof all other themes and movements

---

[1] [From: *The British and Foreign Evangelical Review* (1881), p. 477f.]

tend: 'Unto him be glory in the church by Christ Jesus, throughout all ages, world without end. Amen.'

And now let it be inquired. What is the theme or subject matter of this great doxology which is to fill all ages with glory to God by Jesus Christ? This is no abstract, vague, or indefinite ascription of glory to God. It is well defined and limited. One special perfection of the Divine nature is fastened on and celebrated as the theme of this particular Hallelujah. It is indeed one that is replete with great consolation and grace, hope through grace to the church of God; worthy to be the theme of a distinct and everlasting doxology. It is inspiriting to listen to the very language that expresses it: 'Unto him that is able to do exceeding abundantly above all that we ask or think.' Because of this, because our God is able to do so, let him be gloried in, and glorified for evermore. On this single, most sufficient ground, make his praise glorious. Contemplating him under this one specific title, let us enthusiastically ascribe eternal praise and glory to him; let eternal glory and honour redound unto him in the church by Christ Jesus, the glory implied in his being able to do exceeding abundantly above all that we ask or think.

The marvellous strength and bulging greatness of this language has often been animadverted upon. Inspiration would seem to have done its uttermost in tasking and compelling the power of words to set forth the glory of God in what he is able to do for his people. He is a God able to do 'what we ask'—'what we think'—'all that we ask'—'all that we think.' And this alone were much. Such things can the mind of man think—embracing much and reaching far. 'I think my thoughts in God,' said the pious Kepler, when first he caught hold of the true idea of the solar system. He had found the very thought of God—the thought which had been in God's mind ere yet the heavens were—the thought to which God their Creator had given expression and embodiment when he created the mechanism of planets and their moons moving round the sun, the great central source of light and warmth and power to them all. Great desires, also, as well as great thoughts, can the heart of man entertain—large and wide in their extent, long and lasting in their duration. God is able to fulfil them all. When illuminated by the Holy Spirit, filled with the Divine vision of the glorious things of the kingdom of Christ (John 16:13-15)—purified by Divine grace and quickened by Divine power, great and noble are the things the sanctified reason of man can think,—great and noble the desires the sanctified heart of man can breathe. God is able to accomplish them all—all that we ask or think. But his power transcends this greatly. He is able to do above all that we ask or think. Nay, more: abundantly *above all* that. Yea, rather, he is able to do *exceeding abundantly* above all that we ask or think.

We propose, in the *first* place, to recall to mind certain illustrious cases or instances in God's dealings with every believer, in which he vindicates this claim for himself; in the *second* place, it will be important to point out that he uniformly acts out this designation in the whole of his procedure with his Israel, from the moment of his bringing them out of Egypt till he lands them safely in the promised land; and in the *third* place, the bearing of this on different classes of persons may be briefly indicated.

I. It will give fixity to our meditations on this theme, if we specify illustrious instances in which God vindicates for himself the title under which this doxology glorifies him in what he does for each and every one of his children.

For evidently Paul has not in his eye such interposition as that by which he brought out Israel after the flesh with a high hand and outstretched arm from Egypt, or fed them with manna from heaven, and water out of the rock, but what he does and is continually doing behind that veil which hides him and his movements from the eyes of our flesh and imagination, and from which he is continually, with all and each of the faithful, writing a history which eternity alone will unveil. Thus—

1. First of all, and best of all, and above all else besides, God hath done exceeding abundantly above all that we asked or thought, or could have asked or thought, when he sent his Son into the world to be the propitiation for our sins, that we might live through him. Was not this above all that had been asked? above all that had been thought?— exceeding abundantly so? No one had asked this gift. No one had

thought it. When promised, it was most assuredly what they had not asked, and had not thought; neither had any asked it on their behalf, or thought of it for their benefit It is the unthought-of, the unasked, and, even now that it is given, it is the *unspeakable gift*.

Oh, the complete, exclusive self-containedness of the covenant of grace! 'My covenant,' saith the Lord, as well he may. Who in this matter of the gift of God's Son hath known the mind of the Lord? With whom took he counsel, or who was in circumstances to give him any? From whom received he a suggestion or hint the most distant or indistinct? Surely here was 'the counsel of his own will, according to his good pleasure which he purposed in himself.' And well it was for us that it should be so. For never could man have asked it, never even thought of it. Never could angels have asked it on our behalf, and never could it have come into their thoughts. Even now that, unasked, unthought-of by all creatures, it is revealed, it is the theme of the angels' astonishment, the matter of their holy adoring study. These things the angels desire to look into. For they see that God hath achieved for himself the glory of being able to do exceeding abundantly above all that could be asked or thought.

Nor is it merely in the gift of his Son in general that God vindicates for himself this glorious title; but in all the circumstances and modes of this gift, and in all the effects unto which it is bestowed, and all the depth and intensity of its duration, and in all the grace and glory with which it is completed.

'Unto the Son he saith, Thy throne, God, is for ever and ever;' but thou shalt be my gift to mine enemies—even to them that have lifted up their heel against thy throne, God,—my gift to be light to them that are in darkness, salvation to them that are in ruin, glory to them that are in shame. Is not this exceeding abundantly above all asking, exceeding abundantly beyond all thought? beyond all that we had thought before, or even yet can think? For this gift of God is God, but who can by searching find out God? But the Son, as God the Father's gift, is God's unspeakable, because God's unthinkable, gift.

'Unto the Son God saith, Thy throne, God, is for ever and ever,' and thou dwellest in my boundless bosom of infinite and eternal love and delight. But dwelling still in my bosom, which in Godhead's inviolate blessedness and glory thou canst never leave, thou shalt be found dwelling also in a manger, wrapped in swaddling bands; for 'a body have I prepared thee.' And the Son said, *'Lo! I come!'* Was this asked or thought? It is what we do not need to ask—for unasked it has been given. It is what, even when given, we cannot think—for great is the mystery of godliness, God was manifest in the flesh,—but can only cry, 'To us a child is born, to us a Son is given, and his name shall be called Wonderful'—wonderful beyond our power to think—wonderful beyond all possibility to think. A sweet name Hannah gave her child—'Samuel'—'for I asked him of the Lord.' But sweet and fragrant as it is, it was the very last of names to give with truth to Jesus, for he came unasked, and he is exceeding abundantly above all that we could ask or think.

Ah! and when he came unasked, he came to do what he never could have been asked to do. 'Unto the Son he saith, Thy throne, God, is for ever and ever;' thou dwellest in light that is inaccessible, which no eye hath seen, still less any hand can reach. Yet thou shalt dwell in yon dark world; and that in such form that they may get their hands upon thee, if they please, and nail thee to a tree, if they please,—and please they will. Could that have been asked? Could that have been thought? Nay: no created intellect could have thought it otherwise than as a blasphemy. No intellect save Divine could have thought it in holiness. No man even now can think it in holiness save by the Holy Ghost. 'No man can call the crucified Jesus Lord save by the Holy Ghost.'

'To the Son he saith, Thou art ever with me, and all that I have is thine: for thou art the heir of all things, and by thee also I made the worlds.' Nevertheless, in yon apostate world, created by thyself, as were all worlds, thou shalt be poor. Yea, in that only nation in it in which the poor man's bed dare not be taken as a pledge, but it must be restored to him ere nightfall, thou shalt not have where to lay thy head. Could that have been asked or thought?

'To the Son he saith, A sceptre of righteousness, God, is the sceptre of thy kingdom.' But in the body prepared for thee, thou shalt so stand in the room of sinners, and be made sin for them, that—as if thou wert, thou Holy One, sin's very embodiment, impersonation, and essence—the consuming fire of wrath shall fall upon thee, and the avenging sword of justice smite thee. Could that have been proposed, asked, or thought of?

'Unto the Son he saith, Thou art daily my delight, rejoicing always before me, rejoicing in the habitable parts of the earth—thy delights therein being with the sons of men.' But these sons of men will give gall in thy hunger, and vinegar in thy thirst; and when they hunger and thirst, thou wilt give them bread of life and water of life, and this shall be the bread thou shalt give them, even thy flesh, which thou shalt give for the life of this world: and this shall be the water of life which thou shalt give them, even thy blood, which thou wilt shed for the remission of the sins of many—even shed for the remission of the sin of shedding it.

Could that have been asked or thought? Even when first broached to them by himself, they could not *think* it. They said among themselves, How can this man give us his flesh to eat? Only by the Holy Ghost can we think it in holiness even now. It is the Spirit that quickeneth: the flesh profiteth nothing. 'Yet my flesh is meat indeed, and my blood is drink indeed.'

In every view that we can take of this first and greatest gift, oh, is it not exceeding abundantly above all that we could ask or think! Herein is love, not that we have loved God—not that we even asked God to love us, or thought of such a thing, but that, unasked by us, unimagined and unthought by any, he loved us in his own unanticipated, unsolicited, unthought-of love, and sent his Son to be the propitiation for our sins.

2. When the Lord regenerated us by his grace, and united us to his Son by his Spirit, he does exceeding abundantly above all that we ask or think. When regenerating grace first visits a sinner, it is what that sinner had not asked and had not thought. Herein is that saying of the Lord true: 'Ye have not chosen me, but I have chosen you;' or that other saying of the Lord by the prophet: 'I am sought of them that asked not for me, I am found of them that sought me not.' No man apprehends or finds Christ, but was first apprehended or found of

Christ. No unregenerated man asks regenerating grace. No man dead in trespasses and sins is capable of truly desiring or intelligently receiving the regenerating grace. To think of grace correctly implies and demands the previous possession of grace. To desire grace truly and ask it aright, is the fruit of grace already given and received. Can you ask grace from God in faith?—and if not in faith, it is not his very grace, but some mistaken and deluding semblance of it that you ask. Then whence is this faith of yours, this believing asking of grace? It is not of yourself; it is the gift of God 'By grace are ye saved through faith; and that not of yourselves: it is the gift of God' (Eph. 2:8). Can you so much as even think rightly, that is spiritually, of the grace of God?— and if not spiritually, it is your own carnal imagination that fills your mind, and not the real, true, holy grace of God, for the natural man knoweth not the gracious things of the Spirit of God, for they are spiritually discerned. Whence is your ability so to think? 'We are not able of ourselves so much as to think one thought as of ourselves; but our sufficiency is of God' (2 Cor. 3:5). Your power to ask or think spiritually, your spiritual petition or spiritual idea, is from the grace of God given you when spiritually you could not think at all. Your believing desire and supplication is from the grace of God given you when you could neither pray nor think. The Lord has prevented you, anticipated you with his grace; he has been beforehand with his communication of it, when otherwise you had remained conspicuously destitute of it. His gift of it had preceded both *your asking and thinking*; preceded not only your actual asking and thinking, but preceded your ability to ask or think; has been the very origination, beginning, and cause of your ever being able to ask it or think of it And clearly, therefore, in God's first bestowment of his grace upon you, he did exceeding abundantly above all that you had asked or thought.

'Very bold doctrine,' I hear someone saying. True, it is indeed. But Isaiah is very bold, and saith, 'I was found of them that sought me not; I was made manifest unto them that asked not after me.' Exactly is it this doctrine of God's unanticipated grace, anticipating all solicitation, and transcending and preceding all thought and capacity thereof, that is the doctrine which is called bold, but which Isaiah was bold enough to proclaim with unfaltering voice. Good were it that all successors of his upon the mountains publishing glad tidings of mercy were always as bold in magnifying the sovereign, reigning, royal, prevenient, anticipating grace of God. The heady and high-minded may cavil at it. They may say—they have in all ages said: If none but those who already have it can seek it,—if none but the already regenerate—regenerated before asking or being able to ask or even think of regenerating grace,—if none but those already in possession of this same grace of God can either ask or think about it, we need neither trouble ourselves to think about it or ask it till it comes. It may seem a very clever rejoinder. But it is melancholy work, man, rebelling against God, against the grace of God and the God of grace. Depend upon it, this same grace is on the throne, and you cannot depose it. Grace reigns, and will reign, and it will prove a desperate time to you when it is seen that you cannot bow the knee, nor say, God save the king! but must quibble and cavil, and impudently assail the saving grace of God, and the God of all grace. And it is a most miserable cavil this, about never troubling yourselves about grace until it come, if you are spiritually and eternally dead and damned without it. One would rather think that if you are not insane, the inference with you would have been all the other way. The immediate effect of prevenient grace is to secure that grace shall be rightly thought of, grace shall be earnestly asked for, grace shall be sovereignly, royally given, given into your heart to reign there, till even conscience, that delegate of justice, shall itself become within you a throne of grace, a throne for grace to sit upon and speak from and shine from; and what therefore is your refusal to ask or trouble yourself till it come, as your well-nigh blasphemous suggestion runs, but a rejection of preventing grace itself—a bold and wicked conviction, that as for you it shall not come at all, a determination that it may strive as it may to lead you to ask and pray, but as for you, you see through the whole delusion of our Calvinism, as you call it, and have resolved to have done with its self-contradictions and absurdities? And oh! therefore, are you not a living proof that if Isaiah's bold saying (for the thing is far older than Calvin), if Isaiah's bold saying has been graciously accepted among the Gentiles, to the glory of God and of the gospel of his grace—'I am sought of them that asked not after me, I am found of them that sought me not,'—his counterpart rebuke to perverse Israel is due to you: 'But unto Israel he saith. All day long I have stretched out my hands unto a disobedient and a gainsaying people'?

Yet, gainsay whoso may, it remains a fundamental truth of the 'glorious gospel of the blessed God,' that to be able to think and ask the grace of God, is the fruit of grace already given, given when not asked, given when not even thought of, given when no capacity as yet existed to ask or think of it at all; and in that case is it not exceeding abundantly above all that had been asked or thought? Oh, child of God, when the God of all grace arrested you in your ungodliness and unconcern, when he convinced you of your sin and misery, when he drew a veil to your view over this poor and perishing, unrecompensing, unsatisfying world, and all its semblances and seducing offers, and with it drew at the same time the veil from the world to come, with all its solemnising realities; when he compelled you to cry out, 'What must I do to be saved?' when he revealed to you that Jesus, whom his love and wisdom had appointed without your asking, and beyond all your thought, to be a perfect propitiation for your sins (oh, only think of it!—three persons in the Godhead, *the same in substance*, equal in power and glory—the same in substance, and one of them the propitiation for your sins), a perfect propitiation for your sins, your perfect peace with God, and your life everlasting; when he disposed and empowered, 'procured all, and enabled' you to lay the weight of the grand eternity of your lost wretched soul on the righteousness and love, the all-sufficiency and faithfulness of Christ, thus quickening you to newness of life, and by vital faith uniting you to him who was dead in your desert of death, and is now alive for evermore,—eternal life for you—you now alive in him,—oh! whatever others say in cavilling at the sovereign, anticipating, prevenient grace of God, will not you bear testimony that when God did all this for you, the chief of sinners, the very picture and model of negligence and unconcern,—he did what you had never asked for and never thought of, in all this he did exceeding abundantly above all that you had asked or thought!

3. God vindicates this title for himself, and does exceeding abundantly above all that had been asked or thought, in the view of that estate of grace and privilege into which regeneration or effectual calling ushers those that are persuaded and enabled to embrace Jesus Christ freely offered to them in the gospel, and brought into an estate of salvation. As their former condition was an estate of sin and misery, so their new condition is a whole, complete *estate* also, an *estate of salvation* by a Redeemer. They are not brought merely into new circumstances, in which they may look for a gratuitous mercy merely here and there, a haphazard blessing now and again; they are brought into a perfect and eternal estate of salvation, and they shall never perish, neither shall any pluck them out of their loving and powerful Redeemer's hand. Theirs is an estate of gracious privilege exceeding great and abundant. Being justified by faith, they are adopted also as sons of God, and sanctified into the holy image of God. And there do accompany or flow from those great master blessings of the kingdom such precious enjoyments as assurance of God's love, peace of conscience, joy in the Holy Ghost, increase of grace, and perseverance therein to the end. 'Being justified by faith, we have peace with God, through our Lord Jesus Christ, by whom also we have access by faith into this grace[1] wherein we stand, and rejoice in hope of the glory of God' (Rom. 5:1, 2). Believing souls are liberated from all condemnation, and not only so, but positively justified before God, as possessing a righteousness already adequate to all that the law demands, or ever will or can demand at their hands. They stand in the Lord's throne-room, the objects of the Sovereign's favour, approbation, good pleasure, and fellowship—the honoured nobles of his kingdom. That all the noisomeness of their iniquity is hidden from his sight, and never suffered to come into remembrance, is the least of it, the least portion of their privilege before him. They are represented unto him in all the favourableness which the righteousness of his own Son can secure for them, or even for him, who himself speaks of it with delight: 'I was daily his delight, rejoicing always before him,' and the Father says, 'Behold my servant whom I uphold, mine elect in whom my soul delighteth.' They are welcome at court, where they cannot too often

---

[1] [That is, the state of grace, or favour, or privilege.]

present themselves, and well-pleasing in all the acceptableness that the Eternal Son in their nature can assert in the Father's eyes for himself; finding before God, each one of them, all the grace and favour which God the Son, Immanuel, finds with God the Father. For the Branch of the Lord is for beauty and for glory, for excellency and for comeliness: his blood makes them whiter than the snow, the Eternal Righteousness of all the earth himself being Judge: and they are comely through his comeliness put upon them. Nor is it thought sufficient by him who worketh all things according to the counsel of his own will to make his people accepted in the Beloved: he admits them to the standing of sons in his family—dear children in his household—free of the house, as well as acceptable, well-pleasing subjects and nobles of his kingdom. To as many as receive the Son, no wonder if to *them* he gives power to become the sons of God. And seemeth it to you a small thing to become son to a King? to become the sons and daughters of the Lord Almighty? Nor is it a nominal, honorary, or ornamental—it is a real, a born sonship. No doubt, it must be called—for it must be—adoption. They must be received into the number and acquire a right to share all the privileges of the sons of God. Were they not, each one of them, aliens from the commonwealth of Israel, strangers from the covenants of promise, without God, and without hope in this world? *It must be adoption*: and there is even a charm in that which they never *will* forego. But it is an adoption resting on truth—an adoption resting on, guarded and guaranteed by, regeneration, which is not less real generation, or birth, for being regeneration. These sons are not less born sons, because born again; their generation is not the less generation for being regenerated. We indeed know little about it. But the likelihood is, could we know all, that we would stand in awe before those princes of the blood-royal of heaven, and be admitted into an intelligent appreciation of the indefeasible, inviolable, eternal certainty of bliss and beauty, of the great glory and high destiny of splendid distinction and boundless joy—unique in the wide plains of God's moral government—to which men are born when they are born again. Talk of being born in the purple! *They are* born in the purple who are born of the Spirit; they are the veritable born sons of God who receive the Son Eternal by faith, born not of blood, nor of the flesh, nor of the will of man, but of God; and because ye are sons, God hath sent forth the Spirit of his Son into your hearts, crying, Abba, Father.

Our Father which art in heaven. Hallowed be thy name! Behold what manner of love the Father hath bestowed upon us, that we should be called, and should be, the sons of God! It abundantly exceeds all that could have been asked or thought.

He yet further exalts them to royal dignity, and inaugurates them into the honours of a royal priesthood, clothing them with change of raiment—pure linen, clean and white; he sets a fair mitre upon their head; gives them a censer in which to offer incense at the shrine, which is a throne also—the throne of grace, where grace reigns, and they that receive abundance of grace shall reign too; and incense, pleasing to him in heaven, they need never want; even the breathings of their hearts' desire for whatsoever is agreeable to his large and limitless will. Looking down with delight and paternal appreciation—and whosoever has looked upon his own flock of little ones well know what I mean,—he permits them to compass an altar at which they have no right to eat which serve the tabernacle: feeds them on a paschal lamb and feast of tabernacles such as angels partake not of; accepts their offerings with good pleasure and gleamings of the light of his countenance, which, once seen, electrify them,—for that is nothing short of the light of the land where there is nothing to hurt in all God's holy mountain. Moreover, besides a priestly mitre, he sets a royal crown upon their head. He binds a diadem of tender mercies round their brow, crowns them with loving-kindness, kisses them with the seal of eternal delight and joy; points them right onward to the golden gates of heaven; first, indeed, a journey through the wilderness, but then to the promised land, saying, 'This is the victory that overcometh, even your faith. And to him that overcometh (even to him that believeth), I now give the Morning Star.' Jesus saith, 'I am the bright and the Morning Star.' How sweet it is! Oh the dewy freshness of it! Oh the beaming, brightening hope of the eternal day that is in it! The Morning Star *glowing in your heart* for love and joy; *glistening on your breast* for dignity and honour, such as earthly monarchs wear not; *gleaming on your brow* for high daring in the battle, to flash helplessness and terror on your foes; and *glistening in your eye* for truth and honour bright with all your friends, giving certificate concerning you, that whatsoever things are honest, whatsoever things are true, whatsoever things are pure and lovely and of good report, you habitually think on these things.

No wonder that these things are true of those whom heaven hath certified and established irreversibly as heirs of God, joint heirs with Christ, whom the Father hath embraced as the favourite daughter of the King, the bride and spouse of his own Son, and dowered as such with a chartered and unlimited inheritance, having throughout all high heaven made proclamation to them in these terms: 'All things are yours, whether Paul or Apollos or Cephas, or the world or life or death, or things present or things to come; all are yours, for ye are Christ's, and Christ is God's!' Yes, glorious things are spoken of thee, city, child of God. Thou art a peculiar treasure unto him above all people, people of the Lord; thou art a kingdom of priests unto him, for the Lord's portion is his people: Jacob is the lot of his inheritance. 'There is none like unto the God of Jeshurun, who rideth upon the heaven in thy help, and in his excellency on the sky. The eternal God is thy refuge, and underneath are the everlasting arms. Happy art thou, Israel; who is like unto thee, people saved by the Lord, the shield of thy help and the sword of thine excellency! and thine enemies shall be found liars unto thee; and thou shalt tread upon their high places.' And all this, thine estate of searchless privilege, already conferred on thee in Christ and enjoyed in its first-fruits of the Spirit—the Spirit of love and power and light and sonship—is guarded and guaranteed by a sealed and everlasting covenant: 'For this is as the waters of Noah unto me, saith the Lord: for as I have sworn that the waters of Noah should no more go over the earth, so have I sworn that I would not be wroth with thee nor rebuke thee: for the mountains shall depart, and the hills be removed, but my kindness shall not depart from thee, neither shall the covenant of my peace be removed, saith the Lord that hath mercy on thee.'

Who could have thought of—who could have asked—privileges great and manifold, tender and loving, gracious and abundant, like these? And when, introducing us into the kingdom and fellowship of the Son of his love, he hath given us an 'estate of salvation' such as this, hath he not done exceeding abundantly above all that we can ask or think?

4. But once more, *fourthly,* God will again vindicate and verify the title by which this magnificent doxology glorifies him, when he shall introduce his people into an estate of glory. Then pre-eminently will he prove himself able to do for them exceeding abundantly above all that we can ask or think. It will be an exceeding, a far more exceeding and abundant and eternal weight of glory. As the rapture of holy and eternal glory breaks upon the shining countenances of the ransomed of the Lord, it will be felt by each in himself, and seen by each in all, that the joy of our Lord, into which he hath ministered to us an abundant entrance,—this beatific vision of our Lord's glory which he had with the Father before the world was, and which the Father hath given us because he who hath redeemed us with his blood is worthy of this fullness of joy at God's right hand and before his face—transcends all notions and efforts of our faith and hope. We prayed for it, we longed for it, we asked it, we thought of it. But it is exceedingly abundant above all that we asked or thought.

Take these few eminent instances in which the Lord verifies the designation with which this doxology glorifies him:—*first,* in giving his Son to be the propitiation for our sins, a gift before all others and beyond all thought; *secondly,* in calling us effectually into the fellowship of his Son, training us to ask, and teaching us to think, when as yet we neither asked nor thought of such grace at all; *thirdly,* in bringing us into an estate of grace and privilege—of rights and titles, experiences and enjoyments—a relation which is the ground of our right to ask anything, and our power to think anything; and, *fourthly,* as having in view a prospect in store for us—as having in sure prospect because in eternal purpose for us an inheritance surpassing all possibility of solicitation or conception—a glory which eye hath not seen, nor ear heard, nor hath entered into the heart of man.

II. We have been at some pains to lay a foundation for our second topic, namely, a consideration of the fact that God verifies this title also in his procedure towards his people throughout their whole course and pilgrimage, their whole journey between their introduction into the estate of grace and their introduction into the estate of glory.

Along all the path in which this weak, defenceless, poor, and needy people pass to glory, surrounded and beset by a thousand wants, temptations, necessities, and dangers, he is able to do for them exceeding abundantly above all that they ask or think.

And let it be carefully observed that God's 'ability' here celebrated—his ability to transcend all our solicitations and conceptions—is not a mere abstract ability. It is not a mere ability in possession or distinct from an ability put forth in action. It is not such an ability as leaves the thing contemplated in the position of a mere possibility, a possibility which may never pass into a reality. Rather it implies that what God is thus able to do, he does.

For the glory that God seeks and secures in the Church—the glory that accrues and redounds to God in the Church by Christ Jesus throughout all ages—is the glory of perfection, which, in his marvellous dealings with the Church, he has proved himself possessed of, by actually putting forth for her salvation, preservation, and eternal benefit. The Church does not glorify God for perfections which she may *suppose* him to possess, or may prove by abstract reasoning, or be satisfied on testimony that he possesses indeed. She glorifies God, and is called on to glorify him, by *bearing her own testimony*, by specifying and quoting instances, and setting forth her own experiences, by bearing witness to such attributes of God, and such marvellous degrees and fruits of them as shine forth in her own history, and are inlaid in her own condition, felicity, glory, and perfection. It is ability in actual exercise that she celebrates in the text. Yea, it is expressly said that this ability is put forth in herself and in her members. He is able to do exceeding abundantly above all that we ask or think, according to the power that worketh in us. This very ability is in operation. He does not wait till we can ask or think. The very heart—thought of all this doxology is that if he waited for that, he would wait for ever. And besides, there are no abilities or attributes on which the Church can look abstractly, or as separated in their action and history from her own estate, interest, and condition. This God is our God. In all the fullness in which he is God, he is ours! His perfections, in their multitude, harmony, glory, and action are himself. God's perfections and attributes are not a mere bundle of theological conceptions, though we are too apt so to regard them; they are himself. His power, therefore, is ours to save us, to protect, defend, and avenge us. His ability to do exceeding abundantly above all that we ask or think, is promised, pledged, engaged, by an everlasting covenant, while it is also implicated, committed, and at work with us, according to the power that worketh in us—the working of that mighty power which he wrought in Christ when he raised him from the dead and set him at his own right hand in the heavenly places; which he wrought in us also when we, who were dead in trespasses and sins, were quickened together with Christ, and raised up together with him, and made to sit together with him in these same heavenly places; the power which worketh in us when God worketh in us to will and to do of his good pleasure; the self-same power as will yet again work in us when he shall fashion our vile body like unto his glorious body, according to the power whereby he is able to subdue even all things unto himself.

This glorious and surpassing power of God—this ability to do exceeding abundantly above all that we ask or think—is irreversibly pledged and irrevocably in operation, actually to do for us exceeding abundantly above all that we can ask or think. To quicken grace in us and mortify corruption; to refine and purify our nature; to guard and rule our desires and motives; to support us in our fight of faith, in all our manifold temptations; to keep us at all times from temptation and a snare, or to recover us therefrom with ultimate advantage, if through unwatchfulness we have been ensnared; to sustain, console, and sanctify us in our afflictions and bereavements; to maintain in us a heart for duty and an ability for it; to work in us to will and to do of the will of God; to make us more than conquerors over all our enemies; to fill all our emptiness, and satisfy all our desire, to keep us from falling, or, fallen, to restore our souls, and fill them with marrow and with fatness and with the finest of the wheat, so that we shall not covet and shall not need to covet; and finally to perfect that which concerneth us, and perfect us in all the will of God, that we may be without blemish and without spot before him at his coming; and to carry us in safety, if not in manifest transport, through the river of the water of death unto the land whose children shall never say, I am sick, and where there shall be nothing to hurt or to destroy in all God's holy mountain; to keep us (till then) from falling, and present us (then) faultless, having fashioned our bodies like unto his own glorious body, and transform our souls into his own image from glory to glory as none but the Spirit of the Lord could transform them;—for these and suchlike ends embraced in the history and requirements of the passage from our first entrance on grace to our first entrance on glory, God's ability to do exceeding abundantly above all that we ask or think, is not only pledged by promise and by covenant, but is implicated and operating in fact.

And ye that are escaping to the rest that remaineth for the people of God, exercised under various and ever accumulating proofs of your own weakness, sinfulness, and insufficiency, how precious, how glorious a thought is this! a privilege how sweet! a daily prospect how consoling, how invigorating! You have a God who can do for you all that you ask! Is not that great? Yet it is the least of it. And what this God can do, he is your God to do; yea, above all that you ask, above all that you think; abundantly—exceeding abundantly above it.

And how necessary that he should, in your experience, transcend all that you can ask and think, all along the course and march of your wilderness journey! How necessary, and, I will add, how certain!

1. How necessary! His doing so in those four illustrious instances already specified, renders it necessary—necessary that he should do it always, should do it all along. For it makes the object and the aim of the Christian life high and holy beyond all that we can think.

For, *firstly,* if God so amazingly transcended all prayer and all conception as to give his only begotten Son a sacrifice for our sins—a representative for us, taking our place of sin and shame and death and the grave, that we might be adopted into his place of righteousness and glory and life and heaven,—surely the hatred of sin, the purity of purpose, the disinterestedness, the gratitude, the love, the service, the zeal, the whole galaxy of Christian graces, the excellency and perfection of Christian character we are hereby bound to endeavour to attain are beyond all that we can think!

If, *secondly*, God in sovereign mercy quickened us when we were dead in trespasses and sins, and, when we could neither ask nor think what to ask, did beyond all our askings and all our thinkings, and effectually taught us to think what we ought to ask, and then enabled us to ask what he had taught us to think, graciously taught us to seek, and effectually enabled us to find, nothing less than himself—even this God for our God for ever and for ever—oh! surely the devotion of prayerfulness and love to which he is entitled is beyond all our powers of thinking of it, and cannot be rightly or fully rendered save in heavenly perfection and in heaven itself.

If, *thirdly*, he hath brought us into such an estate of grace and privilege as that wherein the justified in Jesus stand; if he hath effectually veiled, even from his own vision, all our iniquity, and clothed us with his own Son's comeliness—made us sons and heirs, kings and priests, placing us towards himself in a relation so near, so sure, so endearing, so exalted, so replete with privilege and with blessing, and all this freely, without money and without price, without change or the eternal possibility of it, without all risk of failure, removal, reversal, world without end,—oh! how can we think aright of our obligations to him, or how can we express our feelings save by exclaiming, in a species of joyful bewilderment or blessed perplexity, 'What shall I render to the Lord for all his benefits toward me?' I owe him exceedingly above all that I can speak or think.

And, *fourthly*, lastly, if he hath designed for us the glory which is to be revealed, but which flesh and blood cannot inherit, it is so exceedingly abundant above all that we can ask or think; if we, according to his word, look for new heavens and a new earth, wherein dwelleth righteousness, for an inheritance incorruptible and undefiled and that fadeth not away, for a presentation in faultlessness before his throne, and a body fashioned like unto his own glorious body—eyes that are like *his*, even as a flame of fire, a countenance like *his*, even as the sun shineth in his strength,—oh! does not this also convey the extent of our obligations, and the purity and perfection of the holiness to which they bind us, far beyond our present powers of apprehending and appreciating them, and leave us with the similar question of perplexed enjoyment and bewildered gratitude, 'What manner of persons ought we to be?'

We are bound by these noble verifications of our Father's glorious title—bound to a holiness that is beyond all that we can think; but if our powers of attaining it be still less than our powers of thinking it or asking it; if in us, that is, in our flesh, there dwelleth no good thing; if in this world we shall have deadly opposition; if the principalities of darkness (which would seem to be in light compared with us, and able, with hell's own malignity, to take advantage of our weakness) hate us and shoot at us in secret—they secret mysteries to us, we open targets to them, waylaying our weak souls at every turn of the road with manifold temptations; and if, last of all and worst of all, sin dwelleth in us, forcing out the cry, 'O wretched man that I am! who shall deliver me from the body of this death?'—oh! what would become of us were not God, as the text assures us he is, a God able to do exceeding abundantly above all that we ask or think? We feel it absolutely *necessary* that it should be so—that it should be so along all the pilgrimage, were it only that we might be preserved in keeping with the exceedingly abundant great things he hath already done for us at the opening stages, and hath designed to do for us ultimately at its close. But we are not left to exclaim merely. How necessary!—

2. But, how certain! how certain is it that the Lord will vindicate this his glorious title to the believer in all his history!

Yes; it is certain that he will do so. It is certain that he will do so, though it were only that in the noble instance we have given he has done it already, and especially, also, as he has deigned in the heavenly glory to do so again. Is it conceivable that in these three brilliant instances God should exceeding abundantly surpass all asking and all thought, namely, *first*, in giving up his Son to the death and shame of the cursed tree; *secondly*, in calling you into his kingdom, when you had neither thought enough, to think of coming, nor power enough, nor will enough, to ask to be brought; *thirdly*, in establishing you in covenant things, on covenant terms, in an estate of grace unchanging and privilege inexhaustible, and indeed unspeakable, like the fountain and the measure of it, God's unspeakable gift;—is it possible that God should do these three things for you, thus ministering an abundant entrance for you into the Christian life?—

And, *fourthly*, deigning at the close of your believing pilgrimage to minister an exceeding, even an abundant, entrance into the kingdom of glory—the exceeding and eternal weight of glory; and that, nevertheless, between the entrance of grace, so exceeding abundantly above all that you could ask or think, and the entrance on glory so still more exceeding abundantly above the same measure,—is it conceivable that between these delightful and God-glorifying epochs, he should for one moment interpose a blighted, woeful, melancholy, drivelling interval, during which his gracious might slept and slumbered, and came not forth for your protection, deliverance, progress, preparation, and perfecting for his heavenly kingdom? Impossible. 'He that hath begun a good work in you will perfect it unto the day of Jesus Christ.' He will not forsake the work of his own hands. He will not interpose in the progress of it an intermediate or intercalary portion, out of taste, out of harmony, out of keeping with the searchlessly gracious commencement of it, and the searchlessly glorious close. Between the elect foundation and the top-stone, brought forth, as he means it to be, with shoutings, crying, 'Grace, grace unto it,' he will not thrust an incongruous and unseemly piece of parenthetical or inferior, hasty, heartless workmanship. There shall be no one of all God's dealings with you in your Christian life over which it might be written, 'Here God did not act to this believer like a God able to do exceeding abundantly above all his prayers and thoughts.' There shall be no page in all your Christian history to which a foot-note might be appended, saying, 'Here God failed to verify the title under which the Church glorifies him through all ages, world without end.'

'I will sing of the mercies of the Lord for ever.' And all round and round thy walls, city of the Lord, not one tower, even the least, shall provoke the verdict, 'Here the builder began to build, but forgot the cost.' Nor among all his countless myriads who, with open faces beholding the glory of the Lord, are being transformed into the same image from glory to glory, shall there be one single image like that on Babylon's plain, with head of gold and feet of clay. God's gold mines are not so easily exhausted.

> *Deep in unfathomable mines*
> *Of never-failing skill,*
> *He treasures up his bright designs,*
> *And works his sovereign will.*

> *Ye fearful saints, fresh courage take,*
> *The clouds ye so much dread*
> *Are big with mercy, and shall break*
> *In blessings on your head.*

My grace is sufficient for you;—the grace of him who is able to do exceeding abundantly above all that you ask or think, according to the power that worketh in you. To him be glory in the church by Christ Jesus, throughout all ages, world without end. Amen.

III. Let me now close by applying this so precious doctrine to three classes of persons.

1. You have no interest in this God who is able to do exceeding abundantly above all his people's prayers and thoughts. As to the other gods and idols in which you are interested—the other lords that have had dominion over you—I want to know if they can do exceeding abundantly above all that you can ask or think? One would think so, considering your devotion to them and perseverance in serving them. Hast thou not known, hast thou not learnt by sad and sore and long and full experience, that the very reverse is true? Hast thou not, in many a bitter lesson, read the fact that you can both think and wish for exceeding abundantly more than they can do for you? Does not the old commonplace of the insufficiency of all earthly things come out with a freshness and even brilliancy of conviction when contrasted with that special glory of our God which we have made the special

topic of our celebration? Is it not sealed upon your deep conviction, as your own personal and profound experience—the same that has been the experience of all who have gone before you on the same broad road to ruin,—that the portion you have chosen is as much below your power of thought and of desire, as God's ability is above the desires and thoughts of those who put their trust in him? Have you not found, without aught of self-elation—far otherwise—that your capacities of thinking and desiring are far greater than the elements on which you have hitherto tried to satisfy them? The believer's portion abundantly excels his capacities of understanding and enjoying it. But your capacities of thought and of enjoyment far transcend everything on which you have hitherto sought to exercise them. And so, for evermore, will you find that this heart-withering fact is true. You spend your money for that which is not bread, and you labour for that which profiteth not. And wherefore do you do it? Holy Scripture asks you wherefore? 'Wherefore do you spend money for that which is not bread, and your labour for that which satisfieth not?'

2. To the convinced, sin-sick, and anxious sinner. Here is a glorious divine light for you, a glorious view of God in Christ which, by the Divine blessing, ought to do very precious, very perceptible good to you, yea, exceeding abundantly above all that you can ask or think. Will you not, at least, once for all, and now for ever, by faith,—will you not yoke this blessed fact to your actual case as you feel that case now grieving, perplexing, baffling you? What is it that is at the root of all your distress? For I take for granted that you are distressed. I will not think so ill of you as to believe that you could go on in a jaunty dance to eternal doom. No. You think about it gloomily enough sometimes. You know you do. And what is it that always drives back upon you and seals down the perplexity upon your souls, and prevails to keep you from peace and joy in believing? Is it not just the fact that you ask for nothing greater than you expect, and expect nothing greater than you can think? You cannot think how sin like yours can be forgiven. You cannot think how a guilty conscience like yours is ever to be made clean, and free, and honourable, and boundlessly or even averagely blessed beneath the eyes that are as a flame of fire. You cannot think how a worldly heart like yours is ever to be made to find delight in prayer and fellowship with God and things

divine. You cannot think how the doctrine of election is ever to consist with your own responsibility and freedom of choice to receive or reject Christ as you yourself on your own peril shall decide. And you cannot think what this mysterious faith can be on which, for weal or woe, it seems, your everlasting destiny depends. And then you go the weary round of your thinkings, and you fall down in despair at the end of them—as if hope must end when they end, and God's doings must be limited by your thinkings!

Get up, and get rid of these thinkings of yours. What good have you ever got—or will you ever get—from them! Get up and get out of the miserable narrow rut of them! Be not as the horse or as the mule, content to beat, in dull and weary round, with eyes continually earth-prone, the clay-baked track of human thinkings about things Divine. Get up, and do the living God at last, and at least, the justice to believe that he has got a larger mind and greater powers of thought than you. Jesus Christ will have nothing to do with you, the gentle Jesus even will fling you off, if you will not do his Father at least *this* small and poor amount of justice. 'He that hath heard and learned of my Father, *he* it is that cometh unto me.' *That's* the man that I will in no wise cast out: for that really is the man that cometh. Hear, then, and learn of my Father when he says, 'Let the wicked forsake his way, and the unrighteous man his thoughts: for my thoughts are not your thoughts, neither are your ways my ways, saith the Lord. For as the heavens are higher than the earth, so are my ways higher than your ways, and my thoughts than your thoughts.' You cannot think precisely how sin like yours, those very sins that sting you, can be forgiven. But just on that very point 'my thoughts are not your thoughts; for though your sins be as scarlet they shall be white as snow, though red like crimson, they shall be as wool.' You cannot think how corruption and selfishness like yours can ever be eradicated, since instead of the brier there cannot come up the myrtle-tree. You think your evil heart must be improved, and you cannot think how it can be improved enough. 'But that is not in the line, nor in the measure, nor in the kind of my thoughts at all,' saith the Lord. 'A totally new heart will I give unto you, and a new spirit will I put within you, and wholly new things shall spring up before you. Old things shall pass away, and all things shall become new.' Have done with your own thoughts, and have done trusting to your own powers of thinking. Have done carnalising spiritual things, and humanising things Divine by casting them into the mould of human thought and reason. Learn that you are not sufficient of yourself to think one thought as of yourself on any point that concerns your pardon, your peace, your relation to God and Jesus, or that eternal life that is freely placed at your acceptance in him. Not one spiritual soul-profiting thought on these things are you able to think as of yourself. But your sufficiency is of God. Yes, of God. For, in the *first* place, in God's Word God's thoughts are written down before your eyes, and, in the *second* place, God's Spirit is promised to enable you to think God's thought at last and not your own. And with God's written thought in real and definite words before you, and with God's Spirit within you, just as if, with a written page of music before you, the very spirit or soul of music took possession of your breast, and every pulse within you beat responses to the master-mind of the composer, and your whole soul thrilled to find that you had caught the idea, the imagination, the rapture that glorious master-mind meant to express or convey, even so with God's written thought before you, and not the soul of music or the spirit of reason, but the Spirit of God within you, the Spirit of God, who is the Spirit of power, thinking power, and of a sound mind—the very spirit and master-mind of thought—of Divine thought within your mind and spirit;—*then*, according to your limited capacity, indeed, yet truly and in your measure, you will think God's very own thought (where came your power of thinking from if not from him, if not from his?)—you will think God's own thought in unison and fellowship with him. Then will you take in God's thoughts so as to feel that they are the grandest and most solid of facts—his thoughts great facts of love, mercy, forgiveness, peace, and joy; thoughts of love and not of evil, to give you an expected end. 'Many, Lord my God, are thy wonderful thoughts to us-ward; they cannot be reckoned up in order unto thee: if I would declare and speak of them, they are more than can be numbered' (Psa. 40:5), for they are exceeding abundant above all that we can ask or think, each one of them a great deep. Think *for* me, Lord, think upon me. 'I am poor and needy, yet the Lord thinketh on me.' Lord, thou hast finer powers of thought than mine, and good it is for me. Thou art able to do exceeding abundantly above all that I can ask or think.

Yes, anxious soul! poor and needy, I ask you to take hold by faith on this glorious doxology, and begin to be thankful and hopeful, and praise God under this most blessed ascription of glory to him in the highest, above our utmost reach of thought. Yoke your needy case to this heavenly chariot, in which the infinitely amiable Lord God Almighty rideth for the help of his Church in this excellency of his, and it will make your own soul as the chariots of Amminadib. Oh! whence is it to us that the Lord is so willing as then? Whence is it to us that we ourselves are so willing with some little beginnings and pluckings-up of heart as it is this day? There is no anxiety, no fear, no distress, no necessity under which you can now be exercised and pained, or under which you can ever suffer, but faith in God the Father of our Lord Jesus Christ under the glorious aspect of his glory in the Church, will suffice for your relief. No prison this key will not open; no devil this oriflamme[1] will not blind and quell; no shadow of death this glory will not lighten up. 'God is able to do exceeding abundantly above all that we ask or think.'

3. And now for the happiness of giving a word to you that believe. Whence is it to you that you indeed believe? 'Thy people shall be willing in the day of thy power.' Ah! That's it! Thy people have been made willing in a day of thy power. And what a God they have to believe upon! Ah! sure it does and must need Divine power to believe in a God like this.

What can or ought I to say to you? What more is there to say, unless I say this again? I call upon you, this day, again once more to appropriate and praise your God in Christ under this magnificent doxology. I call on you to glorify him, and glory in him as able to do exceeding abundantly above all that you can ask or think. Let this transcendent power of his be one express and very special motive of faith with you. 'Believest thou that I am able to do this?' said Jesus to the blind man. 'Abraham staggered not at the promise of God, but was strong in faith, giving glory to God, and being persuaded that what he had promised he was able also to perform, and therefore it was imputed to him for righteousness.' When, therefore, you come into perplexing circumstances (as what

---

[1] [oriflamme = *lit*. gold flame. From the French word used of the orange-red flag of the Abbey of Saint Denis in France which was adopted as a standard by the early kings of France. An inspiring standard or symbol.]

believers do not?), either in your outward life, or in your inward spiritual experience, and cannot find your way, cannot tell what to think, cannot think what to ask—remember that God can abundantly exceed all your asking, and all your thinking too. Rejoice and give him thanks because of this. And do not require to wait for relief till you are thankful,—there is the cloven hoof of unbelief again.

There is no place for despondency, there is no room to tarry for thankfulness and hang back from the praise of God, till you get everything you want in hand. It is simply not true, in this joyous sphere of rich and reigning grace, that a bird in the hand is worth two in the bush. The whole grove is vocal with a hierarchy of choristers. 'I would have told the very crows,' said John Bunyan. The birds are all a-song, and the fountains all are playing. Spring up, O well, sing ye unto it. And there never shall come a time, with those to whom belongs the short song, 'This God is our God,' when it will be time to despond, far less despair. When staggered by some sudden trial, when all but consumed by some slowly-eating grief, when you know not what to think, and cannot think what to ask (for there are groanings which can neither be uttered nor understood), ask God to think for you, while you stand still and see the thought gradually become a fact—stand still and see the salvation of God. Assuredly it shall be yours to know that his thoughts are not as your thoughts, but as much higher as heaven is high above the earth, and that all things work together for good to them that are the called according to his purpose. Arise in lowliness of mind, and simplicity of faith, and blessed boundlessness of hope, and meet your Almighty God. 'Why sayest thou, Jacob, and speakest, Israel, My way is hid from the Lord? Hast thou not known, hast thou not heard, that the everlasting God, the Lord, the Creator of the ends of the earth, fainteth not, neither is weary? there is no searching of his power of thought. He granteth power to the faint, and to them that have no might he reneweth (bless the Lord, he reneweth) strength. Even the youths shall faint and be weary, and the young men shall utterly fall: but they that wait on the Lord shall renew their strength, they shall mount up on wings as eagles, they shall run and not weary, they shall walk and not faint.'

'Bless the Lord, my soul, and all that is within me, bless his holy name.' μ.

JOYOUS SPIRITUALITY OF CHRISTIAN PILGRIMAGE

OR:

PILGRIMAGE—NOT PENANCE[1]

G ENUINE admiration of the Cross of Christ,—imbuing a man with that evangelical spirituality which is the want of the age, and which alone has been found powerful enough to alienate us from the world at every point—makes him, there can be no reason to doubt, what the psalmist calls himself, 'a stranger on the earth' (Psa. 119:19). Living by that faith which does not, and from the nature of things cannot, in this life 'receive the promises, but sees them afar off, and is persuaded of them and embraces them,' and realises the splendidly dominating power of them, the man wakens up to the dear consciousness, and sees no reason for withholding the confession: 'I am a stranger and a pilgrim in the earth' (Heb. 11:13); 'a stranger and a sojourner as all my fathers were' (Psa. 39:12).

It is of some importance to vindicate this aspect of the Christian life from those objections which intelligent and averagely healthy-minded men of the world are not unnaturally apt to raise against it, as abnormal, melancholy, ascetic, adverse to the cultivation of friendship, and to such interest in the affairs of our own age as that religion must be false which would forbid.

There can be no doubt that the protestation, 'I am a stranger on the earth,' or 'I am a stranger and a sojourner as all my fathers were,' has a

---

[1] [From: *The British and Foreign Evangelical Review* (1881), p. 290f.]

certain air of melancholy about it, a quiet tone of loneliness. The very reference to the 'fathers' gives it an air of the antique or the archaic. It has a little in it, one would say, of the ring of a voice grown old before its time. It is the utterance of a man longing for sympathy and finding little; a man occupied with interests and prospects and desires which obtain no favour in the eyes of those around him. He descends into himself, and discovers there matters of trial and sorrow, which the world in its levity is ignorant of; and he looks forth into futurity, and there he apprehends materials of anxiety and hope to which the world is content to close its eyes. He looks upward to the throne of the Majesty in the heavens, and as one who has been awakened to the knowledge of his responsibility to the King, he realises that he has business in the court of heaven that the world knoweth not of. And looking round upon the very world itself and appreciating its condition of wretchedness and danger as itself seeth it not, his feelings towards that world are unintelligible and unacceptable to it. Whether he look within or around, whether he look forward or upward, he is sensible of emotions in which the thoughtless and ungodly world cannot sympathise; and quietly and with something no doubt of mournfulness in his heart, realising that he is separated in spirit from the vast mass of his fellow-men, he gives expression to the fact in the somewhat pathetic protestation: 'Well, well, I am a stranger now, and a sojourner as all my fathers were.'

It is not that he regrets it. This is not the language of querulousness[1] or of discontent. The fact of his separation and estrangement from the world is not unwelcome to him. It is his deliberate choice that it should be so. Or rather it is the inevitable result of a choice that he has deliberately made already, and which he is not repenting of, but repeating. Be the issue what it may, this at least is certain, 'I am a stranger on the earth.' I have come forth and am separate: and 'I am a stranger on the earth.' My chiefest desires and my chiefest distresses alike tell me that I have lost the sympathy of the world. My deepest sorrows arise from sin; from finding that I am myself so unlike to God; from so frequently displeasing God; from having so

---

[1] [querulous = complaining in a rather petulant or whining manner.]

little heart to seek or to enjoy fellowship with God; from having so little ability to worship and love and serve God; from beholding so little of the light of his countenance, and seeing so seldom his glorious goings in the sanctuary. My deepest desires are for glorious views of the Son of Man, whom the Holy One of Israel hath made strong for himself and for me—strong for the magnifying and manifesting of the glory of God—and for the justifying and renewing of me, a sinner. My peace and joy now are when Messiah, in his infinitely precious righteousness, rises to my view as my shield and hiding-place; my refuge and my deliverer; when in spiritual faith I see the Father reconciling me unto himself, searching all my heart and meeting all my case; telling me that he can be righteous in freely loving me, a lost, rebellious, polluted sinner; and that I can be safe and blessed in fully trusting him, the Just and Holy One. My heart is then opened to its depths, and the light of grace and glory passes through it. And though that light reveals my heart's wickedness, it testifies also its free salvation in the love and righteousness of God my Saviour: though it discloses deep springs of evil and depravity, thus humbling me more and more, it yet gives me a relief from the anguish which the shutting in of that depravity upon the soul to fester there, never fails to create. But this is a light which this world knoweth not of: the things which it discloses both in me and in my God; in me, the sinner, unrighteous and depraved; in God, the Just and Holy One of Israel, are things which the world seeth not, and will by no means believe though a man declare it unto them: the distressing exhibitions of sin and bondage and death in me, which the searching light of the Lord affords; and the disclosures of righteousness, liberty, and life in Christ, my living head and treasure, which the same light reveals;—of these things the world is ignorant,—they are 'foolishness unto them, neither can they know them, for they are spiritually discerned' (1 Cor. 2:14).

But the world's joys and distresses are as much foolishness to me. To mourn, as they mourn, the loss of some perishing portion; to joy, as they joy, in the obtaining of some fleeting idol; I now regard as foolishness indeed. I am crucified to the world, and the world to me. Our judgment and our desire are at variance; and that on no secondary or subordinate themes of interest. On the vital and primary objects of desire, or matters of distinguishing and fundamental interest, we are at variance. The shadow with them is the substance with me; and the shadow with me is the substance with them. They behold me pursuing something which they do not see at all; and little wonder (I excuse them), though that seems to them absurd enough: while I see them following what I know to be a phantom and a dream. Little wonder, then, if a deep and very practical alienation has arisen between us, a separation realised and ratified on both sides. We are fatally and for ever strangers; 'I am a stranger on the earth.'

Let any man read the Psalms of David deliberately, let him look upon them as the honest expression of the writer's actual state of feeling: apart from the credit which he has been taught from his youth to assign to the Scriptures as inspired by the Holy Ghost, so as to form, simply and literally, the Word of God; let him simply contemplate with something like deliberation the state of heart, the character, the principle of conduct, the secret experiences which find vent in these wondrous compositions: and whether he has sympathy with the writer or not, he must come to the conclusion, 'Assuredly this man was a stranger on the earth.' The very revolt which the worldly mind feels from the sanctity and searching holiness of these spiritual songs is an involuntary confession that the writer of them must have been 'a stranger on the earth:' and the very reason why the ungodly man revolts and recoils from them, and never by any chance turns voluntarily to their pages with desire to meditate upon them, and be imbued with their spirit, is because, on the one hand, he is not prepared to be 'a stranger on the earth,' and, on the other hand, cannot but shrewdly know that the actual moulding of his heart and character by these Psalms—the admission of their sentiments into any place of vital love in his heart, and of their principles to any place of influential government over his character and conduct in life, would inevitably make him what, from his love and friendship to the world, he is not prepared to be—'a stranger on the earth.'

But what the world recoils from, the Christian heart desires. Nor will the believer claim for his personal piety any sincerity and progress, except in so far as his heart has been moulded into conformity with the Word of God and the experience of God's people as there recorded. Though it be in every case by a gracious and omnipotent operation of the Divine Spirit that the heart is renewed into the saving faith of Jesus Christ, and brought under the influence of the fear and love of God, the change thus produced is not of such a nature that no account and no explanation can be given of it. Though accomplished by a secret and sovereign energy, it is accommodated to a most express and definite rule. It is achieved by the Spirit, but it is accommodated to the Word. And though the baptism of the Spirit and of fire, under which the heart is melted into self-abasement and kindled into the growing appreciation of the beauty of holiness be beyond our finite comprehension, yet the mould into which the heart thus melted is, so to speak, poured—the impress which it now assumes—is brought most tangibly and fully within the sphere of notice; for it is formed and framed into harmony with that potent Word of God, which he has been pleased to place into our hands, and condescend to entreat us to search: and if a heart, professedly changed by the Spirit of God, whose working we cannot trace, be not in harmony with the Word whose principles we can and may trace, the change professed has not really been undergone.

It follows that if we are true Christians and growing Christians, we will enter with true and growing sympathy into the protestation which the Word of God makes in the name of every Christian of being a stranger and a sojourner on the earth. In proportion as the depth and decision of our personal piety are enhanced, will this sentiment gain ground. As the Word of God dwells in us more richly; as we increase in the study and knowledge of the believing heart, and increase in sympathy with it, in its joys and sorrows, its responsibilities and privileges, its burdens and reliefs, its blessings and hopes, as these are opened up to us in the Scriptures; we will feel more and more alienated from a sinful and unsatisfying, and really very shallow world, and more and more satisfied with our position as 'strangers on the earth.' We will pronounce no censorious and indiscriminate condemnation on those from whom in spirit the grace of God has separated us. We will even watch against giving them unnecessary offence. We will remember, from our own experience, that true spiritual Christianity is sufficiently obnoxious to the dislike of the carnal mind to render it other than highly criminal in the Christian to present it to the unconverted in any additional and unnecessary offensiveness, or shorn of those features of acceptableness of which, even with all its sin-repelling integrity and purity, it is very far from being destitute. And whatever the world is really right in counting excellent and loveable, we will feel bound to show that living Christianity, instead of repudiating, rather sanctions and embraces, and is indeed alone capable of ripening into full maturity. But still we will never fail to see, if living in habits of reverential and lively fellowship with God, that the whole world of unconverted men is one wide waste of utter ungodliness, to which it is no sad doom but a saving grace to be 'a stranger.' The unconverted world seeketh not the glory of God; it acteth not on the principle of fearing and pleasing God; its affairs are conducted with no reference to the will of God; in that world our Father's word, and will, and presence, and claims are habitually, coolly, continually set aside. How then can we ever be other than strangers on the earth?

The secret of maintaining this trying position towards the world in all honour and truth of spirit, to the glory of God, to the promotion of our own spiritual interests and comfort, and to the benefit even of the world itself—the secret of being truly, and comfortably, and usefully 'strangers in the earth,' lies in our being no strangers to God. It is well to give diligent heed to this. It is well to give heed to the process and principle whereby the believer is really enabled to take up and sustain this particular relation to the world. To the worldly man himself it appears exceedingly unnatural and incomprehensible how any human being can have his heart so removed from all that is usually accounted interesting and desirable here below, as to be passing through the world in the real character of a stranger and pilgrim. But if he would attend to the principle on which the Christian acts—if he would but deliberately judge of the process whereby the Christian has become, and still continues to be, a 'stranger on the earth,' he might come to admit, if he be at all ingenuous, that there is nothing unnatural, nothing certainly irrational, and nothing, in the nature of things inaccessible or unattainable, in a man even of an active disposition and a social, and sympathising, and affectionate heart, aspiring to be as the man after God's own heart was a 'stranger in the earth.'

Let us glance at the principle and process as they were seen operating in Abraham, the father of the faithful.

A more decided instance of the believer's relation towards the world, in this aspect of it, cannot be found than in Abraham. The very platform and tenor of his outward life were constructed so as visibly to indicate his spiritual separation from the world. He was not more truly the 'father of the faithful' than he was obviously the Pattern of Pilgrims—the very model of a stranger on the earth. 'By faith Abram, when he was called to go out into a place which he should after receive for an inheritance, obeyed; and he went out, not knowing whither he went. By faith he sojourned in the land of promise, as in a strange country, dwelling in tabernacles with Isaac and Jacob, the heirs with him of the same promise. For he looked for a city which hath foundations, whose builder and maker is God.' And associating with their father all the ancients like-minded with him, the apostle adds—'These all died in faith, not having received the promises, but having seen them afar off, and were persuaded of them, and embraced them, and confessed that they were strangers and pilgrims on the earth.'

Now, what could have prevailed with our father Abraham to assume the pilgrim's staff and the stranger's fare and garb? He had a land that he called his own. He had a kindred. He had a father's house. Doubtless he looked for dying in his nest, his destiny little shaken save by those usual events that gradually change if they do not mar the face of all things in all the homes of earth. Why should Abraham not live, as he has hitherto done, at home among the friends of his youth, the associates of his more active days? What could possibly induce him at one decisive stroke—by one fell swoop—to tear himself away from all that he has counted desirable or dear, and be henceforth a 'stranger on the earth'?

'The God of glory,' says Stephen, 'the God of glory appeared unto our father Abraham when he was in Mesopotamia, before he dwelt in Charran, and said unto him, "Get thee out of thy country, and from thy kindred, and from thy father's house, unto a land that I will show thee: and I will make of thee a great nation, and I will bless thee.'" What could make him a stranger on the earth? 'The God of glory appeared unto him.' That would do it. From that moment he was alienated from the world.

Formerly he had been at home in the world and a stranger to God. Now he is at home with God and a stranger on the earth. Formerly the world had 'appeared' to him—and God was not in all his thoughts. Now 'the God of glory' has appeared unto him, and the world disappears and fades from view. The 'appearance' of God he beholds as real and glorious. The 'appearance' which the world put on, while it beguiled and occupied all his heart, he now discovers to have been false and delusive. He is in circumstances now to choose. The world has appeared unto him with its ease and gifts, its indolent sufficiency lulling his highest faculties asleep, or with its trials and hardships fretting his patience and crossing his aims. And in the counter-revelations of the world's offer and his Maker's glory—with which shall he now consent to be at home? to which shall he now resolve to be a stranger? Ah! but he is not left to weigh his scruples and balance probabilities. He not only sees the glory of God, but he also hears his call; and it is indeed in his call, in the revelation of his character as given in his call—that Abram really sees the glory of God. The word of absolute, supreme authority commands obedience. The word of infinite love commends itself to his acceptance. 'Get thee out of thy country, and from thy kindred, and from thy father's house.' Never was Abram so dealt with before. It is the voice of the King. It is the glory of sovereign majesty. And its effect is immediate and irresistible. Is Abraham dwelling indolently in the world's good,—the spell of its contentment withering his energy of purpose? The voice awakens him:—he starts to his feet. Is he eagerly running his own errand in the world—the strain of covetousness tasking all his effort? The voice arrests him: he stands still to listen. And clear and commanding, as of one having authority, having infinite sovereign right and power, that voice penetrates a secret ear in his heart, and quickens and kindles there a feeling altogether new,—the sharp resistless sense of responsibility—responsibility to One with whom Abram now discovers for the first time that he really has to do. Ah I it is a voice that will brook no disobedience, no gainsaying, no delay. It is the voice of the King,—the King Eternal and Invisible. It is the voice of the King at last: 'Get thee out of thy country, and from thy kindred, and from thy father's house.' No more is Abram's lot in his own hand. 'Get thee out into a land that *I* will show thee.' 'Tis the voice of the Sovereign Disposer. Abram's all is in the hand of 'the God of glory,' and he knows it.

But it is the voice of sovereign mercy also. 'I will make of thee a great nation, and I will bless thee.' I will bless thee: I who have the same authoritative right and power to bless that I have to command and to dispose. I will bless thee,—I whose blessing maketh rich and addeth no sorrow with it—whose blessing is effectual, all-reaching, all-sufficient, eternal:—I will bless thee.' Get thee out, therefore, unto where my blessing shall for ever follow.

Thus did the God of glory appear unto our father Abraham; in sovereign majesty, demanding his unreserved unconditional allegiance; in sovereign mercy, conferring an unlimited and unconditional blessing. And Abraman beholds the glory of God: in the new keen sense of adoring loyalty Abraham welcomes and obeys his King: in the new sweet sense of filial confidence and final and eternal security, Abraham welcomes and puts trust in his reconciled Father which is in heaven.

From that moment he is a stranger on the earth. He has believed God, and parted with the world. He has believed God, and it is imputed to him for righteousness, and the Scripture is fulfilled which saith, 'He was called the friend of God.' But the friend of God is a stranger on the earth: 'By faith therefore he goes out, not knowing whither he goes. By faith he sojourns in the land of promise, as in a strange country.'

In the usual administration of the grace of his kingdom, the King of Zion is not wont to call for a local transference of our persons from one land to another, or away from the society of our relatives into seclusion or to the companionship of those unknown to us. But as to the spirit of our minds, as to the principles which shall govern our hearts and habits, as to the change of purpose and procedure which the sinner undergoes when he returns unto the Lord, and the Lord hath mercy upon him and doth abundantly pardon, there is a transference, a translation, an exchange from one system of feelings and principles, and desires and hopes and efforts to another, as complete, as sweeping, as decisive, as thoroughly producing a revolution upon his nature and character, as the call to Abraham to get him out from his country, and his kindred, and his father's house. Is it not as a pre-eminent example and model in this respect that Abraham is uniformly set forth to us as 'the father of the faithful'?—that we are called upon to walk 'in the steps of our father Abraham'?, that 'they which be of faith are blessed with faithful Abraham'? (Gal. 3:9)—and that 'if we are Christ's, then are we Abraham's seed, and heirs according to the promise?' (Gal. 3:29).

To us, therefore, as to him, if indeed we be of the seed of Abraham, God's friend, the God of Glory hath appeared; to us the word of God hath come. We have seen the glory, and heard the call, of God. And his glory hath appeared to us pre-eminently in the power and privileges of the call. It is indeed in our seeing glory in the call, a glory which the carnal mind never sees, that we realise the call as effectual, or rather that the call realises itself as effectual upon us. The glory of the Sovereign Lord we see in his assertion of his claims over us, his right to command us at his pleasure, his right to dispose of us at his will. 'Get thee up, O slumberer, and flee from the wrath to come. Away to the refuge set before thee! Repent, arise, and flee for thy life.' The glory also of a Sovereign Father we see in his most merciful and most majestic offer and determination in Christ to bless us—to bless us freely, to justify us fully and gratuitously, to reconcile and adopt us in his own Son's righteousness and titles, freely, finally, and for evermore. No longer do we cling to our olden views of God,—our dim and doubtful, hazy and suspicious, and half-slumbering views of the glory of God. No more do we dally,—dreamily tampering,—with the call of God. His majestic and unreserved command, Get thee up and away from the lake of fire—away from thy wicked companions—away from thy worldly idols that are thy gods, thy all:—this unconditional command deals mightily with all that is within thee. And his merciful and unconditional determination, 'I will bless thee,'—bless thee with a free and full forgiveness, if, being guilty, thou needest that—bless thee with an omnipotent regeneration of thy soul, if being depraved and under Satan's bondage thou needest *that*: this sovereign, immediate, unconditional, free and all-sufficient grace deals not only mightily, but deals bountifully with thee. The Eternal King, in short, hath come. He demands thy allegiance: 'Come forth from among them and be thou separate:' but he charges himself with thy lot and thy blessedness for ever: 'I will bless thee, and be a Father unto thee.' And believing his testimony and acquiescing in his proposal,—seeing his glory and hearing his call,—by faith you arise obedient to your Lord, justified by faith, and having peace with God; your faith working by love and overcoming the world: you arise, for this is no more your rest: the Lord is your friend; he is your strength and your song; he also is become our salvation. Your treasure, your citizenship, your home is in heaven. And reconciled to God, and obedient to him, and glad to be so, you are a 'stranger on the earth.'

It cannot, I trust, be warrantably inferred from anything that has now been said, that we could mean to represent the believer as a miserable recluse or a moping solitaire,—as un-companionable,—not formed for or aiming at the duties and enjoyments of friendship. Any such inference would be alike unjust and untrue, alike false and calumnious. The man who is scripturally and spiritually 'a stranger on the earth' has assumed this relation and disposition towards the world, as we have seen, by becoming a friend of God; and that *he* should, and should therefore be indifferent to the sacred claims and the frank and joyous privilege of friendship, is altogether incredible. It is frequently the estimate entertained by the world no doubt concerning the living Christian, that he is of a sullen and morose disposition, looking coldly on the innocent joys of life, and refusing all genial and gladsome association with his fellows. But it is one of many misapprehensions and misrepresentations which the Christian must be content that his character in the eyes of the world should suffer;—one of those many proofs that he cannot expect to be sympathised with or even understood by the world,—that he is, in short, a stranger to the earth. There are those, however, who will deal out to him another measure, and do him justice. They will understand from their own experience how the case really stands.

For it is a grievous misunderstanding. The believer in reality is the only man who has thoroughly fathomed the nature and claims of true and incorruptible friendship. In his friendship with God he has had the glorious opportunity of learning them. And the lessons, which on that high field he learns, he will be prepared and desirous to bring into exercise in those lower spheres of friendship which he may be privileged to occupy among his fellow-men. Nor will he want opportunity for doing so. In this sense he is indeed no more a stranger and a foreigner, but a fellow-citizen with the saints and of the household of God, admitted to a brotherhood of the widest extent and of the most intimate kind. Can it be forgotten that the David who gave utterance to the sentiment we have so often quoted, 'I am a stranger on the earth,' was the friend of Jonathan; and that it was precisely when realising most intensely that he was a stranger on the earth, hunted even as a partridge on its mountains, that he enjoyed most intensely the sweetness and privilege of that most passionate and honourable attachment?

Friendship, indeed, recruits its ranks from the kingdom of grace. The Christian, though separated from the world, is not isolated on a platform by himself, on which he can find none to share or sympathise with him. Unforgiven sin may constitute such a platform—yea, a prison—for the soul. But the fellowship of God is a large and wealthy place, in which all the faithful dwell together in unity. 'Bring my soul out of prison, that I may praise thy name; the righteous shall compass me about, when thou hast dealt bountifully with me' (Psa. 142:7).

Indeed, no man knows the calm, quiet, and confiding joy of true friendship, but he who is a friend of God and a stranger on the earth. For, when once he finds his deepest anxieties settled, and his deepest longings satisfied, in God, so that he needs no more to depend or draw upon created friends for his chief good; he returns now to find in them what it really is in them to yield—not a primary and supreme, but a secondary and subordinate enjoyment. *That* he does find them capable of yielding. He finds them capable now of yielding what he now seeks,—in accession, namely, a supplement, to a happiness already in the main secure. He found them incapable of yielding what he formerly sought,—when he vainly assayed to make them, or any created good, his 'all in all,'—his satisfying portion. Now, therefore, for the first time, he has in the fellowships and friendships of brethren a quietness of enjoyment, a real and full meeting of his expectations, which he never had before. And being now, even if alone in the world and friendless, not friendless and alone, because the Father is with him, he finds, if surrounded by friends, enjoyment in them for the Father's sake.

You are not at liberty merely, it is your imperative duty, to cultivate Christian friendship. Concerning each of his friends alternately, Jesus says to all, 'He that receiveth you, receiveth me.'

One of the first effects, indeed, of living Christianity is seen in those of its disciples who once were, naturally, morose and isolated. Of such, the world will witness with astonishment, and the Church with delight, the expansion which their affections undergo, the enlarged sympathies and genial sensibilities which they display, when grace has *effectually loved on* to its own delighted enthronement ('Grace reigns') And why should not Christian men, and women too (women perhaps we should say, especially), be the very patterns of all that is lovely, and honourable, and frank, and open, and heartfelt, and mutually trustful, and helpful in their friendships with one another? Yea, in point of fact, it is really so. None so joyous and genial as they: and so much the more, as they feel that they are strangers on the earth: and so much the more, as they see the day approaching. Conscious thereby the more truly that all their real treasure is safe; with their relation to the living God settled on his own infinitely holy, infinitely gracious terms, on his own infinitely glorious, and absolutely and eternally sure foundations; with their natures placed under the renewing and disciplinary influence of the Spirit and word and Providence of an Almighty Father; and the continuance and ultimate perfection of that process of renewal secured and guaranteed by an everlasting covenant ordered in all things, and sure: who can afford in an hour of recreation,—when soul and body and spirit, after faithful duty, need to be relaxed,—who can afford, as they can, to unbend and enjoy a brother's society and fellowship,—ay, and with a zest, a cordiality, a quiet, calm, and deep pleasurableness, of which the worldling can form no conception, and compared with which the world's noisy and most excited mirth is unnatural and hollow. 'Rejoice in the Lord, and be glad, ye righteous: and shout for joy, all ye that are upright in heart.'

Equally groundless is another objection that has often been brought against a style of piety so decided as to make a man a stranger on the earth, and to beget the evangelical spirituality of character which we have been describing. It is said that he will be thereby unfitted for discharging his duties in the world.

It were useless to enter seriously on the refutation of this objection. It may be sufficient to reply that it cannot possibly be so, inasmuch as it is precisely *duty*, and not desire, which dictates the entire intercourse which such an one maintains with the world. That the man whose whole *desire* is set upon the world should thereby be greatly disqualified for his *duty*, is natural enough. But that the man, who, by his supreme desire being turned away from earthly things, is thereby left free and unprejudiced to move among them at the dictates, not of inordinate desire, but simple *duty*,—that he should be unfitted, and even thereby unfitted, for his duties in the world, is inconceivable. It is really he, and he only, with whom duty is always constraining, and in whom responsibility is really awake.

Be not afraid, O believing reader, to be a stranger in the earth. Be assured your spiritual safety, comfort, and usefulness are all bound up with your really being so. 'Know ye not that the friendship of the world is enmity to God? whosoever, therefore, will be a friend of the world is an enemy to God.' Whosoever is at home in the earth is a stranger to God. But the more you are alienated in spirit from a passing, shallow, heartless, ungodly world, the more will you feel constrained to apply in livelier faith and prayer to your heavenly Father for friendship and fellowship with him.

It was thus that the Psalmist pleaded his separation from the world as a reason for his obtaining clearer insight into the gracious purposes and holy will of God: 'Open mine eyes that I may behold the wonders that are in thy law. I am a stranger in the earth, hide not thy commandments from me' (Psa. 119:12). The more, also, will you love the worship, the house, the cause and kingdom of Christ upon the earth; and the more liberally, joyfully, and prayerfully will you give for the support and propagation of his gospel. For thus again spake this same stranger on the earth, Israel's sweet psalmist and king: 'For who am I, and what is my people, that we should be able to offer so willingly after this sort? for all things come of thee, and of thine own have we given thee. For we are strangers before thee and sojourners, as were all our fathers; our days on the earth are as a shadow, and there is none abiding' (1 Chron. 29:14, 15).

Nor will this be wanting to you in the hour of sorrow and anxiety, to plead with God as a reason for his hearing and answering your cry, when, as a stranger in the earth for his sake, you cast yourself upon his help and faithfulness: 'Hear my prayer, O Lord, and give ear unto my cry; hold not thy peace at my tears; for I am a stranger with thee, and a sojourner, as all my fathers were.' The appeal is one of inexpressible power with God. His heart warms towards the stranger. He hath most solemnly assured us that he is the stranger's shield. He hath forbidden us, under pain of his especial displeasure, to vex or oppress the stranger. He hath in the most simple and affecting language commanded us to be kind unto the stranger. He hath allured us to the duty of entertaining strangers by beautifully reminding us that some have thereby entertained angels unawares. His dear Son—in whose name we pray, and in whose sympathy we may continually rejoice and enrich ourselves—was pre-eminently a stranger on the earth, and knoweth more than any man the heart of a stranger. In his members, and in his cause, he is a stranger still: and so highly does he estimate the entertaining of the stranger that, on the great day of accounts, one of his tenderest and most affecting commendations of his people's faithfulness will be in these terms, 'I was a stranger, and ye took me in.'

With such affections on the part of the Most High as is thus indicated towards the stranger, let me only be able honestly to plead at his throne, that 'I am a stranger on the earth,' and how can I doubt that in my every need and in my darkest hour he will hear my cry, and not be silent at my tears? Rather—may I not assure myself?—when poor and needy, when pursued by evil and by fear, when perplexed with guilt and with Satan,—when ready to sink under trial and temptation, I flee to his door, he will give me invariable ground to bear this testimony to his grace and faithfulness: 'I was a stranger, and the Lord took me in'? μ.

LETTERS

A SERIES OF LETTERS

These letters were originally published in the first two volumes of The Free Presbyterian Magazine (1895–96). The editor, Rev. James S. Sinclair, referred only to 'a friend' who had made them available. One of the letters had however been published in The Scotsman *as having been written to 'a Free Church minister.'[1] The identity of the minister is unknown for definite. However, the obituary of Mrs Auld, the widow of Rev. Alexander Auld (1819–1904), Free Church minister at Olrig, in the* Free Presbyterian Magazine *for October, 1928, states: 'The pages of the Magazine bear evidence of her correspondence with Dr Kennedy and Dr Hugh Martin.'[2] As the below letters are the only letters of Hugh Martin to appear in the magazine, it might be assumed they were originally written to the Aulds.*

[1] [*The Scotsman*, Monday, 25th February, 1889, p. 6.]
[2] [*The Free Presbyterian Magazine* (1928), Volume 30, October, p. 227.]

⌒

1

Serving with a Guilty Conscience

Lasswade, 2nd April, 1875

My Dear Friend,

First of all, please accept the accompanying copy of those most precious remains of Dr John Duncan[1] in token of the affectionate remembrance I bear towards you, 'being mindful,' if not 'of thy tears,' yet of that blessed and holy question you asked me at ___ 'How can I serve Christ or his Church while I have an unpurged conscience?' Yes, it is a holy question, and an honourable, because a holy one. 'Guilt' (says Dr Duncan, page 40) 'is the relation between disobedience and punishment.' It is a relation constituted by God himself in his holiness and righteousness, and is, therefore, a holy and a righteous thing. And to feel it is, therefore, to feel a holy thing pressing on the soul, and to accept the burden with a resolution to acquiesce in no removal of it, with which God is not well pleased, is a holy feeling, the beginning of truest holiness.

And how can we ever praise God enough that the relief is so holy. Holy, holy, holy! The Holy One himself made sin. The Holy One holily made liable to bear the guilt of all the sins of a people whom no man can number. Immanuel holily slain, holily giving himself in death, holily accepted, holily rewarded for becoming in his holy self the balm, the cure, the comfort, the peace, the all-sufficient and everlasting relief of a guilty conscience. Isaiah heard the seraphim exclaim when they saw the Lord's holiness, 'the whole earth is full of his glory.' Scientific men tell us that the sun is a dark body with a photosphere or atmosphere of light surrounding it. Is not this more certainly true concerning the earth as filled with the Lord's glory, for what is the spiritual photosphere of this dark earth, if it be not a

---

[1] [D. Brown, (Ed.), *The Late Rev. John Duncan, LL.D. in the Pulpit and at the Communion Table* (Edinburgh: Edmonston and Douglas, 1874).]

holily slain Christ? So that from those 'habitable parts of the earth' where he had his eternal delights, there comes, when in this glorious photosphere of a crucified Christ is seen the forgiveness of sins, the echo of his song, 'My delights were with the sons of men.' And when a holy, righteous and real forgiveness penetrates its way into the burning fibres of a guilty conscience, pacifying, cooling, cleansing, then they are given the exact tension for the time which the Spirit of God teaches them, as on shining silver harp strings, to sing, 'Worthy is the Lamb that was slain,' 'the whole earth is full of his glory,' aye, and the whole heaven too! For really, federally, all those fibres of conscience were gathered up into Christ when he died, and then and there they discharged their venom. When Christ, the Head died, his body, which is the Church, died. Head he could not be, nor as Head die, without his body. And when the blessed Spirit of God unites actually to Christ the soul that was federally in him when he died, all the venom of the guilty conscience actually runs up into him and is in him eternally and righteously annihilated; and from him, yea, from his shed blood, there runs down into the fibres of conscience, and into the poor soul's heart's core, the holy peace, purity, love and grace that had their triumph in the cry, 'It is finished.' And we dare not say, 'This cannot be to me;' we are rather bound to say, 'This must be to me.' Surely here, if anywhere, 'the kingdom of heaven suffereth violence, and the violent take it by force.'

Thou knowest, O Christ, what this guilty conscience of mine will grow into to all eternity, if not purged and cleansed and healed by thee! It will be, O Lamb of God, an eternal blasphemer of thee and of thy Father and of thy Spirit. Is that any wish of thine? Thou art its Creator, Creator of this same conscience which I by transgression have made guilty. Hast thou not a desire to the work of thine own hands? A conscience is a more wonderful creature of thine than all suns and stars, with all their photospheres that baffle the search of the sciences. Very glorious art thou as creator of a conscience! But Lord, thou art more glorious far as the balm of a wounded conscience. Father, glorify thy Son by making him the balm of my conscience; and the day will not be far distant when, with those who already sing in the land where they say not 'I am sick,' being forgiven their iniquities, I, too, shall sing to my own heart's solacement and to thy praise the song of my salvation, 'Worthy is the Lamb that was slain, for he was slain for us.'

How near did our blessed Lord come to knowing the agony of having a guilty conscience? That is a wonderful question. We cannot answer it. This only we know, he had a conscience and he had guilt. Holy he was, inviolably holy. 'Such an high priest became us, who was holy and undefiled' even by the sin that he bore, and 'separate from sinners,' even when 'numbered with the transgressors.' But he was numbered with the transgressors and sin he did bear. And the sin which he bore was the procuring cause of his sufferings. And he justi-fied the sword that smote him by an acquiescing reference to the sin that he was answerable for. And to what faculty of his human soul, to what created principle of his nature, if not to conscience, did the Father make appeal when he appealed to him willingly to bear the stroke of the sword which he awoke to smite him? Did the blessed Lamb of God not conscientiously suffer the punishment due to his people's sins? 'I do always the things that please the Father.' Oh, how holy and pure and bright as a burnished mirror was his conscience in all his sufferings! Yet was it not suffering? Yea, its sufferings were infinitely acute because of its perfect holiness. 'The bush burned,' and surely we may here hear the voice, 'Take off thy shoes from off thy feet, for this place is holy ground.' O how little do we know of Christ crucified! The Lord give us the only state of heart that can dare to think of him, the broken and the contrite spirit. Had we more of that we would understand more of him. This, however, we do know, that in his soul agony in Gethsemane and on Calvary, he came so near to the agony of a sin-convinced conscience as that of a hair's breadth. Less would have disqualified him for that sympathy which he has experimentally attained by coming to that point and not a hair's breadth further. Surely this is a guilty sinner's friend, and this is her Beloved, O ye daughters of Jerusalem. The answer then to your question, 'How can I serve Christ or his Church while I have an unpurged conscience?' is just this, he who is the Lord of thy conscience is also the balm, the cure, the peace, yea the everlasting relief and health of it.

Well, I was to have told you of my wanderings and preachings these last three weeks. But what matters it? They are in Christ's hands, there let them rest to bring forth fruit to his glory. I go to Glasgow Communion next Wednesday.

Yours, &c.,

Hugh Martin

2

Healing of Conscience

Lasswade, 20th April, 1875

My Dear Friend,

Please do not be alarmed at my replying so quickly to your last welcome letter, nor think that I expect similar promptitude. The fact is, that my correspondence is so voluminous, that, if I did not reply almost immediately, I would get quite blocked.

I returned from Glasgow communion a good deal fatigued, not having had scarcely any repose since I saw you, and my doctor tells me I must rest from preaching for a time, after the last few months' work. But, as I cannot be absolutely idle, I begin a work today which I have been contemplating for some time, that of preparing for the press a volume, consisting of a series of discourses preached more than twenty years ago. The title of it is, *The Shadow of Calvary.*[1] How solemn these words! Although thinking of them before, this is the first time I have written them, and how weighty I feel them to be! There will be sixteen discourses, five treating of our Lord in Gethsemane, three on his arrest, and eight on his trial. They will be very far from what I would wish; and, though I intend revising them carefully, they are but a feeble contribution towards the elucidation of this wonderful theme. Still, I desire to offer this little tribute of service to our adorable Lord, and may he bless the truths set forth in the book (if it come into existence), and accept my humble attempt to speak of his blessed name.

I am not to make this a long letter, but I must notice your question, 'How can I expect to receive and enjoy that "healing of conscience," of which you wrote in your former letter, while my heart, helped by Satan, keeps whispering to me, your love of sin is unchanged?' Well, you ought to know what I would answer to that. I would answer, 'You

---

[1] [This was most recently republished as H. Martin, *The Shadow of Calvary: Gesthemane, the Arrest, the Trial* (Edinburgh: Banner of Truth Trust, 2016).]

must, you can receive and enjoy that healing, though conscious of sin and Satan raging.' Let me point you to Romans 7. Study the two 'I's' there. 'In me, that is, in my flesh, dwelleth no good thing,' no 'hatred of sin,' which is certainly a 'good thing.' Again, 'It is no more I that do it, but sin that dwelleth in me.' It is no more I that loves sin, it is the sin that dwelleth in me; and that bears no hatred to itself. Paul took his stand between these two 'I's'—I, my sin-inhabited flesh, and I, my willingly spiritual mind—and he made a clean and certain out between them. 'The captive exile hasteth that he may be loosed.' Now, therefore, do not allow yourself to be fettered in this snare of unbelief, that, because you are not what you would fain be, you have no right to Christ and his benefits. I think you work too much trying to unravel these snares, instead of taking the sword of the Spirit, which is the Word of God, and bringing it to deal with them. It has cut, and can cut many a harder knot than that you mention. The Lord give you understanding.

Yours, &c.,

Hugh Martin

3

Seven Eyes

Lasswade, 30th April, 1875

My Dear Friend,

Many thanks for the volume you have so kindly sent me. I read part of it last year at Lodgehill with great pleasure, and please accept my cordial thanks for it, and for this proof of your friendship. Let me also say what a pleasant savour I retain of our last conversation at ___. If we are enabled by grace to help each other in any degree in our efforts after a truly Christian life, O! what help should we expect from that 'Mighty One' on whom God hath laid help, a help that must go for nothing, except for being expended on the helpless; a help, that with all its spending, can yet never be spent.

I was meditating this morning on Zechariah, 3rd chapter. How precious what is there unfolded! A sinner clothed in filthy garments, and the 'seven eyes' reading him right through, gets laid before him a stone with this wondrous engraving, 'I will remove the iniquity of that land in one day.' How precious to a guilty one, whose sin has been read to him under the light of the seven eyes, to read now on this stone set straight before him, the writing, 'I will remove thine iniquity in one day.' O to roll ourselves over on this stone and rest! O to praise God for this most gracious announcement! 'I will remove thine iniquity.' O to build on this stone, and to be built upon it! The psalmist got a sight of this stone with its wondrous engraving when he said, 'Thou forgavest the iniquity of my sin.' He was now in the hiding place, and like Peter on the Mount of Transfiguration, said, 'It is good to be here.' Ah! David would like to abide there always, to have always a sense of pardoned sin, and to sing a song of deliverance, but he remembers that he has still sin within him and around him to meet and to face; and the Lord, as it were, understands the thought, the unspoken thought, for while David says, 'Thou wilt compass me with songs of deliverance,' the Lord replies, 'I will instruct thee and teach thee in the way which thou shalt go, I will guide thee with mine eye.' As if he said, 'Be not dismayed although thy present state is not always realised by thee. Be not afraid to go down from the mount of communion to the tear and wear of everyday life. Do not repine at having to go outside from thy hiding-place within the veil. I will preserve thee, I will guide thee, yea, I will set mine eye upon thee, and with my eye upon thee, lift thou thine eye to me; set thine eye toward me, the Lord, as I set mine eye on thee, and thou shalt have light and direction.' What a deep, tender affectionateness of intercourse between the psalmist and his God do these verses imply. Is it not sad, and sore, and very sinful to see even a little into this, to get a taste of this sweet reconciliation, and yet to wander and backslide, and fret and be impatient, and have many mournful relapses? What have you to say as to that?

But I must now away to write a lecture I am to deliver on Wednesday evening in Glasgow on 'The Relation between the Headship of Christ over the State and over the Church.' Too glorious a topic to be treated by me, but Philippians 2, verses 5-11, would help me could I get into them. I think we should have nothing to do with Christ at all, or else make him our all and never stint.

Yours hurriedly, &c.,

Hugh Martin

4

The Resurrection and the Life

Lasswade, 14th May, 1875

My Dear Friend

Your greatly liked letter I now acknowledge. It did me good to find you asserting so strongly spiritual death. It compels us towards him who is 'the resurrection and the life,' who is the true God and eternal life, the eternal life unsealed to sinners spiritually dead, in and by the glorious sacrifice of himself. The Lord Jesus approaches dead sinners in these words, 'I am the resurrection and the life: he that believeth in me, though he were dead, yet shall he live: and whosoever liveth and believeth in me shall never die. Believest thou this?' (John 11:25, 26). Now, it is not merely that Jesus is the resurrection and the life, but it is that he himself comes and tells us so, comes and tells us what are the immediate consequences to us in our spiritual death of his being the resurrection and the life, and then taking us by the hand and looking us in the face he says, 'Believest thou this?' What a communion with Christ that soul might have who truly realised him putting the question, and not to be put off with no answer or half an answer. What answer can or dare we give but this, 'Lord, I believe, help thou mine unbelief'? Thou art the resurrection and the life, and thou art not any less so because I have to cry, Help mine unbelief. Thou art on that account all the more precious to me, all the more needed by me. In spiritual death, as I am, I need exactly thee, the resurrection and the life. And O suffer me, Lord, to say it, for it is true that thou, as the resurrection and the life, needest dead souls. Thou canst not otherwise be the resurrection and the life. And it is to me that thou hast been pleased to come and say, 'I am the resurrection and the life.' It is between thee and me, here and now, that this wondrous word is passing, and it is to me now thou art saying, 'Believest thou this?' Lord, why askest thou this question of me, unless thou meanest me to know and feel that thou dost really need dead souls in order that it may be possible for thee to be truly and actually the resurrection and the life? Yea, why askest thou this of me, unless it be that so thou mayest give me to understand that thou needest dead and helpless me? It is useless to say, 'Lord, I cannot believe, for I am dead,' because if I were not dead, he who is the resurrection and the life needed not to have come to me. Lord, thou knewest I was dead, and that is why thou comest as the resurrection and the life, comest that thou mayest meet my death and do away with it. Lord, if I am dead and thou hast come to me as the life, what can I say or do, but just break down in wonder, in shame, and in thankfulness that it should be so! Yes, Lord, I break down, an unbelieving dead soul before thee, and thou as the resurrection and the life sayest, 'Arise, live,' and if thou willest that I, dead and helpless, should arise and live, what right, what reason have I to say, 'Lord, I cannot.'? Cannot! even when the Resurrection says, 'Rise.' Cannot! even when the Life says, 'Live.' The soul that says so and sticks to it thereby says, 'Lord, thou art not the resurrection, thou art not the life, I believe not this.'

All the while it remains true, awfully true, that this is just the answer we will give unless the Resurrection and the Life do raise us. He cannot raise us against our will, nor without our will; not that he is limited in power, but because he cannot work self-contradictions and will not work unreasonablenesses. But again, therefore, comes this tender, loving, piercing question, 'Believest thou this? Believest thou that I am the resurrection and the life?' And is the response? 'Lord, I fain would believe, I dare not say thou art not what thou tellest me thou art.' Then this believing acquiescence in his word is just the Resurrection raising you up, just the Life causing you to live. You rise by breaking down; you are raised by being broken down. He himself became the Resurrection by dying; he himself became the Life by rising again from the dead. And his people by breaking down, by dying to themselves, rise in him. He breaks them down that he may raise them up in and with himself. O what a life is that! the life that is obtained by dying and rising again, the life that passed through death and resurrection must be eternal life. The life to which entrance is gained by the gates of resurrection is life everlasting. What will all the splendours of the resurrection of dead bodies be at the sound of the archangel's trump, compared with what my Lord already is as the resurrection of dead souls? And as I hear him say, 'Arise, my love, for the winter is past, the rain is over and gone, death is ended, resurrection is accomplished, life for evermore is entered upon,' does he not thereby cause me to know that a splendour of glory belongs to him, even now, as the Resurrection and the Life, although I scarcely see the most distant tips of the fringe thereof? Ah! well, I think I see this, my great and overpowering need of him as my Resurrection and my Life.

Yours, &c.,

Hugh Martin

5

The Resurrection and the Life

Edzell, Forfarshire, 18th May, 1875

My Dear Friend,

I do not know that it is my turn to write, but I do not deal with a covenant of works in that matter, and I suppose you do not either.

I just write to say that my address will be as above for the next few days, having come to take part in the communion services here. I am pretty well at present, and have been working at the proof-sheets of my book—pleasant enough work if only the printed matter did anything like justice to the theme.[1]

I enjoy this place. The pure air straight from the hills is delightful, and I had a walk this forenoon by a stream overhung with trees beaming in the beauteous childhood of their fresh green leaves. I do like the spring, and was thinking today how I would fain realize in my soul the gospel declaration 'For lo! the winter is past, the rain is over and gone, the flowers appear on the earth, &c (Song of Sol. 2:11-13). I preach tomorrow on the leper's prayer, 'Lord, if thou wilt, thou canst make me clean,' and hope to get some good of it myself, having some sense of need of his cleansing me from all sin—sins of heart, of life, and of service. It will be 32 years tomorrow since I was licensed to preach the gospel of the grace of God. Most glorious privilege! notwithstanding all my sin and shortcoming.

I do not expect to write you again until (*Dv*) after the Assembly, to which I am not looking forward with feelings of pleasure, but rather with forebodings, for there is little seeking of the all-glorifying presence of the Holy Spirit who alone can take of the things of Christ and show them to his servants. Also, many of those fathers and brethren to whom the reproaches of Zion were a burden are like 'the flowers of the forest, a' wede away .'[2] I trust it may not be necessary for me to speak at all,

[1] [*The Shadow of Calvary* (1875).]
[2] [Scots: a' wede away = withered away.]

for the question of our ecclesiastical relationships in Scotland is very far from being ripe for any decision on the subject. The foundations of the old National Church are eminently well worth contending for, her rights and privileges well worth fighting for; but the present occupants of the Establishment exhibit so little spiritual power that one is placed in an excruciating predicament in appearing to defend them when defending the constitution of the ancient Church of Scotland. Of course, it is absurd to say that patronage is not abolished, while it is perhaps equally absurd to say that its abolition has redressed the grounds of our Protest in 1843, and yet the Free Church seems quite indisposed to demand such redress, or to desire to be reinstated in the rights and privileges acknowledged to belong to the Church of Scotland by the statutes of 1592, &c. Indeed, some of our leaders are beginning to pooh-pooh the principle of State recognition and aid. But to say that the State is at present under no obligation to maintain a free, faithful, established church, I would require a fresh revelation from heaven to enable me to believe. Therefore, as I have said, the matter is at such a stage just now as that public discussion can do little good, perhaps harm, and if the Assembly would rather devote a day to discussing how best to promote in our pulpits the maintenance of the doctrines of grace, which are going down in Scotland every day, it would 'set them better.' I read quite lately a sermon preached a few weeks ago by ――― of ――― which was simply horrible. The ground of salvation is wholly cut away. The atonement is nothing but self-sacrificing love, no satisfaction to divine justice, no exhausting of the curse, no removal of guilt, nothing to enable a guilty sinner to approach Jehovah, nothing to pacify conscience, nothing to bring either glory to God or peace on earth, nothing but a senseless, drivelling parody of goodwill to men. I don't see how I for one can hold my tongue as to this sort of thing. We must speak out. Churches that can put up with such doctrine may go to the wall tomorrow for me.

Hoping to hear from you before I return to Edinburgh.

Yours, &c.,

Hugh Martin

6

Rainbows in the Clouds

Lasswade, 6th June, 1875

My Dear Friend,

I was putting on my coat to take some letters to the post when yours came in, so I sit down again, and will take this with me when I go. I regret to learn you have not been quite well, 'down' in body and mind as you say, and that as I am 'Hopeful,' you need a word of comfort from me. As to my being 'Hopeful,' let me first clear off that misunderstanding. On our first acquaintance you represented yourself at your worst, and what could I do but try to fulfil the command, 'Speak ye comfortably to Jerusalem,' which is not difficult to do when Jerusalem is made willing to accept no comfort but such as comes, not only in loving kindness and mercy, but also in righteousness and judgment. Hence, perhaps, 'Hopeful' did make an impression on the line of buoyancy, but he is for all that a very sorrowful fellow, and often after making such impressions, he has to go away by himself and groan, and sob, and sigh, and suffer deserved chastisement. As to needing a word of comfort from me, if your need touches my sinful heart, how must it tell on his heart who is the gracious and sympathizing High Priest, and who is infinitely more tender and more ready to help than any fellow-sinner? I think, however, that this depression of spirit of which you speak is one of the 'manifold dispensations' through which the Lord sometimes takes his children—one of the 'ways of the wilderness' through which he sometimes leads them round about, so that they may learn the rich variety of covenant provision made for all their need. You know the science of the rainbow. We cannot have the rainbow, unless there be the cloud for it to rest upon. The beautiful rays are there, streaming away into invisible space, but in order to the revelation of the beauty, the interception of the cloud is essential. 'I do set my bow in the cloud, and it shall come to pass, saith the Lord, that when I do bring a cloud over the earth, the bow shall be seen in the cloud, and it shall be for a token of the covenant between me and the earth.' May we not say that when the Lord brings a cloud, not over the earth, but over the heart, then he 'sets a bow in the cloud,' such a bow as this—'Why art thou cast down, O my soul, and why art thou disquieted within me? Hope thou in God, for I shall yet praise him who is the health of my countenance and my God.' Do you not see the bow? 'Hope thou in God who is the health of my countenance and my God.' 'My God'—is not that the token of the covenant, the echo of the covenant promise, 'I will be to them a God, and they shall be to me a people'? And a people that shall 'yet praise him.' So you see the 'praise' is in the covenant with all else, but you and I would stint the praise until we are relieved from our cast-down state. 'Gratitude,' says a sardonic writer, 'is thankfulness for favours received that have satiated the greed of human nature.' But in the kingdom of grace gratitude is thankfulness for favours to come, favours that will come, because they are in the covenant, and faith is already the substance of them, and the evidence of them, while yet they are unseen and unenjoyed; therefore 'why art thou cast down, O my soul?' Really, though I am not 'Hopeful' you make me write as though I were, and why should I not be, and you too? Answer that if you can, at least if you can consistently with your duty to glorify him who is the Hope of Israel.

I was meditating this morning on the words, 'The Lord is gracious and full of compassion,' and I thought, 'The Lord is gracious,' that is true, because he says himself he is so. It is also inexhaustible, because it reveals the character of him who is infinite, therefore, being true and inexhaustible it should be enough for me—enough to live upon, and enough to die upon. But is it apprehended and appropriated by me? there's the weak point of the argument. Well, is he not gracious enough to enable me to apprehend and appropriate it? Is he not gracious enough to be willing that I should apprehend and appropriate it? He is; therefore it just comes round again to the simple but blessed statement, 'The Lord is gracious,' and more or better cannot be.

You would observe from the newspapers that I took no part in the Church and State debate, didn't even vote. I could have voted with

Sir Henry Moncrieff, for his motion was harmless, but I knew it was framed not so much with the view of emphasising our Free Church position as of keeping in check our more advanced men, and I was glad on that account it got such a large following. But I am happy to tell you that I expect soon to be out of earshot, for a season, of the alarm of war, as I am looking forward to a six weeks' sojourn in the Highlands. I go to Dornoch (*Dv*) on the third week of this month to the Communion there, afterwards to Rogart, and there will remain on until after the Dingwall Communion, first week of August. Indeed, my heart's in the Highlands already, so I add no more at present, but that I hope soon to have good accounts of your improved health, and remain,

Yours, &c.,

Hugh Martin

7

The Work of the Spirit and the Merit of Christ

Montrose, 30th January, 1877

My Dear Friend,

I was purposing this morning to devote the afternoon to letter-writing, and you were the fourth on my list. But since then your welcome letter has come in, giving you a double claim, and therefore I begin with you.

So it seems, I have not yet earned the right to be called 'a brother indeed.' Now to think of that! For you say, 'If you could help me in at the strait gate you would be a brother indeed.' Well, I give it up! Because if you were once in, and were questioned as to your mode of entrance you would be in a sorry plight; for were you asked, 'How came you here? Did you enter in according to the command?' and you were to answer, 'No, Dr Martin, shoved me in,' you see yourself that such an answer would not do, you would be condemned in your own eyes. But suppose you answered, 'Yes, I entered in,' and the questioner were to add, 'Then what means this twist that I see?' and you should say, 'Oh! that came from Dr Martin shoving me in.' Would you not then be very properly told, 'He must be a great fool that man who would presume to put his hand to the work of the Holy Ghost.' Ah, dear friend, do you not rejoice that the bringing in at the strait gate of regeneration is inseparably bound up with the nature and provisions of the everlasting covenant? Do you not rejoice also, that it follows inevitably from the essential nature and intrinsic value as well as designed effect of the death of Christ? He died, 'the just for the unjust, that he might bring us unto God.' The 'he died for' secures the 'he will bring,' because he, the Just One 'died for the unjust that he might bring them.' If he died for every human being as some allege, then the 'he died for' does not involve the 'he will bring.' What then does it involve? We may well ask that! It involves something foreign to the revelation of Holy

Scripture, something new, something which is a figment of proud human reason. An indefinite atonement may satisfy superficial enquirers, but the belief of it indicates a decline in vital religion, and marks a shallow age as to personal piety. But a definite atonement satisfies souls taught of God, because such souls seek the glory of Christ, and could not endure the thought that Christ's death should have been for those not one whit the better of it. The United Presbyterian Church is wrong on this doctrine,[1] and too many in the Free Church would compromise it also, although they may defer openly avowing it until I am dead, or unable again to speak out in its defence.

There is a thought—as you ask me for help—that has sometimes helped my own faith—it is this—Christ's death is meritorious of its own application. I have, and perhaps you have a miserably hesitating habit, which treats Christ and his salvation very unworthily. Godly jealousy of ourselves is very right and proper, but to *jalouse*[2] away Christ out of the place which is his in the covenant of grace, as the performer of all its conditions, and the administrator of all its provisions, this is very wrong. Paul desired that believers should not only be rooted and built up in the faith of Christ, but should abound therein with thanksgiving. They were to 'abound' because of the abundance that was in Christ. Abundance of grace there was in him, leading him to take up the case of sinners and to go through with the work of their redemption, and abundance of merit there was in him to bespeak the fulfilment of the Father's covenant engagement, that his work, when finished and accepted, should be placed to the account of all those on whose behalf it was accomplished. And is there not abundant declaration made in the Word of God of this wondrously gracious arrangement? 'This is the name whereby he shall be called, the Lord our righteousness.' 'He hath made him to be sin for us, who knew no sin, that we might be made the righteousness of God in him.' 'Christ hath redeemed us from the curse of the law, being made a

---

[1] [For an overview of the drift in the United Presbyterian Church on the subject of the atonement, see: Ian Hamilton, *The Erosion of Calvinist Orthodoxy: Drifting from the Truth in Confessional Scottish Churches* (Tain: Christian Focus Publications, 2010).]

[2] [Scots: jalouse = to suspect or to be suspicious of; to have doubts about.]

curse for us.' And have we not abundant presentations of Christ made to us in the gospel by himself, by his Father, and by the Holy Spirit, as a Saviour not only able and willing to save all who come to God through him, but to save them with a complete and perfect and everlasting salvation? And is not he in the gospel made over to you and to me if we have no objections (and I am sure we have none), to be indebted to him for an out-and-out, an absolute and unconditional salvation? And since, therefore, Christ is exhibiting and offering himself to us in the Word of the gospel as the 'Living Bread' and the 'Living Water' that can alone refresh and satisfy our souls, let us have done with our miserable questionings—may we eat? can we drink? have we ever drunk? Let us rather seek to rejoice that in him there is ever a fountain of grace for all our need, and let us ask him to enable us to drink, and to drink copiously, out of 'the wells of salvation.' It is little I can say to help you for I am but a child, but I would desire that through the riches of infinite, free, and ever faithful mercy, our intercourse may not prove altogether indifferent to him who has the name that is above every name, and that while we must not be too dependent on one another, or even on our dearest Christian friends, we yet may obtain upon our friendship some glint of blessing from the Well-beloved, enabling us to say with increasing heart truth—

> *Dear dying Lamb, thy precious blood*
> *Shall never lose its power*
> *Till all the ransom'ed Church of God*
> *Be sav'ed to sin no more.*

> *E'er since by faith I saw the stream,*
> *Thy flowing wounds supply,*
> *Redeeming love hath been my theme*
> *And shall be till I die.*

Yours, &c.,

Hugh Martin

8

Praying for our Children and for the Church

Montrose, 15th April, 1877

My Dear Friend,

I hope this will find you well. My own health is fairly good at present, at least, as the Scotch say, 'I canna' complain.'

I have been, for the last hour or two, revising the proof sheets of a small treatise I am writing on the 'Inspiration of Scripture,'[1] and of which I hope to send you a copy shortly; and, as a relief from the strain of thinking, I now take up my pen to have a quiet talk with you. And if we at times find that it is a relief to unbosom our minds to a friend, what ought it to be to us to have the privilege of drawing near to a throne of grace, there to unbosom all our wants, our cares, and our griefs, aye, and our poor praises? We would not be presumptuous with the Lord, but holy familiarity is not presumption. People that live together in family have intercourse and communing that those outside do not know anything about; and does not our living in family as redeemed, adopted children, with the Father, the Son, and the Holy Ghost, suggest and warrant a holy liberty and intimacy of communion with God which the world knows nothing of? 'Because ye are sons, God hath sent forth the spirit of his Son into your hearts, crying, Abba, Father.'

For example, when we pray for our children, are we not ourselves to speak to God as children to a Father able and ready to help us? Are we not to be earnest and importunate in asking from him what we most of all desire for them, and that is their salvation? And can we contemplate

[1] [A reference to his book: *The Westminster Doctrine of the Inspiration of Scripture; With a Prefatory Note on the Free Church College Committee's Report, and with Remarks on Marcus Dods's Recent Sermon.* The preface was signed 'Montrose, April, 1877.' This was republished by the Free Presbyterian Church of Scotland in 1964.]

seriously the possibility of not getting an answer in peace regarding them, and not be stirred up to further solicitude and importunity on their behalf? Can we bear the thought that any one of them should be an enemy of God, and in a state of guilty and irrecoverable rebellion against him to all eternity? We cannot. And are we not in our prayers to tell this to God? We are. Are we not to tell him that we cannot and dare not anticipate anything less at his hands than the salvation of each one of them? Will he be offended if we tell him that we cannot endure the thought of their everlasting perdition—of their being left to be blasphemers of his name to all eternity? Will he be displeased if, in our infirmity and agony of feeling, we thus bring before his grace and power the case of their immortal souls? I do not believe that he will. Has he not said that from those who walk uprightly he will withhold no good thing (walking uprightly does not mean, as some foolishly imagine, walking in celestial perfection on earth, but walking within the bounds of the covenant of grace), and is not the salvation of the children whom God has committed to my care a 'good thing?' It may be true that in this matter I know not what spirit I am of, when I tell God that I cannot bear to think of any one of them being shut out for ever from his favour. But whatsoever spirit I am of in the matter, I shall tell the Lord of it fully and unreservedly, and he will know. And I will ask him, what did he give me the example of Jacob for, who wrestled for the blessing? What did he give me the promise of his word for, 'a seed shall serve him that shall be accounted to the Lord for a generation'? And what did he give me the name of Christ for, of whose name it is written that 'men shall be blessed in him, and all nations shall call him blessed'? And what did Christ leave the promise of the Holy Spirit with his church for, who, 'when he is come, reproves or convinces the world of sin, of righteousness, and of judgment'?

Also, when we pray for the church of God, for the cause of Christ, and for the advancement of his kingdom in the earth, are we not to use holy boldness? Have we not the Lord's own words—'The kingdom of heaven suffereth violence, and the violent take it by force'? Do we give Christ credit for the loving kindness and condescension manifested in such a prediction—'The kingdom suffers violence, and the violent take it by force'? Christ is there evidently contemplating with satisfaction his children importunate on behalf of the kingdom; he is contemplating some of such wrestling as he had seen done in the past, as to be done still, and again in the future. It is our supposed vindication of ourselves in getting quit of a troublesome beggar, 'O, the man was getting quite violent.' But it is Christ's vindication of himself for granting the victory and for bestowing the blessing—'O, the poor beggars are getting quite violent, I must suffer myself to yield, to be taken by them.' 'And he blessed him there!' And if Christ and his poor beggars understand one another, is not that enough? If he and they are of one mind—they not content without the blessing, and he not content without bestowing it—who else has any business or right to interfere? The devil, does he gainsay them? Ah, but Christ and his children are standing together in the heart of the promise—'I will put enmity between thee and the woman, and between thy seed and her seed'—and are thus railed in within an impregnable barrier which has been placed there by God's almighty hand. And, while Christ and his children stand together there within the fortress of the promise transacting their love-matches, Satan has been cursed off the ground with the beastliness of a creeping thing, awaiting in helpless rage and enmity the day when he and his seed shall be for ever shut out into the outer darkness.

This reminds me that I have a question to answer your A___, 'Is Satan glad at people's troubles?' God bless the boy and teach him, and lead him early into the paths of his salvation. What can I answer? I hope he doesn't think I have any special means of knowing the mind of the arch-enemy! Well, tell him from me that Satan is a being—a person—of pure unmingled malignity and venom, without a single good point to mitigate the unalleviated fullness that is in him of sin, and nothing but sin; not a single redeeming point about him to make him even pitiable or deserving of anything but the unrelieved eternity of woe that is before him. Perhaps this is not a direct answer, but, as I have told A___ what sort of a being Satan is, let him answer his own question himself. And tell him from me, moreover, that to incur Satan's hatred for fleeing to Jesus Christ—who is unmingled love and holiness, and who has in his cross triumphed over Satan and is blessed for ever, and blessed specially in blessing—to incur Satan's hatred for fleeing to Jesus is nothing to speak of, cruel and fearful though his hatred be. Yea, rather, if his hatred is incurred for Christ's sake it is something not only not to be dreaded but something we should be glad and thankful for having got grace to do.

But I have given you enough 'talk' to-night. With affectionate interest in you and yours.

I am, &c.,

Hugh Martin

9

Kindness, Scripture, Light

Edzell, Forfarshire, 28th May, 1878

My Dear Friend,

I came here for change of air last week, and am happy to say that I have not had a touch of headache since I came. My old friend, Mr Inglis, shows me much kindness, and wishes me to remain a month at least.

That expression which I have just used, 'shows me much kindness,' reminds me of a sight which I got lately of the dire unbelief of my heart. You know that when we say a man 'shows us kindness,' we mean that he gave us, or bestowed on us, kindness. Well, I was the other day reading and pondering over the 85th Psalm, and on coming to the 7th verse, 'Show us thy mercy, O Lord, and grant us thy salvation,' it struck me that 'showing' and 'granting' were here identical terms. Thus, if one is 'shown' mercy by God, it means that mercy is granted to him and given to him. Hence those to whom God has in any measure shown his salvation, ought not to doubt of his granting it to them, revelation being communicative, as in those other words, 'Show kindness and do good, O Lord, to Zion, thine own hill.' But I, in my dreadful unbelief, do often attribute less to God than I do to my fellow creature, for while I may have obtained some view of God's salvation in and through Christ, and have been 'shown' it as glorifying to God and suitable for sinners, I yet too often doubt God's willingness to grant or bestow it upon me. Yea, I may have obtained some spiritual knowledge of Christ and him crucified, and after all may doubt his willingness to give himself to me. As if the Holy One, the fountain of all blessing and blessedness, should show his salvation to a poor sinner, and then in effect tantalise him by saying, 'Do you not wish you may get it?' That be far from thee, O Lord, thou giver of all good; and yet that is in reality the language of unbelief! Oh, what would become of us if we had not a merciful and faithful High Priest, who has compassion on the ignorant and on those who are out of the way? 'Lord, I believe, help thou mine unbelief.'

Of course I am anxious today, and who is not, as to the debate in the Assembly.[1] Being here I will be a day behind in getting the newspaper, and shall not know the result of the vote until Thursday, unless my brother William wires to me tomorrow. Although not a member this year, I have made known my mind pretty freely to some of the brethren who are members, and although not at present in the high places of the field, yet my voice may be listened to none the less from the quiet places, where one can speak more calmly. And, indeed, by God's blessing that is already true, for my pamphlet on *The Inspiration of Scripture* has met with a good reception not only from able men in our own church, but also from honoured names in other churches, some of whom have written to thank me for what they are pleased to call 'a service to the cause of truth.' No doubt a few extreme folks blame me for being too hard on the College Committee, but I can bear that, so long as the positions I have laid down are unassailed, which, indeed, they cannot be, except at the cost of the assailant. And yet last Assembly uttered no whisper when the 'Report' of the Committee was laid before it, as to their divergence of view from that of the Confession, and to which I animadvert in my pamphlet. The Confession says: 'It pleased the Lord to commit the revelation of himself and of his will wholly unto writing,' &c. The Committee says: 'The revelation of God and of his will are committed wholly to writing,' thus avoiding to state by whom they were committed to writing; and if divine authorship is not maintained, divine authority falls to the ground. Alas! I fear there will soon come to light throughout our church courts an amount of sympathy with these unsound views such as will startle us. The United Presbyterian Church, by her recent action, has, in my opinion, 'made shipwreck'—neither more nor less. And the evils which she sanctions usually appear in the Free Church two or three years afterwards, so we may look out! Indeed, ____ has got into the habit of looking out,

---

[1] [Possibly a reference to the trial of Professor William Robertson Smith for heresy on account of his higher critical views of Scripture.]

and paving the way for the evils as they come. How sad that men in important positions do not ask themselves as to any undertaking they are about to engage in, 'How will this bear on the glory of God, and on the honour of his Word, which he has magnified above all his name?' but ask, 'How will this bear on our standing as before men?' We are all liable to regard the church of Christ too much as a 'business concern,' to be managed by experts; whereas it is the ordinance of God for the custody of his truth, 'set' in the world by his appointment and under his control 'for the defence of the gospel.' And as there is not in any land a nobler sight for the sun to shine on than a general assembly of a free, faithful, Scriptural church, for 'there is the testimony of Israel, there do sit the thrones of judgment, the thrones of the house of David,' so, therefore, it is with overwhelming dread and sorrow of heart that we contemplate anything occurring that would tarnish, or even compromise, our profession of holding that high and solemn position.

I observe your question as to getting light on the path of duty. My own experience is, that if I believe a certain course to be warranted by the Word of God, I must go forward, although I have not light given me on probable issues and consequences. If, under a sense of my weakness, I stipulate for light and liberty before I go forward, the Lord may withhold it, because I am not yet in the actual need of it, and would most likely abuse it if I got it. It is usually in the performance of duty, and not before it, that the Lord vouchsafes that light and strength which supports the poor weakling, and confirms him in the all-graciousness of him 'under whose wings he hath come to trust.'

And now, 'my right trusty and well-beloved cousin' (as the Queen says of the Lord High Commissioner), let me just add that I hope to hear from you soon. I do not know that I can visit you this summer, but if not, it will not be for want of grateful recollections of my former visit. Indeed, the remembrance of the extent to which I drew upon your kindness is often simply oppressive.

Yours, &c.,

Hugh Martin

10

Word and Spirit

Montrose, 19th November, 1879

My Dear Friend

Do you understand the state of things in our poor church? I do not. What I am afraid for is the doctrine of the Trinity. Of course shallow folks (and they are too numerous) would laugh at my saying so. But although I cannot enter on it here, yet let me tell you that a church's hold on the doctrine of the Trinity is affected by her hold of the doctrine of the inspiration of Scripture. There is an inevitable certainty that when the infallibility of inspiration is questioned, in that measure Sabellianism gets a footing. For it is in virtue of a truly inspired Word—his own Word—that the Holy Spirit acts as a person. It is degradation to the Third Person of the Godhead to suppose that he would speak by the word or words of any person less than himself. He does not speak at all as a person by any word less than his own Word, or the Word of the Son, or the Word of the Father, all which are one. To suppose the Spirit coming by a new and fresh revelation is of course Quakerism, but in his coming by a previously written inspired Word, he acts as a person. As a person he speaks, enlightens, convinces, persuades, and renews. Deprive him of his own Word, of Christ's and the Father's Word, then the Spirit is made to be only a force, overcoming just as force overcomes, as a hatchet knocks down a bullock. Deal falsely with personality here, then the Holy Spirit does not combine with the Second Person, but falls back upon an impersonal Deity—a Thing. You have merely what is implied in 'God is a Spirit,' but Word is gone, Father is gone, Sonship is gone, Messiahship is gone, Mediatorial position is gone, infernal robbery has been committed, and the mists of darkness have settled down upon the church! Yea, we are not a church at all, for we are robbed of a divine revelation, of a divine record. The privileges and position of a church are given 'chiefly because unto them were committed the oracles of God.' Alas! that so many who ought to be teachers deal as falsely and irreverently with the oracles of God as a cat playing with her kitten, or a kitten with a cork.

I am sorely afraid that there is to be a great decline in our church, a great lack of holy courage in contending for the infallible truth of the entire Scriptures, and truly men that can tolerate the substitution of the natural for the supernatural, of human reason for divine revelation, are not only no longer worth their sustentation, but are no longer 'worth their salt.' May God raise up men taught from above, and valiant for every jot and tittle of divine truth, for it shall stand should heaven and earth pass away. And if you meet any after I am gone who do courageously stand for all revealed truth, give them my compliments, and tell them to be strong and of a good courage, for now, even at this present time, their heads shall be lifted up above their foes. Let them yield not to the current sentimental Christianity that would convert men's faith in a living, glorious, inexhaustible, infallible Word into empty-headed, empty-hearted speculations no better than Chinese puzzles or acted charades. God will avenge such trifling. 'The Scripture cannot be broken,' is the testimony of him who is himself the eternal Word. And will he suffer it to go unpunished if the divine truth which he has in infinite condescension been pleased to make known to men by means of an infallibly inspired record—will he suffer it to go unpunished if that truth be broken up into bits and shreds, into fragments and fancies? And if the 'Lord will not hold them guiltless who take his name in vain,' he will not, assuredly, hold that church guiltless, which tolerates any profaning or abusing of that Word by which he hath made himself known. We pity poor silly papists who ascribe infallibility to mortal men, but what are we to think of proud, self-blinded Protestants who deny infallibility to the written words of the God of truth?[1]

Yours, &c.,

Hugh Martin

---

[1] [Part of this letter was quoted in *The Scotsman*, 25th February, 1889. It was republished in *The Bulwark: Magazine of the Scottish Reformation Society* (2011) January–March, p. 4.]

P.S.—I cannot get myself satisfied speaking of the blessed combination of Word and Spirit. What is it but the very manifested light of Jehovah. God dwelleth in light that is inaccessible and full of glory, and which no man can see or approach unto; with thee, O God, is the fountain of light. Nevertheless, the church says, 'In thy light shall we see light.' In thy light which would otherwise be inaccessible, we, through the illumination of thy Word and Spirit—thy light—'shall see light.' Thus, whoso of the children of men hath in any measure come into this light, becomes one of God's 'hidden ones,' hidden in this world, not from dread of that light into which they have been brought but hidden because of the excess of its purity, its brightness, and its glory.

H. M.

11

A Crumb is Not Enough

Montrose, 4th January, 1880

My Dear Friend,

I will have to be brief today, and you will not grudge brevity when I tell you that I have quite a number of new year's greetings—friendly souvenirs in the shape of books, &c.—to acknowledge, all which kindnesses on the part of friends should fill my heart with gratitude, although I have many trials and tossings to act as ballast. But I believe it is best for us to be kept in our own place by the stinging thorns of affliction, if nothing else will do, than to be allowed to take our own way—the way, too often, of folly and of pride.

I hope this will find you well—well in soul and in body. I trust also that ___ is getting better, and that it may please the Lord to spare him for service in the church on earth; but, if otherwise designed, it is because the Lord has a higher sphere of work for him in the church above. And yet I have sometimes thought, as to the office of the ministry in the church on earth, that if we realized in the least measure the inconceivably momentous issues to immortal souls— issues of either an eternity of bliss or of an eternity of woe, according as they receive or reject the gospel message—we must feel that we know not if, even in heaven itself, there will be work more important than the proclamation to sinners of the blessed gospel of the grace of God, which brings 'glory to God in the highest,' and in which all the adorable perfections and attributes of the Triune Jehovah are harmonized and magnified to the very uttermost.

I observe that you say in your last letter, 'The communion is to be observed in Dingwall first Sabbath of next month, and I wish I could be there in spirit, if only to get a crumb of what will be going; come you too.' With all my heart, but your invitation is after all too late, for I am there in spirit already. I had a letter from the dear host announcing the forthcoming solemnity, and in replying to him, I enclosed a card to be placed on the parlour mantelpiece so that the assembled friends and brethren might see it, and on the card I wrote, 'A brother, cast down but not destroyed, desires a place in your supplications and sympathies.' But then, as it is with 'all my heart' that I respond to your invitation, there comes as usual a scolding for you. For what? For saying you would like to be there to get a *crumb*. Now, it is very right and proper that after a feast of Christ's is over, we, in view of our ill-deservingness and nothingness, should be thankful for the smallest crumb—the very least taste of Christ and him crucified that may have been vouchsafed to us. But that is a very different thing from preparing and arranging beforehand to be content with just a crumb, seeing that the Lord says, 'Open thy mouth wide and I will fill it.' This systematic cutting down and limiting and diminishing of the grace that is in Christ's words is very far from being honouring or pleasing to him, and it ought not to be allowed to go on, as if our object was to get the minimum or smallest portion consistent with our getting anything at all. Christ has not stinted the provision of the covenant. 'He gave himself for us.' Neither has he stinted the bestowal of the provision. 'Ho! every one that thirsteth, come ye to the waters, and he that hath no money; come ye, buy, and eat; yea, come, buy wine and milk without money and without price.' Are we then, as it were, to stint our own mercy, so far as in our power, by our unbelief, our unwillingness, and our unthankfulness? O! be not content without getting Christ—a whole Christ—to dwell in your heart by faith. Be importunate with him to give you soul appetite, yea, heart relish for the provision of Zion.

Am I too hard upon you? Well, say, 'his bark is worse than his bite,' and you know that the bark of the St. Bernard's dog has sometimes done good service to poor travellers. So do not think I have been scolding you, or if you do, take it as a very affectionate scolding, for I would desire, especially in this first week of a new year, to greet you well and lovingly in the name of him in whom all time centres, and who inhabiteth the praises of eternity.

Yours, &c.

Hugh Martin

~

12

A Terrible Answer

Montrose, 12th February, 1880

My Dear Friend,

I wrote you very briefly last time, and have not heard from you since the Dingwall Communion. I therefore do not know how it fared with you in your attempt to join the dear people there in spirit at that time, but I shall tell you how it fared with myself.

You will remember that I told you I had sent a card for the mantelpiece, with the words, 'A brother cast down but not destroyed desires an interest in your supplications;' and I believe the card was placed where I directed, and was observed by the assembled friends. Well, on that Sabbath forenoon (the 1st *inst.*) as I went out at the house door to go to church, I suddenly felt a strange giddiness come over me, such as I never felt before, and my head reeled and my sight seemed to fail, and I would have fallen with all my weight to the ground had it not mercifully occurred to me to seize hold of an iron chain that was on the gravel walk, and letting myself down gradually I lay for some minutes in a half-conscious state. By-and-by, feeling a little better, I got up and staggered back into the house, but was sufficiently ill to have to go to bed, where I had to remain for a day or two. The doctor attributed it to something wrong with my stomach, but I myself accounted for it very differently. I considered that it was sent for daring to call myself 'A brother cast down but not destroyed,' for one who truly is such is one who bears about in his body the dying of the Lord Jesus, and if I took the title presumptuously the Lord was to teach me otherwise. For, my dear friend, it is no light matter to take to oneself any of the characteristics of the humbled, emptied children of God. The Scripture cannot be broken, and he who is 'A brother cast down but not destroyed' is one that has been brought low in soul as deserving the wrath of God due to him for sin; he is 'cast down' because he sees no hope or help in himself whereby he can be delivered from the just consequences of his apostasy from God, and he feels that if he is not utterly 'destroyed' it is because a possibility of deliverance has been opened for such as he is, through the casting down even unto death of God's Eternal Son, who was 'sent forth, made of a woman, made under the law, to redeem them that were under the law, that they might receive the adoption of sons.' Therefore, the Lord saw fit that I should be cast down literally that I might learn that there is but a step between me and death, and that I might also examine and see to it, that my life is a living in the fellowship of the humiliation of the Lord Jesus, 'bearing about in my body his dying, that I may become conformable unto his death,' and which means a seeking and cherishing by grace, somewhat of that spirit of lowliness, of meekness, of self-denial, of hatred of sin, and of zeal for righteousness and truth, which animated the holy Jesus in all that he did and suffered. Moreover, the Lord by this incident showed me that the prayers of his dear people were not to be offered for me on a misunderstanding, but that I should in spirit, in soul, and in body, be in the very case indicated. 'By terrible things in righteousness dost thou answer us, O God of our salvation.' And if God shows me that I am not to take his words and apply them to myself, except in their true connection, for the Scripture cannot be broken, may I not with adoring prostrate reverence say to him that therefore I expect that he will not either apply them except in their true connection?—that if he gives me in answer to prayer terrible things in righteousness, I expect he will give them to me in the connection in which he himself has put them in his own word, when he says of those to whom these terrible things in righteousness are given: 'Blessed are they whom thou choosest and causest to approach unto thee, they shall be satisfied with the goodness of thy house, even of thy holy temple.'

I heard from Dingwall that Dr [*John*] Kennedy's subject on the Sabbath was, 'God is love, and he that dwelleth in love dwelleth in God, and God in him.' Would it not have been a feast to have heard him? Dr [*Gustavus*] Aird's text on Monday was, 'As ye have received Christ Jesus the Lord so walk in him, rooted and built up in him, &c.' I would like to have heard that too, for that passage of Scripture has long been a favourite one with me, although too good for me ever to have tried to preach upon. How exceedingly rich and gracious, and encouraging, that there should be in Christ for the poor, weak believer the advantages to be derived from both a foundation and a root. 'Rooted and built up in him.' Their state and standing is laid or built on Christ as the foundation, and he is also the root from whence they draw all the life and nourishment needed for their being established in the faith, and enabled to offer that thanksgiving which is the dutiful form in which their adherence to him ought to be expressed—'abounding therein with thanksgiving.' Still, Dingwall is not heaven, and preaching is not Christ, although, after all, the chief desire of my soul is to be enabled so to preach Christ as that by the power of the Holy Spirit he would be received and welcomed into the hearts of some sinful men and women who should be to me a crown of rejoicing in the day when I shall have to give account of my stewardship. And if this will be the 'glory and joy' (as Paul says) of the poor earthen vessels, what will it be, my dear friend, to behold the King himself in that day, to see him, ay, and to share in 'the joy that was set before him'—the joy of wearing the crown wherewith his mother crowned him in the day of his espousals and in the day of the gladness of his heart!

Hugh Martin

13

Getting the Benefit of the Promise

Montrose, 17th March, 1880

My Dear Friend,

Your last letter pleased me much, with the exception of one sentence in which you say, 'I wish I could believe that God was as favourably disposed towards me as you are.' You will next be saying, in the supremacy of your theological attainments, 'I wish I could believe that God was as wise and as good as you are.' Now, why am I doomed to be thus always affectionately finding fault with you? Suppose that my letters are, as you say, 'cheering and helpful,' are they not very far from being 'good and perfect'? You know well that 'every good and perfect gift cometh down alone from above, from the Father of Lights, with whom is no variableness, neither shadow of turning.'

Why are you still 'off and on' in this way? Why ever saying, 'I could not take this, I would not presume to believe *that*, I fear such and such a promise of the Word was not meant for *me*.'? Who was it meant for, if not for you and the like of you? We read that 'it is a faithful saying, and worthy of all acceptation, that Christ Jesus came into the world to save sinners,' and if I say, 'That's for me, that suits me—a sinner—a chief sinner,' would you take the bread of life out of my mouth and say, 'No, that's not meant for you'? Well, if you would scarcely do so to me, why do it to yourself? Do you think God is honoured thereby? Far otherwise; for if we are not, as sinners, to bring our needs and our wants alongside the promises of God in his Word, and plead their fulfilment to our own special case, I do not know for what reason he has put these promises in his Word, or how else we are to get the benefit of them. O! it's a grand thing to gather up, as it were, everything—everything—all that we are and have been and have done, as lost, self-destroyed sinners, and all that we need that

Christ should do for us; and lay the weight of all, over on the grace and faithfulness of the promise that tells of a Saviour to the uttermost, and give that promise a fair trial, and see if it will bear us, and all our weight of sin and guilt, of helplessness and misery. For the promise was not to Abraham and his seed through the righteousness of the law, but through the righteousness of faith; and if they which are of the law be heirs, then faith is made void and the promise made of none effect. 'Faith made void and the promise made of none effect'—what a collapse! Then all from Abraham downward who have relied on the promise have their foundation taken away, and heaven is made empty if the promise is made of none effect. It need not now be asked—'Who are these that are arrayed in white robes, and whence *came* they?' but 'whither are they *gone*?' Also these holy beings who never sinned, but who stand confirmed by the Word of the Lord, they may call on the rocks to pity them and fall on them, for if the promise is made of none effect their foundation is insecure and uncertain. But these are only creatures placed in jeopardy, but what of the unchanging Jehovah, our Lord and our God? What of him? Is his Word, by which the heavens were of old and by which all things consist, is his Word to go out in smoke and to vanish into eternal falsehood? For so it would be if faith is made void and the promise made of none effect. 'Oh!' you say, 'these are terrible thoughts.' Not more terrible than true, for if we are to contemplate faith made void and the promise made of none effect, we must contemplate all the consequences that would relentlessly follow thereupon. If there were reason to doubt by one hair's breadth the veracity of that Word which upholdeth all things in heaven and in earth, if there were reason to suspect by one jot or by one tittle that faith would be made void and the promise made of none effect, there were equal reason to assume the eclipse and collapse of all that glory of God which by his unalterable Word he has manifested and made known. But blessed for ever be he who hath said—'The Scripture cannot be broken. Heaven and earth shall pass away, but my Word shall never pass away.'

Somehow I cannot help thinking that the time is not far off when it will please the Lord to batter and break down these secret nooks and corners of unbelief that you are too fond of hiding in, to bring you out from these false refuges that you are too fond of sheltering in, and to make you see that they will never do. It is when we are hunted out from every vain confidence that we are fitted to hear the Lord's declaration of free saving mercy, and to listen with silent adoring wonder to such gracious avowals as this—'I have loved thee with an everlasting love, therefore with lovingkindness have I drawn thee.' 'Let me see thy countenance, let me hear thy voice, for sweet is thy voice and thy countenance is comely.' And should her disconsolate countenance be that day blurred and blotted with tears—as well it may be—and should her voice be broken and discordant—as indeed it is—yet when Christ's voice is heard in accents of grace and love, her countenance will be no more sad but will be worthwhile even for him to look upon, and her voice will be no more songless but will be worthwhile even for him to listen to, for all that is within her shall that day leap for joy; and there shall be none in heaven or in earth to hinder her, yea, not a voice raised even in hell to say, 'What doest thou?'

Somehow, as I said, I think this day is not very far off. Go away then and seek it, and plead for it on the ground of Christ's own promise—'Blessed are the poor in spirit, for theirs is the kingdom of heaven. Blessed are they that mourn, for they shall be comforted.'

Yours, &c.

Hugh Martin

14

To a Bereaved Friend

Montrose, 22nd April, 1880

My Beloved Friend,[1]

I want to come in spirit beside you, for I would fain turn aside and see the voice that speaks with us, even although I should fall at his feet as dead; for he lays his right hand upon us and says—'Fear not, I am he that liveth and was dead, and behold, I am alive for evermore, and have the keys of the unseen world and of death.'

We have all heard the sound of these 'keys,' as they hang at the golden girdle of our risen, ascended Lord, and which have been the means, I believe, of bringing to dear ___ the first ecstasy of perfect love, perfect certainty, and perfect bliss, and of calling forth the first rapturous cry—'Unto him that loved us and washed us from our sins in his own blood, and hath made us kings and priests unto God and his Father, to him be glory and dominion for ever and ever, amen.' And we shall all soon need the use of these 'keys' for our own poor weary souls, and sweet music shall they be to those who have already heard the sound of the 'golden bells' that adorn the hem of the garments of our great High Priest, as from within his holy place he is the minister of peace to his sin-stricken people—that peace from which spring true humility, holiness, and love, and which springs itself from forgiveness of sin, even from redemption through the blood of the Lamb.

I cannot write to you, but I have wept sore with you and for you these days. What did the Lord mean by making me—a blind, ignorant creature, give you warning that he was coming?—coming, as I said, to break down the secret fortresses in which you were hiding, and to bring you out to meet with himself. And now that he has come, I trust it is in order to his enabling you to fall down before him and to say—'Thy will be done. Be it unto me even as thou wilt.' Seize, then,

---

[1] [Written on getting notice of a bereavement.]

the opportunity of his coming very nigh, and seek by grace to make an absolute and complete surrender of yourself, and of all that concerns you, into the Lord's hands. O! it is a sweet sight—a sight that even Jehovah delights in—when a humbled sinner is brought to lie low at the feet of the sovereign Lord, at the feet of infinite love, at the feet of crucified grace, and, while recognizing his holy smiting hand, yet looks up, even amid breaking heart-strings, and says—'Thy will be done.' For, in a love that hath been from everlasting, are there never to come moments of rapture?—moments giving token of the time when, the flesh being abolished, that which is born of the spirit and is spirit shall look forth through creation and providence with an eye like unto God's own eye, and in response to his 'I am the Lord thy God, worship thou me,' shall reply in deepest, lowliest adoration, 'Thou art the Lord my God.' Ah! a broken-hearted sinner at Christ's feet has a keen scent and a tender feeling, though it may have poor logic, and then is the time when one may be trusted not to abuse grace but to welcome it, and to rejoice in it, and in it alone.

I shall not intrude further. It may be a little while before you can write to me, but never mind, I shall get a letter by-and-bye, when it will be no effort. Remember David's gracious meekness, how he arose and anointed himself and went into the house of the Lord and worshipped. Grace and peace be with you.

Your smitten brother,

Hugh Martin

15

Vital Faith

Maryton, Montrose, 12th May, 1880

My Dear Friend,

I long to hear from you. Have I never an affliction that you seem to wish to be apart from me in your sorrow; I, from whom, what is it can you tell, that the Lord hath not taken? What would become of such as I am, were it not that the 'will of God' is to be seen coming forth in and through the sufferings of Christ to 'sanctify, or set apart and make godly' the lonely ones for himself, and to bring them more and more into experimental conformity with him who had to say, 'I am become a stranger to my brethren, an alien to my mother's children.' Therefore, though we be afflicted it is for your sakes, as Paul says; or whether we be comforted it is also for your sakes, for our hope of you is steadfast, yes, steadfast as the everlasting hills, that as ye are partakers of the sufferings, so shall ye be also of the consolations.

I do not know when I have suffered more in sympathy with a bereaved one than with you, not only at the first, but since I got your message, that you lacked the faith that would follow the forerunner within the veil. But, my dear friend, the glory within the veil does not need your faith of it in order that its tides of blessing may keep pouring in upon the spirits of the just made perfect. We are sometimes apt to mistake between faith and imagination, and to think that if we have not lively views of heavenly things we have not faith. But faith is not a view. At least it is not a view of a scene, it is a crediting and honouring of God on the ground of his own Word, and he has himself told us by the mouth of the apostle what is the place and the work of faith both as regards Divine truth and human destiny when it is said that salvation 'is of faith, that it might be by grace.' That text is like a delicate and beautiful balance—its two scales being grace and faith—'it is of faith that it may be by grace,' and you cannot touch the one scale without affecting the other also. Now, in self-jealousy you doubt concerning the one scale—your faith, but do you doubt concerning the other—God's grace? Do you not believe that in and through Christ grace reigneth, grace aboundeth, yea, that Christ is grace and gives grace, and is given by grace? You do believe that. Then let that scale alone, and let us examine the other—your faith. Both God and you are agreed that salvation is by grace, but that in order to your actually obtaining it, it must be of faith. The grace is certain and undoubted, certain on God's part and undoubted on yours. But the faith must exist also, in order to our salvation. But have you not just said that salvation is by grace, and is not that faith? If you believe in grace, is not that faith? If you accept of grace, is not that faith? If you welcome grace, is not that faith? If you submit to grace is not that faith? What are you puzzling at? The only need-be for faith is, that it may be by grace. Are you to make a god of your faith, as if it were the source of salvation, whereas it is only the empty space into which grace pours a free, full, and finished salvation? Therefore, look up to God, and confess your unbelief, your ignorance, and your folly, and tell him that you must be indebted to him not only for salvation from sin, but for salvation from unbelief, and from error too. Is not that as good faith as there is need for? And tell him also that you are resolved to stick to his own terms, that salvation is by grace; and since he has said that it is to be by grace, your believing his Word makes it yours by faith.

Now, I have given you a few sentences, which may the Lord be pleased to bless, for your help and comfort.

Hoping to hear from you soon.

Your true friend,

Hugh Martin

〜

16

Christ's Offices

Montrose, 8th June, 1880

My Dear Friend,

I was glad to see your handwriting again, and to know that you found cause of thanksgiving and praise, as well as of mourning and sorrow in the recent dispensation with which you have been visited. Believe me, or rather believe the Word of the Lord, 'Yet God is good to Israel.'

I am sending you by this post a small treatise I have written and published, *The Prophetic Office of Christ*[1] the proof sheets of which you saw last winter. I myself see no merit in the little work except perhaps its catholicity. All the leading doctrines of Christianity may be gathered from it, yet not one word indicating to what branch of the visible Church the writer belongs. That is something, and something attained without being thought of or aimed at by me when writing. But the treatise itself is simply a shell from the shores of the ocean of divine truth. The glory of Christ's prophetical office—the combination of Word and Spirit—which is truly and fully just Christ himself as the ever-living and ever infallible Teacher in his Church, is far too little regarded in present-day thinking and teaching. Ah! it is when the Church hears Christ's own voice in and through the written Word, that she will have a testimony for him to give such as shall convince an unbelieving world—a testimony the voice of which is 'Whom having not seen, we love, in whom, though now we see him not, yet *believing,* we rejoice with joy unspeakable and full of glory.'

I am not to write at length today, for I am troubled with rheumatic pains which flit down even to my fingers. And yet you were carving out more work for me. Well, if spared and able, I should like next to bring out something on Christ's kingly office; if only the thoughts were God-given. A running commentary on the kingly Psalms would be the line I

[1] [See page 403 of this volume.]

should like to adopt. For example, the 2nd, the 8th, the 24th, the 45th, and the 89th. Then the 90th, and those that follow with their repeated anthem, 'The Lord doth reign.' Next would come, 'Grace reigns,' a glorious theme, and lastly, '*They* shall reign, they who receive grace and the gift of righteousness, they shall reign in life by one, by Christ Jesus.'

Do you know I sometimes think I hear the words said, 'Ye ought to be strong, and to remember the infirmities of the weak'? Who are to help 'the weak' if such do not who have been long fed and watered in the pastures of divine truth? Is it right to be expecting to be always nursed and dandled, taking up, as it were, the time of the Great Physician with simply one's own case, when the professing Church and a world lying in wickedness need him so sorely? Who are to help 'the weak' if they do not who have again and again received help at the Lord's gracious hands? His word to his followers was, 'Freely ye have received, freely give.' Are we prepared to turn round and say, 'Lord, we did not receive very freely, we did not receive very much, we will wait until we receive more fully and more largely before we endeavour to give out?' Truly, if that is our way of it, we need not wonder although we are left to be useless and unsavoury; 'That which was kept of the manna until the morning bred worms, and stank.' Therefore, while we ought to wait on the Lord for the opportunities and the encouragements to engage in his service, we ought to be ourselves in our hearts and lives that very workmanship which would glorify him, and which might be a means of blessing to others. We ought to be his witnesses, witnesses to the power of his grace and truth; and we ought to be his remembrancers giving him no rest till he arise and build up Zion, and make her a praise in the earth.

What did you think of last Assembly? It appears to be forgotten that some of the views now called 'new' were known and debated in the Church centuries ago, so that our young critics seem to me like so many relics of the middle ages!

But I am not to begin another sheet, so conclude at present.

Yours, &c.,

Hugh Martin

17

The Foundation Blessing

Montrose, 3rd July, 1880

My Dear Friend,

How are you? 'Faint,' perhaps, 'yet pursuing,' the Lord doing you good. I mean doing you good to your obvious perception thereof, for he cannot do you other than good, world without end.

I wish to tell you that you may help me to praise the Lord for it, that during the past few weeks he has been graciously pleased to be revisiting and reviving my poor and needy soul. Humbly let me say it, yet to the honour of his grace, he has been leading me to the green pastures and beside the still waters, and restoring me in the paths of righteousness for his own name's sake. Therefore, 'extol the Lord with me, let us exalt his name together.'

In considering what were the *means* which the Lord was pleased to employ, and through which he drew near, I may say it was in connection with that too much neglected and despised invitation of his Word. 'Turn you at my reproof, behold I will pour out my Spirit unto you, I will make known my words unto you.' O! do we! do we realise the exhaustless supply there set before us, and to which we are bidden welcome? Do we realise the wondrous privilege of being warranted yea encouraged 'to turn'? Do we realise the greatness of the blessing promised by him who cannot lie, 'I will pour out my Spirit unto you, I will make known my words unto you'? It is in substance the same blessing as was held out to the woman of Samaria. 'If thou hadst asked of him he would have given thee living water.' Are we, therefore, dry and parched as we may be, but on the warrant of God's own invitation 'turning' and 'asking' these blessings which he has been pleased to declare he is willing to bestow? In speaking thus, it is with myself I am reasoning, though it may not be inapplicable to you too.

I have also been thinking lately of that glorious foundation of all our blessings—the death of Christ. How ashamed we should be of our low and superficial views of that blessed mystery into which even angels desire to look! Christ in and by his death defeated and destroyed death—the death that was the penalty of his people's sins. He was even in death a powerful triumphant conqueror, a slain Lamb yet a living Priest. His death, although it was the separation of his soul from his body, was the separation of neither from his Godhead or from himself, for his personality is in his Godhead. He was the Living One while vanquishing the death due to his people in and by his own death. He also went to the grave; not his dead body merely, 'Come see the place where the Lord lay.' He likewise rose from the dead; not merely 'was raised,' but re-uniting his paradisaically-blessed soul and his lifeless body, he arose. 'The Lord is risen indeed.' And all this he did as his people's surety, and this triumph they will share with him, he the first fruits and afterwards they that are his. Pity poor Unitarians and praise God for a Divine Saviour! I have expanded these thoughts in an article I have written for next issue of the *British and Foreign Evangelical Review,* and shall send you a copy when it is out.[1]

I have also an article in this month's issue on 'Justification by Faith.'[2] It may not be relished by those who hold erroneous views of the atonement, but if any seekers after scriptural views of it are benefitted or helped, I don't care should a thousand whipper-snappers call me 'an old wife.' I have an impression that my writing days are nearly over, that the time is not very far off when Christ shall be, not to my fitful faith, but to my endless enjoyment, the 'Pearl of great price.' Indeed, with my broken health, it will be but a fight to the end, but in the hope that the end will end the fighting, all is well.

Write soon.

Yours affectionately,

Hugh Martin

---

[1] [See page 193 of this volume. This mention, and the fact that the article referred to is signed 'μ,' is one of the proofs that Martin used 'μ' as his pen-name.]

[2] [See page 221 of this volume.]

18

Time as Reckoned by God

Montrose, 20th July, 1880

My Dear Friend,

I have been 'learning my questions' according to your authoritative directions, but to be fair to me, was it not on the supposition of continued broken health that I spoke as I did? I am also ill of a disease without something of which I could hardly keep up any sense of self-respect, *viz.*, a grumbling and grudging over my uselessness in the Church and in the world. That sense of uselessness along with my broken health affords little reason why I should wish to live always. But the Lord's will be done. If he is pleased to give me health wherewith to serve him and his Church a little longer, I am willing, although as regards our own Church, alas! the more abundantly I love her the less I am loved!

Did it strike you that I have been too rash and ready of late, to say things that indicate an assurance of my own personal salvation? It may have been so, but you know I have been, as a rule, so sorely kept down, that if the Lord has been pleased to give a faith's glimpse of what he has provided for his children, surely a little bit of joyous scamper towards the confines of that everlasting inheritance may be allowed? Especially when all is seen to be the provision of grace, when Christ himself is seen as the gift of that grace, ready, fit, yea, waiting to be received by the poor sinner that has nothing, not the least coin wherewith to purchase the least blessing. We may think we ought to give, if not a price, at least some return for blessing received, but I have come to feel myself so strengthless, so helpless, so empty and dependent, that even if I had something to give (which I have not), I have not strength to give it. Giving, therefore, can no longer be my investment, it must be taking. And in the measure in which the freeness, the fullness, and the all-sufficiency that is in Christ is apprehended by faith, in that measure will I become content to take at God's hand what he is pleased to give, and to say, 'Even so, Lord, be it unto me as thou wilt.'

But I am writing too much about myself. It is, however, almost my settled persuasion—although I am not saying anything about it to any one—(what good would that do?)—that I shall not long be able to hold intercourse with you. For one thing, I see truths with which I have been familiar from my childhood in a new light, the light of eternity. When reading this morning the first chapter of Genesis, where it is written 'the evening and the morning were the first day, the evening and the morning were the second day,' &c., &c.; it occurred to me that men do not reckon time as God reckons it. He says, 'The evening and the morning are a day,' we say, 'from the morning till the evening is a day.' But soon we shall reckon as God reckons. We shall begin our reckoning in the 'evening' of this mortal life, looking back on all its darkening clouds and deepening shadows, on all its precarious paths, and sorrowful stumblings, and we shall end our reckoning in the 'morning' of the bright rising of the 'Sun of Righteousness,' whose glorious beams shall usher in the full noon-day light of glory. Of that glorious noon-day we may reverently say that it shall be 'infinite, eternal, and unchangeable.'

Yours, dear friend, until its dawning,

Hugh Martin

THE PROPHETIC OFFICE
OF CHRIST[1]

A Letter to My Daughters on the Prophetic Office of Christ

*'Thou art fairer than the sons of men: grace is poured into
thy lips: therefore God hath blessed thee for ever.'*
—Psalm 45:2

My Darlings,

It has occurred to me that, as I have so little opportunity of fellowship with you, I might put in form for you some views of the person
and character of our ever-blessed Redeemer, not doubting that you will
accept this as a true and good expression of the profound love I have for
you, and the deep interest I take in your spiritual and eternal welfare.[2]

It is characteristic of living Christians that they are anxious to be
able to answer the question, 'What think ye of Christ?' They know of no
question of equal importance. Politics and science are valuable; literature
and art are ornamental to the character. To be able to answer such
questions as—'What think ye of Milton? of Shakespeare? of Spencer?
of Wordsworth? of Tennyson? or (let us say), of Moses? or, of Paul,
as contributors to the literature of the world?'—is something. But
towering above these, in infinitely greater grandeur, is the question
which men and nations will soon have to answer with a promptness
to which they have seldom hitherto been shut up:—'*What think ye
of Christ?*'

[1] [Originally published as a pamphlet: *Letter to my Daughters on the Prophetic
Office of Christ* (Montrose: George Walker, 1880).]

[2] [This was an actual, *bona fide*, letter. There was no intention of its publication
until the writer and his dear correspondents agreed that it might be useful.]

Many answers may be given, all more or less accurate, so far as they go: being unsatisfactory chiefly through defect. I am very conscious that this is true concerning the following answer; but I give it for all that, because it seems to awaken interest, and to lead to a good deal of thought—a pretty full following up of which, if done justice to, might give a somewhat complete view of the person, and character, and position of our Saviour. I would say, then, that,—Jesus Christ is that man (being God also) for whom God, the Holy Spirit, hath done everything that God could do, inwardly (subjectively), by the working of grace, to qualify him for being the loving, powerful, effective Redeemer of lost men; and for whom God, the Father, hath done everything that God could do, outwardly (objectively), by communications of power and glory, at his own right hand, to qualify him for carrying out his redemption work, unto the actual salvation and eternal blessedness of a people whom no man can number.

Besides these two mutually supplementing statements, I would say,—That, thus sustained of the Holy Ghost, and to be thus rewarded of the Father, he did, himself, the Son of God, and Second Person of the Godhead, in human flesh and blood, lay down his life and resume it, in glorious freedom from all manner of compulsion, in actings of love and power and holiness, commanded (John 10:18) thereunto by the Father's authority, and securing therein the Father's approbation (John 10:17). And this he did by way of redeeming—and that righteously, effectively and eternally redeeming—to God (to be his servants and children and portion,—the travail, moreover, of his own soul, unspeakably beloved to all eternity, the ransomed friends and followers of the Lamb) the same people whom no man can number, and who, consequently, shall have to all eternity, a standing under God's government, a place near his throne,—a relation to, and powerful bearing upon, his purposes, and council, and government,—like unto which, there shall be no other. 'A peculiar people.' 'The Lord's portion is his people: Jacob is the lot of his inheritance' (1 Pet. 2:9; and Deut. 32:9).

It is meet and suitable, therefore, that Jesus Christ should occupy a place in the love, gratitude, and admiration of his redeemed, quite peculiar and unique; and a place in the praises and celebrations of heaven, and in the power, and public dignity of the universe, altogether unapproachable. Accordingly, we find all reasonable beings—all who are around the throne, and acknowledge the reign and government of God—well-nigh exhausting the powers which God has given them, in heaping honour, and glory, and power, and praise upon the Lamb of God—the actually redeemed from among men adding. '*For he was slain for us.*'

It certainly ought to be matter of ambition with us to have our understandings filled with knowledge concerning this adorable person, and our hearts filled with love to him. In spirit, we should be able, already, to join with genuine enthusiasm in these heavenly songs; and we ought to cherish the desire—to foster, strengthen, confirm, cherish into enthusiastic hope and longing, the desire—to be in due time present in the scene of such holy joy and sacred delight.

And if it promote this end, that I now attempt to think and speak somewhat carefully about Jesus, as the supreme office-bearer in the Church, my labour will not be in vain. Be it understood, then, that I mean to speak, especially of,—*Christ in his Prophetic Office.*

It is not easy to separate the actings of Christ as a Redeemer into such distinct lines as shall be clear from each other. Yet there are evidently certain such lines of action wherein Christ is seen communicating light and knowledge, understanding and wisdom, and counsel, for instance, rather than exercising authority or power, or obtaining gifts and blessings;—such lines of action as entitle us to say that in all this he is acting out the calling, claims, and requirements of a particular office: and without either giving the predictive element a very high place in it, or yet entirely excluding it, we call this the Prophetic Office.

'Christ executeth the office of a prophet, in revealing to us by his Word and Spirit, the will of God for our salvation.'

The Father repeatedly testifies of Jesus in this office. Clearly he commends Christ to us, as a prophet, when in his baptism he testifies of him—'This is my beloved Son, hear ye him.' We are here commanded to take all knowledge and instruction from him: to make him in all things our source of intelligence, our fountain of light and wisdom. At the transfiguration it was the same. In the prophecies of Isaiah, also, there occur frequent commendations of this heavenly prophet to our respectful and obedient regards:—'Behold my servant whom I uphold: mine elect, in whom my soul delighteth: I have put my Spirit upon him...A bruised reed shall he not break, and the making flax shall he not quench...He shall not fail nor be discouraged till he have set judgment in the earth: and the isles shall wait for his law' (Isa. 42:1-4). Again, in Isaiah, chapter 49, we find Immanuel demanding the regards of the Church for himself, on the ground that the Father hath called and qualified and sustained him in this office: 'He hath made my mouth like a sharp sword.' In chapter 61, the Redeemer is still more express: 'The Spirit of the Lord God is upon me, for he hath anointed me to preach glad tidings to the meek; he hath sent me to bind up the broken-hearted, to proclaim liberty to the captives, the opening of the prison to them that are bound.' The Church, in the 45th Psalm, speaks of this office of Christ, very briefly, but very distinctly, saying—'Grace is poured into thy lips: therefore God hath blessed thee for ever,'—made thee a recognised, trustworthy, most blessed tutor in all wisdom, and knowledge, and understanding to the Church for ever. With this view the Father gives to the Son, as Immanuel, access to all his mind, will, love, purposes—'The Father showeth him all things that himself doeth,' that he may tell the same to his people, that he may make them known in the transactions of his office. Hence 'no man knoweth the Father but the Son, and he to whom the Son shall reveal him.' And the intimacy, lovingness, and familiarity of Christ's revelations to his people are evidenced by this, that he lays no stint upon what the Father reveals to him, but opens it all up to his people: 'I call you not servants, but friends, for *all* things that I have heard of my Father I have made known unto you' (John 15:15).

The love of God in giving, as the prophet of the Church—as the official, regular, standing instructor of the Church—none less than the Son of his bosom, is beyond our power of understanding or celebrating. What more, in this kind, could he have done for his vineyard, than this? And then he gives his Spirit that the communications of knowledge and light may not fail. Pollock's singularly beautiful remark is here to be remembered: 'If I could give you not my word only, but my very mind and spirit—my personal mind and spirit—it is certain that you would understand me: my words would suggest to you nothing but exactly what they are the representations of to my mind and very spirit. And thus exactness and certainty of knowledge is secured.'[1]

There *is* a certain infallibility in the Church. And the Protestant Churches have been too chary to claim it. It is not the privilege of pope, or cardinal, or archbishop, or council, or holy father of any rank or grade. 'All thy children shall be taught of God, and great shall be the peace of thy children.' And those taught of God, taught of Christ, taught outwardly by the lips and words of the man Christ Jesus, and inwardly by his Spirit, are taught savingly, so as that in all things pertaining to the salvation of their souls, unto the glory of God, they shall truly and practically be infallible. What less attribute ought to attach to such a style of teaching? If Christ taught only by his Spirit, it might be very awful; but it would be little else than a solemn atmosphere—no distinctness, no exactness, no definite proposition: solemnity—perhaps almost horror—would be the predominant feeling. If he taught only by his words, pedantic accuracy might characterise everything, without spiritual efficacy, power, glory, freshness, or heavenly beauty: with no attractiveness, no living power, no effectiveness and certainty of acquisition and retention attending the doctrine. But when the word and Spirit combine, everything requisite is provided for a fair, full, true, sure, effective, and lasting acquisition of the very truth; and the pupils of Christ have an unrivalled teacher.

Moreover, when we think here what the Spirit hath done for Christ himself, as God-man, to fill him with love for his work and office, we see with what right Christ is entitled to say,—'learn of me, for I am meek and lowly, and ye shall find rest to your souls' (Matt. 11:29). 'Then I was by him as one brought up with him; I was daily his delight, rejoicing always before him, rejoicing in the habitable parts of his earth, and my delights were with the sons of men' (Prov. 8:30, 31). A good, a wonderful qualification for the entire prophetic office; and no wonder,

---

[1] [Who and what work Martin refers to here remains unidentified.]

therefore, that it is followed up by Jesus himself, with a special claim to our attention:—'Now, therefore, hearken unto me, O ye children, for blessed are they that keep my ways. Hear instruction and be wise, and refuse it not. Blessed is the man that heareth me, watching daily at my gates, waiting at the posts of my doors' (Prov. 8:32, 33). The force of the argument on which this appeal is based is 'I am, from eternity, the confidant of the Father—partner and partaker of his purposes: sharer of all his thoughts and plans; joint-proprietor in all his joys; most intimately acquainted with all his ways; entitled also to take to deal with all that is the Father's, because I am the heir of all things having by inheritance obtained a more excellent name than the angels.'

Fear not, therefore, that I will in any way do injustice to the Father's interests, and purposes, and love, and kingdom, and government, and honour. I am myself too intimately related to them all; I am, myself, personally too closely bound up with them to do them any injustice, or have any temptation or inducement to injure, misrepresent, or obscure them, in communicating and making them known to you. You may implicitly intrust me with the work of instructing you concerning all that is the Father's. The Father trusts me, and surely well may you! I give a good account to my Father of all that he commits to me; and well may you expect that in making it known to you, it shall suffer no damage at my hand, but be the very truth and mind of God, the very truth and love and loving heart of the Father. 'No man knoweth the Father save the Son, and he to whom the Son doth reveal him.'

When, therefore, Jesus makes known to you, for instance, by his Word and Spirit, that God is reconciled, is pacified, is seated on a throne of grace, to receive sinners who approach unto him through this propitiation; when he makes this known in the light, force, sweetness, efficacy, and hearty and unfailing certainty and splendour of it by his Spirit (the same Spirit convincing you of sin, of righteousness, and of judgment—of sin, because of unbelief; or righteousness, because Jesus hath gone to the Father; and of judgment, because the prince of this world is judged); when the poor self-condemned soul sees, in the Spirit's light (which is just Christ's own light and the Father's) the reality, excellence, beauty, grace, and authority, and divine majesty of the throne of grace; till he is drawn to come boldly to it to obtain mercy, and to find grace to help in time of need: when he is enabled to see the reality of all this so distinctly, that he is constrained to make the experiment,—to try if God will not open the windows of heaven and pour out a blessing—to taste and see that God is gracious:—here is teaching of such a nature as is felt to deserve the utmost confidence, gratitude, and joy, and such reciprocations as imply in them a perpetual, practical, making use of the opportunity of obtaining heavenly understanding, and all things of any real importance, which, in the Prophetic Office of Christ, there is thus provision for believers enjoying continually.

It is of importance to bear in mind that this office is a perpetual, regular, standing ordinance: a constantly existent channel, through which light and wisdom may be flowing from the depths of the supreme Godhead into the heads and hearts of all the members of the Church continually. It is not an occasional event, having its seasons of recurrence, like astronomical events: but it is the maintenance in the Church, and for the enlightenment and joy of the redeemed here below, of a continual Sun of Righteousness, with healing in his wings. The office of the Prophet is not something to be found in the Church during jubilee days, Ascension days, Easter Sundays, and such like. But, constantly, equably, at all times, Jesus is in the Church, exercising his office, and open to the prayers of his people everywhere;—'O send forth thy light and thy truth. Let them lead me, let them guide me, to thy holy hill, to thy tabernacle, unto God, my exceeding joy.'

It would be desirable to contemplate some of the more striking qualities of Christ as a teacher.

I. He is a loving teacher.

He takes a profound interest in his pupils. He has loved them with an everlasting love; therefore with lovingkindness does he draw them. It is not with him as with some formal teachers—a matter of no importance whether their pupils derive benefit or not, provided they get creditably through the discharge of their office, and perhaps earn the wage due to it. With Jesus, the discharge of the office is the actual and successful communication of knowledge and wisdom in the will of God for our salvation: where this is not affected to some one or more souls (otherwise ignorant) there his office is not discharged at all. And lovingly to see that that this really takes place, is an integral part of his duty.

O, to be taught of him! O, to see the love of the Father, in the face of the Son, in the light of the Spirit, in the truth of the Word! O, to be thus shone upon!—thus illuminated!—thus 'made light in the Lord'! 'Ye are the light of the world'—said Jesus to his pupils. Well they may be so called, since such is their teacher. 'Unto you that fear my name, shall the Sun of Righteousness arise with healing in his wings.'

The glorious combination of the 'word and Spirit of Christ.'— whereby he is the everlasting, real, present, and effective teacher, prophet, or illuminator of his people, is nowhere more wonderfully and emphatically brought out than in the words of the prophet—'This is my covenant with them, saith the Lord, *My Spirit that is upon thee, and my words that are in thy mouth, shall not depart out of thy mouth, nor out of the mouth of thy seed, nor out of the mouth of thy seed's seed, from henceforth even for ever*' (Isa. 59:21). It is evident that this is the voice of the Father, addressing the Messiah, to whom personally the Spirit is given without measure. To him, also, the word, the whole counsel of the Father in salvation is given, not merely that personally he may understand it—that as the man Christ Jesus, he in his human understanding may use it, and in his human heart may love it, but given into his 'mouth,' that in his office of prophet he may communicate it—(for why else is it said to be in his 'mouth'?)—that he may teach it to his redeemed ones, to those who are the travail of his soul. For 'he shall see his *seed*:' he shall be satisfied when he sees his Word and Spirit abiding in their mouth. 'His Word and Spirit,' also, 'shall not depart out of the mouth of his seed's seed:' that is to say, not out of the mouth of the Church's children, which of course are just his seed also; but the idea of the successive generations of the Church is thus brought out: and the Church's perpetuity—'from henceforth and for ever.'

This, therefore, is the distinguishing characteristic of the true Church of Christ—that both the Spirit of God and the Word of God abide therein, from age to age, from henceforth and for ever. This is the true doctrine of infallibility, which the Church of Rome has done so much to parody, pervert, and profane, and turn men's minds away from, as if there were no infallibility to be affirmed at all, except the infallibility of the persons of the Godhead. To reduce the matter to that is to bring it to a tame enough, and lame enough conclusion. We are indebted to the Church of Rome for almost entirely banishing the truth on this point from nearly the whole Catholic Church on the earth. The Protestant Church has to a large extent become frightened to confess any doctrine of infallibility at all, except the personal and Divine infallibility of the Godhead. Under this reaction from Popery, a good deal of profound truth has been ignored altogether. And this applies to many a doctrine, such as that of 'the keys,' and to some duties, such as the love and veneration which the Scripture claims at our hands for the Virgin Mary—'from henceforth all generations shall call me blessed.' The discriminating considerations by which the real doctrine may be distinguished from the Popish perversion have in these areas become so delicate, so nice, so exact, so difficult to do real justice to them, that, partly through a kind of pious dread, and partly through a carnal laziness, the Church has evaded the duty of at once fighting Popery, and *rescuing from her grasp the fullness of the truth, which all of the truth, which all round and round she perverts*; and been content with proving (in some respects) her error, without going on to show what exactly the real truth is which she has turned into a false-hood in the particular case concerned.

And this applies nowhere more exactly than to the indefectibility and infallibility of the Church. For these are true doctrines (under proper explanations and qualifications) which the Church should never allow herself to be robbed of. There is a society on the earth of which Jesus Christ is the head; and in its heart the Holy Spirit shall for ever dwell, and in its mouth the Word of God shall for ever abide. The covenant of God is so completely at stake in seeing that this shall be, that it is even spoken of as if this were the sum and substance of the covenant—nay, as if this, to all intents and purposes were the covenant itself. '*This is my covenant* with them, O thou my servant, whom I uphold, mine elect, in whom my soul delighteth; my Spirit that is upon thee, and my words that are in thy mouth, shall not depart out of thy mouth (and that means also the Spirit shall no more be withdrawn from thee than the word—a part being taken for the whole) nor out of the mouth of thy seed, nor out of the mouth of thy seed's seed, from henceforth even for ever.' It is precisely the same as in the intercessory prayer. The idea of continuity and perpetuity is brought out there in very much the same manner. The apostles, there, personally have the place of what Isaiah calls immediately Christ's 'seed;' and those taught by the apostles have the place of what is called 'the seed's seed.' 'Neither pray I for these alone, but for all them which shall believe through their word,' i.e. really 'their seed's seed from henceforth, even for over.'

Then, because of this glorious distinction—this infinite and ever-lasting distinction, the Church of Christ, with Christ himself as the ever living head, and indwelling heart of it—the Church of Christ, I say, is, in the next verse, called upon to arise and assert her privilege, position, and power. Consequent on this being true of her, consequent on her possession, illimitably, of the Spirit and word of Christ, the command is given her—'Arise; shine: for thy light hath come, and the glory of the Lord hath arisen upon thee.' Unto what less than this should the Church of Christ be called, in the promises? Is it too much to expect, considering the arrangements and preparations, the privileges and advantages implied in her having the Word of God without error, and the Spirit of God without limit, and both of these without end? Is it not reasonable, is it not simply what might be expected, when God—in the promises, or on the presupposition of all this—says: 'Arise; shine: for thy light hath come, and the glory of the Lord hath risen upon thee'? Is not thy 'light' indeed come, when the words of God, expressing God's glorious mind and intellect and purposes, are come, and shone upon, illuminated, and protected from misrepresentation and misunderstanding, and possibility of misunderstanding, by God's own intelligent Spirit seeing to it that God's word shall be found bringing out to view in your mind nothing but exactly God's thought, just as *he* thinks it, in all the moral beauty in which he thinks it and means it? Is not thy 'light' indeed come when *this* is come?—when the word and Spirit of God are come? And what 'glory' more in God is there than this, to arise upon thee, or on any of his creatures in heaven or earth? Yea, the glory of the Lord is arisen upon thee, when the Spirit of the Lord and the word of the Lord are in thy mouth, and in thy heart. And, 'the word of God is nigh thee, even in thy mouth and in thy heart' (Rom. 10:8). Therefore, realise thy position now, and 'arise; shine: for thy light hath come, and the glory of the Lord hath arisen upon thee; and kings shall come to thy light, and princes to the brightness of thy rising.'

Another verse in which this ever-blessed and remarkable combination of 'the Word and the Spirit' is strikingly brought out, is John 3:34—'He whom God hath sent speaketh the words of God, for God giveth not the Spirit by measure unto him.'

Here it is not affirmed, as usual, that God gives his word and Spirit. It is affirmed only that he gives the Spirit. But it is inferred that he whom God hath sent speaketh the word of God from his receiving the Spirit wholly, without division, or partiality, or stint, or measure. It is admitted that a teacher might have a measure of the Spirit, and yet speak words that might not be of God,—words that might be against the truth, or aside from the truth. The Spirit dwelling in him by measure, might not, according to that measure, feel himself called upon to act on the man's mind, and through his mind, in every direction and on every question, so as to make his utterance of error impossible. He would not hold himself responsible for that. The man might hold and give forth error in the directions, or departments, over which the measure of the Spirit given to him ranged not. The Spirit given to him, specially as a Spirit of adoption, would see to it that nothing went wrong fundamentally, as to the man's taking God in Christ by faith as his heavenly Father, and crying 'Abba, Father,' in Spirit and in truth. But it would not follow that such a man should be a great or correct theologian, the Spirit not being given to him specially as a spirit of knowledge and of understanding. But if the Spirit is given to him in all his characters, in all his gifts, in all his graces, in all his capacities—then there is no direction in which this man can deal with the truth of God, without error on his part being injurious to the glory of the Spirit. That is not the case where it is only a measure of the Spirit that is included or involved. But where the whole fullness of the Holy Ghost is bestowed on a man (and such a man, it seems to me, it should be easy to prove must also be the God-man), then anything but the word of God—the truth of God—it is impossible that that man could utter. God hath 'sent' him, and sent him to 'speak;' and he hath secured that he shall speak God's word, not in the particular way of prescribing to him this message or that message—this special lesson or address—and so on, everyone in its course, one by one till the completeness and summation of them have been reached, seeing to it that each in its turn and all in their sum are 'God's words;' not in that particular way does the Father secure that his 'sent' 'speaker' shall speak God's words. But, giving him in his office, and for the ends of it, the Holy Spirit without measure, as none but the Son of God could receive him in his Divine fullness, he makes it certain that such a teacher shall speak God's words, and nothing but God's words, not by particular arrangement for each case when he is to speak, but by the general and all-embracing rule, that the infinite and infallible Spirit of God would be dishonoured by anything but the truth of God proceeding from his mouth. Therefore, with even an inspired man, if a mere man, we must have the assurance that each separate message is inspired; and not on any other ground do we receive it as the word of God; so that to all practical intents and purposes, the 'inspiration' which we value so highly, is ultimately a quality of the writing and not of the *writer*—of the speech and not the speaker. That is not so when the teacher is Jesus. The Father giveth not the Spirit by measure unto him. He cannot speak outside the sphere of the Spirit. What he speaketh, writeth, uttereth in any way, is the word of God, and he has command over it in every direction. He hath it, to say it reverently, at his finger ends. 'The Father loveth the Son, and hath given all things into his hands:' therefore, 'he that believeth on the Son hath everlasting life; he that believeth not the Son shall not see life, but the wrath of God abideth on him.'

II. This is a *teacher who understands* the capabilities of his pupils, and will not over-drive them.

Jesus is the author of those very faculties with which he has to deal in instructing his children, and he knows what each one of them can do. In the days of his flesh he taught the people generally, and his disciples in particular, 'as they were able to bear it.' He expressly told his disciples, 'I have many things to say unto you, but ye are not able to bear it now.' And he will continue to act in this gentle and genial manner, for he saith, 'Learn of me, for I am meek and lowly.' This implies that he will not over-drive his scholars: on the contrary, he will carry the lambs in his arms, and gently lead those that are with young.

III. At the same time, he is such a teacher as cannot only make known the truth to those who have the capability to receive it, but can strengthen the faculties of his scholars.

A more human teacher may say, 'I can give you statements of truth, but I cannot give you understanding.' But Jesus can give understanding. He can give light, and the eye to see it. 'Oh! send forth thy light and thy truth.' Nay, he can make those 'light in the Lord' whom he undertakes to teach. He can produce such a change on their understandings, as to make them (as it were) constituent elements of the kingdom of light, 'children of the light and of the day;'—'out of darkness into God's marvellous light.'

No creature-tutor or teacher, can do anything approaching to this. He may deal so kindly and affectionately with his pupils that they shall exert themselves, in reply to his efforts, so effectually, that their very faculties shall be strengthened and improved under such dealings. They may acquire information; and more than that, ability to deal wisely with it. In this way, they may grow in knowledge and understanding exceedingly. But Christ can so influence and affect the soul by his Spirit, that things formerly disliked shall be loved and sought after for their own sake and the enjoyment that is to be found in them. A carnal mind that delighted only in earthly things, shall become full of love to, and chiefly characterised by, spiritual and heavenly things; for the Spirit of light by which Jesus operates his mind and will upon his people in them, is the Spirit of wisdom, and love and peace, and of a sound mind. Hence, we find Paul praying in various of his epistles for his converts, that they may be filled with the Spirit in all knowledge and wisdom, that they may know the hope of their calling, and what is the riches of God's inheritance in the saints, and what is the exceeding greatness of his power to themward who believe. How Jesus acts directly upon the human understanding in teaching his people, we know not; but we know that he hath the hearts and minds of all men in his keeping, and can influence, change, alter, the disposition and receptive faculty of them at his pleasure. However worldly, carnal, stupid, and earthly our minds, therefore, may be, in subjecting ourselves to the teaching of Christ, there is no room for dullness or despondency. Jesus can make them as a flame of fire for ardour, or a flame of lightning for brightness. It is said of John the Baptist, 'he was a burning and a shining light.' Can there be any doubt that it is as a pupil of Christ that this is said of him?

How delightful to think that when omnipotent operation is needed on our minds and hearts, so as that the truth may be received in true intelligence of it, and in its spiritual effects of saving and comforting the soul, such operation is put into the hand of the Eternal Word made flesh, originally the soul's very creator, in whose image also the soul was created, and who can create it again in himself—unto good works that we may walk in them—unto God's holy light that we may rejoice and dwell and shine in it. Nor is it after his own image, considered only as God, that he conforms the spirits of his people when he makes them to be light in the Lord. He is God-man. He himself has a human soul; and after his own image as man, does he conform his people. Beholding, as in a glass, the glory of the Lord Immanuel, they are transformed into the same image from glory to glory as by the Spirit of the Lord. Nor does the use of the word 'as,' imply any diminishing resemblance—any distant similarity or similitude. 'From glory to glory'—progressively—are they transformed, so 'as' none but the Lord, the Spirit, could transform them. Dwelling in the presence of revealed truth—vital and vitalising truth, truth instinct with light, sparkling and brimming over with light—they see light in God's light:

they become light in the Lord. They themselves, and the truth revealed to them, become so germane to one another, that an atmosphere of light becomes natural to them. They play and disport themselves in light. They are pupils of the light—children of the light—an intelligent and enlightened band of truth-seekers, and truth-finders, and truth-bearers, (Phil. 2:15) phosteric ones, or light bearers—shedding light everywhere around them; seen in their own light—their own, though it is the light of the Lord; yet not as by mere reflection, but by inherent light do they shine: they are luminous: and when times become darker, they become brighter, and more and more precious: and the darkness which devoureth up evil things, instead of injuring them, brings out more and more to view, the beauty of their heavenly glory: yea, and as all darkness that is in them passes away, and the light that is in them gets growing scope to shine, they shall at last shine as the sun in the kingdom of their Father. Meantime, it is of infinite importance that they watch and keep the light that God has given them—that God hath made them; and for this end, it is indispensable, that in their dealings with God, they deal often, deal truly, deal effectively, and intensely, with God as light, the Father of lights. 'This is the message which we have received of him, that God is light, and in him is no darkness at all: if we walk in the light as God is in the light, we have fellowship with him, the blood of Jesus Christ cleansing us from all sin.' Meanwhile, God, who commanded the light to shine out of darkness, will go on shining in their hearts to give the light of the knowledge of the glory of God in the face of Jesus Christ; and beholding as in a glass the glory of the Lord, they shall be transformed into the same image from glory to glory, as none but the Spirit of the Lord could transform them. Thus will their light so shine, that men will take knowledge of them that they have been with Jesus, and will glorify their Father which is in heaven.

IV. This is such a teacher as cannot have his time overdrawn upon by any number of pupils, however great.

And that, not because it is in his character as God that he teaches, for that is not true. Christ, as Mediator, as God-man, as our Redeemer, executeth the office of a teacher. He hath come into relations with time, in taking human flesh and blood; and he cannot, as man, be in more places of space than one at a time. Yet certainly it is as God and Man, in two distinct natures and one person, that he teaches the countless thousands of his Church. And yet he does not require any, or even one, of his children to remain in waiting, till he is finished with another's lesson. What glorious capacities, in this regard, may have been bestowed on his glorified body and glorified mind, in their exaltation to the right hand of God, we cannot know. There have been such gifts, occasionally possessed and enjoyed by mere men, as should, in contemplation of them, lead us to have less difficulty in understanding how the Father might, in infinite love and delight, give the same Spirit of his love to the humanity of him who is daily his delight—(rejoicing always before him, rejoicing in the habitable parts of the earth, in the dwellings of Zion, and the homes of his hidden ones, his countless and beloved pupils)—to effect therein the most extraordinary increase of natural faculty, as well as gracious operation; so that the human nature of our Lord might consciously be in intelligent communication with thousands and tens of thousands of pupils at a time. When Jesus prayed, saying, 'Father, glorify thy Son, that thy Son also may glorify thee,'—who shall tell what glorious extension and enhancement of natural faculty, in all directions and in all kinds, was included in that prayer! We know, however, that through the mind and heart (the human mind and heart) of Jesus, countless multitudes—ten thousand times ten thousand, and thousands of thousands—of cases (his peoples' states and wants, their sins and sorrows, and their necessities) are continually passing, and that he is infinitely well able for, and accurate in, the conduct and on-carrying of them all.

The subject of the Mediator's relation to time is a very wonderful one. The mediation was, of course, designed from everlasting, but it has its conduct in time. His goings forth have been of old from everlasting; but it was in the fullness of times that God sent forth his Son. Ascending up in the same body in which he had obtained 'eternal redemption for us,' he kept his person still in relations to time. He is to come again the second time without sin unto salvation; and he saith, 'Behold I come quickly.' He is the first and the last: *time centres all in him.* One day is with him as a thousand years, and a thousand years as one day; yet he accommodates himself to our rate and impressions of time: and in a moment, by retiring to our closet, we may have the master with us, for as long as we please, as if there were not another to call for his gracious presence. He is always at home. He is never over-burdened. His time is never fully occupied. He cannot, by overcrowding of his pupils be distracted. However many may have come, the cry is still, Come; Come unto me:—the weary, for rest: the thirsting, for the water of life: the guilty, for pardon: the troubled, for peace: the ignorant, for knowledge, and wisdom, and truth, and light. Come: learn of me, for I am meek and lowly. I am always busy and always free.

Here it occurs to me to ask, if ever you have tried to get an answer to the question, *What is that*

'CROWN OF LIFE'

which the Lord hath promised to them that love him? I can only tell you what I think. I think it is,

'A Physical Brain like his own.'

And I think this extremely likely to be the correct answer.[1] When I speak of his 'physical brain,' I venture to form no idea concerning it, except that it is that supremely glorious material instrument or engine or organ, by means of which primarily his human soul or spirit communicates with matter, and thereby with the external world generally. In that case, it must be that divinely perfect material instrument through which there is continually pouring the stream of all his thoughts and emotions, all his sympathy with

---

[1] [This is perhaps a surprising conclusion. However, although we do not know the full details of Hugh Martin's state of mind, it would seem that he suffered from a nervous condition, and possibly had a psychiatric disorder. In any case, for Martin, the thought that one day his mind would be renewed was evidently a source of great comfort. Martin is not dogmatic in his conclusion.]

his people, and all the actings of reason (the human reason of the God-man!) wherein, or in respect of which, he is continually governing his kingdom, which 'ruleth over all.' What a prospect—to have a brain like that!¹ A brain which is for ever worked by the Holy Spirit— by the Holy Spirit in that character in which Jesus gives his Spirit in a measure to his pupils and people on earth—'the Spirit of love, and of power, and of a sound mind.' Well is Jesus able to give those who are his pupils and his children a brain like his own. Why, it is as if we were telegraphing to heaven, and the wires were bearing back the answer:—'He shall change our vile body, that it may be fashioned like unto his glorious body, according to the working whereby he is able even to subdue all things to himself' (Phil. 3:21).

And how splendidly the promise reads in this sense—the promise of James 1:12, which I have been long accustomed to render to my own mind thus:—'Blessed is the man that stands out his provings, for when he is proved—(he could not bear it sooner—it would break him down before his 'provings' were done, and thus ruin him)— when he is proved, he shall receive the *crown of life*, which the Lord hath promised to them that love him.' And how well, in the light of this thought, does the beautiful expostulatory and stimulating thought of Paul read:—'Now, they do it to obtain a corruptible crown, but we an incorruptible.' *Incorruptible!*—when 'this corruptible shall have put on incorruption!' And how fine in this connection, are the other adjectives, of Peter (1 Pet. 1:3, 4):—'Blessed be the God and Father of our Lord Jesus Christ, who, according to his abundant mercy, and by the resurrection of Jesus Christ, hath

---

¹ If I had been that delightful, darling English lark, Fanny Havergal, I would probably have said here, 'Wasn't it so kind of him to give me such a pleasant thought as that?'—and I would probably have added, 'He that gave the thought can give the thing,'—and 'faithful is he that hath promised.' But being, at the best, only an old Scotch black-bird, *tashed* [Scots: *stained, soiled, tarnished*] with many a storm now, I can only leave this thought with my compatriots, not expecting that it will be any objection to them that it identifies their *croons* wi' their *heeds*!

begotten us again to a lively hope, to an inheritance *incorruptible* and *undefiled*, and that fadeth not away.' *Undefiled*: unsoiled by any physical humours, or black headaches, or unworthy thoughts, whether silly or unholy or weak. Fading not away: a brain never fatigued, never needing rest, ('they rest not, day nor night') never needing any kind of *pabulum*:[1] but wherein-soever it may resemble a telegraphic machine, it shall be for ever in prime good working order: a brain worthy to be the fulfilment of Christ's promise when he says, 'Be thou faithful unto death, and I will give thee a crown of life' (Rev. 2:10).

Now, whether this be the *Crown of Life* or not, it is certainly in the promise (Phil. 3:21). It is certainly there. And if anybody object, and say, This cannot be the *Crown of Life*, because a crown is something to wear,—I answer, My interpretation may stand for all that, for there is the besides. They can take it, and wear it. And if they can give me as good an answer to the question.—What is it? as I have given to the question, What's the *crown of life*? I will be very much obliged to them.

V. This is such a teacher, as inspires his pupils with an irrepressible love for each other.[2]

And no wonder; for they have all an adoring and enthusiastic love for him. They have all, with more or less distinctness, as it were, on bended knees, laid hold of his hand, with the adjuration, 'My Lord and my God!' And he has, as it were, laid his warm hand, like a Father's, on their heads; and they have worshipped him, nothing doubting. He *saith unto her 'Mary,' she saith unto him 'Rabboni.'* Yes,

---

[1] [pabulum = bland, insipid entertainment.]

[2] It is astonishing and delightful, the amount and intensity of love entertained for such loving labours in our Lord's vineyard as Frances Ridley Havergal; A.L.O.E.; Hesba Stretton; and the authoress of the 'Last Words of Samuel Rutherford.'

Now that Miss Havergal has gone to her well-earned rest, who is to be her successor? I suspect it will require to be as in some Free Church congregations, when a good contributor is removed, the only way to make up the loss, is by *everybody doing a little more*. I could hardly put a nicer wreath upon her bier than by saying that.

he is a master: beloved as master never was nor will be; for he is such a master, as has died for his pupils, and risen from the dead that he might reign over earth and heaven and hell, for their protection and salvation: and under his benignant reign they live now not unto themselves, but unto him that loved them and gave himself for them. Ransomed by, and sprinkled with, his precious blood, they have now the right, the incentive, the obligation, the will, and the power to glorify God and to enjoy him for ever. He often reveals himself to them—makes himself known to them in the breaking of bread and in the learning of lessons. He shines in their souls till they see his glory, and the Father's; ('shew us the Father and it sufficeth'); and their souls return unto their rest, for he deals bountifully with them. We cannot tell the confidence we have in him. We know that he is our brother: we believe and are sure that he is our God. In him are hid all the treasures, riches, wonders of wisdom and knowledge: and what with his omniscience as God and his tender sympathy as man, we find in his person a fascination that is glorious in holiness, fearful in praise-worthiness, perpetual fountain of wonder upon wonder. There is nothing wherewith—nothing wherein—we do not trust him. We know whom we have believed, and we ask each other's growing love and glad enthusiasm in singing to him,[1] in lauding, and blessing him, by his grand and gracious titles, his names of majesty and grace; while we evermore renew the doxology wherewith the fathers at the time gave welcome to him; 'To us a child is born, to us a Son is given: and his name shall be called Wonderful, Counsellor, the Mighty God, the Everlasting Father, and the Prince of Peace.' We would sooner have five minutes of his love—five minutes of the light of his face, of 'the light of the knowledge of the glory of God in the face of Jesus Christ,'—than all the thrones, and crowns, and banks of Europe unto eternity; and yet he gives us love infinite, eternal, and unchangeable, without money, without price, and without end.

As to how *we* have dealt with *him*, since he first began to reveal his love to us, making us, in one and the same light, see at once our need of it, and our welcome to it, our wretchedness without it, and

---

[1] 'And with my song I will him praise' (Psa. 28:7).

its all-sufficiency and delightsomeness;—As to the reciprocation and responses we have made to this love; the less we say, the better. But *this* we can say;—*he* has been faithful. He has never indicated weariness of us; though we may often have seemed as if we would weary him and grow weary of him. He has never cast us off; though we would seem oftentimes to have gone far towards casting *him* off. We have never sought him without finding him. He hath, indeed, made it a rule of his kingdom and his school, 'Let the heart of every one rejoice that seeks the Lord,'—'And it shall come to pass that whosoever shall call upon the name of the Lord shall be saved!' We can, however, say, that 'now is our salvation nearer than when we believed:' and our love for him groweth, as it well may, while in quiet judgment and in warm affection equally, we can say, we know no limits which it should not out-grow. 'Extol the Lord with me, and let us exalt his name together. This poor man cried, and the Lord heard, and delivered him from all his distresses.' 'We know whom we have believed, and are persuaded, that what we have committed to him against that day, he is able to keep:' and he will come again for us at last (and it will not be long), and all his saints with him, and we shall be for ever with the Lord. Even already, by faith in 'Jesus the mediator of the new covenant,' and faith in 'God the Judge of all,' we are already 'come unto Mount Zion, the city of the living God and the heavenly Jerusalem, to the innumerable company of angels, and to the spirits of just men made perfect.' Our beloved dead who have gone before, we have, and hold in Jesus. And we cannot tell the love and gratitude wherewith we regard him as the author of their salvation from before all ages, their Redeemer upon the cross, and the present guardian of their blessed rest.

No wonder, therefore, that as the pupils of such a master, we have an irrepressible love for one another. Nor is it necessary that we should often see each other, to exercise, and cherish, and foster, this delightful love. With the pupils it may be as with the master: 'Whom having not seen, we love.' They are, indeed, scattered over all lands, and through all ages. The promises that we live upon every day, *they* too, in their various days, have lived upon. We are blessed with faithful Abraham: with Isaac, the son of the free woman, we are free: we are walking in the light of the Lord with the house of Jacob: and *non numquam* (not never) we prevail, like Israel, both with God and man. All a-down the ages, we call the excellent of the earth our mother, and our sister, and our brother: and 'we know that we have passed from death to life, because we love the brethren.' The great things we have all alike learned from Jesus; the overwhelming importance of them; the subtle and pervasive spirituality of them; and the substantial identity of them, create among us a sort of free masonry, a sort of telegraphic sympathy of each with all; and our delight in those we believe to be his, is without stint and without end. We have all alike asked of Jesus and got a glorious answer to the question, 'Who will shew us any good?' The light of his Father's countenance, whose delight he daily was from eternity, rejoicing always before him, was to us an answer far grander than all possible abounding corn and wine. We have all asked him, 'How can guilty man be just with God his maker!' And as *Jehovah Tsidkenu*, (the Lord our righteousness) he has told us neither to go up to heaven above, nor to go down into the deep below (Rom. 10:6-8),—neither to go up nor down—not to move a foot, nor waste a minute, but here and now he will be of God made unto us righteousness: and being justified by faith, we shall have peace with God, access by faith into a standing of grace and favour with the Lord, and warrantable joy in hope of the glory that is to be revealed (Rom. 5:1, 2) And then,—to take another hard question of the many wherewith we have all alike proved him,—feeling the Augean stable[1] of impurity and hell of restlessness, that is by nature in each of us, and is bound to remain in the heart that remains in 'an estate of sin and misery,'—we have all alike asked him, 'Who can bring a clean thing out of an unclean!' And he hath assured us that 'to as many as receive him to them gives he power to become the sons of God;' born of God; spirit, born of the Spirit; pure as God is pure; and to be perfect soon as our Father in heaven is perfect.

From a common experience, therefore, of strange things like these; of gifts of light and grace; God's marvellous light, and God's rich and

---

[1] [A reference to Greek mythology—a cattle shed that had not been cleaned out for many years.]

reigning grace; we love one another, being alike all begotten of him; loving, therefore, both him that beget, and those that are begotten. Numerous as the sound of many waters are the voices of those that have gone before: numerous as the dew drops from the womb of the morning over all the earth, will those be that shall follow after. Nay, very many have we seen following on to know the Lord, of whom we rejoice to believe that already they have gone to be with Jesus, which is far better: and in no long time we hope—not because we are faithful, but because 'faithful is *he* that hath promised'—we hope, after a little more suffering, and all needed sustaining grace (1 Pet. 5:10). that we also shall overcome through the blood of the Lamb, and the word of our testimony. And the gracious Spirit to whom we owe so much, hath long ago written for us a song of anticipation:

> *But as for me, thine own face*
> *In righteousness shall see;*
> *And with thy likeness, when I wake,*
> *I satisfied shall be.*
> (Psa. 17:15)

μ.

Other Books by Hugh Martin
published by the Trust

The Shadow of Calvary: Gethsemane, the Arrest, the Trial
paperback, 264pp.
Also available as an eBook from banneroftruth.org

Christ for Us: Sermons of Hugh Martin
paperback, 262pp.

*The Atonement, in Its Relations to the Covenant,
the Priesthood, the Intercession of Our Lord*
cloth-bound, 248pp.
Also available as an eBook from banneroftruth.org

Jonah
Geneva Series of Commentaries, cloth-bound, 384pp.

About the Publisher

The Banner of Truth Trust originated in 1957 in London. The founders believed that much of the best literature of historic Christianity had been allowed to fall into oblivion and that, under God, its recovery could well lead not only to a strengthening of the church, but to true revival.

Interdenominational in vision, this publishing work is now international, and our lists include a number of contemporary authors, together with classics from the past. The translation of these books into many languages is encouraged.

A monthly magazine, *The Banner of Truth,* is also published, and further information about this, and all our other publications, may be found on our website or by contacting either of the offices below.

THE BANNER OF TRUTH TRUST

3 Murrayfield Road
Edinburgh, EH12 6EL
UK

P O Box 621, Carlisle
Pennsylvania 17013
USA

banneroftruth.org